Micro-Analysis of Computer System Performance

Boris Beizer

Director of Research and Development,
Data Systems Analysts, Inc.
Pennsauken, New Jersey

VNR **VAN NOSTRAND REINHOLD COMPANY**
NEW YORK   CINCINNATI   ATLANTA   DALLAS   SAN FRANCISCO
LONDON   TORONTO   MELBOURNE

Van Nostrand Reinhold Company Regional Offices:
New York Cincinnati Atlanta Dallas San Francisco

Van Nostrand Reinhold Company International Offices:
London Toronto Melbourne

Copyright © 1978 by Litton Educational Publishing, Inc.

Library of Congress Catalog Card Number: 77-27822
ISBN: 0-442-20663-1

Manufactured in the United States of America

Published by Van Nostrand Reinhold Company
135 West 50th Street, New York, N.Y. 10020

Published simultaneously in Canada by Van Nostrand Reinhold Ltd.

15 14 13 12 11 10 9 8 7 6 5 4 3 2 1

Library of Congress Cataloging in Publication Data

Beizer, Boris, 1934–
    Micro-analysis of computer system performance.

    Includes index.
    1. Microcomputers—Evaluation. I. Title.
QA76.5.B373   001.6'4'04   77-27822
ISBN 0-442-20663-1

Dedicated to: *"the perplexity of man-*
kind, who can give no answer to the ques-
tion you've just put me, Zorba."

Nikos Kazantzakis

Preface

This book concerns a body of analytical techniques which can conveniently be grouped under the title "microperformance analysis." This is to be contrasted with another group of techniques, not covered here, that could be called "macroanalysis." It is not so much in technical details that these techniques differ, but in objective, starting point, and the systems to which they are best applied. The point of view in microanalysis is to start at the most detailed level of a system—the code—and to build upward to a model of the entire system. Macroanalysis, conversely, seeks to deduce the system's characteristics on the basis of its over-all, topmost level behavior. Microanalysis is dominated by analytical techniques while macroanalysis is based mostly on measurement and simulation. The boundaries between these two approaches are not clear at present, and to some extent they are arbitrary.

Wholly analytical approaches to performance analysis and optimization are limited. They are best suited to the analysis and optimization of small, relatively simple systems, such as might be implemented with a micro- or minicomputer, or to the analysis of a component of a large system, such as a program or subroutine. While it is in principle possible to apply these techniques to the analysis of a large scale system, such as a commercial operating system, the analytical effort and computational resources required make such applications impractical in most cases.

This book emphasizes practice rather than theory. Consequently, there are few derivations—and those only where they serve to clarify the application. Formulas, models and algorithms are presented with an emphasis on delimiting the areas to which they may be safely applied. References to collateral reading are given for the reader interested in the derivations.

The following is assumed about the reader:

1. Junior to senior level training in computer science, software engineering, computer engineering, mathematics, or some combination thereof.
2. An introductory course in probability and statistics and at least a first year survey course in university mathematics (i.e., algebra and elementary calculus).

3. Programming experience with some exposure to assembly language programming and a general understanding of simple computers such as mini- and microcomputers.

These prerequisites limit the range of analytical techniques that can be presented. Specifically, I have included only closed-form analytical expressions, or such algorithms as can be programmed with ease in a language such as BASIC or FORTRAN. The scope of these techniques, particularly in queueing theory and latency models (chapters 10, 11, 13) can be substantially expanded by using the referenced material and by introducing moment-generating functions and numerical procedures for inverting them.

This book is intended to serve as a self-contained, self study text and reference for the computer professional, or as the basis for a one semester course on performance analysis and optimization. When supplemented with additional material on queueing theory and latency models it can be the basis of a one year course on performance analysis with a theoretical orientation. Alternatively, when supplemented with additional material on simulation, it can be used for a performance analysis workshop course.

The entire subject area is one in which practice is essential. Exercises have been given to illustrate the general nature of the problems the reader should be able to solve at that point. Also featured are variations not explicitly discussed in the text. The variety of available mini-, micro-, and pedagogical demonstration computers is overwhelming. Rather than selecting one or two computers to be used for tutorial purposes within the book, I recommend that the instructor or reader pick a specific computer with which they are familiar and modify the exercises to apply to it. A similar approach is suggested for application areas.

BORIS BEIZER
Abington, Pa.

Acknowledgments

Deep appreciation is rendered onto Data Systems Analysts, Inc., and the United States Air Force, Rome Air Development Center for the support they gave to this work; and my appreciation and affection to Adrienne Bilotta who heroically typed the manuscript (and kept it all under control).

Contents

Micro-Analysis of Computer System Performance

1
Introduction

1. OVERVIEW OF THE BOOK

1.1. Performance Analysis

Performance analysis to the uninitiated appears to be a complicated activity dominated by higher mathematics. Superficial appearance aside, in principle and in practice, performance analysis is analogous to the system design process itself. The following distinctions between performance analysis and design are noteworthy:

1. Analysis can be done by a few individuals rather than a team of design specialists.
2. Bugs are more obvious and less catastrophic.
3. Absolute perfection is neither achievable nor desirable.
4. Reality can be simplified; most complexities of the real system can be ignored without danger or error.

The purpose of this book is twofold: (1) to provide a framework for doing the performance analysis of a simple system, such as one based on a microcomputer, or to analyze a segment of a larger system, and (2) to introduce the techniques needed to conduct such analyses. This book can be divided into four sections: (1) Chapters 1-3, Introduction;(2) Chapters 4-8, Timing Analysis; (3) Chapters 9-14, Systems Analysis; and (4) Chapters 15-16, Epilogue.

1.2. Chapters 1-3—Introduction

The first chapter sets the stage for the analytical process by investigating the reasons for doing an analysis in the first place, examining the alternatives to analysis, and reviewing the steps of an analysis.

The next chapter explores the structure of typical computers, highlighting features that are important to performance evaluation.

A definite idea of what "performance" means is prerequisite to analysis. Three concepts are introduced: **throughput, delay**, and **resources**. A performance analysis is defined as the process of determining the relation between these three things. Systems are asked to do work. The unit of work is called a **transaction**. Transactions may be further divided into **tasks**. The **load** to which a system is subjected is expressed as the arrival rate of transactions or tasks (e.g., tasks per second).

1.3. Chapters 4–8—Timing Analysis

These chapters contain the meat of the subject—calculating the processing time and resource usages. The point of view is statistical, but only elementary concepts are assumed. The reader is led, step by step, through a series of techniques that convert a program or flowchart into algebraic expressions that describe processing time and resource usage.

1.4. Chapters 9–14—Systems Analysis

Knowing how many microseconds it takes the computer to process one transaction in the absence of other transactions is only the beginning of the analysis. These chapters introduce the analysis of the realistic complexities that exist in most systems. The effect of interrupts, DMA, and program level changes is the subject of Chapter 9. Systems interface with peripheral devices such as moving and fixed-head discs. These devices exhibit large delays which must be evaluated and integrated into the analysis: this is covered in Chapter 10. Chapter 11 is a short introduction to queueing theory which is a prerequisite to almost all system level analysis. Systems are then subdivided into two major categories: cyclic systems and noncyclic or asynchronous systems. The analytical approaches to these two types are distinctly different. Their analyses are covered in Chapters 12 and 13, respectively. Finally, the estimation of memory requirement is a subject unto itself that can only be tackled after the other aspects of performance have been determined. Memory analysis is treated in Chapter 14.

1.5. Chapters 15–16—Epilogue

Analyses, like programs and systems, are bug-prone and must therefore be subjected to rigorous testing intended to verify that the analysis does indeed represent the reality to which it aspires. Procedures analogous to those used to test and verify programs are discussed. The means by which measurements of performance in working systems are made, and the problems associated with such measurements, are also discussed, as is the role of analysis in rectifying errors inherent in the measurement process.

The last chapter concerns tuning, what it is and isn't, and how the principles that apply to analysis are also valuable adjuncts to the tuning process.

2. PERFORMANCE ANALYSIS

2.1. Why Do An Analysis?

Analyses are generally done for one of three reasons: (1) defensive, (2) exploratory, and (3) as a means of control.

The objective of a defensive analysis is to prove that the system meets the specification, i.e., that it "works," or, if you happen to be on the buyer's side rather than the vendor's side, that it doesn't work. Defensive analyses are usually done after major design decisions have been made, the design frozen, or so far along that the result of the analysis is unlikely to influence the design. The analyst under these conditions may be subjected to pressures that he "prove" something. What is to be proven depends on which side the analyst is on. Often, by the time things get around to a defensive analysis the system is in operation and it is easier to determine its performance by direct measurement. Defensive reasons are the worst reasons for analyzing a system's performance.

An exploratory analysis is aimed at determining the limits of the system's performance, and incidentally, demonstrating that those limits meet or exceed the specified performance. Here again, physical measurements on the real system may prove to be the tool of choice, but sometimes considerable analysis is required to interpret and/or correct the measurements.

The best reason for analyzing a system's performance is to exercise control over the design process. Analyses are done continually to assure that the system's performance tracks the specification. They are done to provide a rational basis for crucial trade-off decisions that may not be intuitively obvious. They are done to provide early warning of the impact of a specification or hardware change. This type of analysis is a continuing effort, mostly done by the designers themselves.

2.2. The Analyst Analyzed

If the subject was the performance analysis of large scale systems, such as a commercial computer's operating system, rather than microanalysis, I would characterize not the analyst, but the analysis department. It would consist of several subdepartments, service groups, specialties, etc., with an organizational structure not unlike that of a small corporation.

The situation in the microcomputer or minicomputer based system project is distinctly different. Most of the analysis is done by designers. If the system is complex it may pay to employ a specialist to bring together the subsidiary analyses done by the various project members into an over-all model of the system's performance. The analyst then, rather than being a mathematician or specialist, is a designer; a designer primarily interested in analyzing performance as it affects his aspect of the design.

2.3. The Results of Analysis

A performance analysis produces numbers; numbers that characterize the system's performance. What is more important, the analysis results in a process (think of it as a special purpose computer) into which situations, hypotheses, parameters, etc., are entered and from which answers to such questions as, "What will happen if . . . ?" or "Is . . . better than . . . ?" are produced. A process or special purpose computer of this type is generally called a **model**. The result of an analysis, then, is a model of the system and numerical answers to the questions whose posing led to the construction of the model in the first place.

2.4. Models and Model Building [RIVE72, BUNY74, SVOB76].

Most large cities have a museum with a technology section. Some of them have collections of ship and aircraft models. The model collection ranges from sloppy, hastily assembled, amateurish constructs that barely represent reality to cleanly elegant, professional works, to laboriously built models so crowded with poorly executed details that one wonders at the senile masochism that must have led to such abominations. They all purport to give a true semblance of the thing which is modeled, but only a few achieve the necessary artistic balance between simplicity and detail. It is evident that if too much detail is put in, the model fails to satisfy us with its representation of reality. It is clear that the good modeler must know two technologies—that of modeling and that of the thing being modeled. No matter how well versed the modeler may be in ship lore, he will produce garbage if he does not know how to handle a knife and how to apply paint; while the most skilled woodworker will produce unfortunate jokes if he does not know that the rudder belongs aft.

Some of the best ship models were produced in the seventeenth and eighteenth centuries before the invention of copying machines. In those days, the ship's architects and builders did not rely on drawings or plans, but instead constructed detailed models from which the shipwrights scaled their measurements. The model would sit in the ship loft and other models, such as cross-sectional models, would be scattered throughout the construction site for reference. These models were not merely works of art, but an integral part of the ship design and building process.

Today, this tradition of model building in the engineering profession is best exemplified by the use of models in the aircraft industry. Many different models are constructed, each with a specialized purpose, and, therefore, each with a different emphasis. A wind tunnel model, intended for the examination of aerodynamic characteristics, is exact in external configuration but its insides are stuffed with instrumentation probes rather than miniature seats. An internal model, used to examine the placement of seats, the traffic pattern during emergencies and the like, has no validity with respect to aerodynamics. In addition to these physical models, abstract models are constructed of subsystems to examine their stability and dynamic behavior. These models employ simulation or analytical procedures and are known in the trade as **mathematical models**. In principle, a mathematical model of a device or system is a philosophical extension of its earlier counterpart constructed of wood.

This brings us to the hobby shop. In any large hobby shop you can pick out an aircraft, say, and find a dozen different kits for it. They vary in scale, price, detail, performance, and what they model; from simple plastic models at a dollar, to fully operational, radio controlled, flying scale models at several hundreds of dollars. The radio controlled models sacrifice detail in order to fly, while the best scale models cannot fly at all and are intended solely for display. One is not inherently better than the other; they merely have different objectives.

The analytical process consists of building a good model (i.e., suitable to the purpose) and playing with it. Whether the model is the system itself on a test bench, a simulation program running in a computer, or a pot full of mathematical expressions, it is a model and its validity depends upon the amount of detail that has been used to construct it and the simplifying assumptions made.

2.5. Justifying the Analysis

Analysis is not cheap. A detailed analysis can consume 10% of the software development effort.* A reasonably accurate, but less detailed analysis can consume 5%, and it would be difficult to conduct a system analysis that had any value at all for less than 2% of the software development effort. Since analytical activities contribute to the system in an indirect manner (after all, the analysis doesn't do anything in the final system) it is often difficult to justify its cost to a sponsor already suspicious of the ephemeral content of software—never mind analysis, which in his eyes must appear to be software squared.

For these reasons, it is incumbent upon the analyst (or the designer when wearing an analytical hat) to justify at least to himself the effort required to do the analysis, because sooner or later (more often sooner) he will have to justify it to someone else. The analysis of a system, particularly a small system, should be conducted with a definite end in mind; an end which is translatable into something substantive, such as cost.

---

*Why analysis cost is intimately tied to software costs rather than hardware complexity or system complexity will become apparent in what follows.

The key to justifying a special analytical effort, whether it be of the running time of a minor subroutine or the performance of an entire system, is to determine the expected payoff for the cost expended. While the expected payoff may be difficult to judge, it is usually not difficult to calculate the theoretically maximum payoff. For example: a junior programmer proposes to analyze a common subroutine with the intention of improving its performance. The probability of executing it is 0.01. The system's performance appears to be adequate. The production run for the system is 1000 units, at a cost of $15,000 each. The analysis will take five days, at a cost of $175 per day or 88¢ per system. If the routine were eliminated, 4¢ worth of memory would be freed and the net reduction in processing load would work out to about 20¢ (after multiplying by the 0.01 probability). The best expected payoff is therefore 24¢ per system and the proposed analysis is worthless. The programmer now proposes an analysis that may save five words of memory—five words on a ROM chip which has been committed to capacity. The payoff is several dollars per system and the analysis is clearly worthwile.

In large scale systems with high production runs, such as a commercial data processing system, because of the costs, the analytical effort is almost always justifiable. In low cost, moderate run systems based on small computers, the decision is more delicate, because the cost of the analysis and the expected payoff are often close. In very high volume systems, such as might be used in an automobile, appliance, or camera, again the payoff tends to be obvious, and in favor of doing the analysis. It is in the middle ground of most micro and mini computer applications that the question can be tricky. Common sense and an honest assessment of maximum and expected payoff, weighed against the cost of analysis, will determine the course.* See [RIVE72] for appropriate techniques.

2.6. Performance Evaluation Alternatives

There are three groups of techniques that can be used to evaluate a system's performance: (1) analytical methods, (2) simulation, and (3) measurement. Each has advantages and disadvantages. Analytical techniques are best applied to small systems or to small to moderate-size elements of large systems. Simulation is the method of choice for very large or complicated systems. Measurement, when properly done and controlled, is desirable for all systems. This book is mostly about analytical techniques.

In simulation, the system is represented by statements in a simulation language which are run by a simulation system. The program generates transactions, which the simulator then "processes," not in actuality, but rather by determin-

---

*One should not get carried away and consider the cost of analyzing the analysis. If that can't be done intuitively, it probably shouldn't be.

TABLE 1-1. Comparison of Analytical, Simulation, and Measurement Techniques for Performance Evaluation

Factor	Analytical	Simulation	Measurement
System size appropriate	micro/mini/midi	mini/midi/macro	all
Labor to do analysis on a scale of 1 per instruction in program	0.05	0.04	0.01
Tools	smart calculator/mini/time shared system	large computer	instrumentation
Cost to set up analysis	moderate	high	very low
Running cost per data point	low—pennies	high—dollars	cost of running the system very high—$10's
Accuracy	±10%	2-3%	1-2%
Flexibility	high	low	low
Special training	analytical techniques	analytical techniques simulation language	analytical techniques instrumentation package data processing package
Turn-around time to answer questions	short—hours	days	days
Trade-off evaluation	moderate	difficult	very difficult
Response to system change	change numbers or equation	change simulator program and debug	change running code and debug
Change in load assumptions	change numbers or equations	change simulator program or parameters	observe change
Elapsed time for analysis	developed as system is developed	analytical and simulator debug time	must have live system

ing how many instructions would have been required to perform that processing step. It is an analogue of the real system.

Measurement is just that: measuring the performance under a simulated or real load. It can be complicated because it may be difficult to generate a controlled driving load, and because the act of measurement may distort the measured performance.

Analytical techniques are used to simplify simulations and to correct measured performance for instrumentation effects. Therefore, analytical techniques are fundamental to all three approaches and in fact are prerequisite to simulation and measurement. Table 1-1 compares the three approaches from several different points of view. See [GORD69, WYMA70, REIT71, DRUM73, SAMM69, BUNY74, PRIT69, PRIT74A, PRIT74B] for further information.

2.7. Overview of the Approach

These are the steps in a performance analysis:

1. Clarify the specification so that the performance objectives are complete, consistent, and understandable.
2. Characterize the load to which the system will be subjected, also in a consistent, complete, and understandable manner.
3. Identify the performance limiting characteristics of the system—specify numerical quantities.
4. Start building models at the lowest subroutine level—including only those segments and paths of programs which are significant.
5. Incorporate the smaller models into larger models, much in the same way that software and systems are integrated.
6. Debug the model.
7. Set up the test conditions of interest and observe (i.e., calculate) the values of the performance parameters of interest and/or the resources that will be needed to meet those performance objectives (how much memory, how fast a ROM, etc.). In other words, play with the model.
8. After a decent interval, validate the model, preferably by comparison with the real system under identical conditions. Be prepared to gloat, sulk, or run, as suits the results.

2
Computer Structure, Resources and Application

1. SYNOPSIS

A computer consists of a number of units each of which is capable of performing its operations at specified rates. These units represent the **resources** of the system. The computer is examined from the point of view of resources rather than from the more traditional point of view of the functions performed by the component units. Resources are categorized into types and relations between resources are qualitatively examined.

2. A REPRESENTATIVE COMPUTER

2.1. General

Figure 2-1 depicts the architecture of a representative microcomputer. It is not intended to correspond to any specific computer, but rather to illustrate principles which are germane to performance issues. See [BARN76, CARS76, SOUC76, WEIT74, FLOR69, BEIZ71A] for related information on system architecture.

2.2. The Bus

The computer has a common bus. Every memory bus operation consists of a transfer of a single eight-bit character from one unit attached to the bus to another unit attached to the bus. Not all possible combinations of transfers are meaningful or possible. The bus can transfer characters at a maximum rate of R_b characters per second. This is a hardware limitation which cannot be exceeded—attempts to do so will result either in lost data or a refusal to execute the transfer.

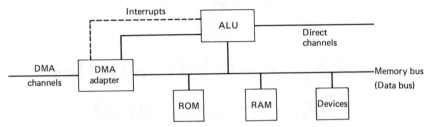

Figure 2-1. Block diagram of a typical microcomputer.

Initiations of transfers on the bus are not done directly by program control (i.e., by the execution of an explicit instruction to that effect), but rather are implicit in the operation of the units that are served by the bus. The units typically attached to the bus are: memory units of various types, DMA (Direct Memory Access) adapters, channel adapters, and ALUs (Arithmetic and Logical Units). Transfers are normally initiated only by ALUs, DMAs, channels, and interrupts. Only one pair of units can use the bus at any instant. Access to the bus is controlled by a bus controller, which can be an explicit unit or can be distributed among all the units attached to the bus without an explicit bus control unit. The controller (implicit or explicit) is designed so that it can always keep up with requests for transfers at the maximum bus rate. Therefore, from the point of view of resource usage, the bus itself and its controller (whether centralized or distributed) represent the same resource—R_b transfers per second.

There may be several buses in the system, used to provide intercommunications among different sets of units. Each bus represents a resource and each will have its own maximum operating rate. A bus may be dedicated to a specific function—e.g., to provide communications between a memory and an ALU. In such cases, the bus is usually sufficiently fast to handle the transfer of data at the maximum combined memory rates (assuming there is more than one memory unit). This kind of bus would not be a ponderable resource, since it could not limit the performance of the system.

2.3. ROM

The ROM (*R*ead *O*nly *M*emory) is typically used for program and permanent table storage. In actuality, the ROM may be modifiable, either in a special operating mode or by means of a "programmer" device. In this case it is called a PROM (Programmable ROM). Programming speeds are generally much lower than reading speeds. Furthermore, the programming is rarely done while the system is doing the job for which it was designed. Consequently, ROM write rates are rarely considered a system resource. From our point of view, ROMs and PROMs are much the same.

A ROM is characterized by two resource parameters: (1) access rate in characters or words per second, and (2) capacity in words. ROM capacity plays a secondary role in performance analysis. The capacity is typically limited by the total memory address span. Since ROM contents do not change (for us) there can be no fluctuation of the demands for storage made upon the ROM. The rate at which accesses are made, however, is subject to fluctuation and can influence performance; therefore, ROM access rate is a resource parameter. ROM access rates are typically higher than ALU execution rates (see below) and slower (but not by much) than bus transfer rates.

2.4. RAM

RAM (*R*andom *A*ccess *M*emory) is used for program storage, table storage, working space, and for dynamically allocated buffers, queues, and stacks. Read and write rates are generally equal to each other and slower than ROM as well as bus transfer rates. RAM access rate is a significant resource parameter, often the only one of interest. The demand for RAM space may fluctuate with system load. RAM space availability can have a profound influence on performance since the execution of a job may be deferred or curtailed if the required space is not available. RAM space is, therefore, a resource parameter.

2.5. The DMA Adapter

The DMA (*D*irect *M*emory *A*ccess) adapter provides a connection between a peripheral device and a memory unit. It typically performs block transfers of data at a rate dictated by the device. That rate is perforce less than the bus rate or the memory rate. The DMA adapter may be used to terminate several devices; that is, the adapter may have more than one channel. The DMA adapter itself has a maximum transfer rate. Each DMA channel appears to have a private connection to the memory, and can transfer data at its rate. However, at any instant the sum of the transfer rates of the attached devices must be less than or equal to the DMA transfer rate. The DMA transfer rate, therefore, is a system resource parameter.

Each transfer of a word or character to memory may require more than one memory access. DMA transfers are usually block transfers and therefore the address of the next location in memory to be accessed (read or write) must be known. Furthermore, how many characters have been transferred must be known. This information may be stored in whole or in part in the DMA adapter or in the DMA channel logic. In many systems, however, this information is stored in memory (RAM). This means that in addition to the memory access required to take care of the actual data, additional memory accesses must be made to access the control words for the data. There are typically two additional accesses, although four is not an unusual number. The DMA then, while having one resource parameter, implies additional load on the bus and the memory.

2.6. Devices

Any number of devices may be attached to the memory bus, to the DMA adapter, or (in some computers) directly to the ALU. The specifics depend upon the device and the computer's architecture. However the device is connected, its use will typically impact several resources in much the same way as the DMA does. The device also represents a resource. It too may have a maximum performance rate. It may, like the DMA, influence the utilization of several other resources, and it may itself be characterized by several parameters.

2.7. ALU

The ALU (*A*rithmetic and *L*ogic *U*nit) executes instructions at the maximum possible rate. This does not necessarily correspond to the rates associated with other units, especially memory. It may be faster or slower than memory depending on the specifics of the units involved. Typically it takes one memory cycle (and therefore one bus cycle) to access the instruction and one memory cycle to access the operand (if any). The instruction execution thus implies two bus accesses and two memory accesses. The ROM and RAM do not necessarily operate at the same speed, and this can influence the rate at which instructions are actually executed. The ALU speed should be carefully distinguished from the bus speeds and/or the memory speed(s). This is readily done by assuming that the bus and memories are infinitely fast. The time to execute a single instruction under this assumption is a measure of the ALU's speed. Specifications are not always clear and some digging, and/or prodding of the computer manufacturer's representative may be necessary to disentangle which of the several units truly limits the ALU's instruction execution rate.

2.8. Interrupts

The system may be fitted with one or more interrupt lines. In a typical microcomputer, interrupt lines are OR'ed together and activity on any one line causes the interrupt. When an interrupt is activated, the instruction presently being executed is completed, after which control is transferred to an interrupt program. In the larger computers, several other things take place; the present value of the program counter is stored on a push-down stack and the contents of one or more registers may be stored as well. The interrupt program must (typically) execute instructions to determine which line caused the interrupt. The first instruction in this sequence is used to block further interrupts. After the interrupting device has been detected, the interrupt is acknowledged (by an instruction) and the interrupt program may store the device's identity and some other information on a stack or in a dynamic memory area. Some cleanup is then done prior to enabling the interrupts again and returning control back to the interrupted routine. This entire process may consume anything from a few ALU instruction times, memory bus cycles, ROM cycles, RAM cycles, etc., to several hundred cycles of each type. The details are highly context-dependent, but usually readily determinable. The total resources consumed by an interrupt is called the Raw Interrupt Overhead (RIO) and is an important parameter of the system. The RIO is determined by assuming that nothing else is going on, and that exactly one interrupt occurs with no other interrupt occurring while that interrupt is serviced by the interrupt routine. Since a DMA transfer typically ends in an interrupt, it represents at least the RIO resource consumption in addition to that required for the actual transfer.

2.9. Direct Channels

Direct channels are connected to the ALU. They are activated by the issuance of an I/O instruction. The ALU cannot execute the next instruction until the device has acknowledged completion of that instruction or that phase of the instruction. The execution time of a direct channel instruction is therefore device-dependent, and can range from a few bus cycles to a long time. During that time at least the ALU is locked out, and depending upon the structure of the machine, other units may be locked out as well.

3. RESOURCES

3.1. What is a Resource?

The various units of which the system is composed represent resources and those resources are measured by one or more parameters, such as an execution rate or a capacity. Thus, a memory has two resource parameters: memory access rate and memory capacity. The term "resource" will be used in the sequel to mean "resource parameter," where the specific parameter is obvious from the context. It is often convenient to consider a system resource that cannot be associated with a single device. A bus, under this definition, is a single resource—bus transfer rate; while a moving head disc is several—character transfer rate, sector access rate, track access rate, and capacity. An interrupt rate is an example of a resource that involves several devices—bus, ALU, and memory. Nevertheless, it is represented by a single number: the maximum rate at which interrupts can occur.

A resource may be created by software. I call these **synthetic resources**. For example, a portion of memory can be allocated to a pool of shared buffer blocks.

This pool, then, becomes a resource measured in buffer blocks. Similarly, processing time can be subdivided (and, therefore, bus transfers and memory accesses) into convenient time slices, say, one millisecond long, creating a processing resource which is available at a rate of 1000 per second. Ultimately, all synthetic resources must be expressible in terms of physical resources, but it may be convenient at times to think about something in terms of synthetic resources rather than the physical resources from which they are actually created.

Physical resources have the additional property that they are available only in finite quantities. Resource parameters are always positive numbers. Resources can be increased by spending more money and decreasing them may (or may not) reduce cost.

3.2. Resource Demand, Relative Demand, Utilization, and Efficiency

If we examine any resource over a period of time we find that it is sometimes gainfully employed and at other times not. A memory location may this instant be used by some routine and the next instant returned to the pool. The bus may momentarily be transferring data and the next instant not. An opportunity to access a memory may or may not be taken advantage of. If we keep track of the time during which the resource is in use and divide this by the total time of observation, assuming that everything was steady, we would surmise that the resource was in use a certain percentage of the time. That percentage is called the resource **utilization**.

$$U = \text{Utilization} \triangleq \frac{\text{observed time in use for resource}}{\text{length of observation period}} \qquad \text{(D2.1)}$$

Utilization is expressed by a dimensionless number to which the pseudo-unit **erlang*** has been given. A utilization of 1.00 (one-hundred percent) is called 1 erlang. If analysis shows that 1.25 erlang of CPU is required, i.e., the computer is using 125% of the available time, rather than having said something ridiculous, we have merely noted that one computer is insufficient to do the job. N erlangs, then, mean that at least N devices will be needed. The resource **usage** is defined as the quantity of the resource required for a specific task (e.g., instructions executed, number of memory accesses, etc.). A memory has two resource parameters, one erlang of transfers, and for reasons that will be apparent later, N erlangs of storage, where N is the number of blocks into which storage has been subdivided.

---

*Named after Agner Krarup Erlang of the Copenhagen Telephone Company, who, working on the theory of telephone systems, had by 1925 inadvertently developed the basis for much of computer system performance analysis.

Transactions enter the system at a specified rate. The transactions themselves lead to processing tasks which therefore make demands on resources at a specified rate. The **demand rate** is the rate at which request for the resource is being made. Evidently:

$$\text{Demand rate} \triangleq \text{Task arrival rate} \times \text{resource usage per task} \qquad \text{(D2.2)}$$

For example:

1. Tasks per second $\times$ instructions per task = instructions per second.
2. Tasks per second $\times$ transfers per task = transfers/second.

The ratio of the demand rate to the available resource rate is called the **relative demand**.* It is denoted by the Greek letter ρ:

$$\rho \triangleq \text{relative demand} \triangleq \frac{\text{demand rate}}{\text{resource rate}} = \frac{\text{task arrival rate} \times \text{resource per task}}{\text{resource rate}}$$

$$\text{(D2.3)}$$

The relative demand (or simply "demand" when the context is clear) is also dimensionless and expressed in erlangs. The relative demand does not necessarily equal the utilization. In fact, it can never exceed and must generally be lower than the utilization. There are many reasons why the utilization and the relative demand may not be equal. The relative demand might be 0.05 erlangs, but the system's design may be such that a utilization of 0.15 may result, perhaps because of intervening gaps caused by blockage of one resource by another, perhaps by intent, perhaps because the system is out of tune. While the relative demand is easily determined, the utilization can only be found through analysis. In fact, analysis of the entire system is usually required.

When the utilization equals 1 erlang, the resource is said to be **saturated**. Since relative demand is always smaller or equal to utilization, a relative demand of one erlang (and typically less) will likewise cause resource saturation. The ratio of the relative demand to the utilization is called the **efficiency**.

$$\text{Efficiency} \triangleq \frac{\text{relative demand}}{\text{utilization}} \qquad \text{(D2.4)}$$

One-hundred percent efficiency is not usually a desirable goal, mainly because it can rarely be achieved unless the resource is saturated, and the consequence of resource saturation (as will be seen) is infinite processing delay.

---

*Terminology is very confused in the literature here. What I have called relative demand many writers call utilization. In fact, the common practice is not to distinguish between these two concepts. This is fine as long as they are equal, which they can be, but can lead to much confusion when they are different.

Determining the relative demand for a resource expressed in erlangs is straightforward. Assume that the system is called upon to process R tasks per second; that each task requires the execution of C instructions, and that the computer takes K seconds to execute an instruction. The relative demand will evidently be:

$$\rho \triangleq R\,\frac{\text{tasks}}{\text{second}} \times C\,\frac{\text{instructions}}{\text{task}} \times K\,\frac{\text{seconds}}{\text{instruction}} = RCK \text{ erlangs.}$$

The imposed load R is a characteristic not of the system but of the application environment. C is a characteristic of the system design and depends on the hardware *and the software as implemented in that particular computer.* K is typically a fixed hardware parameter. More generally:

$$\rho \triangleq R\,\frac{\text{tasks}}{\text{second}} \times C\,\frac{\text{resource unit*}}{\text{task}} \times H\,\frac{\text{seconds}}{\text{resource unit}}$$

Resources can be subdivided into three categories which have the following names: Type 1 resources = constant H; Type 2 resources = bounded H; and Type 3 resources = unbounded H.

Type 1 = constant H:
$$P_1 = R\,\frac{\text{tasks}}{\text{second}} \times C\,\frac{\text{resource units}}{\text{task}} \times K\,\frac{\text{seconds}}{\text{resource unit}}$$

$$(2.1)$$

Type 2 = bounded H:
$$P_2 = R\,\frac{\text{tasks}}{\text{second}} \times C\,\frac{\text{resource units}}{\text{task}} \times H\,\frac{\text{seconds}}{\text{resource unit}}$$

$$(2.2)$$

Type 3 = unbounded H:
$$P_3 = R\,\frac{\text{tasks}}{\text{second}} \times C\,\frac{\text{resource units}}{\text{task}} \times H\,\frac{\text{seconds}}{\text{resource unit}}$$

$$(2.3)$$

In all three cases, R is a parameter of the environment, expressing how many tasks of the given type the system is to process, P is the demand, and C is a system design parameter expressing how many units of that resource (e.g., instruction executions) are used to process the task. The difference between the three resource types is in the third element K or H as appropriate.

---

*Note that the use of the term "unit" in this context should not be confused with its usage as a description of part of the system. The present usage is in the sense of dimensional analysis—as in stone, furlongs, centimeters, coulombs. It would have been better had computer scientists and physicists gotten together on this, but such is the tyranny of evolution.

In the case of a constant type resource, H is a constant and is not influenced by either the load or the manner in which the processing is accomplished. Generally this corresponds to physical resources, especially rates. For example, instruction execution time, bus transfer time, and memory access time, are all constant resources.

In Type 2 resource, the number of seconds required to do one unit of work is variable and may depend upon the load and several other factors, but that time is always larger than some parameter K which is physical. Consider a disc access; the demand is:

$$\rho = R \frac{\text{tasks}}{\text{second}} \times C \frac{\text{accesses}}{\text{task}} \times H \frac{\text{seconds}}{\text{access}}$$

The accesses per task probably do depend upon the load, but the number of fractions of a second required to access the disc decreases with increasing load, since there is an ever higher probability that more than one access can be made during the same revolution or be found on the same track. H is therefore a function. Furthermore, various techniques can be employed in the software design to minimize H. It is clear, however, that we can never do better than be on the right track and the right sector precisely at the instant we wish to access this particular disc sector. The bound, in this case, is the time required to transfer one sector of data. This is a physical parameter, and clearly no design or load can modify it.

In a Type 3 resource, the time required per unit of work is not only not constant, it is also not bounded by physical system characteristics at all. It will, however, still be a positive number. As an example, consider memory capacity:

$$\rho = R \frac{\text{tasks}}{\text{second}} \times C \frac{\text{buffer blocks}}{\text{task}} \times H \frac{\text{seconds}}{\text{buffer block}}$$

H is now a measure of how long the particular buffer block will remain in use. For example, if the system must store a copy of an output for ten years, then $H = 3.16 \times 10^8$ seconds, and it presumably will need a lot of memory unless tasks come very infrequently. In this case, there is neither a physically inherent upper or lower limit on the value of H. In common parlance, H for an unbounded resource is called a **holding time**.

3.3. Resource Characteristics

In general, C and H are functions of the load and the other resource demands. It is instructive to distinguish between several different categories that recur in many systems.

3.3.1. Characteristics of C

The following distinctions on the nature of C, resource usage per task, are noteworthy:

- *Constant C.* The resource usage per task is constant and independent of the load. This is the simplest case and is often a useful approximation to the real situation. As an absolute truth, it is rare.
- *Linear C.* The resource usage per task is a linear function of the load. For example, $C = K_0 + K_1 R$. This is typical of a process which has some overhead which is to be executed independently of the load. K_1 can be positive or negative. A negative K_1 implies increased processing efficiency as load increases. This is common. If K_1 is negative, then this too is probably an approximation to a more complex real situation corresponding to one of the relations discussed below. Generally, K_0 tends to be much larger than K_1.
- *Polynomial C.* C is given by a polynomial in R. Say, $C = K_0 + K_1 R + K_2 R^2 + \cdots$. While second and third order polynomials are not uncommon, it is rare that we find a fourth or higher order polynomial. Usually the coefficients get smaller with higher order terms. In systems where there is much processing whose duration depends upon the length of internal queues, K_2 may not be a small coefficient and may dominate in the higher load regions. The polynomial C is often an approximation for the next case, which is also common.
- *Inverse polynomial C.* C is given by a function of the form

$$C = \frac{K_0}{1 - K_1 R - K_2 R^2 - \cdots}.$$

This may be an exact expression for C. Terms higher than the fourth power are rare. Note that this can be converted to a polynomial approximation by synthetic division.
- *General, NonLinear C.* The relation between C and the load may follow a general, nonlinear expression, of which an exponential is a common case, i.e.,

$$C = K_0 + K_1 e^{-K_2 R}$$

This can also be approximated by a polynomial, if desired.

3.3.2. Dependent and Independent Resource Demands

Considering any two resources, their demands may be interdependent or independent. Some degree of dependency is common. For example, a DMA channel input affects the DMA hardware, the bus, and the memory. Whichever one of these resources saturates first will limit the others. For example, DMA transfers will saturate if the DMA itself is saturated, or if the bus or the memory is saturated. Probably the most common kind of dependency occurs for bounded and unbounded resources. The holding time is almost always a function of the other demands as well as the load. For example, if processing demand is high, it is reasonable to expect that memory holding times will increase. Note that this high processing demand, while containing load-dependent factors, could also be high for reasons that are not directly related to load. In the general case, then, demands are not independent; however, for some resources the degree of interdependency may be small and can be ignored without introducing significant error. Recognizing that resource demands are interdependent, it may often be convenient to ignore this fact in order to simplify an analysis or to obtain bounds on how the system behaves.

Physical resources tend to have the least degree of interdependency, load dependency, and functional complexity. Synthetic resources tend in the opposite direction. Ultimately, since it is physical resources that one pays for, it is important to express things in terms of physical resources. It is obvious that the demand for a synthetic resource must impact the demand for the physical resources used to create it.

4. OBJECTIVES RESTATED

A system has inputs that arrive at a rate which may or may not be controllable and which may or may not be affected by the system's performance. It responds, after some delay, to those inputs and produces outputs. In so doing, it uses resources. The objectives of performance analysis include:

1. Given the throughput and resources, determine the system's performance.
2. Given the throughput and a target performance, determine the resources or resource mix required to achieve that performance.
3. Given a resource mix and a performance objective, determine the throughput that the system can handle.

5. EXERCISES

1. Some of the following are resources, some are resource parameters, and some are merely system facilities or characteristics. The category may depend on context. Categorize these items as being either a resource, resource parameter, or system characteristic, and specify the context (if any) for resources:

   (1) Teleprinter; (2) teleprinter control routine; (3) teleprinter polling rate; (4) telecommunications line; (4) a job; (5) a job queue; (6) job control lan-

guage; (7) job control language interpreter routine; (8) job queue length; (9) the FORTRAN compiler; (10) the FORTRAN language; (11) a routine written in FORTRAN; (12) the common subroutine library; (13) a particular common subroutine; (14) the multiply instruction; (15) the subroutine call instruction; (16) instruction execution rate; (17) an I/O channel; (18) I/O handler routine; (19) I/O job queue; (20) an entry on the I/O job queue; (21) the storage block used to hold an I/O job queue entry; (22) the job's priority; (23) the job priority processing program; (24) a program label; (25) main memory; (26) a main memory location; (27) the operating system; (28) a human operator; (29) a system user; (30) a file; (31) an entry in a file; (32) a block used to store file entries; (33) a file manipulation program; (34) an execution of a file manipulation program; (35) a disc unit; (36) a disc control subroutine; (37) a program stored on disc while it is stored on disc; (38) the CPU; (39) a card reader; (40) interrupts; (41) interrupt control hardware; (42) interrupt execution rate; (43) the computer's priority structure; (44) time slices; (45) a satellite link; (46) the satellite link's transmission capacity; (47) the satellite link delay.

2. *Continuation.* For resources in Exercise 1, identify the resource parameter(s) and give typical values and dimensional units.

3. *Continuation.* For resources in Exercise 1, categorize as synthetic or physical. If synthetic, identify the component physical resources.

4. *Continuation.* For each resource in Exercise 1, specify the tasks that consume it.

5. *Continuation.* Identify the sets of dependent resources (if any) in Exercise 1 and explain the nature of the dependencies. Identify those resources that are independent.

6. Can the resources of a real system be saturated? If so, what are the consequences? Can the relative demand for a resource exceed 1 erlang? Can the mean relative demand over a long period of time exceed 1 erlang?

7. A routine places items on a single queue in accordance with five priority levels. The number of entries on the queue is proportional to the rate at which items arrive for service. Processing consists of two components: one to compare the new entry with those entries already on the queue in order to find the proper place at which to link it, and one to do the actual linking. Show that the demand rate is a quadratic in the task arrival rate.

8. The principality of Gratislavia, which is in the Carpathian mountains, near the conjunction of Bukhavina, Moldavia, Bessarabia, and Transylvania, has a central telephone exchange serving a thousand subscribers. National policy prohibits calls to and from the outside world. Gratislavians are very talkative and spend half of their time on the telephone. How many erlangs does the telephone exchange handle?

9. *Continuation*. On alternate Tuesdays, the subscribers make an average of one call an hour which lasts 20 minutes. How many erlangs must the exchange handle then?

10. *Continuation*. During the fast of Mad King Ludwig, the call duration on alternate Tuesdays goes up to 35 minutes. What is the minimum number of telephones in Gratislavia? Why do I find it so irritating to make calls there? What can you infer about the Gratislavian language?

11. *Continuation*. If the thousand subscribers spend half of their time on the telephone and the average call duration is 3 minutes, how many calls per hour does the typical Gratislavian make?

3

Performance Measures and Parameters

1. SYNOPSIS

The performance of a system is ultimately measured by its ability to handle a workload presented to it at a statistically steady mean rate. "Handling" implies that the workload is completed without excessive delay. Load and delay are intimately related. For every system there is a load which makes the processing delay potentially infinite. At that load, at least one resource (e.g., memory speed, channel capacity) is saturated. All performance questions can be resolved in terms of the relation between suitably defined loads and the corresponding delays.

2. THE STATISTICAL POINT OF VIEW

Systems process inputs. Decisions are made in the course of that processing. There is a branch point in the program, and the usage along one branch is rarely identical to that of the other. Inputs arrive on the several inways with varying time gaps between them so that while the *mean* time between arrivals, and therefore the mean arrival rate, is predictable, the absolute time between inputs is random. A floppy disc is used as a mass memory and its position beneath the read heads is random relative to the stage of processing. It is only in the most trivial systems in which all inputs and outputs are synchronized and in which resource usage is fixed for every task that some type of randomness does not occur. Thus "processing time" really means "mean processing time;" similarly for input rate, resource demand, utilization, and delay; in fact, for almost every numerical parameter of interest in the system.

This statistical point of view is probably the most basic assumption that must be made in analyzing the system. It is of course possible to set up a scenario of inputs, disc positions, initial conditions, etc., to trace the actions of the system, and to determine just for that scenario what the performance would be. This is occasionally interesting, but it is better done with an emulator, or on a carefully monitored real system.

There are pitfalls to the statistical point of view, however, as the following example shows. I was measuring the performance of a system whose specification stated that the delay at a given load should not exceed two seconds. Over a period of several minutes, not only did the delay at times exceed two seconds, but it exceeded 30 seconds. The mean delay for which the system was designed was, however, well within the specification. The user was upset, but incorrect. The specification had not stipulated maximum delay, nor was it necessary that it do so; the mean delay was adequate to the purpose. Conversely, there are systems in which an absolute maximum delay should have been specified, but for which a mean delay was provided—again an ambiguous specification.

It is an unfortunate fact of life that for most systems the dispersion in performance about the mean is very large. The more complicated the system, the larger the deviation from the mean is likely to be. Another way of putting this is to say that almost every performance-related parameter which is not a physical characteristic of the hardware (and some of those too) is represented by a probability distribution. "Processing time" really means the mean value or expected value of that probability distribution of the processing time. Furthermore, experience has shown these distributions to be broad with a standard deviation of five to ten times the mean not unusual. The distributions are rarely Gaussian, but most often are exponential or geometric.

It is fortunate, from a manipulation and analytical point of view, that we do not often need to use anything but the most elementary statistical concepts and we can blithely add the means of two distributions and not worry whether or not this is the same as the mean of the distribution of their sums and such other esoterica. However, this is not always true, and therefrom stems another possible source of analytical inaccuracy.

It is not unnatural to forget that we are dealing with probabilistic events and situations, and to ascribe absolute verity to our results. This leads to such erroneous statements as, "The processing delay *is* 345.6789 milliseconds," rather than the more correct statement, "The mean of the delay is 340 milliseconds with a standard deviation of 800 seconds." Dealing with statistics can lead to occasionally strange results, such as predicting a behavior that cannot occur in real life. The value of a parameter can only be an integer, yet we speak of 3.53 units of whatsits. This may lead to apparent contradictions between the actual behavior of the system, as seen by the designer or user, and the probabilistic behavior of the system as seen by its analyst. There is no real conflict if all parties realize the differences in their points of view.

3. DEFINITION OF THROUGHPUT

3.1. Transactions

Systems, particularly those based on microcomputers, perform a small set of repetitive operations (time the wash, adjust the fuel flow and spark advance, etc.). These operations are performed on inputs, resulting in outputs. A functional operation as viewed by the user does not necessarily entail a single input, nor even a sequence of inputs followed by a sequence of outputs. Generally it is more complex, consisting of several steps with some feedback, either directly or indirectly, between the outputs and inputs. At some point the system has reverted to the state it was in prior to the first input and is ready to accept a new input/output set. For example, while the individual keystrokes on a hand calculator constitute individual inputs, from the user's point of view the entire sequence of keystrokes including the decimal key, the "enter" key, the "add" key, and so forth, constitutes a single transaction of interest. Just what one wishes to call a "transaction" is arbitrary. In the above example it could be the individual keystrokes, the add operation including output display, or the execution of a routine involving input, output, and their interaction. As an example of the opposite extreme, the transaction to a microcomputer used to control a private telephone system is a "call." A detailed examination of a "call" from off-hook to hang-up entails hundreds of complex steps of which the user is not aware—that totality of steps, in that context, constitutes a single transaction.

While the designer may find it convenient to deal with a more microscopic transaction than that which the user acknowledges (after all, the telephone user is interested in how long it takes to place the call, not what the trunk signalling acknowledgement delay is), performance should ultimately be measured in terms of functionally oriented transactions that are sensible to the user. After all, who pays for the system?

The rate at which transactions are presented to, and disposed of, by the system is called the **throughput**. In some systems it pays to distinguish between input and output rates, but generally, such distinctions cannot readily be made and the more general term "throughput" is applied.

System load is measured in transactions completed per second, or transactions per minute, per hour, or on some other convenient rate scale. The term "throughput" is usually taken to mean the maximum load (transaction rate) which the system can handle without excessive delay. This, however, is a vague usage requiring further definition of "handle" and "excessive delay." I shall use the terms "throughput" and "load" interchangeably to mean the rate at which transactions are being presented to the system for processing. The term "ulti-

001.6404 B397m
c.1

mate throughput" or "maximum throughput" will be used when I'm discussing what is generally (and loosely) called "*the* throughput."

3.2. Simultaneous Transactions

Most systems of interest do not have a single set of inways and outways;* a calculator being an exception in that it has only one keyboard and one display. Most systems can accept several transactions quasi-simultaneously on several different inway sets, and can produce several outputs also quasi-simultaneously on the several outway sets. I say "quasi-simultaneously" because true simultaneity is not possible in most computers. Events will differ by one instruction, by the delay of single gate, or by a delay of several milliseconds due to the execution of a handling routine. I shall not be so precise in what follows, and will use "simultaneous" to mean quasi-simultaneous, but sufficiently close that the time difference is imperceptible and unimportant. For example, a counter could be counting elapsed times on several different inways. The event or transaction consists of the interval starting with a positive-going polarity and ending with a negative-going polarity. The elapsed time for the transaction might be several seconds (i.e., the pulses are a few seconds long); however, new pulses could arrive at a rate of 100 pulses per second (obviously not on the same inway).

3.3. Different Transactions

There is no reason to assume that only one kind of transaction is being processed by the system at a time. It could be simultaneously counting on some lines, sampling analog voltages on others, adjusting the air conditioning on a third set, and running the elevator on a fourth set of lines. Most systems of interest are designed to handle more than one kind of transaction, which transactions occur concurrently with others of a different kind.

Transactions vary in yet another way. A given type of transaction may entail different processing steps depending upon the value of inputs. For example, the system is receiving pulses. If the pulse is less than 5 milliseconds long, count it. If the pulse is more than 5 milliseconds long, measure its length and add that to some memory location. The distinguishing characteristic in this example is the pulse length, but it could just as well have been a signal level, a character pattern, or a logical pattern of some of the inways that dictated (implicitly or explicitly) what was to be done with that type of transaction.

Given a diversity of responses such as this, it is tempting to lump all trans-

---

*That is, the lines along which inputs arrive and outputs depart, as distinguished from the events or signals on those lines—inputs and outputs.

actions together and to create an artificial "average" transaction. This can and should be done where proper; however, it is not always easy to tell what "proper" means without detailed knowledge of the hardware and the software which is going to process the transaction. The following criteria are useful.

- If the differences in the various transactions affect only the value of the results, or the contents of the memory locations used to process the transaction, then it is safe to lump them together and deal with an average transaction.
- If the differences in the various transactions are manifested in different paths through the programs, the validity of an averaging approach to transactions cannot be determined except by analysis.
- When in doubt, don't pre-average. If done incorrectly it can invalidate the analysis.

3.4. Some Necessary Simplifying Assumptions

It would be nice if it were possible to do a complete analysis without making simplifying assumptions. The model that requires the fewest assumptions is the system itself, in operation, being monitored by equipment that has absolutely no effect on the measurements. Simulation models require fewer assumptions and analytical approaches require the most. The following assumptions are appropriate. If any cannot be made with a clear conscience then a possible source of error has crept into the analysis. Alternatively, if these assumptions do not hold, you are beyond microanalysis and into macroanalysis.

3.4.1. Transaction Independence

Every transaction is independent of every other transaction. That is, the specifics of the processing of a given transaction is independent of the processing associated with any other transaction of the same or a different type. If two transactions are interdependent, then they are both really part of a larger transaction that encompasses them both. This is not always true in real life and at times care must be exercised in modeling the system and the load to assure that such dependencies have been taken care of.

3.4.2. Statistics Are Independent of Load

The statistical characteristics of transactions (e.g., their length, the probable paths that will be taken in processing, etc.) do not change with load. While the behavior of the system may change, the users do not change their habits as a result of what the system does. Again, this may not be the case in reality. If the transaction statistics change with, say, increasing load, subdivide the load into ranges each of which has its own kind of transaction statistics. If the statistics of the transaction does change with load, and the above subdivision approach is unacceptable, one should look to simulation for an answer. Alternatively the system can be analytically enlarged to include the generation of transactions as a process within the enlarged system, finding some type of "external" event which serves the purpose of a transaction.

3.4.3. Steady State Assumptions

It is assumed that the statistics do not change over the time period considered by the analysis; that the system has been operating under the postulated load from time immemorial and will continue to do so into the indefinite future. That is, the analysis is a steady state analysis. There are many queueing problems imbedded within the analysis of a typical system. Almost all reasonable, analytical solutions to queueing problems are based on steady state assumptions. The simplest transient queueing problems are analytically abominable. If transient solutions to system behavior are required, simulation or experimentation is the approach of choice. However, transient behavior can often be explored by piecing together a number of steady state analyses; that is, a quasi-steady state approach is used. The most significant thing that the steady state assumption gives us is *every second is the same as the previous and future seconds*. This assumption is often what makes an analysis possible.

3.4.4. Continuity—Well-Behaved Events

Things are assumed to be statistically continuous. That is, it makes sense to talk about 3.4 characters, a fraction of a bit, a fraction of a sector of memory, etc. While in reality nonintegral values may be impossible, or the behavior of the system at integral values may change discontinuously, for the most part such discontinuities and anomalous behavior will be ignored. This is not a bad assumption actually; it is another way of saying that we can, if we choose to, average things without doing violence to the statistics. Most systems and loads are sufficiently complex that this assumption is satisfied. While strange distributions may occur, we will ignore them and plow ahead with naive statistics.

3.5. Summary

- Load or throughput is expressed as transaction arrival rates (typically in transactions per second).
- The definition of a transaction is arbitrary but should be related to what makes sense to the ultimate user.
- Transactions can arrive quasi-simultaneously.
- The system can handle transactions of different kinds quasi-simultaneously.

- Do not average the characteristics of different kinds of transactions unless you are sure it can be done safely.
- Every transaction is *assumed* to be independent of every other transaction.
- The characteristics of transactions, or their arrival rate, are not changed by the behavior of the system.
- Every second is statistically the same as the next or previous second—steady state assumptions reign supreme.
- Transactions can be treated as a continuum. It's a digital world, but we have to use analog mathematics.

4. OF TASKS AND TRANSACTIONS

4.1. Definitions

Until now I have been loose about the use of the terms "transaction," "task," "work," "load," etc. It is now necessary to define some of these terms more formally to avoid possible confusion in what follows.

A **transaction** is a unit of work as seen from the user's point of view. Specifications usually give the load in terms of transactions per day, per hour, or per second. A transaction consists of operations, some of which are performed by the system, but some of which are also performed by persons or devices that are outside of the system. The specifier does not usually distinguish between those parts of the transaction that are in the system's purview and those that are not.

A **task**, by contrast, is a component of a transaction that can be identified with a processing function. A transaction might consist of the following operations:

1. Accept input.
2. Validate input.
3. Transmit acknowledgment to sender.
4. Do input processing.
5. Search file.
6. Request directions from sender.
7. Accept input.
8. Validate input.
9. Do processing.
10. Update file.
11. Transmit output.

The user would consider the entire scenario as a single transaction. From the system's point of view, the transaction consisted of eleven steps and there were nine different task types.

Most systems process several different types of transactions. These transactions, while requiring different processing operations, do have operations in common. The common elements may be defined as tasks. It is generally simpler to analyze a system's performance in terms of the tasks that it performs than in terms of the transactions it performs. The boundary between tasks and transactions is not fundamental, merely convenient, and the specifics will depend upon the organization of the system's software, and to a lesser degree on its hardware. Generally, task boundaries are decided by application of one or more of the following criteria:

1. The processing routine is batch-oriented and works on an ordered list of transactions. The work done by the routine on one transaction is a task.
2. The routine is called on demand or scheduled by the executive to operate on an entry identified on a process queue. The call/operate/return sequence is a task.
3. The routine stops at some point to issue an I/O order and waits for the completion of the I/O operation before resuming work. The processing leading to the I/O order is a task, the execution of the I/O order itself and the associated wait is a task, and the subsequent processing is another task.
4. There is a branch point in the routine and the branching is directed by a characteristic of the transaction. Thereafter, some paths lead out of the routine, or through essentially independent paths in the routine. The differences between the several paths are obvious, and/or functional, and/or otherwise noteworthy. The execution of each path corresponds to the processing of a task.

A flowchart is a natural form for describing transactions in terms of their component tasks. Every transaction should be described in a flowchart whose component elements denote processing steps, I/O operations, user actions, waits, etc.

4.2. An Example

Figure 3-1 is a segment of a transaction. A microcomputer is used to act as a smart terminal controller for several VDU terminals. The terminals are used to process orders for parts, say. The order forms are complicated. The user specifies what action is required and the terminal controller requests the proper form from a remotely located central computer complex. The forms may be several pages long and may contain many fields per page. The form is transmitted by the central computer in a highly encoded format designed to minimize transmission time. This is translated by the terminal controller for the user's benefit. The terminal controller only transmits the answers (i.e., the contents of the blanks) back to the central computer. As each page is com-

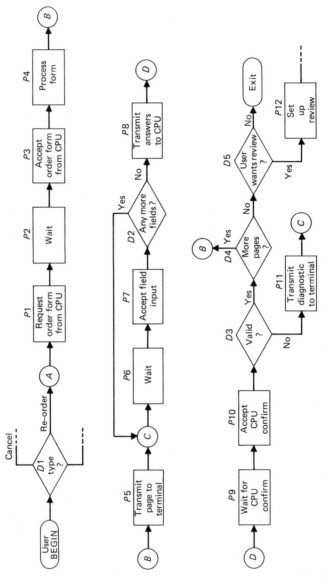

Figure 3-1. Example of a transaction.

pleted, the micro computer transmits the answers to the central computer, which either accepts them or rejects them. If the answers are not valid, a diagnostic code will be transmitted which the controller will translate and transmit to the terminal. Finally, the terminal allows the user to review the entire form.

Decision *D1* is not part of the process as such—it is really a characteristic of the kinds of transactions that the terminal controller handles. However, there is probably a decision of this type someplace in the computer's program. Process *P1* probably consists of several subsidiary processes which are completed by the transmission of the request for an order form from the central computer. The next step is "process" *P2*, which is really not a process. What the terminal controller will do here depends on the structure of the software; typically it will process the transaction for some other terminal. Process *P3* is a true processing step, as is process *P4*, which does the translation. Process *P6* is another wait for input. This has no direct correspondence to a program step and the length of the wait depends on user habits. Decision *D2* and Decision *D4* depend on the structure of the form. Which branch is taken on Decision *D3* is again determined by the user's behavior. The computer's program does not necessarily have an actual decision corresponding to any of these (*D1, D2, D3, D4,* or *D5*). "Decisions" *D1* and *D5* could correspond to different interrupts caused by special keys on the terminal. Decisions *D2* and *D4* could be implicit in a count, or could be mechanized by termination characters in the encoded form. While there may be a loop from *D2* to *C* and from *D4* to *B*, it may not be identifiable as such in any program, being implicit rather than explicit.

4.3. Transaction Flows Versus Process Flows

Figure 3-1 has the appearance of a flowchart; it does not necessarily correspond in a simple manner to a processing flowchart. Figure 3-1 is an example of what is usually called a **transaction flow**, which distinguishes it from the more normal type of flowchart referred to as a **process flow*** or "process flowchart."

Decisions in a transaction flow are generally functionally oriented and correspond to characteristics of the transaction, the user habits, and the system's environment (e.g., the wait for the central computer to get back with a confirmation, the expected rate of typographical errors, the number of fields on a page, etc.). Processes in a transaction flow consist of anything that could take time or consume resources. A transaction flow therefore is annotated with copious references indicating the how, when, and where of all things that could affect performance and resource consumption.

Another difference between transaction flows and process flows is that a trans-

---

*Many things apply to both process flows and transactions flows. The term "flow" will be used to mean both.

action flow, by design, deals with only one transaction at a time. Conversely, a process flow deals with one transaction at a time if and only if that is the way the software is organized. This difference is clarified by comparing Figure 3-2(a) with Figure 3-2(b). Figure 3-2(a) shows a simple transaction flow, consisting of tasks $A, B, C;$ I/O operations; and task D.

The process flow of Figure 3-2(b) is distinctly different. The program is structured as a loop. While in this loop all tasks for all awaiting transactions are completed as far as possible. Each process ($A, B, C,$ and D) is a batch processor. The entire loop from X back to X might take a few dozen milliseconds, or a few seconds. The program starts by setting up the read requests that were accumulated during the previous pass through the program. This is followed by the A processing phase. It is done here so that by the time the A's are finished, the reads will have been completed and no time will have been wasted waiting for the I/O operation to complete. Once the reads have been done, process C can be activated to work with the data that was read. When C is done, the write operations can be initiated for those transactions that just went through the C process. While the writes are going on, the B process is being done. By the time the B process is done, the write operations are done and the D process can be finished. Each transaction will take two passes through this program.

The principle to be noted here is that the process flow is a program, but the transaction flow is a trace of a transaction through that program.

4.4. Why Transaction Flows?

The starting point of every performance analysis is a careful development of complete transaction flows for every statistically significant transaction. The transaction flow acts as an organizer of the load characteristics, particularly when expressed in terms of tasks. Questions of the following form will have to be answered throughout the analysis, "How many read operations per second?"

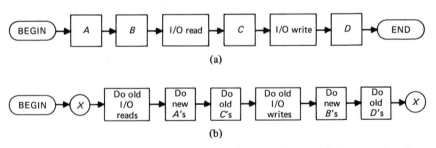

Figure 3-2. Distinction between transaction and process flows. (a) A transaction flow; (b) its corresponding implementation.

"How many input characters per second?" "How many output characters per second?" "How many interrupts per second?" "How many . . . ?" If the transaction flows have been developed in proper detail, then the answers to such questions can be obtained by analyzing the flows, using the same techniques that are used to analyze resource usage (as described in Chapter 5). In both cases something that has the appearance of a flowchart will be analyzed.

5. DELAY, DELAY, DELAY, DELAY, AND DELAY

5.1. Just What Delays Are We Talking About?

Just as there are different types of transactions, it is reasonable to expect that there will be different delays associated with the processing of such transactions. That might knock off one of the "delays" that headed this section, but not all of them. The problem is that even with a single, simple transaction consisting of input/processing/output, there are several different delays and it is important to identify which are caused by what, and for which ones the system (and therefore system designer) should be responsible.

5.2. Input Delays

An input is a sequence of events—a string of pulses, a string of characters, etc. Suppose we are asked to count pulses arriving on several inways. The user defines "arriving" as the trailing edge of the pulse. The user specifies that the "pulse count delay" (i.e., the delay between the "arrival" of the pulse and the new count display) shall be less than 5 microseconds at a pulse arrival rate of 100 per second. The pulses are several seconds long. It would not make sense to measure the delay from the leading edge of the pulse, since in such circumstances no system could ever meet the specification.

Suppose the user had specified that we merely count pulses, leaving it to us at what point we should do the counting. If we have that freedom, then it would make sense to count the leading edge of the pulse, since this would reduce the delay. If, however, we elected to count the trailing edge, the specification could not be met. When an "input" is a sequence of events, with possibly intervening outputs and feedback, things can be muddy and the notion of delay must be clarified.

Input delays are those delays which are inherent in the transaction and not controllable by the system. A simple test for determining if there is an input delay is to assume an infinitely fast processor. Whatever delay remains under such circumstances is inherent in the transaction and cannot be ascribed to the system.

5.3. Output Delays

Just as there are input delays for which the system is not responsible, there may be output delays for which the system is not responsible. For example, an input to the system results in a string of pulses whose duration is several minutes. It would not be fair to say that the system's delay is several minutes since the transaction takes that long to complete. Again the user who measures by this criterion is being unfair; a rational person would have specified the delay to be measured to the point where the output began, rather than the point at which it ended. We can make the same test here again. Let the processor be infinitely fast—what delay remains cannot be ascribed to a fault in the system.

5.4. Strange Delays

There really is no problem, is there? The idea is to stick the system with only the portion of the delay for which it is truly responsible. A pulse is going to come in and as a result of that pulse, the system will produce a string of output pulses. We measure the delay from the *trailing* edge of the input pulse to the *leading* edge of the output pulse train.

- Clever designer—elects to trigger the output pulse stream from the *leading edge* of the input pulse stream (user didn't specify). Result—a negative delay; no it's not a time machine, just specsmanship. ("Ready or not, here I come.")
- Unscrupulous designer—starts the first pulse out immediately, all precalculated and set up, and waits an abominably long time between successive pulses. ("Good morning! Barton, Barton, Snurdle, Price, and Watershed, could you hold please?")

5.5. External Congestion Delays

The system is to produce outputs in response to inputs, but the user can accept the outputs at only a specified maximum rate. Either he will introduce commands that will hold back the output rate, or the outputs will simply drop on the floor. The system starts stacking the outputs (in buffers, queues, or whatnot) and is soon saturated.

Delays which come about by the user's inability to accept outputs cannot be blamed on the system. On the other hand, if nothing the user does can affect the rate at which outputs are produced, then the user cannot have caused a congestion delay. For example, if the output lines are properly part of the system, and they are inadequate to handle the load, then the system designer is responsible and not the user.

Congestion delays do not occur solely on output. If there is feedback and the user must await a signal from the system to continue with the next input, then the system's slow response could result in input congestion. That is, congestion in the user's shop. One might adopt an out-of-sight-out-of-mind attitude because as far as the system is concerned the inputs appear to be arriving at a slower rate, but this is not an effective attitude, since it will not take long to find out that the system is responsible for the congestion.

Congestion delay then, is delay caused by the inability of the system or the user, or both, to accept each other's signals.

5.6. Processing Time, Processing Delay, Delay

Processing time, execution time, and **CPU time** are synonymous terms. They all mean the time spent by the CPU processing the transaction. To eliminate any doubt, this time is determined by counting the instructions required to do a process and multiplying that count by the time required per instruction. If a routine takes 200 instructions at 2 microseconds per instruction, the processing time is 400 microseconds. Processing time is determined under the assumption that there is nothing else going on at the time. No DMA transfers, no interrupts—nothing.

Because of the possible action of interrupts and I/O transfers, the time interval over which the process takes place is greater than the processing time. Thus, if the above 400 microsecond routine had to be executed in a CPU that was committed 50% of the time to some other operation (quasi-concurrently) the *elapsed processing time* would be doubled—800 microseconds. The **elapsed processing time** is the time over which a particular process is actually executed.

The **processing delay** is the time it takes to clear a transaction excluding the delays for which the system is not responsible. Typically, this time includes the effect of waiting for I/O operations, interrupts, cycle stealing, other processes, etc., but excludes congestion, input, and output delays. The processing delay may or may not be related to the processing time or elapsed processing time; although it is usually larger than both. The term "delay" without modifier means "processing delay" as defined above.

The term **transaction delay** means the total delay suffered by a transaction including all internal and external congestion delays. "Delay" is also used to mean any of the above delays when that being discussed applies to all of them. Where otherwise unclear, an appropriate modifying adjective will be used.

5.7. Summary of Delays

- There are many factors contributing to the delays that a transaction will suffer in being handled by the system.

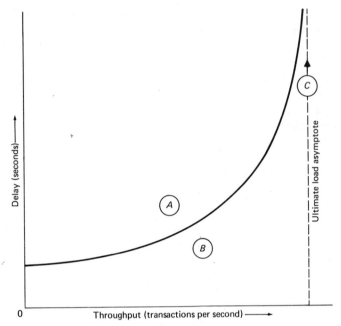

Figure 3-3. Typical throughput–delay curve.

- Some of these delays are the system's responsibility and some are the user's. "Render unto Caesar what is Caesar's . . .".
- Because the delays can interact in a complicated way, it is not always easy to tell to whom the delay belongs. However, the delay that remains after assuming an infinitely fast system clearly does not belong to the system.
- The user's specification of delay (if any) will often not be correct. Negotiations may be needed to resolve the conflict.

6. THE THROUGHPUT–DELAY FUNCTION

6.1. Throughput and Delay

Figure 3-3 shows the typical relation between throughput and delay. Figure 3-4 shows a similar curve for a system model. There is a minimum delay at zero throughput equal at least to the time required to process one transaction. As the throughput increases, so does the delay, until it becomes infinite. The throughput at which this occurs is called the **ultimate throughput** or **maximum throughput,** and often corresponds to what is loosely called "the throughput" without modifying adjectives. It cannot be achieved, because most sytems will either

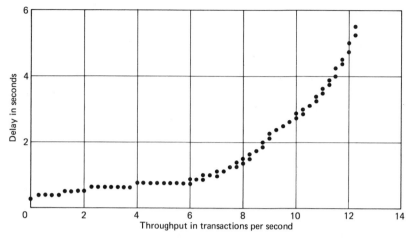

Figure 3-4. Throughput–delay function for a model system.

take steps to curtail inputs, drop inputs on the floor, run into illogical conditions, or merely blow up.

Every system has a characteristic curve like this, although it may not be obvious. Remember that we are doing a steady state analysis, which means that things just keep going as they were. If the system cannot process a transaction and lets it drop on the floor, then in accordance with our assumption of steady state it will drop transactions on the floor at a constant rate. These transactions are thus delayed. Since the arrival rate is assumed to go on forever the same, the delay for the dropped transaction is also forever. This may seem like analytical chicanery, but it isn't. In the context of computing systems where instructions are executed in a few microseconds and long routines take milliseconds to execute, a delay of ten or so seconds might as well be infinite. Furthermore, the general characteristics of the curve shown can be demonstrated experimentally on live systems with suitable instrumentation.

6.2. What the User Expects

The user has specified (if we are lucky) a delay and a throughput. Referring again to Figure 3-3, say that it is at point *A*. The system shown clearly meets the user's requirements, since it can perform its work with a lower delay than specified at the desired throughput. If the specification is *B*, then the system is inadequate, for while it does provide the necessary throughput, the delay is excessive. All too often, the user has specified throughput without specifying the delay, and he gets a *C* system for his trouble. It handles the load all right, but takes forever doing it. While perhaps satisfying the letter of the specification, it clearly does violence to its spirit.

6.3. Cat and Mouse Games

Figure 3-5 shows a single specified point S and a number of system characteristic curves. System A is an honest system, meeting both the intent and letter of the specification. While the user might desire a smaller delay, or a higher ultimate throughput, these are things that he did not pay for, and consequently cannot expect.

System B appears on the surface to be a better system. It has lower delay throughout the throughput range of interest, but has a smaller ultimate throughput. It might be better if the user is interested in performance today; it might be worse if the user cannot accurately predict his load in the future and wants a little safety margin to play with. Both systems A and B, however, are honest.

System C is not only dishonest, but has a bug! How can we say that without even looking at the design, the nature of the tasks, what not? Nevertheless, this system *must* have a bug. If it did not have a bug, since it provides higher delay at lower throughput rates, one would only have to include within the program a generator of dummy transactions that would see to it that the throughput rate was always sufficiently high to take advantage of the lower processing delay that the higher throughput provided. It is clear that any such system either has very strange specifications, or more likely has a bug. In general, when the throughput delay curve dips down, there is a bug someplace.

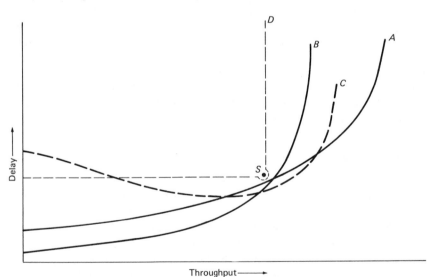

Figure 3-5. Reasonable and unreasonable throughput–delay functions.

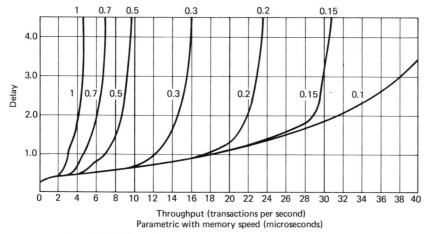

Figure 3-6. Effect of memory speed on throughput–delay function.

System *D*, also dishonest, is a salesman's dream. Look how it hugs the maximum delay line and then takes off, straight up, failing catastrophically. The user got precisely what he paid for, and presumably not one iota more.

6.4. Families of Throughput–Delay Curves

Given two systems identical in all respects except for one system parameter, say instruction execution time or memory speed, we would expect similar throughput–delay curves. The break for higher speed memories would occur further out, and the delay at any given throughput would be lower for the higher speed memories. This is in general true to a first order approximation. Figure 3-6 shows a family of throughput delay curves for identical systems that differ only in memory access time. The memory access time is given in microseconds and ranges from one microsecond to 100 nanoseconds. These curves were taken from a very detailed system model. Note that the delay at low throughput levels has not been reduced. The primary effect of the higher memory speeds is to extend the break point of the curve. This is typical of real systems.

6.5. Reconciling Real and Ideal Specifications

The ideal specification would consist of an identification of all throughputs, all associated delays, and a presentation of the minimum points on the appropriate set of throughput-delay curves. This is ideal, but hardly ever occurs. More typically, the user will not specify anything, although sometimes a throughput is given, but no delay. Furthermore, proper operation, in the mind of the user, may not have anything to do with either throughput or delay, and consequently the relation between throughput and delay seems to be far from the user's objectives.

As an example of a typical specification, consider the following:

The computer is to act as a buffer unit for a number of teleprinter terminals. It accepts characters from N terminals, stores them, transfers them to the central facility, and when the facility acknowledges their receipt, the computer will cause the character to be printed by the terminal. Similarly, it will print all other characters transmitted by the central facility.

Nothing has been said here about throughput or delay. However, we can convert this specification by the following steps:

1. The terminal can input characters or output characters at a maximum rate of 15 characters per second. Therefore, we can say that the maximum throughput per terminal will not exceed 15 characters per second to be split between input and output.

2. We have not been told how much delay the central facility has in accepting a character and returning an acknowledgment. However, we know that a person sitting at a teleprinter could type up to 10 characters per second. If the system takes much more than 100 milliseconds for the entire round trip, the user is likely to perceive it, therefore 100 milliseconds is a maximum acceptable over-all delay.

3. Substracting the round trip transmission line delay for which our system is not responsible from the 100 milliseconds (say, the round trip transmission delay is 70 milliseconds) leaves us with 30 milliseconds to play with. Part of this is to be allocated to input and part to output. Since input tends to be more complicated than output, we might allocate 20 milliseconds to input and 10 to output.

4. With these observations we revise the specification to read thus:

   The system will be able to terminate N terminals. Each terminal shall be capable of accepting up to 10 characters per second in without output, or 15 characters per second out without input. Delay for characters coming in from the teleprinter shall not exceed 20 milliseconds at the rated throughput. Delay between receipt of character from the central computer and the initiation of printing shall not exceed 10 milliseconds.

Another example: the microcomputer is being used to control video games. As usual, there is no quantitative performance specification, although there are functional specifications that describe what the game is, the options, etc. An intermediate specification might read as follows:

The system shall have a linear screen resolution of 525 points (number of lines in TV screen). It shall be capable of accepting a control slew rate without perceptible delay of 525 points per frame in each axis.

This would in turn be translated into:

The system shall be capable of accepting four positional changes per frame, or 120 per second, with a delay not exceeding 33 milliseconds between control stick change and appearance on the TV screen.

Again, we have managed to take a nonspecification and convert it into a single point on the throughput–delay curve.

Doing the above conversion is not always trivial. It may constitute a significant part of the analysis and the design. But it must be done, lest we be later faced with ambiguities and an inability of the two parties to agree on what constitutes adequate performance. I have found the following procedure useful.

1. Do not allow a non-numerical performance specification to stand. Whatever the user establishes as a performance measure, insist that it be made quantitative, i.e., do not accept: "adequate," "sufficient," etc., but get a number, even if it has nothing to do with throughput and delay.
2. Use your knowledge of the application to convert the vague specification into equivalent statements regarding throughput–delay functions. Try to get agreement to tie down the delay at zero throughput, the ultimate throughput, and at least one intermediate throughput–delay point for every transaction of interest.
3. Restate the specification in terms of throughput–delay functions showing how they were derived. Discuss them with the customer and obtain agreement on the appropriateness of these performance measures. As you do this, be sure to have in mind a means for measuring, or otherwise demonstrating that the proper relation has been achieved.

By "customer" here, I do not necessarily mean some outside individual user or consumer. The customer might be another corporation, the marketing department, a technical director, or a project manager—to some extent it is all of them.

7. OBJECTIVE AND SUBJECTIVE RATES

7.1. The Concept

Let us shift our point of view a trifle. Consider a system which is serving a number of inway sets with one user at each set of inways. For simplicity's sake, assume that there is only one kind of transaction, and that the users behave independently. The user enters transactions as fast as he is able. There

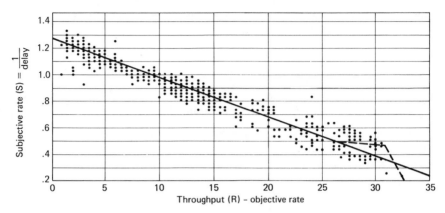

Figure 3-7. Subjective rate (SR) function for actual system (921 data points).

is a delay, say, of three seconds between initial input and final output. The user surmises that the system can process transactions at a rate of one every three seconds, or 0.333 transactions per second. If more users call for service, the delay might increase to 5 seconds, whence the user's subjective evaluation of the system's ability would be that it can process 0.2 transactions per second. The reciprocal of the delay, then, appears to the user to be a rate, which we shall call the **subjective rate** S, to distinguish it from the rate at which the system actually processes transactions (the throughput) which in this context we shall call the **objective rate** R.

If we now plot the reciprocal of the delay (subjective rate) against the throughput (objective rate) we might obtain the pattern shown in Figure 3-7. The points shown in Figure 3-7 were measured on a live system. The line drawn through those points is a best fit line. The surprising thing about this relation

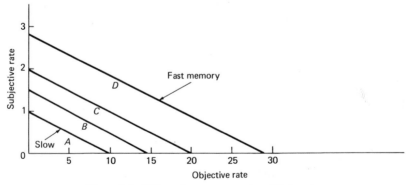

Figure 3-8. Effect of memory speed on SR function.

is that the "curve" is a straight line. The dashed line is actually a slightly better fit, whose characteristics will be discussed later.

Figure 3-8 shows another idealized case. It shows subjective–objective rate (SR) curves for several systems that differ only in memory speeds. The system represented by D has the highest speed memory, while the system represented by A has the slowest memory.

Figure 3-9 shows some other subjective–objective rate curves. Curves B, C, and D are typical. Notice the slight curvature and break near the tail of the dashed curve on Figure 3-7, and compare this with curves D and C of Figure 3-9. Knowing nothing more about these systems, I would be inclined to make the following observations.

- *System A.* Either a very simple system or not real.
- *System B.* High performance, relatively simple system.
- *System C.* Probably running out of memory—possibly I/O bound or possibly some nasty buzzing up and down queues.
- *System D.* Reasonably complex system—well designed and operating well.
- *System E.* Has a bug.

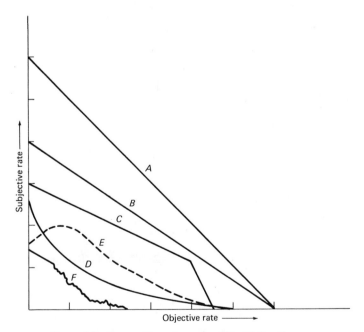

Figure 3-9. Reasonable and unreasonable SR functions.

- *System F.* Fair system in the early stages of debugging. Surely in need of tuning.

These are mighty strong assertions to make on the basis of a few kinks in a curve. The curve, either the throughput–delay curve, or the more revealing subjective–objective rate curve is the cardiogram of the system. The objective of analysis is to gain understanding of a system, not only when it is working well, but when it has bugs, or is otherwise failing to meet its objectives. These are not the only types of behavioral curves for systems, nor the only way to look at them. These are merely the curves that are relatively easy to derive or to measure. As we proceed with analytical techniques aimed at obtaining these curves, the reasons for the above assertions will become obvious.

7.2. A Simplistic Model of Delay

Consider a system in which there is only one resource of interest, say, instruction execution time. It is clear that at least statistically, we can in principle convert throughput to an equivalent demand on the resource. With many simplifying assumptions and some elementary queueing theory we can show that delay is inversely proportional to the unconsumed resources. Let $R, C,$ and H be defined as follows:

R = throughput in transactions per second;
C = instructions executed per transaction.
H = instruction execution time in seconds per instruction.

Then the demand is RCH; if there is only ALU binding the unconsumed portion is at best $1 - RCH$, giving us a delay of

$$D \cong \frac{K}{1 - RCH},$$

and, more precisely,

$$D = \frac{CH}{1 - RCH} = \frac{CH}{1 - \rho}.$$

If the system were ideal, it could process $1/CH$ transactions per second. Define this as the processing rate P or

$$P \triangleq \frac{1}{CH}.$$

With a little algebraic manipulation, we readily arrive at:

$$D = \frac{1}{S} = \frac{CH}{1 - RCH} = \frac{\frac{1}{P}}{1 - \frac{R}{P}} = \frac{1}{P - R},$$

or

$$\frac{1}{D} = S = P - R$$

or

$$R + S = P, \qquad\qquad (T3.1)$$

which is a straight line sloping downwards at a $45°$ angle intercepting the axes at P. I call equation (T3.1) the subjective rate law:

The subjective rate plus the objective rate equals the processing rate.

This statement is not only intuitively appealing; it also says that our systems have justice. Would that real systems behaved so simply. This point is worth repeating if only to warn the reader about using this law indiscriminately; it does not hold except for the simplest, most trivial systems. Systems for which it does hold we shall call **ideal**. They are ideal because it is not possible (with a few insignificant exceptions) to obtain better performance than this.

7.3. A Note for the Faithless

For those readers who are either impatient, incredulous, or statistical sticklers, we offer the following. Assume a classical M/M/1 queueing system, i.e., the ideal, single-server, poisson-exponential system. The waiting time (time in the system) is given in Chapter 11 as

$$T_s = \frac{1}{\mu - \lambda}$$

where

T_s = the time spent in the system,
μ = the mean service rate,
λ = the mean arrival rate.

The time spent in the system is the delay, and by definition its reciprocal is the subjective rate. The arrival rate is, of course, the throughput, and the service rate is what we have called the processing rate. Rearranging the terms gives us the "law." The M/M/1 assumptions do not really hold, except as a crude approximation; the system is a network of internal queues, with multiple priority levels, and the processing rate is hardly constant over the range of throughputs.

7.4. Multiple Resources

In reality, the system has many different resources available at rates H_i, and requiring C_i per transaction. If we were to plot several of these for the highly idealistic model we are talking about, the result of Figure 3-10 might be obtained. The system has three resources of interest; call them A, B, and C. A is in short supply, but its usage is low. If the system utilized resource A alone, the straight line A would be the result. Resource B is available in large quantities, but also has a large usage. Alone, line B would result. Resource C is intermediate, both as to availability and as to usage. Typically, the system will behave as if it is responding only to the most critical resource for that particular throughput. As a rule of thumb, sharp breaks in the subjective–objective curve mean that the delay-producing factor is shifting from one resource to another or from one process to another. While this is observable on the throughput–

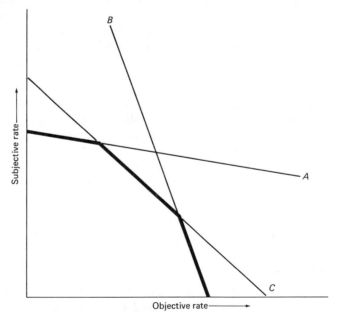

Figure 3-10. Several resources.

delay curve as well, the kink is not as noticeable as on the subjective–objective rate curve.

The lesson to be learned here is that performance (meaning the relation between throughput and delay) is, at any given throughput, determined (mostly) by that resource which is in shortest supply at the throughput.

8. PERFORMANCE REVISITED

8.1. How to Achieve the Desired Performance

Let's start by assuming that system is close to where you want it to be and that you wish to improve it in some region of the throughput–delay curve.

1. Determine what the limiting resource is at that throughput.
2. Try the following alternatives, individually or in combination:
   A. Increase the binding resource (cheap shot).
   B. Decrease its demand by reducing the usage per transaction.
   C. Trade it with some resource which is in greater supply at *that point of the curve.*
3. There is nothing to be gained by going beyond the point where other resources begin to bind the system without doing something about them too.

To determine how much of resource X you need, reduce it to a point where it is binding the system throughout the region of interest. This establishes a lower bound on resource requirements. Other factors, such as standard product line characteristics, safety, and expandability will undoubtedly increase this value.

To find the impact of a new function or a modification of an old one, determine how it affects the coefficient of the throughput–delay curve for each resource in those areas where that resource is the binding resource or the potentially binding resource.

8.2. Restatement of Objectives

Whatever the ultimate objective of an analysis might be (e.g., determine performance, tune the system, optimize the design, examine impacts, etc.), that ultimate objective requires that we first know the precise relation between throughput and delay. In principle, the analysis consists of determining both the throughput delay curve, and the family of such curves that may come about through changes in resources. In other words, we want to determine the functional relation between throughput, delay, and resources; alternatively, between objective rate, subjective rate, and processing rate. The following factors complicate this:

1. Few systems have only one kind of throughput. Most are required to handle several types of transactions, each demanding different resources.
2. There are usually several delays of interest—typically, a different delay for each transaction type.
3. The resources are not really independent; e.g., CPU instruction execution time is of necessity bound by instruction fetch time, which is a memory resource parameter.
4. Resource availability, especially memory, may be interrelated with delay.

9. SUMMARY

A system's performance is described by the various throughput delay functions of that system, or where convenient and more revealing, the equivalent subjective-objective rate functions. All systems behave in such a way that when any one resource is saturated, the delay becomes infinite in the steady state. A complete specification, therefore, must consist of at least a pair of numbers (throughput and delay) and preferably a sufficient number of points on the throughput-delay curve to achieve satisfactory performance throughout the system's operating region. Demand and utilization are not performance parameters, since the user should not care what they are. They are, however, important measures of what performance might be. All substantive performance issues can be resolved in terms of appropriate throughput-delay functions. Design issues and trade-off questions are ultimately understandable in terms of their effect on various throughput-delay functions.*

10. EXERCISES

1. Define transactions and suitable measure(s) of throughput for the following applications: a digital watch, a batch processing service bureau, a supermarket checkout counter, a road, a vehicular traffic control system, a TV game, an office building elevator control system, and the Gratislavian telephone system.
2. "Throughput" in some applications is defined as the sum of the input rate and output rate rather than just the input rate or output rate alone. In

---

*One might argue that other measures, such as "degree of multi-processing" are also important performance parameters. However, degree of multi-processing, is a special kind of throughput measure applicable to closed queueing network models. This is discussed in further detail in chapter 13.

other applications it is defined as the mean of the input and output rates. Justify conditions or application characteristics that would make such definitions convenient and explain why, fundamentally, it does not really matter.

3. Gratislavians enjoy all the same telephone services that we do, and other than their talkativeness, they use the system in much the same way. Identify six different types of telephone call transactions and give estimated proportions among them.

4. Find systems or applications in which one or more of the simplifying assumptions of Sections 3.4.1 through 3.4.4 do not hold.

5. Draw a simplified transaction flow and the corresponding process flow for any of the applications of Exercise 1 above.

6. Fit an approximate function (hint: $1/[A + BX + CX^2]$) to the curve of Figure 3-4. Express the delay as a function of the load with the CPU's processing rate as a parameter. Assume that the mean instruction execution time is 4 microseconds.

7. *Continuation.* Explore the behavior of the system using several different computers that differ only in the instruction execution time. Use 0.25, 0.5, 1, 2, 4, and 8 microseconds.

8. *Continuation.* Assume that the cost of the equipment is given by:

$$C = 25,000 + \frac{5,000}{M},$$

where C is the cost in Gratislavian gridnicks and M is the instruction execution time. It is desired that the delay not exceed 2 seconds. You could design the system using several slow computers or fewer fast computers. Minimize the system cost. That is, pick the number of computers required and the instruction execution time. Assume that all computers in the configuration must be identical. Do not worry about how they can be made to play with each other or the system architecture. Solve this problem for a maximum throughput of 1, 2, 4, 8, 12, 16, 24, 32, 48, and 64 transactions per second.

9. *Continuation.* Redo Exercises 6, 7, and 8, converting the throughput-delay curve to the corresponding subjective rate curve.

10. Redo Exercise 8 assuming that the system cost function is given by

$$C = 25,000 + 5,000 (1.3)^{(4/M)-1}.$$

11. Pick up your telephone and call a friend at about 3 PM on a Friday. Carefully identify all delays from the instant you pick up the handset to the point where you first hear the called party's voice. Record the scenario and identify all delays as to input, output, processing, or congestion.

12. *Alternative.* Log in to an available time-shared system to which you have legal access at the following times: 8:30 AM Tuesday, 2:30 PM Friday, 1:00 PM Wednesday. Record the scenario from off-hook to the point at which you successfully execute the first command on a specified user's interactive program. Identify all delays as to input, output, processing, or congestion.

4
First Cut Performance Analysis

1. SYNOPSIS

This chapter describes analytical procedures of questionable accuracy and dubious validity that are nevertheless useful; it's all right to use a bad technique at the right time and for the right reasons.

2. OVERVIEW OF THE ANALYTICAL PROCESS

2.1. The Ideal

The following steps are essential to a proper and complete analysis of a system's performance.

1. Obtain a complete, unambiguous, statistically proper specification of all throughput-delay functions as system objectives.
2. Obtain a complete, unambiguous, statistically proper characterization of the load.
3. Obtain a complete, etc. hardware specification.
4. Obtain completely debugged program flowcharts, source code, and all necessary system documentation.
5. Do a complete analysis of each subsidiary processing routine.
6. Generate a system model or an event simulation of the system, based on the information of steps 1-5, above.
7. Debug the model.
8. Obtain the theoretical throughput-delay functions and resource utilizations from the model.
9. Validate the model by means of suitable experiments on the live system.

2.2. The Real

That's the ideal—how about the real? The client calls on Wednesday. He is about to go to court with the system vendor over a performance issue. The vendor has a performance analysis purporting to show that the system will hack the load. The client has experimental data that purports to show that it doesn't. The conflicting analyses arrive late in the afternoon. It takes the better part of Thursday and Friday to find out what the system was supposed to be doing in the first place and a final position paper, suitable to the client's intention, is needed by Tuesday. Your long lost uncle has just arrived after 20 years in an Australian penal colony, so that kills Saturday and the better part of Sunday. Tuesday morning you call saying, "Don't go to court. The vendor is right for all the wrong reasons."

Another scenario—the Belchfire Corporation, manufacturer of the new, hot, Curmudgeon 204 microproc (to which you are committed) calls apologetically saying that the prototype you've been testing was a fluke and production quantities won't be available for six months to a year. You're supposed to sign the contract tomorrow. He offers, as a stopgap, the completely compatible Curm 104 which is half as fast, making it no better than Blitzencorp's KO4, at a 20% lower price. You bounce the numbers off the wall like the hero you are and recommend that you stick with Belchfire and the lesser Curm 104, if they agree to throw in another 4k of RAM.

A third scenario—you did the beautiful analysis and now you wait breathless while they run the little bastard up on the test bench. Your analysis is so far off that the engineering department is accusing you of having been stoned. What's more, your first impulse is to agree with them. This time, it's not the company's money, the vendor, the buyer, or all them others, but your credibility which is at stake, especially after you conned them into the fancy model—the many hours of playing with time shared system and all that. At two o'clock in the morning you heave a sigh of relief when, by juggling a few numbers around, you can prove what's wrong with the test setup.

Reality lies someplace between the steps of the ideal analysis and the above scenarios. The dubious practices to which I alluded in the synopsis are not really dubious, but rather means for establishing bounds on the performance. While it's nice to be able to say, "The performance is given by this curve within ±5%, with a confidence of 95%," it is occasionally just as useful to be able to say, "The performance will be at least such and such," or, "The performance can never be better than thus and so." If you think about it, the purpose of any further analysis is to reduce the gap between "such and such" and "thus and so," and if everybody is satisfied with the gap, there is no point in going further.

2.3. Hardware versus Software

You may have noticed by now an unseemly tendency to concentrate on software issues rather than the hardware. After all, it's the hardware that represents the ultimate resources and the hardware that does the work. Yet it looks like most of the analytical effort will be related to software.

Let's examine a few cases:

1. The machine has no multiply instruction: The processing requires multiplication of two numbers. The first number lies between 1 and 8. The second number lies between 1,000,000 and 2,000,000. Never mind what the programmer should have done, which number did he add over and over how many times?

2. Identical products using identical computers and identical (functionally) algorithms: Manufacturer A thinks the product is a dead end and takes the quick and dirty approach to the software with little or no consideration for long term product viability or enhancements. Manufacturer B is committed to the product and puts in all kinds of bells and whistles.

3. A data logging system: The input is a ten-bit binary number. The output is a ten-bit binary number. The system does a calibration conversion to get rid of all sorts of nasty nonlinearities in the sensors. The calibration conversion involves substituting the input number into a fifth order polynomial whose terms include Bessel functions (of the first kind) as well as a sprinkling of incomplete elliptic integrals. Designer A struggles with the nasty math and provides a separate microproc per sensor and can barely keep up. Designer B precalculates the entire function for the ten-bit input and uses the input as an address to a 1024 word ROM where she looks up the answer—one microproc for the entire set of sensors.

4. Designer Y ran out of resource A and had lots of B left over on his last two projects; so he biases the design to conserve A at the expense of B. Designer X had the opposite experience and biases everything the other way. The net result of either approach is insignificantly different.

The reason for the emphasis on software and system organization rather than on hardware is that the effect of hardware on performance tends to be relatively simple and easy to predict; consequently the bulk of the analytical effort is spent on software issues whose effects are not obvious.

A hardware parameter change tends to have a proportional effect on performance. For example, doubling the memory doubles the memory. Doubling the channel capacity allows twice the number of transfers to take place. Doubling the memory speed has a more complex impact since it could simultaneously double the ultimate throughput and halve the delay.

The impact of software parameter changes is far more complex. For example:

1. By making several programs permanently resident, rather than overlaying them from disc, the total memory utilization went *down*. Overlaying the programs in an attempt to decrease memory had actually increased it.

2. By using a full-size buffer block for a transaction that required an average of only a few characters of storage, memory was *reduced*—i.e., the "waste" paid off.
3. A system was CPU-bound. The code that accounted for most of the processing was drastically tightened—cut in half. Performance was not affected.

I have always liked the following analogy. Performance is a box of a desired size and shape. The system is a water-filled rubber balloon with the amount of water representing the available resources. The whole thing is covered with grease and wiggles a lot. Furthermore, if you approach with anything sharp, it will burst and leave you with a mess. Software pushes the thing this way or that way, with the intention of making its shape conform to that of the box. It does not change the volume of the water, however. Analysis is the act of trying to measure the thing.

3. SOME "BAD" APPROACHES

3.1. General

It is simply amazing that despite theory, despite experience, and despite common sense, numerous attempts are made to analyze a system's performance without due consideration of software.

There are some restricted situations in which this can be safely done; e.g., when existing software whose behavior is understood will be simply transferred to a new machine. The one virtue of these "softwareless" methods is that they are simple, and generally you get what you pay for.

3.2. Instruction Mixes

The instruction repertoire is divided into several broad classes of instructions, such as: load/store, fixed point arithmetic, floating point arithmetic, multiply/divide, branch, etc. Each group of instructions is given a weight, say 30% for load/store, etc. This is called an "instruction mix." Different mixes are given for different applications, leading to "business mixes," and "scientific mixes," to name the two most popular. See [BENW75, SVOB76]. Presumably, if you have an application that is characterized by a particular mix, then a comparison of the instruction execution time for two computers gives a fairly direct measure of relative performance. If you know how the Belchfire 809 performed, and you evaluated its mix, then a comparison with the Curd 4040 can be readily made.

The trouble with this approach is that it assumes too much: (1) it assumes that the application is the same in detail; (2) it assumes that the instruction usage by type will be more or less the same for two different groups of programmers; and, worst of all, (3) it ignores all other resources. Some of these ills can be rectified by including I/O operations in the mix as well. When you get down to it, instruction mixes are just slightly better than saying that A's memory is twice as fast as B's, therefore, everything else being equal, A should have twice the performance. In commercial data processing, where software is written in a higher order language, and is indeed transported to the new machine, this approach is not as invalid as it may seem at first, since performance comparison is the issue and not actual performance.

As valid as it may be under restricted circumstances in large commercial data processing systems, it becomes increasingly invalid in small, and particularly in microcomputer- and minicomputer-based systems. Large systems have to contend with a host of applications. Not one or two transaction types, but hundreds or thousands. Not one or two programs of several thousand instructions, but thousands of programs, comprising millions of instructions, programmed by hundreds of different programmers. Under these assumptions, there is a lot of statistical smearing that tends to make the simplistic measure useful. If one programmer is very clever, there will be another who is proportionately dumb. If one program optimizes time, another will optimize space.

3.3. Benchmarks

This is another popular and valid method in commercial and scientific data processing whose validity in systems software, particularly in small systems, is almost nil. The idea is that you cook up a number of programs that, as a set, characterize the load. For example: invert a 40 X 40 matrix; process one hundred payroll checks; enter one deposit. The benchmark is run on the target computer and the performance measured. If your objective is to buy a data processing system, and you are trying to select among several potential vendors, this is not a bad approach. However, it presumes that the benchmarks are stable and truly represent the application. This can be done in large scale data processing centers with stable software and applications which have been run for years. See [JOSL68, BENW75, DRUM73, BUNY74, SVOB76] Applying it to a small system whose application is unique is foolhardy. It will take less effort to model the actual software than it will to prepare and execute the benchmarks. It tells you little or nothing about which direction to go in a trade-off, and is no help in tuning.

3.4. Extrapolation from Known Systems

You know the performance of the combination of software X and hardware A. You want to determine the performance for hardware B. You compare the hardware characteristics of computers A and B and adjust the measured or analytically determined performance of A, resulting in a prediction for B. This is not too bad if it is really done that way—that is, if the applications are really identical. All right, they're not identical. Application B will require this modification to the software resulting in further changes to the model. It isn't bad as long as the resource usages are the same. All right, disc B is slightly slower by comparison, but we can fudge that too. The principle is that it's all right to do this when the deviations are small, but there is always the danger that they will not be small.

Here is what typically happens. A detailed analysis and model is made of system A. The model is confirmed experimentally from live testing of A. The model is adjusted so that it tracks reality to within a few percent. Application B comes along. It is similar to A in all important respects. The A model is modified to predict B. It also tracks when compared to actual measurements at a later date, but not quite as well as A did; the model is not corrected. The next application, C, evolves from B, and so does the model. Now as applications evolve, the model evolves, but in a direction which tends to degrade its correlation with reality. There may be three reasons for this: (1) the software is really getting much better, making the model pessimistic; (2) the hardware is getting better, and the model is pessimistic; (3) the applications are getting more complicated and sophisticated, and the model is optimistic. The result is that we don't know what the model is except, hopefully, in the ballpark.

3.5. Faith, Hope, and Charity

Faith in the brilliance of your lawyer and hope for the charity of the customer— with these, who needs a performance analysis? I have included this as a "method," because the practice is so widespread that it *must* be a method for determining the system's performance. Too often, the one who has the faith, hope, and charity is not the one who will be responsible for making the system work.

4. ESTIMATING PROCESSING TIME

4.1. General

To analyze a system's performance one must be able to determine the relation between the load and demand of every resource. Most resources generally entail a delay. Given the resource demand and the delays associated with the subsidiary processes of a system, it is possible to determine the overall relation between throughput and delay. It is easier to determine some resources and some delays than others. For example, delays and resource usage associated with channels are generally easy to calculate. Memory utilization in general cannot be determined until after the entire throughput-delay function has been worked out. Transfer delays for moving and fixed-head discs are difficult to determine precisely but can be easily estimated. Determining the processing time and the associated delay, while not difficult in principle, is generally the most time-consuming part of the entire analysis if only because there is so much of it to analyze. In most analyses, the action is centered on determining the processing time—the time that would be taken to process a transaction in the absence of any interference from other resource demands, delays, interrupts, etc. Detailed methods for determining this accurately are given in subsequent chapters. This section deals with an introductory approach aimed at getting reasonable approximations.

4.2. Where to Start

1. Draw a flowchart of the program or routine to be analyzed. Every junction (i.e., connector) and decision should be explicit*, using the conventions of Figure 4-1, or the equivalent. The particular convention is not important but consistency is.
2. Decide for every branch whether the basis for it is related to a characteristic of the transaction or to an internal aspect of the program's design.
3. If the decision is transaction-based, estimate the probability of going along each path. Erase all paths whose probability is low, say, of the order of 0.05 or less. This will typically eliminate all the exception processing and about half the total software.
4. If the decision controls a simple, local loop, estimate the number of times you expect the program to loop. Annotate the loop accordingly.

---

*The reason for showing junctions explicitly is intimately tied to the analytical procedures discussed in later chapters. While the undesirable forms shown in Figure 4-1 are common, they are to be avoided because they confuse or obscure structure which is important to an analysis.

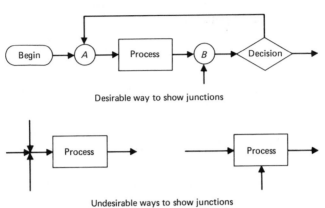

Figure 4-1. Desirable and undesirable notation.

5. For all other decisions, estimate the probability associated with each branch and annotate the branch accordingly.
6. Trace what you intuitively believe to be the most likely path through the routine. Keep track* of it and keep track of the product of all the probabilities you meet along the way.
7. Look at the final probability. If it is greater than 0.8, quit this phase of the analysis. If not, go back to step 6, tracing the next most intuitively likely path and add the resulting probability. Keep going until you have accumulated a probability of about 0.8–0.9.

Let's take the procedure through step by step on a simple example, starting with a flowchart of the process of interest.

These four paths accounted for 80% of the contribution to the processing time that could occur from all paths. If more accuracy is required, then you could trace more paths, but each additional path will have an increasingly lower probability and this could be tedious—it were better to use the techniques discussed in subsequent chapters. If you can't account for the bulk of the processing in a few paths, then explicit path tracing is just not the way to do it.

At this point, it is easy to obtain an expression for the mean processing time for this routine. It is the weighted sum of the processing times for each path, i.e., the processing time along that path multiplied by the probability of that path, summed over all paths.

Path 1: $A + D1 + B + D3$ (0.56)
Path 2: $A + D1 + D + D2 + D3$ (0.06)

---

*I make multiple copies of the flowchart and use a yellow highlighting marker to show the path.

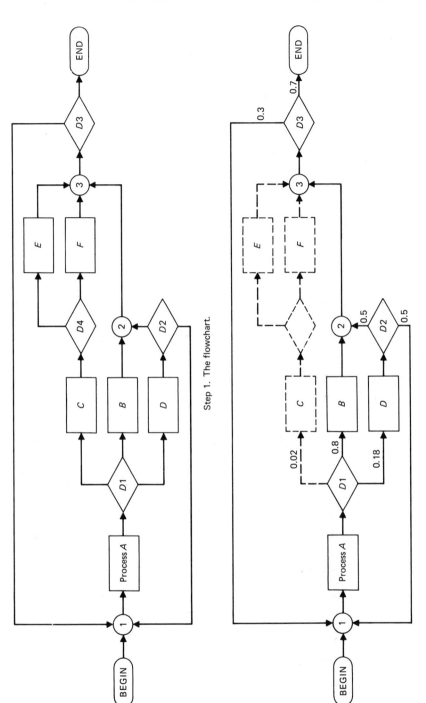

Step 1. The flowchart.

Steps 2, 3, 4, 5. Annotating probabilities and simplifying the model.

59

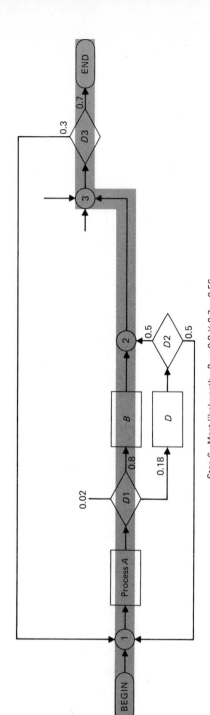

Step 6. Most likely path. $P_1 = 0.8 \times 0.7 = 0.56$.

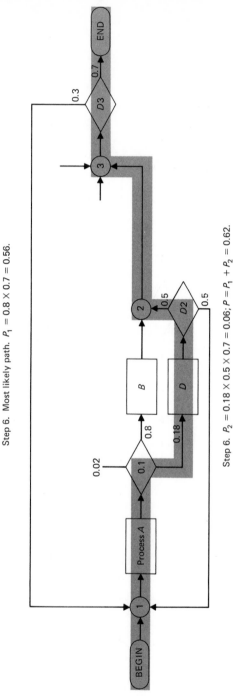

Step 6. $P_2 = 0.18 \times 0.5 \times 0.7 = 0.06$; $P = P_1 + P_2 = 0.62$.

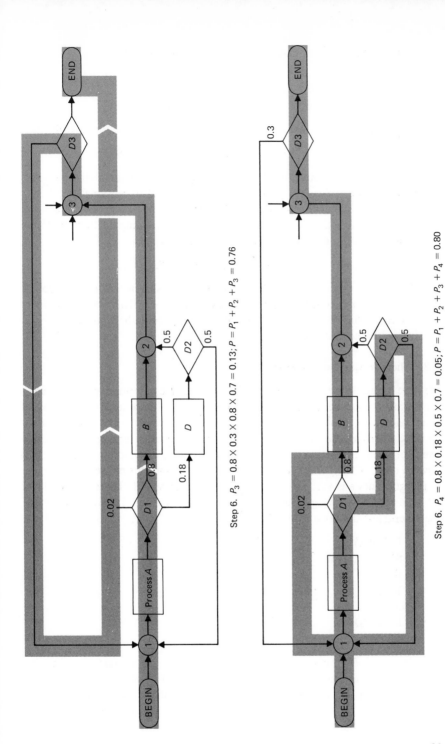

Step 6. $P_3 = 0.8 \times 0.3 \times 0.8 \times 0.7 = 0.13; P = P_1 + P_2 + P_3 = 0.76$

Step 6. $P_4 = 0.8 \times 0.18 \times 0.5 \times 0.7 = 0.05; P = P_1 + P_2 + P_3 + P_4 = 0.80$

61

Path 3: $A + D1 + B + D3 + A + D1 + B + D3$ (0.13)
Path 4: $A + D1 + D + D2 + A + D1 + B + D3$ (0.05)

Multiplying by the probabilities, collecting terms, and simplifying, we obtain:

$$0.96A + 0.87B + 0.10D + 0.96D1 + 0.1D2 + 0.92D3$$

Since we did not account for all paths, having quit with a cumulative probability of 0.8, we must divide the entire expression by 0.8 to renormalize. This is equivalent to assuming that the statistical behavior of the paths not analyzed will be more or less like that of the paths we did analyze. Doing this, we obtain the following expression for the estimated mean processing time:

$$1.2A + 1.09B + 0.13D + 1.2D1 + 0.13D2 + 1.15D3$$

Note that the processing time for each decision has been taken into account. A common error is to leave decision processing time out. This is an unfortunate error because 20–30% or more of the processing time could be consumed by such conditional branch instructions.

4.3. Where to Get the Processing Time

We have an algebraic expression for the running time, but ultimately, we want a real number—microseconds. Where do we get that? I have some good news and some bad news. The bad news is that you must actually count instruction by instruction, using the programmer's reference manual to obtain the execution time for each instruction in process A, process B, etc., which implies that you have to do something that looks an awful lot like coding the entire routine.

The good news is that the *code does not have to work*! There is a whole lot of difference in looking at a processing step and saying, "I'll do a load, store, increment, left shift two, add some register, load, . . ." and,

```
LX  MXYZ
SNXL MUVW
RAL
RAL
AC
L  ABCD
etc.
```

It doesn't matter where the data is to be stored, all addresses in the same memory are equivalent from a processing time point of view. It doesn't matter which register you use, they all take the same amount of time. Furthermore, if you look at the repertoire, you'll find that from a processing time point of view, you can ignore the difference between add, subtract, AND, OR, EXOR, etc., since they also take the same amount of time. In a typical microcomputer with an instruction repertoire of 64–128 instructions, the programs you write will mostly use only 10 or 12 of these instructions. If instead of concentrating on what the instruction does, you concentrate on how long it takes to do it, you'll come up with a mental picture of a very small repertoire that covers almost all cases. I call this an **estimating repertoire**. The specifics depend upon the machine and your own coding style. I settled on the following one which tends to fit almost all machines of interest:

LOAD/STORE MEMORY	LSM	
DO REGISTER	DRS	(almost all inter-register operations)
SHIFT/ROTATE REGISTER	SRR	(left, right, logical, arithmetic, etc.)
DO MEMORY	DOM	(set bit, reset bit, add, subtract)
CALL SUBROUTINE	CALL	(does subroutine call)
RETURN SUBROUTINE	RETR	(return from subroutine)
MULTIPLY/DIVIDE	MDV	
SKIP IF CONDITION	SKP	(covers most conditional skips)
JUMP	JMP	(covers most unconditional jumps)
JUMP IF	JIF	(covers most conditional jumps)

In developing such an estimating repertoire you must be careful about addressing modes; these basic instructions are to be fleshed out with an immediate mode, direct mode, and indirect mode (M, D, I) as appropriate. The CALL and RETURN "instructions" may actually be macros. Treat them as if they were real instructions with appropriate (long) execution times if they do not exist as such. For that matter, any oft-repeated process can be handled by creating an "instruction" with the appropriate execution time. Before starting the analysis of a new machine, I make it a practice to construct the estimating repertoire for that machine. If it has no indirect addressing mode, say, I create one. This may mean that the direct addressing mode takes 2 microseconds and the "indirect" mode takes 10.

4.4. Existing Code, Timing Analyzers, and Other Programmers

Quite often the analysis is undertaken when part of the code has already been written, and is in varying stages of debugging ranging from completely solid to very dubious. If it's your own code you presumably know where to make corrections and exercise caution.

Working with already existing code is about the same as estimating. There are minor difficulties, such as learning the assembly language, project coding conventions, etc. It is a good idea to make up a timing sheet for the instruction repertoire—the one provided in the manual usually has a lot of irrelevant information that gets in the way; important when designing, but annoying when estimating.

Sometimes, the processing time may be given as a byproduct of the assembler or may be gotten from a simulator utility program. Extreme caution is advised here. Typically, you get the processing time for the path taken, or for a selected path, where the rules of selection are not too clear. If the timing analyzer does not ask you to supply branching probabilities, then it cannot be right, unless of course the routine has no conditional branches. This point is sufficiently important to warrant repetition. *Any timing analyzer or timing data produced by a utility program in which you are not required to specify the probabilities associated with each and every conditional branch instruction cannot be correct and has absolutely no validity.* That takes care of about 99% of all timing analyzers. It may provide you with some useful information, if you can find out just how the timing algorithm works. A typical procedure is to take the straight path (if any). This may be a reasonable approximation to the processing time of the most likely path, and then again it may not.

Timings provided by a colleague (say, the author of the routine) are likewise to be treated with suspicion, unless you know for a fact that the author is using a correct procedure (e.g., he has also read this book). The problem is that programmers will provide timing for the cases of interest to them. That might be a worst-case time, the time for a functionally crucial path, an "estimated" time, etc.—in fact, anything but the statistically correct mean time that you are looking for. It is a good practice to ask for a run-through on how they got the time and to satisfy yourself that it does indeed suit your purposes.

4.5. Subroutines and Subprocesses

In the above examples, I labeled things as "processes," the implication being that these were relatively small strings of code unbroken by conditional branch instructions. They could just as well have been subroutines, macros, or entire subprograms. The procedure is the same as it is for individual instructions, except that instead of absolute time, you put down mean processing time, arrived at by the same procedure. You start at the top and work down. You reach process A, get out its flowcharts and analyze it, coming to process $A1$, which in turn leads you to $A2$, etc., down to the bottom level of code. This could take you down several levels in a microcomputer and 50 or more in a large scale system.

As you get lower and lower in the call tree two things happen. The routines tend to get simpler and easier to analyze, but the probabilities tend to get more obscure and difficult to estimate and relate back to functional characteristics of the transaction. However, there are fewer probabilities and their impact is less significant as you get lower. Overall, things are simpler at the lower levels of the call tree.

5. THE "BRICK WALL" AND OTHER ESTIMATING APPROACHES

5.1. Bounds

It is not necessary to precisely determine a system's performance if it is possible to find reasonably accurate bounds on that performance. More often than not, it is sufficient to prove that the system's peformance is adequate; e.g., "The delay at a specified throughput is less than . . . . " Furthermore, if we can complete the picture by saying, "The delay is always more than . . . " sufficient accuracy may have been obtained. This is what I mean by "upper" and "lower" bounds on the performance. It is obvious that if the upper and lower bound are close enough, then we have obtained an accurate analysis. The important fact about upper and lower bounds is that it is usually easier to calculate them than it is to develop a full blown, detailed, mathematical model of the system.

5.2. The Brick Wall*

The system's ultimate throughput is determined by that resource which has the highest utilization (at the throughput). While occasionally it is possible that two or more resources may reach the limit simultaneously, this is so unusual that it is hardly worth agonizing over. If a task demands a fraction x of a resource, then the most the system could possibly handle is $1/x$ such tasks per second. This is the first "brick wall." For example, each task requires 150 instructions to be executed and the system is capable of executing 1,000,000 instructions per second. Evidently, the delay will be infinite at or before 6666.67 tasks per second. If the channel is capable of transferring 125,000 characters per second, and each task requires that 1,000 characters be transferred, then clearly the system cannot possibly handle a throughput of more than 125 tasks per second. If we draw the objective–subjective rate curve for each such resource, assuming an ideal system, we have a straight line at a 45° angle, as shown in Figure 4-2. We obtained this by recalling that in an ideal system,

$$\text{objective rate} + \text{subjective rate} = \text{processing rate.}$$

We are given the processing rate; therefore, the above curve is completely determined. Taking the reciprocal of the subjective rate, we obtain the more commonly used throughput–delay curve as in Figure 4-3. The brick wall is more obvious here. While resources A and B could support a higher throughput, C being the limiting resource establishes the brick wall.

---

*I am indebted to Jack Brennan of North American Philips Corp. for this term.

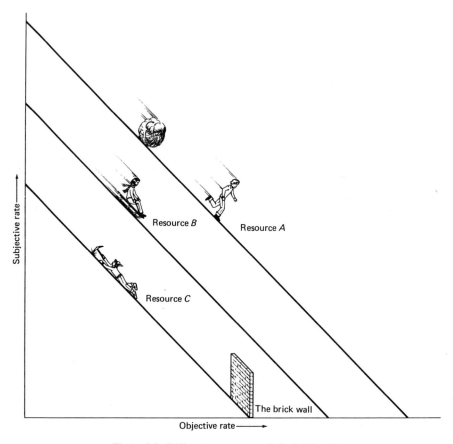

Figure 4-2. Different resources and the brick wall.

5.3. A Slightly Better Wall

The observations of the above paragraph established the ultimate throughput, but not the entire curve. Let us now bring together a few more facts and try to bound the system a little better. The processing time, say, of the limiting resource is rarely equal to the delay for a single transaction. After all, there may be data transfers to inways and outways, disc accesses, and other unavoidable delays. Take a path through the *transaction flow* of the transaction of interest and add up all the delays that you can readily ascertain or estimate, under the assumption that this is the only transaction being processed. That delay is surely greater than the delay caused by the action of the limiting resource. Take its reciprocal and plot that on the subjective–objective rate curve, as in Figure 4-4.

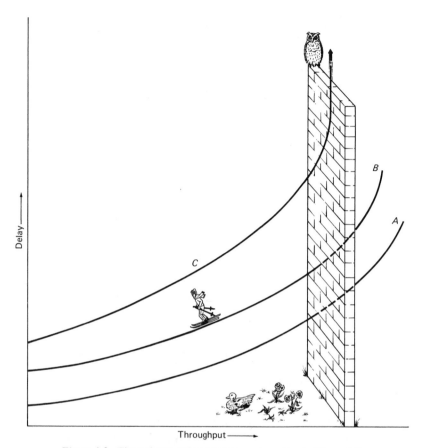

Figure 4-3. Throughput–delay curves corresponding to Figure 4-2.

There, I plotted the limiting resource as before, and the subjective rate corresponding to the minimum sensible delay (for whatever reason). I then extended that in a straight horizontal line to cut off the resource line. I did this because:

1. If the line joining A and X went through a point such as B, the system would be silly. That is, between A and B we should be pumping in spurious transactions to obtain the potentially better performance.
2. It is possible that the curve goes through some other point, such as C; it most assuredly does, but we are trying to establish bounds here; upper bounds for the present, so we won't speculate about the possibility of going through C.

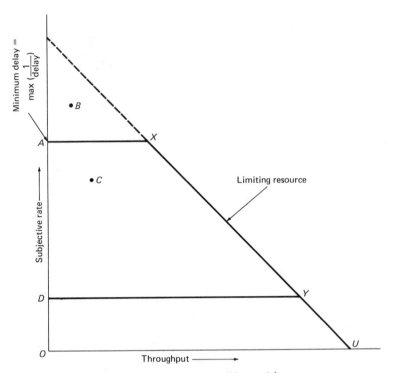

Figure 4-4. Including the minimum delay.

We now know that the system's actual performance curve lies within the area delineated by points A, X, U, and O in Figure 4-4. This may be suitable for our purposes, in which case we can quit. In a similar manner, we can (if we can) determine the worst-case delay for the entire transaction, assuming that every-thing has gone wrong. (For example, instead of assuming that a disc transaction will have a latency of zero, requiring only the transfer time for the data, we assume that a full revolution will be required to fetch the data.) Doing this, we might come up with the point D, and playing the same game, extend the curve to Y, bounding the system's performance a little better. Note that the resulting lower curve, DYU, is not necessarily a lower bound on the performance. It is merely a hint that the system will generally be better than this throughout the region of interest.

5.4. Some Not So Ideal Systems

Go back for a minute and look at the empirical data of Figure 3-7. It does not slope downward at a 45° angle, although it does approximate a straight line.

One might be tempted to say that this system is far less than ideal, yet it exhibits some of the simple behavior of ideal systems. Consider now two independent processes, call them 1 and 2. A transaction consists of doing process 1 followed by process 2. It is evident* that the total delay will be the sum of the individual delays.

Let

S_1 be the subjective rate for the first process by itself;
S_2 be the subjective rate for the second process;
S be the overall subjective rate.

Similarly, define P_1 and P_2 as the processing rates for the first and second processes, respectively. Since the two systems are in series, the throughput R is the same for both, and

$$\frac{1}{S} = D = D_1 + D_2 = \frac{1}{S_1} + \frac{1}{S_2}$$

or

$$S = \frac{1}{\dfrac{1}{S_1} + \dfrac{1}{S_2}}.$$

Moving along,

$$S = \frac{1}{\dfrac{1}{P_1 - R} + \dfrac{1}{P_2 - R}}.$$

Suppose now that $P_1 = P_2$; that is, both processes require identical resources per task. Then with a little manipulation we have

$$R + 2S = P.$$

This is a line with half the slope of an ideal system. Continuing in this manner, we could cascade several identical processes leading to a system whose characteristic curve was a straight line with a smaller slope yet. If the processing rates are not identical, the curve will not be a straight line, but rather a slightly curved, downward sloping line. The purpose of this exercise is not develop any profound conclusions about cascades of processes, but merely to illustrate one of several mechanisms that can lead to a straight line function that does not correspond to an ideal system (one with slope of -1). Systems whose subjective-

---

*Not really evident at all, and not in general true. Always true for ideal systems—e.g., M/M/1 queueing systems.

objective rate curves are straight lines (but not necessarily at a 45° negative slope) will be called **quasi-ideal.**

The ideal system was a good upper bound to the performance of a system. The quasi-ideal system is a good approximation to the performance of many systems. Furthermore, while a system may not fit nicely to a quasi-ideal model throughout its operating range, it may fit well enough over a small segment thereof. That is, the real system could be approximated piecewise by quasi-ideal models.

Probably the most appealing thing about the quasi-ideal approximation is that we only have to know two points; the location of the brick wall (i.e., the ultimate throughput) and the delay at zero throughput. In Figure 4-5, I have taken the data of Figure 4-4 and drawn two straight lines from the subjective rate axis to the ultimate throughput point. Recall that point A was the minimum reasonable or expected delay (actually subjective rate) and point D corresponded to the expected worst-case delay. Point U for both of them corresponded to the maximum throughput point. The shaded region in Figure 4-5 represents a good guess as to where the system curve is likely to be.

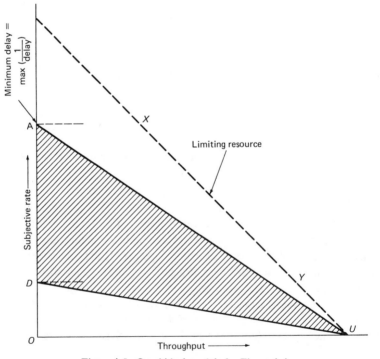

Figure 4-5. Quasi-ideal models for Figure 4-4.

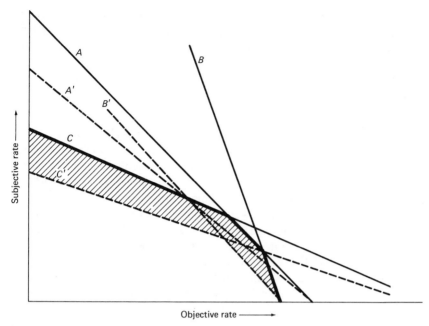

Figure 4-6. Further bounds using several resources.

5.5. Several Resources

In Figure 4-6, we have a system dominated by three resources. The solid lines correspond to estimates based on expected or minimum delay values for each resource separately. Since the system's performance will be limited by the least available resource, the system must be on the lowest of the three solid lines. This is represented by the heavy solid line. In a similar manner, the dashed lines represent the functions based on a worst-case delay assumption for each resource. The heavy dashed line is the function obtained by taking the worst of the three resources at each point. The shaded region represents an approximation to the system's behavior.

6. WORST-CASE/BEST-CASE ANALYSES

6.1. Motivation

It should be clear by now that much labor can be expended to determine the re-source demand: not so much the labor of converting, say, a detailed flowchart into an expression for CPU usage per transaction, but in doing the flowchart itself and the associated trial code. The problem with design flowcharts and code is that they have many paths. Since the analysis is often being done to investigate the desirability of a design approach, it does not seem to pay to have to go through the entire design. The object of a worst-case analysis is to find a lower bound on the performance without having to go through (most of) the detailed design. Similarly, a best-case analysis is aimed at an upper bound.

6.2. Principles

To find the mean resource usage we must have all statistically significant paths of the transaction flow at hand, and what is worse, we must have a good handle on the probabilities associated with every branch along those paths. A worst-case or best-case analysis requires only that we examine one path: the pessimistic or optimistic path. The corollary to this is that there are no branches, and consequently no probabilities to worry about. It does not obviate, however, having to think that path through. Since it is a simple path, determining the resource usage is trivial; it is the sum of the resource usages of all the components of the path. If the CPU is the resource, add all the instruction execution times; if channel or bus time, add all the transfers; if latency, assume that the transaction will always "miss"—e.g., will have to seek from the most disadvantageous track, etc. Conversely for a best-case analysis.

6.3. Worst-Worst and Best-Best

In doing an extreme case analysis, it is tempting to be extreme about the resource usage of the components of the path. For example, in a worst-case analysis, one might be tempted to be very pessimistic about how many instructions will be required to do something. Intuition might say 100 instructions and a pessimist, 200. If this is added on top of having chosen the worst-case (best-case) path, then the analysis is doubly pessimistic (optimistic) and likely to be close to useless. Such multiply extreme analyses are only useful if it is necessary to prove that the system definitely will (will not) work. If the worst-worst-case analysis shows that adequate performance has been reached, then the system will clearly do the job. Similarly, if best-best-case analysis shows inadequate performance, the system will not do the job. If this is not your objective, then multiple levels of pessimism or optimism should be avoided. The process consists of many levels. An extreme case analysis, since it is intended as a shortcut, should be extreme only at the topmost levels. The lower levels should be as close to the mean as possible.

6.4. Some Pitfalls

- Programs have many loops. If you always assume that every branch will be taken only the worst way, then your analyses will predict an infinite resource demand. Be realistic about the worst-case loop; let it be bad, but not awful or ridiculous. Similarly, the best-case analysis should loop a sufficient number of times to accomplish the program's objective i.e., to do the processing.

- Branching probabilities that are related to the characteristic of transactions in a simple and direct manner should not be arbitrarily shoved to one extreme or the other. This too could lead to overly extreme results. If two different transaction types have slightly different resource usages, take the bigger (smaller) one, but if the difference is extreme, and the big (small) one has a low (high) probability, use caution.

- Don't take conflicting path segments. If there are four processes, say, A, B, C, and D, requiring, respectively, 1, 2, 3, and 4 units of resource usage and physically a transaction that enters at A must complete with process D, while one starting at B must complete with C, the two paths are equivalent because $A + D = 5$ and $B + C = 5$. It would be wrong to take the impossible paths $A + C = 4$ or $B + D = 6$. The impossible should not be included.

6.5. How Good, How Bad?

There is no universal guiding principle that can be used to tell how far off an extreme case analysis is. Things are too application- and implementation-dependent to allow such generalities. Generally, the more complicated the system, the more extreme the difference between the worst-case (best-case) and the mean. A ratio of 10:1 is not unusual, yielding a ratio of 100:1 between worst-case and best-case analyses. When used at the topmost level of an analysis, then, extreme case analyses are qualitative at best, so working things out to 12 decimal places is merely an act of masochism or a confusion of precision with accuracy.

The lower the level at which the extreme case analysis is done the less the impact on the overall results. Consider a system in which routines are nested several layers deep. If we use worst-case analysis at the bottom two levels or so, there will (usually) not be much of an impact on the overall predicted performance. Worst-casing the bottom levels can save a lot of work, because that is where most of the code is. So that while it was not worst-case analysis you were after, you could use worst-case analyses at the lower level to save some work. This kind of pessimism might just take care of all things you left out.

7. EXERCISES

1. Consider the instruction repertoire of three different microcomputers with widely varying capabilities, but without built-in floating-point operations (e.g., a 4, 8, and 16 bit computer of the same family). Assume that instruction executions for a given application occur in accordance to the following frequencies.

Load/store	35%
Arithmetic/logic	20%
Conditional branch	20%
Unconditional branch	10%
Increment/decrement	5%
Other	10%

Compare the relative speeds of the three computers you selected for this application.

2. *Continuation.* Develop a common estimating repertoire for each of the above three machines. Apply that repertoire to the analysis of processing time for the following operations: floating-point multiplication, floating-point division, floating-point square root. Use a 16 bit mantissa and an 8 bit exponent. Assume that all numbers are equiprobable. How would your analysis change if the numbers were not all equiprobable?

3. Convert all models of Appendix II for which flowcharts are not given to flowcharts.

4. Use path tracing to obtain approximate values for the mean resource consumption of the following models in Appendix II. Models are given in (roughly) order of increasing difficulty.

(a) T003(A1-ASD)	(e) T006(Z1-A1)	(i) A44
(b) T003(AB-QSW)	(f) T006(LAM1-LUX)	(j) A41
(c) T004(AB-A3)	(g) T006(71-D)	(k) A5
(d) T004(A1-B3)	(h) A36	

5. Flowchart a routine for the *exemplar* microcomputer that will link an 8 character queue block to a specified queue chain. Assume that all registers (except the program counter) must be stored upon entry and restored upon return. Use the estimating repertoire developed for Exercise 2 above and the flow tracing technique to approximate the processing time for linking one queue block.

6. *Continuation.* Modify the routine so that it clears the contents of the queue block prior to linking it to the queue. Furthermore, let the routine be capable of linking N queue blocks whose addresses are given in a list. Plot the processing time as a function of the number of queue blocks in the list.

7. Flowchart a 16 bit binary to 4 bit BCD conversion routine for integers as programmed on the *exemplar* microcomputer. Assume all numbers to be equiprobable. Find the approximate mean processing time.

8. *Continuation.* Do Exercise 7 assuming that the probability of a 1 bit in a given position is 0.005 for the highest order bit, 0.01 for the next higher order bit, to 0.08 for the lowest order bit.

9. *Continuation.* Do problem 7 assuming that all numbers below 2^8 are equi-

probable with a probability of 0.003891 and that all larger numbers are equiprobable at approximately 5.96×10^{-8}.

10. Explore how the subroutine's design might be changed as a result of the different assumptions for Exercises 7, 8, and 9.

11. Do a best case and a worst case analysis of the following models.

(a) T004(A1-B3)	(e) T010	(h) A41
(b) T005(LAM1-LUX)	(f) A36	(i) A5
(c) T008	(g) A44	(j) A37
(d) T009		

12. Do best and worst case analyses for Exercises 7, 8, 9 above. Estimate the probability of the best case and worst case. Compare to the estimated means for Exercises 7, 8, and 9.

13. The processing time for a transaction is 0.005 seconds at the blowup point. The delay at zero load is 0.01 seconds. The delay at 20 transactions per second is 0.1 seconds. Draw an approximate throughput–delay curve.

14. *Continuation.* The number of transactions in the system is given by $2RD$, where R is the load in transactions per second and D is the delay. Plot the number of transactions in the system as function of the load.

15. *Continuation.* There is an I/O process which consumes 100 channel cycles per second for every transaction in the system. Plot the throughput–delay curve or subjective-objective rate curve assuming the channel's capacity is (a) 50,000 Hz; (b) 100,000 Hz; (c) 200,000 Hz.

16. The main road in Gratislavia, between Z'Gorsk and Phrizbeoua, is 15 kilometers long. The mean length of a Gratislavian car is 6 meters. Traffic laws are very strict and require that a gap of one car length for every 10 kilometers per hour be maintained, and that no gap shall exceed the length of the road. The minister of transportation decreed that they should drive so as to maximize the road's efficiency. What did this do the average speed of cars in Gratislavia?

17. *Continuation.* Gratislavians are mad drivers and they love exceedingly fast cars. They obey no laws (jurisprudential or physical), except the spacing law. What is the speed limit in Gratislavia?

18. *Continuation.* The highway's throughput is measured in cars per hour and the delay is the time it takes to go between Z'Gorsk and Phrizbeoua. Plot the throughput–delay function for the highway. *Hint:* do it algebraically. Find an expression for the gap and solve by cases.

19. *Continuation.* On Mad King Ludwig day they hold a race—back and forth between Z'Gorsk and Phrizbeoua—1000 laps. There are only 500 cars in the country. The first time they held the race, all the cars were on the road. How long did the race take? How many cars were in the race the day the record was broken?

5
Statistical Analysis of Processing Time and Other Resources

1. SYNOPSIS

The tedious and inaccurate explicit path tracing is replaced by a more accurate and simpler flowchart reduction method.

2. WHY? HOW?

Our intermediate objective is to obtain the mean processing time (i.e., the mean number of instructions executed) by a routine as a step in the over-all analysis. Similarly, though relatively less frequently, we want to get channel usage, memory references, and other resource usages. In principle this is not difficult; it is done as follows.

1. Trace every possible path through the flowchart from entrance to exit.
2. Count the number of instructions executed (memory references made, characters transferred, etc.) along each of those paths.
3. Find the probability of the path as the product of all the probabilities of all decisions met along that path.
4. The mean processing time is

$$T = \sum_{\substack{\text{all} \\ \text{paths}}} P_i t_i,$$

where: T is the mean processing time or other resource usage of interest; P_i is the probability of the path; and t_i is the resource usage along that path.

While in principle this is simple, it is impossible in practice for the following reasons.

1. If there is just one loop, there are an infinite number of paths through the program.
2. Assuming that you approximate the number of loop traversals, or assuming that there are no loops, even modest flowcharts have hundreds or thousands of paths.
3. If the routine has multiple entrances and/or exits, the problem is further aggravated by the product of the number of entrances by the number of exits.
4. If you want to evaluate a trade-off, so that it is desirable to keep some aspects of the problem parametric rather than numerical, explicit path tracing is hopeless.
5. There are so many terms to be summed that it would be difficult to maintain any semblance of accuracy.

Most important, it is not necessary.

3. SOME DEFINITIONS

3.1. What Is a Flowchart?

A flowchart is a pictorial/graphic representation of a process. It consists of the following parts:

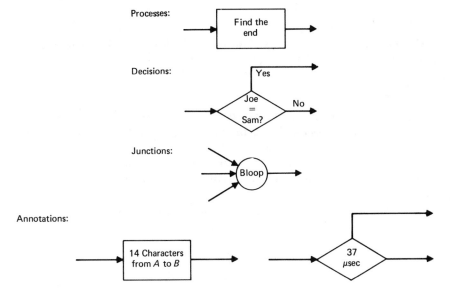

Probabilities:

$P = 0.8$

$P = 0.2$

$P = \dfrac{3MT}{3MT + 1}$

$P = \dfrac{1}{3MT + 1}$

3.2. Processes

The **processes** describe what the system is to do, or what activity is taking place at that point of the flow. Often, the process in question is a computer process and represents a hunk of coding that does some recognizable function. A process as defined here has only one entrance and one exit. If a process has more than one entrance or exit, such as

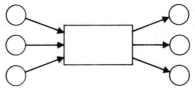

a deeper examination will reveal that something like the following is actually the case.

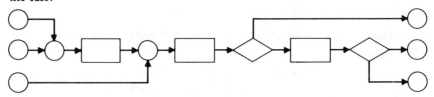

The process can be broken down into subsidiary processes, decisions, and junctions in which each process has only one entrance and one exit.

3.3. Decisions

Decisions result in at least a two-way branch in the flow. Often, particularly in the use of jump or vector tables, the branching is multi-way. Decisions are themselves processes when actually implemented. That is, resources are consumed to execute the decision. It is convenient to represent all decisions as a combination of processes and pure decisions that consume no resources, as follows:

3.4
μsec

becomes

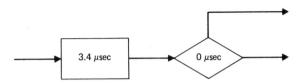

This separation of the decision aspect and processing aspect of branches is the first step, but a crucial step, in the transformation of a flowchart to a mathematical model.

3.4. Annotations

Each process or decision, when executed, represents the consumption of one or more resources of interest. The resource consumption must be known for all processes. This can only be determined from knowledge of the hardware and the application. However that information is obtained (say it is processing time), annotate the appropriate process box with its numerical or algebraic value. In the case of decisions, allocate the resource (say processing time) to the fictitious process preceding the decision that was added in the previous section. Similarly, if a junction point takes processing time to achieve, the processing in question is attached to the lines that precede the junction. The end result is a revised flowchart in which all junctions and decisions consume no resources, such resource usage having been tacked on to preceding or succeeding processes (real or fictitious).

3.5. Probabilities

A probability must be associated with every exit branch of every decision. These are the probabilities that the program will go in one direction or the other. Determining these probabilities is the most difficult part of the analysis. They are derived from characteristics of the postulated load, from consideration of the internal structure of the programs themselves, or sometimes from sheer guesswork. For the moment, assume that such probabilities can be obtained whenever needed.

4. SOME SIMPLE REDUCTIONS

4.1. Processes in Series

Two processes in series can be replaced by a single equivalent process. The resource used by the combined process is the sum of the resources used by the component processes:

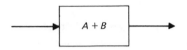

is replaced by

4.2. Junctions in Series

A number of junctions such as those shown below, without intermediate processes or decisions, can be combined into a single compound junction:

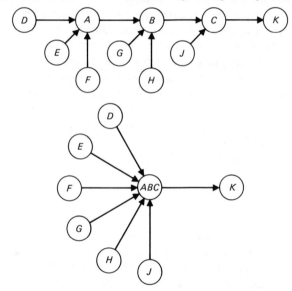

Similarly, again assuming that there are no intervening processes or decisions,
a junction can be "taken apart" in a number of ways. For example,

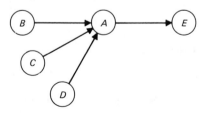

can be transformed to

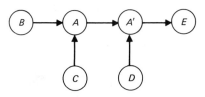

or to

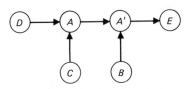

Note, however, that if there *are* intervening processes or decisions, junctions cannot be manipulated so freely.

4.3. Junction Splitting

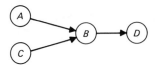

can be changed to

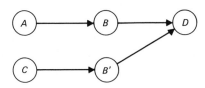

4.4. Decisions in Series

A pair of decisions in series with probabilities as indicated below can be transformed as follows:

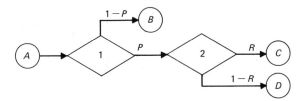

becomes

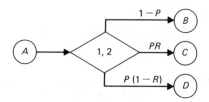

A quick check of the probabilities shows that

$$1 - P + PR + P - PR = 1$$

as expected.

Note that the probability resulting from two decisions in series is the *product* of the component probabilities. A multi-way decision can be broken down into a number of two-way decisions as follows:

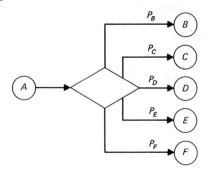

where

$$P_B + P_C + P_D + P_E + P_F = 1$$

becomes

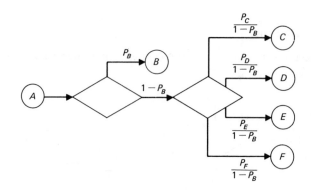

A check of the probabilities reveals that

$$P_B + (1 - P_B)\left(\frac{P_C}{1 - P_B} + \frac{P_D}{1 - P_B} + \frac{P_E}{1 - P_B} + \frac{P_F}{1 - P_B}\right) = 1.$$

Note that in every case the sum of the probabilities at the exits of a decision when considered without respect to the rest of the flowchart must equal unity.

4.5. Decision/Junction Merging

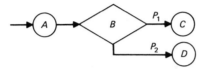

can be changed to

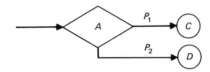

4.6. Junctions and Processes

Processes may be moved about in front of or behind associated junctions as long as the accounting is kept straight. Keeping the accounting straight means the process resource values for every path is to be unaffected by the transformation. For example,

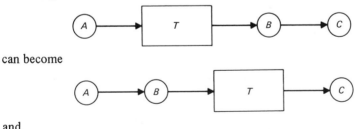

can become

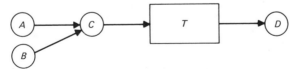

and

can become

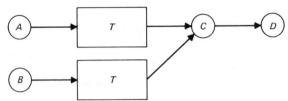

Similarly,

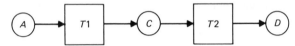

can be transformed to

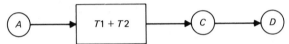

or

Furthermore,

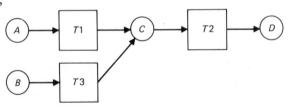

can be changed to

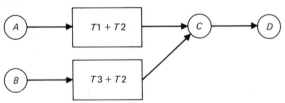

but not to

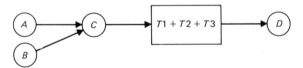

because the *ACD* path now consumes *T*3 more of the resource than it did before the transformation, and similarly the *BCD* path has an excessive *T*1 component.

However, the following transformation *is* valid:

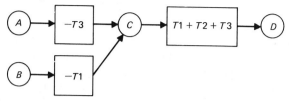

because the books balance.

This last transformation may seem a bit hokey, or may excite a few programmers who would dearly like to have processes that consume negative time. However, from an analytical point of view, there is nothing wrong with this transformation; the overall effect will be the same as the original. The resource usages from A to D and from B to D are still $T1 + T2$ and $T2 + T3$, respectively.

4.7. Decisions with Processes

A set of analogous transformations for combinations of decisions and processes can also be used to simplify flowcharts:

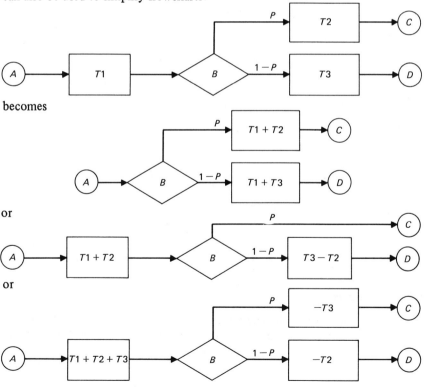

5. SIMPLE ANALYSES

5.1. General

The mean (expected) value of the resource (say the processing time) of a flow-chart can be exactly derived by the application of three rules: those for series, parallel, and loop connections. These rules, together with the transformation of Section 4 above, are sufficient to analyze any flowchart.

5.2. Series Rule

A. The resource usage is the sum of the component resource usages.
B. The probability is the product of the probabilities.

5.3. Parallel Rule

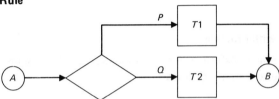

becomes

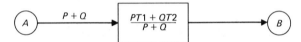

5.4 Loop Rule

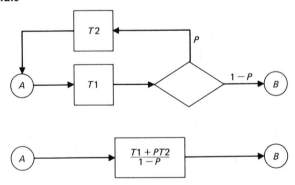

5.5. An Example

We will now apply these rules and transformations to the analysis of a flowchart. We will start with the original flowchart, annotated with appropriate probabilities and resource values, and end up with a trivial flowchart whose resource usage is the mean of the original.

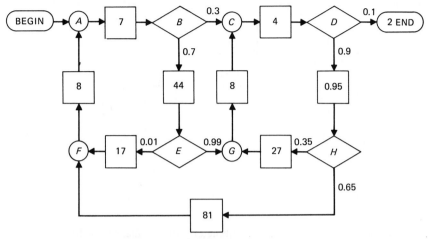

The mean processing time is not obvious.
Start by splitting node G and applying the series rule.

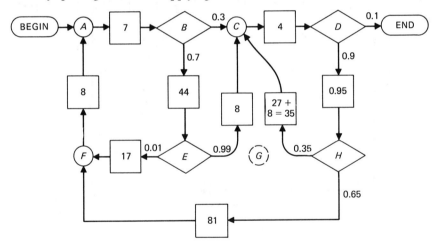

Next, knock off node E (decision) and obtain

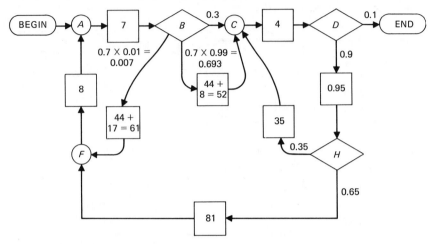

The links between B and C can be combined by the parallel rule as follows:

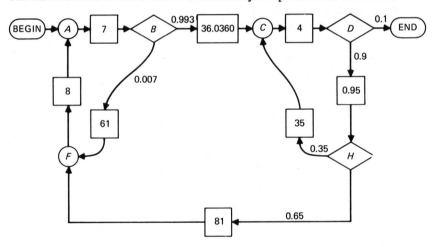

Then clean up the *ABF* loop to make things neater:

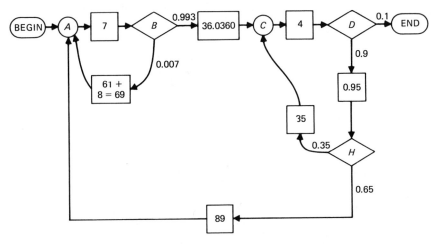

Apply the loop equation to the section between *A* and *B* and combine this with the contribution of the *B-C* link to obtain

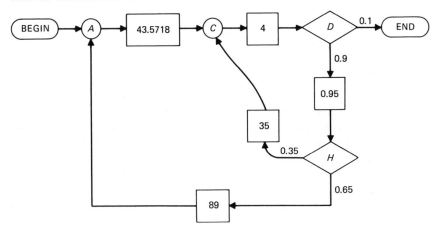

A little playing* with nodes D and H result in

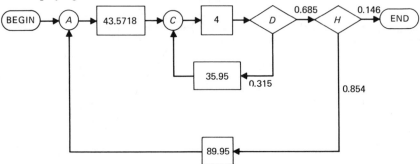

Apply the loop equation to nodes C and D to get

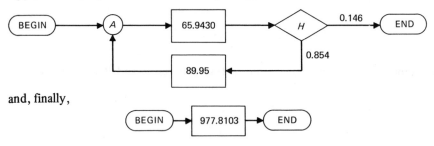

and, finally,

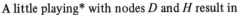

5.6. Review

The procedure is a node-by-node (junction or decision) elimination procedure that transforms flowcharts into analytically equivalent, simpler flowcharts. There are three cases (series, parallel, and loop), each with appropriate equations. Having done as much simplification as possible as a result of the elimination of a node, select another node and continue the process until there are no more nodes left (other than the entrance and exit of the flowchart). The resulting flowchart has a single **link** connecting the entrance to the exit. The resource usage of that link is the mean value of the resource usages as averaged over all possible paths through the flowchart.

5.7. Tricks and Things

A random approach to the analysis of a flowchart by the above algorithm can lead to an escalation of labor rather than a saving. There is a strategy to this kind of analysis. The basis of that strategy is creative procrastination: if it looks tough, put it off. A more formal way of saying this is: *do that first which complicates the flowchart least.*

---

*Try it out!

At any point you have one of the following choices:

1. Eliminate a node by applying the series rule.
2. Eliminate a link by applying the parallel rule.
3. Eliminate a loop by applying the loop rule.

Start the analysis by combining all series links that have no intervening junctions or decisions. This does not complicate the flowchart; it reduces it by eliminating processes. This had already been done in the example: the process between node H and F (81 resource units) probably consisted of several successive processing steps in the original flow.

Next, eliminate all remaining parallel links, i.e., links that begin and end on the same node pairs. This is followed by reducing all loops, if any. By "loop" in this context I mean fairly obvious ones that fit the loop equation directly without further manipulation. For example, in the fifth step, a loop was apparent about nodes A and B and was ready to be reduced. The earlier versions of that loop, while discernible at the third and fourth steps, should not be reduced.

Multi-way branches should be left to as late a point as possible. Loops should not be reduced until unavoidable. Do the innermost loops of a set of nested loops first; work outward to the outermost. If it appears that a rearrangement of the decisions might be beneficial, pick some other area to work on that does not require such a rearrangement; similarly for moving processes to the other side of a decision or any other such transformation. If some of the processes are algebraic (i.e., algebraic expressions rather than numbers) go as far as you can with the numerical processes before you tackle the algebraic processes.

The most tedious thing about this reduction method is drawing and redrawing the flowchart at every step. This can be avoided by using a blackboard: but that does not leave a permanent record. (Oh, how often we have to go back!) I like to make multiple copies of the model flowchart. I eliminate a node and draw in the new section of the transformed flow. I erase the old section with opaque correction tape of the sort secretaries use for correcting masters. I then make two copies of that step, keeping one for posterity and the other for marking up during the next stage of the reduction process. This is allright if you have a copier a few feet away. If you have to run down the hall, or across the street, you'll have to batch the copying or find some other approach. Tracing paper with overlays for each step in the reduction process is not bad either.

6. NUMBERS, PARAMETERS, AND ALGEBRA

6.1 Why Parameters

You will often find that it is not possible to express everything numerically. This is particularly true of probabilities. Often, the probability associated with a decision is a function of the load, and since the objective of the analysis is to determine behavior as a function of load, such probabilities will be represented by algebraic expressions rather than pure numbers. Occasionally, the resource value associated with a process will also be an algebraic expression. In most small systems the analysis of the topmost level flowcharts will entail a small number of parameters (of the order of 4 or 5). In very large systems with complete models 400 or 500 parameters are not unusual. There comes a point at which the number of parameters is simply too large to handle by manual tools. At that point, a time-shared system with algebraic processing programs becomes indispensable.

6.2. How to Avoid Parameters and What to Do about Them

Every analysis will have at least one parameter—the transaction arrival rate. Most analyses will have two parameters: a load-related parameter, and a performance-related parameter that will have to be solved. The labor tends to be proportional to $N \log_2 N$, where N is the number of parameters. If analysis with two parameters required one unit of labor, an analysis with four parameters will require eight times as much work, and one with eight parameters will require twenty-four times the labor. It is clearly in our interest to avoid the introduction of marginally useful parameters and to eliminate parameters in favor of numbers, however and wherever possible. The following observations can be used as a guide:

1. Keep hardware characteristics such as memory cycle time, instruction execution rates, transfer rates, etc., parametric. They factor out of most expressions and are therefore relatively easy to accommodate. Besides, these are the ones most likely to be changed as a result of the analysis.
2. Do some judicious worst-casing for parallel paths. The difference between two parallel paths may be slight. If you pick the longer path (say it is only a few percent bigger) you may be able to eliminate a probability.
3. Loops complicate algebraic expressions horrendously. Nested loops lead to truly miserable expressions; but the complexity is often associated with terms which are "down in the dust." Worst-case the loops by minimizing the denominator. By analytically decreasing the denominator a few percent you may be able to cancel all sorts of things. Similarly, by adding a small term to the numerator you may be able to simplify things.
4. Make your simplifying assumptions as you go—i.e., at each series, parallel, and loop combining operation. There is no need to have these simplifying assumptions be consistent with each other as long as they all result in (slightly) pessimistic answers. If you wait until the end to eliminate parameters you will have too big a mess on your hands to handle. Try the pre-

vious example with everything parametric—the resulting algebraic expression will barely fit on a page.

5. Probabilities that arise as a product of several probabilities by virtue of the series rule can similarly be simplified, but caution is advised. The sum of the probabilities leaving a node must be equal to unity lest you have expressions with negative resource consumptions. Furthermore, it is not always obvious whether increasing or decreasing a given probability is a pessimistic or optimistic assumption.

6. Recognize in advance that, if a loop is to be traversed N times, the looping probability is $N/(N + 1)$, so that $P/(1 - P)$ is simply N. Distinguish between those loops in which the looping probability is a random variable and those in which the looping probability is merely a way of expressing the number of times the loop will be taken [e.g., $N/(N + 1)$]. If N is related to load it will usually be factorable.

7. Eliminate parameters as you go. KEEP YOUR WORKSHEETS AND NOTES, AND RECORD ALL YOUR PARAMETER-ELIMINATING ASSUMPTIONS; THERE IS AT LEAST ONE CRITICAL PARAMETER YOU WILL HAVE ELIMINATED AND WILL SUBSEQUENTLY HAVE TO REINSERT.

6.3. Numerical versus Algebraic Results—Problems

The more parameters in the analysis the more difficult (i.e., algebraic) it is, the more error-prone the results, and the more flexible. Trade-off evaluation demands that the trade-off variable be kept parametric. As the number of parameters is increased, it becomes more difficult to maintain quality control. The model becomes ever more bug-prone. In this respect the model's behavior is much like the program it is a model of. I think that if you made everything parametric that could be made parametric, the model would be about as complicated and labor intensive as the program, if not more so. The number of parameters you can handle depends on the tools you have. With nothing but a pocket calculator (even a programmable scientific calculator) three to four parameters are routine, five to ten are for the hardy, and more than ten are for the compulsive masochist. If you have access to a time-shared system or a small on-line computer with BASIC or FORTRAN, then you can handle up to thirty parameters with relative ease. For more than this, a large computer with an algebraic manipulation package and/or specialized modeling software is indispensable.

The problem, then, is not in deciding what should or shouldn't be parametric (after all, most requirements for parameters are rationally based), but in making sure that whoever foots the bill is aware of the cost of every additional parameter, and that such costs do not obviate the utility of the analysis.

6.4. The Other Side of the Coin

Having scared the reader into the eternal forswearing of parameters, we'll now look at the obverse side of the coin. We'll assume that in every case we will have to examine the system's behavior at a sufficient number of load levels to determine the throughput–delay curve. Therefore, throughput or something closely related to it, is always a parameter of the analysis. Typically, you are not asked to examine one case, but several cases. That is, you must produce several throughput–delay functions.

1. Are the cases related to each other by different values of one parameter? If so, make it parametric. If N cases are to be examined, it is easier to hold the parameter as such than to do the analysis N times.
2. Are the cases related to each other by different values of several parameters? Can *those* parameters be expressed, by means fair or foul, physically sensible or not, as functions of a single new parameter that may or may not have functional meaning? If so, make them parametric.
3. Most of the model does not have parameters. Separate the parametric parts from the numerical parts and simplify the numerical parts using the reduction technique to the maximum extent possible. Simplify the parametric parts by means of the procedures of Section 5 above, and then re-examine the role of the parameters. A few of them may disappear.
4. Check each case of interest. The cases are typically suggested on the basis of functional and operational considerations. Several cases will combine because they have identical performance. For example, despite intuition, performance is uninfluenced by the relative proportions of transactions A and B.
5. Has X been selected as a parameter because you can't know its value at present? Make it parametric and plow ahead with the analysis, leaving the resolution of the value of X till later. Maybe it will go away. In any case, it beats waiting around sitting on your hands while some committee agonizes over the value. Besides, the first value you get will be wrong and you would have to backtrack anyhow. Similarly for values you find dubious or questionable. Make them parametric, go ahead with the analysis, and come back to them later. The same applies to routines and processes that have not yet been designed.

7. EXERCISES

1. Use the flowchart reduction technique on the following models of appendix II to obtain the mean value of the resource usage.

(a) T003(A1–ASD)	(i) T008
(b) T003(AB–QSW)	(j) T009
(c) T004(AB–A3)	(k) T0016
(d) T004(A1–B3)	(l) A36
(e) T006(Z1–A1)	(m) A44
(f) T006(LAM1–LUX)	(n) A41
(g) T006(71–D)	(o) A5
(h) T006(LAM–LU)	(p) A42

2. Modify the following models as described and determine the mean resource usage.

    (a) Replace links (D1, N3) and (D3, N5) of model A39 with model A5.
    (b) Replace link (D1, N3) of model A39 with model A39 (once).
    (c) Replace link (D1, N3) of model A39 with model A39 recursively.

3. Do Exercises 1(a)–1(k) above, replacing all resource values with parameters.
4. Do Exercises 1(a)–1(k) above, replacing all probabilities with parameters. Recall that the sum of the outgoing probabilities must equal unity. You may find it convenient to use related letters for the complement of a probability. For example, replacing 1–PABC by QABC.
5. Do Exercises 1(a)–1(k) above, replacing all numbers with parameters.
6. Examine the following models under the assumption that all probabilities are parametric and determine which case holds. Assume that probabilities are correct (i.e. the sum of a nodes outgoing link probabilities is unity, and all probabilities are positive numbers between zero and one inclusive).

Case 1. Finite value for all values of probabilities.
Case 2. Finite value for some values of probabilities; specify the permissible range of probabilities as a set of inequalities.
Case 3. Finite value for no probabilities.

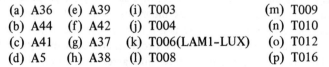

(a) A36	(e) A39	(i) T003	(m) T009
(b) A44	(f) A42	(j) T004	(n) T010
(c) A41	(g) A37	(k) T006(LAM1–LUX)	(o) T012
(d) A5	(h) A38	(l) T008	(p) T016

7. Develop and use a node-by-node elimination procedure to find the *length* of the shortest path for the models of exercise 6. *Hint:* min (A, B).
8. Explain the difference between finding the shortest path and finding the *length* of the shortest path.

6

Transaction and Process Flow Revisited

1. SYNOPSIS

Transaction and process flows are re-examined as multi-resource models rather than in the more restrictive sense of models of processing time and delay. Procedures and approaches for extracting the usage for other resources from the basic flows are examined and explained.

2. TRANSACTION AND PROCESS FLOWS AS MULTI-RESOURCE MODELS

2.1. General

Transaction flows have been, thus far, considered mostly as models for the delay incurred by a transaction. Similarly, process flows have been used almost exclusively as models of instruction executions. This, however, is a too restrictive point of view and can obscure much of the information contained in these flows. *The flowchart, be it a process flow or a transaction flow, is an organized, consistent, description of the usage or demand for every resource of interest.*

It is easy to prove that the flows are (potentially) models of the usage or demand for every resource. Consider this: the computer does nothing except what it is programmed to do. Every action has a program or program segment associated with it. Complete flows incorporate all such program segments. Resources can be used only if there is a program designed to use them. Therefore, every resource is reflected in the program and consequently in the flowcharts. The trick to converting a flow into a resource model for other than CPU time is to identify the instruction or instructions at which the use of the resource occurs or is initiated. This means digging into the program and understanding it, at least insofar as the particular resource of interest is concerned.

2.2. Procedures

The flows, then, are annotated not merely with the processing time for each link, but with the values of all other resources that may be used at that link as well: in general, N resources in all. This may at first seem like multiplying the effort by N. This was hard enough to do for processing time; doing it for N other resources in addition is clearly impossible.

It is not really as bad as all that. The processing time model is typically the most complicated of all, since something is happening at every link: In all, the analysis of the rest of the resources combined is comparable to that of the processing time analysis alone. The following observations are appropriate:

1. While there will be N models, one for every resource of interest, the flows are identical, as are the probabilities. The probabilities have to be derived only once. Since much (perhaps 30-50%) of the effort revolves around deriving probabilities, the effort for additional resource analysis is considerably reduced.
2. Most links contribute nothing to most resources. Most of the work consists of multiplying and adding probabilities. Most paths can be eliminated wholesale because it is clear that nothing happens along those paths with regard to the use of the resource.
3. You have the processing time model to use as a guide. The reduction steps you used for it are still valid. Get out the copier and change the numbers.
4. Many parameters (those not associated with probabilities) disappear. If the model is algebraic, the resulting algebra tends to be simpler than that of the equivalent processing time model.
5. Many of the other resources do not even appear in subsidiary models such as subroutines, and this fact is immediately obvious.

While there are many similarities, it is not true that the same simplifications that were used for the processing time model are valid for the model of some other resource. For example (compare to Chapter 5, Section 6.2):

1. Parallel paths that differed only by a small amount with respect to processing time (thereby allowing you to simplify the model by picking the longer of the two paths) are not necessarily close with respect to some other resource; e.g., one branch may initiate an I/O operation, while the other does not.
2. Worst-case assumptions and tricks such as minimizing the denominator of an expression and maximizing the numerator in the interest of analytical simplification are not necessarily the same for all resources; they often are, because they are tied up with probabilities. The simplifying assumptions of other resources should be made independently of each other unless (as is often the case) the simplifying assumptions work the same way for all the resources being analyzed.

2.3. Activity Counts

The flows can be used to determine the mean numbers associated with activities that are not directly translatable into resources, although such activity counts may be useful or necessary to determine the demand for other resources. For example, if you want to know how many lines of printing are generated by each transaction, analyze the flows with only the printing instructions shown, rather than the processing time. Typically, this would be a call to a print-initiate subroutine. Similarly, to determine the number of interrupts generated (directly or indirectly) by the system, annotate the flows with all the instances in which routines or instructions which directly or indirectly result in interrupts are executed. True, the printer can be considered a resource capable of printing N lines per second. Similarly, there may be an upper limit to the number of interrupts that can be handled per second, etc. Often however, we want to count activities that are not directly translatable into resource demands; e.g., what output rate will the system generate in response to a given input rate? Since a sufficiently well annotated flow reflects everything of interest in the system, the analysis of anything of interest—resource or activity count—is centered in the analysis of the flow.

3. RESOURCE ANALYSIS—SPECIFIC COMMENTS

3.1. Instruction Execution Time versus Memory Access Time

If, as is the case in many computers, the relation between instruction execution time and memory access time is constant, then there is little to talk about. Executing an instruction requires X memory accesses, and the one is derived from the other in a simple manner. There are, however, many computers for which this is not true. A typical case is a CPU that is slower than its memory. This may be because several CPUs share the memory, as well as channels, and perhaps other devices. Two sets of annotations must then be provided: one for CPU instruction execution time, and one for memory cycles consumed by those instructions. More complicated situations can occur in generalized-register microprogrammed machines. Microinstruction sequences are stored in a high speed ROM. Instructions are stored in a RAM, as are data, but the programs are written to take maximum advantage of the registers, favoring inter-register operations that do not make RAM references. An instruction then, is annotated by several numbers: (1) the time required to fetch the instruction, (2) the time to execute the instruction, (3) the time (if any) to fetch the operand, and (4) the number of ROM cycles taken to execute the instruction. The CPU time is the instruction fetch time plus the operand fetch time, plus the instruction execution time. The RAM time is the instruction fetch cycle plus the operand fetch cycles, and the ROM time is the time required to execute the microprogram.

Large scale computers (and some minicomputers) may be complicated by one or more of the following features:

1. The presence of an instruction look-ahead mechanism and stack that allows instruction fetches to take place independently (almost) of instruction executions.
2. The presence of multiple ALUs and sufficient smarts to allow several instructions or segments thereof to be executed in parallel.
3. Memory interlace organization that reduces access time for consecutive memory fetches.
4. Split cycle operations (read–modify–write) with a different timing than a simple memory fetch or memory load.
5. Data-dependent instruction execution times typical for shift, rotate, multiply, and divide instructions.
6. Pipeline operations that reduce the per instruction time in a sequence of identical instructions.
7. Device-dependent timings. This is especially so for devices that are controlled directly by CPU instructions.

If several of the above characteristics apply to the computer being analyzed, then purely analytical techniques may be obviated because it is simply not possible to include all that data in a reasonable model. Again, simulation may be the tool of choice.

An alternative to simulation, in the face of a complicated situation, is to model the typical case or cases. This, presumably, is obtained by a statistical analysis of instruction executions. Annotate the flows for high frequency routines to reflect the situations of interest (e.g., shift instructions, multiply instructions). Then, determine the mean numbers of instruction executions for single instructions, instruction sequences, etc. This can be followed by a detailed analysis of those sequences of instructions with their own microscopic models. This gives us models for the execution times and memory accesses of the instructions as they appear in the program being analyzed; these models can then be used to estimate the over-all processing time as if none of the fancy hardware existed. This may sound complicated, but in principle it is no different than the "analysis" you made to determine that indirect operation required an extra memory cycle.

3.2. Channel Use

You are interested in determining channel use measured in characters per second. A central bus is treated the same as a channel. There may be several channels or buses. Consider them one at a time. Annotate the flows by noting all instances at which a channel operation takes place. If you put a "1" down for each such place, the analysis of the flow will tell you the mean number of channel operations or bus operations, or what not. If you annotate the flow with the mean number of characters transferred by that operation, the analysis of the flow will tell you the mean number of characters transferred. A separate model (in principle) is required for every channel. I find it easier to do them simultaneously by assigning dummy parameters to each channel. For example, say we have channels 1, 2, and 3, and the bus. I'll call them B (bus) and $C1$, $C2$, and $C3$. A transfer is initiated at a particular step in the flow with the following characteristics:

$$350 \text{ characters on the bus,}$$
$$120 \text{ characters for } C1,$$
$$75 \text{ characters for } C2,$$
$$0 \text{ characters for } C3.$$

I annotate that link of the flow with:

$$350B + 120C1 + 75C2.$$

Similarly for all other links. If everything has been done correctly and there are no interactions between the channels, then, typically, B, $C1$, $C2$, and $C3$ will factor out of the final expression.

3.3. Buffer and Queue Requests

A segment of main and/or mass memory may be divided into blocks that are allocated to tasks as required. Such blocks are resources. Typically, we may have main memory data storage blocks, queue blocks, and mass memory storage blocks. There may be one or more pools of each type (e.g., small buffers and large buffers). The analysis of such dynamic pools is treated in Chapter 14. Several components go into that analysis. The first component is the rate at which requests are made for such blocks. This may or may not be a simple multiple of the transaction arrival rate.

The flows are annotated to indicate all points at which a request for a buffer is made. As with the channels, if there are several pools, a separate annotation is made for each such pool. Note that we have only asked for the point at which the blocks are requested and not the point at which they are returned. This is not an oversight, for the following reasons.

1. If the mean request rate does not equal the mean return rate, the system quickly runs out of buffer blocks—it's a bug. They must be equal; therefore, only one of them need be analyzed.

2. Early in the game the flowcharts have bugs. Forgetting to return a buffer is an embarrassing but common one. Most systems at some time or another run out of buffers for this reason. Programmers rarely forget to get a buffer; therefore, the request instances are more likely to be correct than the return instances.
3. Returning blocks to the pool may be done by a variety of complicated routines, and it may be difficult to determine just how many blocks are being returned. Requests are generally made singly, or in small groups of fixed size, which size is usually not data-dependent.

In one painfully meticulous analysis we did keep separate track of requests and returns. It was not obvious that the expressions were equal because of the large number of parameters. Of course you know what happened—the model kept predicting a need for an infinite number of buffers. That's the way the system behaved. There was a bug and the model was faithful.

I don't recommend this (keeping separate track of buffer requests and returns) as a means of catching bugs. First of all, you have to prune many paths from the program to make it analytically tractable; right there is a reason why the requests do not necessarily equal the returns (in the model). Secondly, you won't catch all the instances. You round off one expression one way and round off another expression a different way, and thereby create a loss of blocks, or, equally ridiculous, a return rate that exceeds the request rate (the system is manufacturing memory). Furthermore, the loss of blocks becomes painfully obvious in the early phase of system testing; an analytical model won't make it more so. Finally, it is just not necessary. If by some fluke it is easier to identify the block return instances and the number of blocks returned is given by a simpler expression than the number of request, then by all means model the returns instead of the requests.

3.4. I/O Operations and Interrupts

An appropriately annotated flow can be used to determine I/O operation rates as a function of the input load. Many I/O operations terminate in an interrupt, typically signalling the completion of the operation. The interrupt is processed by an interrupt routine. There is typically no direct relation between the interrupt routine and the routine that initiated the I/O operation. By annotating the flows with the I/O operations and with the number of interrupts of each type that those operations produce, you can determine the relation between the load and each type of I/O operation and between the load and each type of interrupt caused by I/O. This will not identify all interrupts, since some of them may be directly caused by inputs. The latter, however, are usually easy to find. It is then relatively easy to calculate the probability of each kind of interrupt as a function of the input load; this gives you the information you need to analyze the interrupt routines.

I/O and interrupt routines can be tricky. The following example is typical. The program operates at two priority levels. The lower level is used for most of the processing, while the upper level handles the interrupts. The system is designed to transmit blocks of data from memory. The blocks are linked in a chain. The transmission of the blocks is initiated at the lower priority level. The interrupt routine examines the interrupt and the data, and if there is another block in the chain to be transmitted it issues the I/O instruction directly from the high priority level. Analysis of the lower level only tells us how many *chains* will be initiated, but not the total number of blocks and, therefore, the total number of I/O operations and interrupts that will occur. To find that, we need additional information, such as the expected number of blocks on the chain, which could depend on all sorts of things. It is not necessary that the routines operate at different priority levels; the same kind of effect can be obtained with other program structures.

I/O operations are typically controlled by centralized driver programs that handle all I/O transactions for a particular device type. Similarly, interrupt routines are centralized programs that handle all interrupts of a given type (or perhaps all interrupts). In the interest of efficiency, I/O operations and interrupts associated with several different transaction types may be merged insofar as these routines are concerned, but this may obscure the number of such operations or otherwise make it difficult to determine.

Interactions of this kind (i.e., things happening in several different places as a result of a relatively far removed event) are not limited to I/O operations and interrupts, though it is in these areas that such problems typically exist. The interaction, furthermore, may not be related in a direct causal manner (i.e., "this thing causes that thing"), but may be implied in the contents of the data base (e.g., a number stored someplace). There is no snappy algorithm for discovering and analyzing such things; I can only recommend a thorough knowledge of the system.

4. DELAY ANALYSIS—A MORE COMPLETE TRANSACTION FLOW

4.1. Transaction Flows as Models of Delay

Recall that the principal distinction between a transaction flow and a process flowchart is that the transaction flow represents one or more paths through a program which is represented by a process flow. Furthermore, recall that the transaction flow does not necessarily correspond in a direct manner to the process flows, although every process identified in the transaction flow must directly or indirectly be represented by appropriate process flows.

If the processes identified in the transaction flows are models of processing time, or processing delay for individual processes, then the overall transaction flow is a model of the mean delay that a transaction suffers in passing through the system (see Chapters 12 and 13).

The simple transaction flow with appropriate corrections for interrupts and cycle stealing is a valid model for the simplest kinds of systems: those that cannot carry on concurrent processes. However, even a microcomputer is capable of carrying on concurrent processes, as in the following cases:

1. operation at multiple priority levels, either by software or interrupt hardware;
2. concurrent and independent I/O operations, typically through one or more DMA channels with termination signaled by an interrupt.

In more complicated systems (also based on mini and microcomputers) the ability to attach several computers to a common system bus adds:

3. concurrent operation of several computers;
4. independent operation on several memories.

Furthermore, progress of a transaction through the system may depend upon external events, such as:

5. input delays, output delays, and feedback.

Any one of the above situations, singly or in combination, can occur. Their analysis requires an expanded notation.

4.2. Another Model

Figure 6-1 shows a situation that cannot be modeled by the simple kinds of transaction flows I have been discussing until now. The figure represents the following statement:

The system performs process A on the transaction. At the conclusion of A,

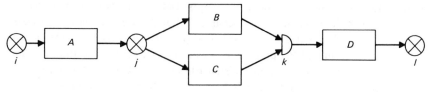

Figure 6-1. A more complicated transaction flow.

it simultaneously initiates processes B and C. It does not progress to the next stage until both B and C have been completed. Thereafter it does D.

There is some new notation here. A, B, C, and D represent processes. They are annotated with the elapsed time of the process. The circles marked i, j, and l, are junctions in this new type of flow diagram. Note that j, while having two outgoing branches, does not carry a probability. The half-moon labeled k is a new kind of symbol, indicating that all incoming conditions must be satisfied before the transaction can continue.

Symbol	Name	Meaning
	PROCESS	Elapsed time for process X.
	MUST	All outgoing branches are initiated simultaneously.
	AND	All incoming legs must be satisfied for the flow to continue.
	OR	Any one incoming flow initiates the subsequent activities.

The PROCESS box represents the elapsed time for the indicated process. Note that this is not the same as the processing time, but must take into account a number of factors, such as interrupts, DMA, and queueing, all of which are discussed in detail in subsequent chapters. For the present, because processing time usually dominates the elapsed time (i.e., it is the biggest contributor), if the box represents a CPU process, you can think of the elapsed time as being the processing time. If the process is an I/O process, then the elapsed time is the time required to complete the I/O operation. Note also that in this type of model it is time that is emphasized. While this type of model can be applied to the analysis of other aspects of the system, its principal utility is in the analysis of processing delay.

The MUST junction indicates that *all* outgoing legs must be taken concurrently. There are no probabilities associated with these junctions; all are equi-probable.

The AND junction indicates that all activities coming into it must be completed before the transaction is taken to the next step.

The OR junction indicates that any activity will trigger the next step and that subsequent activities will have no effect.

4.3. Discussion of the Model

Assume that process C, in Figure 6-1, takes longer than process B. The elapsed time will be that of process C. What, however, is happening along the B line? If C is an I/O operation, say, and B is a CPU operation, might not the CPU (which had finished first) not proceed with some other task, while waiting for C to complete? This is indeed the case. However, the fact is not represented on this kind of flow (called an **activity flow**). Activity flows deal with elapsed time and not resource usages. Furthermore, they are drawn from the point of view of a transaction, and not from the point of view of system and program structure.

Activity flows have no loops. If there were a loop, it would have to have the form of one of the two following diagrams:

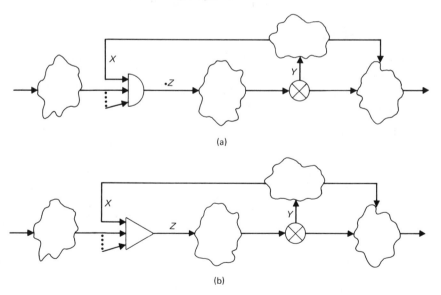

(a)

(b)

The cloudy regions indicate details of the activity flow that are of no interest at the moment. If the flow was as in (a), then we are asking that condition X be satisfied before we go on; but condition X cannot be satisfied until condition Y has been satisfied, which in turn depends upon Z, which is waiting for X. This is a contradiction that can only be resolved by saying that everything to the right of the AND can never be satisfied.

Analogously in (b), if X is satisfied then so is Z, and ultimately Y. Therefore, the whole feedback loop is superfluous, since from our point of view, it is constant.

One might be tempted to leap onto an erroneous conclusion, galloping off into the sunset with a hearty "Hi-yo Silver." After all, these are AND gates, OR gates, throw in an inverter, and you have a sequential switching network: not only are feedback loops possible, they are the only thing that makes sequential switching networks interesting. STOP! These are steady state models of processes and systems. While it is easy to fall into the habit of talking about this particular kind of model using terms such as "event A cannot be realized until event B has been satisfied," which has a decidedly sequential ring to it, this is not at all what we intended to model. Every process indicates an elapsed time. To have feedback means that either there is a time machine in operation, or the condition pre-existed. If the condition pre-existed, then by the steady state assumptions it has always existed and will always exist. Feedback could, you could argue, affect subsequent transactions. By definition of steady state, this means it will affect and has affected all transactions.

4.4. Reduction Process

The activity network can be reduced using a node-by-node elimination procedure similar to that used for other types of flows. To do so, we need only allow AND or OR nodes to do double duty as MUST nodes; that is, allowing several outgoing links from AND or OR nodes. The procedure is as follows.

  1. Start with the MUST junctions.

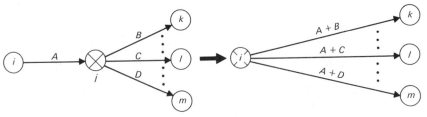

Transform all MUST junctions as shown above with the new elapsed time as the sum of the elapsed times of the links traversed.

2. Remove AND and OR parallels as follows:

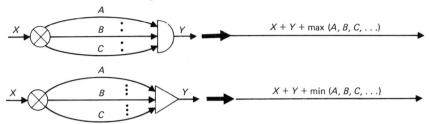

3. Continue until all MUST, AND, and OR junctions that can be removed by the above rules have been eliminated. If you are done, you are done; otherwise, continue with the following rules.

4. In the following rule, a circle indicates any kind of node without specifying AND, OR, or MUST. Transform:

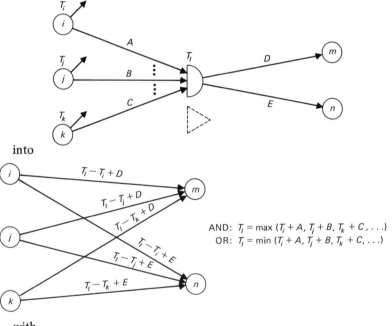

into

$$\text{AND:} \quad T_l = \max (T_i + A, T_j + B, T_k + C, \ldots)$$
$$\text{OR:} \quad T_l = \min (T_i + A, T_j + B, T_k + C, \ldots)$$

with

$$T_l = \max (T_i + A, T_j + B, T_k + C, \cdots) \quad \text{if } l \text{ was an AND node,}$$

$$T_i = \min (T_i + A, T_j + B, T_k + C, \cdots) \quad \text{if } l \text{ was an OR node.}$$

T_i, T_j, T_k, etc., are new numbers associated with the *node* that specify the time at which the event will take place (i.e., the conditions at the node will be realized). T_0 is the time for the beginning node and is (usually) set equal to zero. To keep things numerical and to simplify the work, it is convenient to start at the left hand side (the beginning) of the activity flow and to work toward the right (the end). OR nodes are removed by the same rule except that min (the minimum) is used for the new event time rather than max (the maximum). T_l may, because of the previous removal of other nodes, appear in the expression for D, E, or other links. Substitute the expression for T_l wherever appropriate.

5. After each application of rule 4, check to see if there are any opportunities to apply rules 1, 2, or 3, and do so if they occur.

4.5. Mixed Models

The various processes in the activity flow could themselves be the results of a subsidiary activity flow analysis, or, for that matter, a probabilistic transaction flow or process flow analysis. Immediately we see the possibility of a more generalized model yet, in which we have AND's, OR's, MUST's, DECISIONS, JUNCTIONS, and possibly a few more kinds of symbols. This time, the masked rider of the plains goes galloping off into the sunset without benefit of horse. This type of model, called a **generalized activity model** does indeed exist and can be analyzed. However, there is no neat node-by-node reduction procedure, and the statistical issues become somewhat exotic. This does not mean you should not attempt to represent a system by a more generalized model if that is the way it seems to behave. In most cases, you will be able to reduce it by alternatively applying activity network modeling to those segments that are represented by an activity network, and transaction flow modeling to those segments that are best represented that way. In fact, I have said before that the process times shown in the activity model were probably the result of a process flow (statistical) model. Thus, we had transaction flow models nested within an activity flow model. If such nesting does not occur, and a truly generalized activity model seems inevitable, I suggest the following course of action:

1. Look again. Is that really the way the system behaves?
2. Do some explicit path tracing from the transaction flow (probabilistic) point of view. This may generate several subsidiary models, each of which is reducible.
3. Consider the use of a generalized activity network processing program such as GERT. [PRIT69, PRIT74A, ELMA70].
4. Consider the use of simulation.
5. Get heavily involved in network theory, graph theory, et al.

5. EXERCISES

1. In model A41, replace link (D1, D2) by an assignment of one queue block and link (D3, N1) by the return of one queue block. Does this process increase or decrease the number of queue blocks in use?
2. Do Exercise 1 again, but this time solve the model only once. Hint: resources do not have to be positive *always*.
3. In model A5, assume that link (DO3, A134) represents I/O initiations and that link (DO1, A761) represents I/O completions. Compare the mean number of initiations to the mean number of completions.
4. In model A42 replace all even numbered resource values by a call to subroutine A and all odd numbered resource values by a call to subroutine B. Find the mean number of A and B calls for all combinations of inways and outways.
5. In model A5 replace even digit probabilities by X for the smaller value of the pair and by $1 - X$ for the larger value of the pair. Similarly, replace odd digit probabilities by Y and $1 - Y$. Find the mean value expression.
6. Repeat Exercise 5 above with $X = N/(N + 1)$.
7. In model A42, replace probabilities as follows and find mean value expression (use appropriate complementary probabilities).

$$
\begin{array}{ll}
\text{Link (D2, N3)} & N/(N + 1) \\
\text{Link (D3, N2)} & (N + 1)/(N + 2)
\end{array}
$$

8. In model A36, let D1 and D2 be MUST nodes and N2 an AND node and find the expected delay.
9. In model A36, let D1 and D2 be MUST nodes and N2 an OR node and find the expected delay.
10. In model A44, let C and D be MUST nodes and B an OR node and find the expected delay.
11. In model A41, let D1 be a MUST node and N2 an AND node. Find the expected delay. Can you always count on being so lucky?
12. Modify model A36 as in Exercise 8 above and use it as a subroutine to replace link (D1, D3) of model A41. Similarly, and simultaneously, use the results of Exercise 9 above to replace link (D1, D2) of model A41.

7
Analytical Barriers and Subtleties

1. SYNOPSIS

The correct derivation of model probabilities is so large a part of the effort that a more detailed discussion of this problem is warranted. Probabilities are categorized and approaches to deriving each kind of probability are discussed. Further techniques for representing and modifying model flows are presented, intended this time as aids to deriving probabilities. Most of the real program can be ignored, but intuition is only marginally useful. Better procedures for deciding what part of a program may or may not be significant are presented. Models must be tested and validated; procedures for this are also given. Finally the question of higher moments is discussed.

2. PROBABILITIES AND HOW TO FIND THEM

2.1. The Problem

Converting an annotated flowchart (meaning probabilities and resources) to an equivalent algebraic expression, or a number (if there are no parameters) is essentially a mechanical (albeit occasionally tedious) process. Finding the resource usage of a link in a flowchart is also straightforward. It requires either another analysis or the equivalent of counting instructions. In either case there is not much mental labor involved once facility with the techniques has been obtained. Furthermore, it is possible to automate a large part of the entire process.

The results of the analysis, however, depend completely on the probabilities associated with the decisions in the flows. Unfortunately, there is no simplistic algorithm by which probabilities can be derived. If probabilities were merely a matter of determining how many ways this can be combined with that and what percentage of the load has such and such a characteristic, the problem would not be central to performance analysis, but would be relegated to a minor role comparable to arithmetic. Unfortunately, the model is often correctly described in terms of one or more probabilities whose derivation can be difficult. The following complications contribute to the problem.

1. The probability is not constant. It is a function (ultimately) of the load.
2. The probability is (often) a function of the processing delay or some other delay.
3. The probability is a function of the utilization of other resources.
4. The probability is a function of the total number of transactions in the system awaiting or undergoing processing.
5. The probability is a function of several of the above.

A probability which is a function of the arrival rate of transactions occurs when the system processes some transactions or tasks in a batch. The higher the arrival rate, the larger the batch, and consequently, there is at least one probability (that of looping in the batch processor) which is load-dependent. A probability which is a function of a processing delay can occur in a system which has processing queues. If there exists a priority scheme in the system, and tasks must be ordered by priority, some (but not all) mechanizations of a priority scheme will require the examination of successive entries in the queue. The higher the processing delay, the longer transactions will remain on queue and the longer the queues will be; therefore, the probability that controls the queue examination loop will depend on the processing delay. A simple example of a probability that depends on the utilization of other resources comes about in memory management. Say the memory management processor uses a garbage collection technique to clear memory segments that have been returned to the pool. The routine is activated periodically and also whenever a process requires memory and finds none. The routine then examines the buffer pool and relinks blocks that are no longer in use. If memory utilization is increased, the probability of activating the garbage collector is similarly increased. Probabilities which are functions of all the above factors are more the rule than the exception. Load increases processing delay, which increases queues and the utilization of other resources. High resource usage initiates corrective activities, which in turn increase the processing per transaction over and above that which was due to the load alone.

Ultimately, the general system model has the following appearance:

$$D = f(D, R, P)$$
$$P = g(D, R),$$

which is to say that the delay is a function of itself, the transaction arrival rate, and the processing rate. The processing rate is in turn a function of the delay and the transaction arrival rate. This means that getting the throughput–delay curve of a system will require the solution of an equation, or possibly several simultaneous equations.

2.2. Transaction-Dependent Probabilities

Most systems handle several different transactions. There must therefore be at least one decision that distinguishes among them. If there were none, the transactions would undergo the same processing and would be identical from a processing point of view. Consequently we can expect to find decisions which reflect the type of transaction being processed scattered throughout the program. It is unfortunate for the analyst that most branching instructions have only two directions—skip or not skip, jump or not jump—on the condition being tested. To add to the misfortune, there are usually more than two transaction types. Consider a system that handles four different transaction types. It would be nice if the decision looked like this:

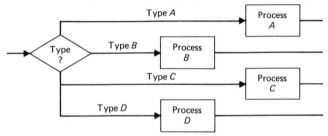

Specifications will usually provide a count or rate for each transaction type, say, in transactions per hour or transactions per day. The probability associated with this decision is simply determined as the ratio of that transaction type to the total transaction arrival rate.

In principle, this is what we do; however, the principle may become obscured by the detail. What the real flowchart looks like is:

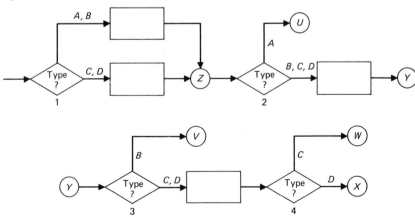

The first probability is determined as the sum of the A and B transaction rates divided by the total. The second takes a little more effort. The over-all structure is that of a tree. The terminal probabilities at points U, V, W, and X must be the same as if there had been a four-way branch. To find the probabilities keep track of how many transactions are left on each side of the branch after the others have been "diverted" onto the other path. For example, $B + C + D$ transactions enter at decision *3* and $C + D$ go one way, with B going the other. The probabilities are evidently $B/(B + C + D)$ and $(C + D)/(B + C + D)$. Tracing the tree from node Z to node X reveals the following sequences of probabilities:

$$(B + C + D)/(A + B + C + D), (C + D)/(B + C + D), \text{ and } D/(C + D).$$

Multiplying these yields $D/(A + B + C + D)$.

Assume for now* that there are no loops in the *transaction flow* (i.e., transactions pass through the system once and do not re-enter; if they do, it is in such a way as to allow them to be treated as new transactions). The sequence of decisions which distinguishes among transaction types can be expanded into a simple tree, albeit one with many branches. To do this analysis, it pays to work with a simplified transaction flow which includes only the decisions that relate to transaction types. The following steps are productive.

1. Simplify the transaction flows so that processing steps are eliminated, leaving only decisions.
2. Label each decision as to whether it reflects a transaction type or something else.
3. If there is a grouping of decisions with one entrance (to the group) and one exit (from the group) and in which no decision (within the group) reflects transaction types, eliminate the entire group, replacing it with a straight line.
4. Trace every path through the tree. In most cases, the probability of taking each path will depend only on transaction type.
5. Wherever the flow converges back to a single line, as in point Z of the above diagram, split the flowchart and treat the parts separately.
6. Consider the total arrival rate for each such subflow. Allocate to each branch of each decision those transactions (rather, rates) appropriate to the branch, and determine the probabilities as in the above example.
7. The sum of the probabilities at each pinch point should equal one. You should not be losing or gaining transactions. If you are, you have an analytical or conceptual error.

2.3. Transaction Type Flags

A significant amount of processing may be expended in determining a transaction's type. Because of this, where processing details will depend upon type,

---

*But see flow balance equations in Chapter 11.

the programmer will resort to flags to indicate the type. Alternatively, the type may be implicit in the path; this was the case treated above. Flags contribute to the difficulty in deriving probabilities. They are sometimes set deep in a subroutine, so that at the level of the flowchart being examined it is not obvious what it was that set the flag. There are no shortcuts here. The specific conditions that cause the flag to be set or reset must be determined by digging as deeply as necessary. Where there is one-to-one correspondence between a flag (perhaps a type number) and a transaction type, there is little difficulty. However, most flags of this kind are set and reset by a variety of conditions. For example:

SET FLAG A IF TYPE A OR TYPE B OR TYPE C, RESET IF TYPE D OR E.

Naturally this activity does not occur in a single statement, but, rather, is scattered throughout the program. Documentation and a cross reference list for the flag are indispensable. You must look up every reference to the flag and create a logical expression corresponding to the setting and resetting of the flag. Every OR term in this logical expression implies addition of the transaction rates (since they are assumed to be mutually exclusive); every AND implies multiplication; and every NOT implies subtraction from unity (complement). In short, apply rules of elementary probability theory [FRYT65, PARZ60].

2.4. Transaction Characteristic-Related Probabilities

A decision may be based not on a transaction type as such, but rather on a characteristic of a transaction which may be common to several different transaction types. For example, we could have types A, B, C, and D. In cases A, B, and C, we can distinguish between, say, "fast," and "slow" as characteristics which cut across types. Other examples are: short/long, correct/error, logical/illogical, accept/reject, act/ignore, old/new, begin/middle/end, etc.

These are treated exactly as are decisions which relate to transaction types. That which constitutes a transaction type is arbitrary and relates to functional characteristics of the system; i.e., transaction types are usually dictated by the user and may have little or nothing to do with the way the processing is organized.

It may be, and often is, that what are conceived of from an external point of view as different transaction types, are internally treated the same. Alternatively, two transactions, because of seemingly minor functional differences, may undergo radically different processing. The characteristics-related probabilities, then, are the general case. An external (i.e., user's point of view) typing being merely one of several characteristics of the transaction. The principle, then, is to list all the characteristics of a transaction, and to do the entire tree in the manner discussed above. The following procedure is workable.

1. There is at least one decision (someplace) corresponding to every characteristic of a transaction. If there isn't, either the distinction is external
(user's point of view) and embodies no processing differences, or you have
overlooked something.
2. A decision relates to a characteristic of a transaction if that decision's
probability is independent of the load, of the history of the transaction,
of the state of the system, of other transactions, etc. If the branch can
be taken either way on a given transaction it is not related to a statistical
characteristic of the transaction.
3. The procedure of Sections 2.2 and 2.3 above is then applied to determine
the probabilities.

2.5. Probabilities Related to Batch Size

2.5.1. General

Say that the program or a segment of it operates in a main loop as a batch
processor. There is a certain amount of loop overhead, and thereafter a reasonably constant amount of processing per transaction or task in the batch.
The probability of looping is simply $N/(N + 1)$, where N is the number of items
in the batch. It now remains to find N.

2.5.2. Constant Collection Period

Transactions are collected over a period of time which is constant or readily
determinable and not related to load or the system's performance. Given the
transaction arrival rate and the collection time period, the number of items in
the batch is simply the rate multiplied by the time period.

2.5.3. Load-Dependent Collection Period

The collection period is variable and depends in some (unknown) way on the
load. Leave the collection time period parametric and worry about it later.
Typically, it will turn out to be directly related to the processing delay, or
some other performance parameter, which means there will be an equation
to solve someplace along the line.

2.5.4. The Collection Period Includes the Batch Processing Time

This is a nastier situation. Not only are the tasks collected during some pre-
determined or variable period of time, but the collection continues throughout
the time that the process is in operation. A typical example is an interrupt
processing routine that not only processes the one interrupt that initiated it,

but all others that may have accumulated while the previous interrupts were being processed. Exact models are difficult, and if too much of this is going on, simulation may be the answer. However, the following observations are appropriate: ignore it, make believe that no new transactions enter the batch while the process is going on. In support of this approach, consider the following arguments.

1. The additional time during which the process is active is usually very small compared to the time during which the bulk of the batch was accumulated. That is, 95% of the tasks entered the batch between activations and only 5% while it was active.
2. The error made by assuming that all the transactions came during the accumulation period is pessimistic. It tends to decrease the batch size, thereby increasing the pertask overhead.
3. The error is increasingly pessimistic or increasingly smaller depending on which grows faster with load. If the collection period grows faster than the processing period, the model is getting better (even though it is still pessimistic). If the processing grows faster than the collection period, the model gets worse, that is, more pessimistic.

2.6. Queue Length-Dependent Probabilities

2.6.1. General

The system has internal queues and the processing for one transaction or task entails a loop whose duration is determined by the number of transactions (or a fraction thereof) in the system. My first impulse is to tell you to redesign the system. There is a better way to utilize resources than by buzzing up and down task queues. The following questions should be raised.

1. Could you have avoided buzzing the queue by keeping one or more pointers to the entry of interest?
2. Is that really the most efficient sort routine?
3. Does FIFO (first-in-first-out) really have to be maintained, or is it merely simpler to think about the problem that way?
4. How about splitting the queue up into several queues?
5. There must be a better way to find the entry than by a brute force, sequential search. How about binary halving interpolation searches? How about trying another search key?
6. Is this queue necessary?

It's not my purpose to crash on designers and their (sometimes kinky) love for queues. However, it is simply amazing how many queue length dependencies show up during the course of analysis which were not suspected by the designer. When the system exhibits such dependencies with deleterious impact on the system's performance, a design change may be the answer. Usually, "the queue" is not a single, simple, easily identified queue as such; if it were, the designer would have spotted it and avoided it if he could. It is usually spread out among several processes which operate sequentially, some having queues as such, some having a dedicated work area, some making reference to the tables, etc.–all of it very devious and becoming obvious only when you try to determine how many times around a loop a process will go, or try to find some probability or another.

Assuming that you have deduced the existence of a queue length-dependent probability, your first step should be to try to eliminate it, not merely because it may make your analytical task difficult, but because it may hurt the system. If the responsible designer is yourself, you have yourself to blame, to thank, and to find the solution. The more interesting case is when it is someone else's design. Don't say the following:

1. "Wow! You have a queue length dependency that will blow the system sky high under load. Aren't you dumb!"
2. "Why don't you redo your program using a Fibonacci search with second level indirect indices?"

Try the following approaches:

ANALYST: I'm having some difficulty deriving a probability in your routine. Can you give me a hand?

DESIGNER: Not now. I'm busy.

ANALYST: Please?

DESIGNER: I don't know anything about probabilities.

ANALYST: Here's the big loop–I want to make sure I've got all the cases. I'll derive the probabilities.

DESIGNER: O.K., go through it as you see it.

(*After some time*)

ANALYST: And when I add them all up, it looks like this equation (expression, etc).

DESIGNER: Huh?

ANALYST: Well, among other things, it seems to depend upon x, y, and z, which in turn seem to depend upon the length of the following queues. . . .

DESIGNER: (*Alternative 1*) I'll be damned. Look, I have some patches to make, could you come back tomorrow?
(*Alternative 2*) Oh that. Sure, but you can ignore it. The queue can never build up that big because. . . .

(*Alternative 3*) That's an error path. You forgot switch *ABCDEX2*.
(*Alternative 4*) Yup! That's the way it works all right. It's unavoidable because. . . .

2.6.2 Queue Length Dependencies

After you have gotten rid of all possible queue length-dependent probabilities
by redesign, approximation, or by fiat, there may nevertheless be several of these
that cannot, with a clear conscience, be ignored. If there are too many, and the
derivation is difficult or otherwise intractable, it may be beyond the realm of
microlevel analysis, and more advanced queueing theory methods or simulation
may be indicated. If the dependency is strong (i.e., has a major impact on the
system's performance), then accurate modeling is essential. While there may be
one or two probabilities with major impact on performance, and which also are
queue length-dependent, it is rare that there are many. The following approximation procedure can be used for weak dependencies with little or no error.

1. Do a brick wall or other crude upper bound analysis of the performance.
2. Determine the approximate throughput–delay function.
3. The queue has to build because the process (the server) has delay. The
   number of items queued in the system is approximated by the process
   delay multiplied by the arrival rate for transactions (see Little's Theorem,
   Chapter 11).
4. Only a portion of the total delay concerns the queues of interest. Multiplying the transaction arrival rate by the fraction of the total delay gives
   you an approximation of the number of items queued on the particular
   queue or queues of interest.
5. What you have now is an expression for the number of items on the queue
   as a function of the throughput. From this you can readily determine the
   probability associated with the loop or loops that involve queue buzzing.

The following steps can be used to obtain a closer approximation to reality.

6. Solve the model (i.e., obtain the throughput–delay function) based on the
   probability determined above. (See Chapter 12 or 13.)
7. Repeat steps 3 to 5 with the new probability (function).
8. Is there a significant difference between the two models? If not, quit.
   Otherwise, continue with step 9.
9. Repeat the above, noting if the model is converging or diverging. If successive approximation causes the model to diverge, (i.e., the resulting throughput–delay functions are getting further and further apart from each other)
   there is probably an analytical error, or else the probability and queue
   length dependency is more significant than you thought. If the model

converges, it doesn't prove it's right, but it does give you a warm feeling in the tummy.

2.7. Process Control Switches

Switches are a perennial source of modeling trouble. In trying to determine a probability, I have found otherwise intelligent designers telling me, "It's equal to one the first time through and zero the next." When the switch is mechanized by a jump table, giving rise to a multi-way branch, you can find the sum of the probabilities equal to an arbitrary positive number, rarely less than 2.5. There is clearly a communications problem.

There is no general procedure that works in deriving these probabilities, except to apply basic statistics and to properly enumerate all cases and paths. This is a fancy way of saying that you will have to trace paths and count. The procedures of Section 3 below may have to be invoked. Extreme caution is advised in deriving switch probabilities. It is a common place to make analytical errors. The following observations may be helpful in your derivation.

1. The past, present, and future seconds are statistically the same. There is no need to trace a specific transaction through the switches. The same process on a previous or future transaction should give the same result.
2. Every transaction is statistically the same. Don't worry about how the transaction got there; assume it's there. Don't worry if this transaction sets the switch. The previous transaction is just as good.
3. Keep track of all cases and make sure the probabilities add to unity.

3. UNFOLDING PROCEDURES

3.1. Why, What, and When?

We have explored algorithms for determining the mean resource usage without recourse to explicit path tracing. We adopted the node-by-node reduction procedure because it was efficient and it allowed us to determine the mean value of a resource's usage without the explicit enumeration of a large (potentially infinite) number of paths. There is nothing wrong with explicit path tracing if you keep it reasonable. The unfolding procedure described in this section is a form of path tracing (or rather flowchart expansion) that can considerably simplify the analysis of an otherwise intractable routine or probability. Consider this flowchart:

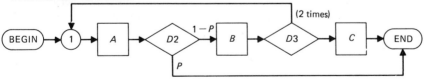

Assume that the probabilities of either *D2* or *D3* are difficult to find. The following flowchart is equivalent:

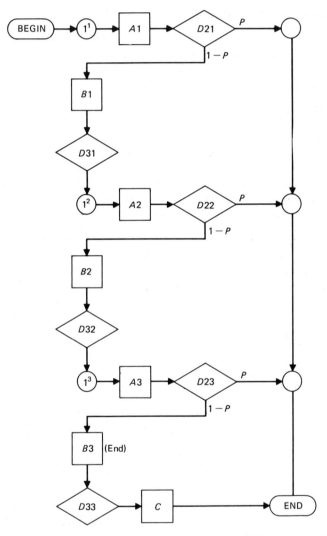

What we have done is trace around the loop the requisite number of times, unfolding the process as we go. The resulting flowchart is more complicated, but it is analytically equivalent, and may render the derivation of a balky probability tractable.

There is never any point in unfolding when the probabilities are readily determinable. Why bother—the reduction techniques give the answer directly. The main reason for unfolding is to allow you to keep track of cases, to model switches, etc. If it doesn't serve that purpose, don't do it.

3.2. Further Analytical Equivalences

Unfolding is a specific example of the use of **analytical equivalence**. The principle behind simplifying the analysis (particularly probability derivations) is to replace the intractable part of the code by an equivalent hunk of in-line code. The following examples are noteworthy:

1. The program is written to compact space by taking advantage of common code sections, either as explicit subroutines, or as returns to the common code with switches. Put the code in line, since there is no point in saving space in the course of an analysis. Make sure, however, that you properly account for all processing associated with setting up the use of the common segment.

2. The program uses instruction modification (Lord forgive us) to thread devious and wondrous paths through itself. Use explicit, equivalent, unmodified code in the model. Be sure you account for the processing required to do the instruction modification.

3. The subroutine is a complicated, multi-inway, multi-outway thing, whose probabilities are truly challenging. Analyze the subroutine separately for each instance of the call, replacing it with N different subroutine models corresponding to the N different kinds of calls.

4. The program is recursive (i.e., there is a segment that calls itself, directly or indirectly, as a subroutine). It can, with some distortion, be remodeled as a loop. Furthermore, unless the program is for a doomsday machine, the number of recursions is small and readily determinable. It was probably written as a recursive routine for programming convenience, not because recursion was essential.

5. There are co-routines (routines that call each other as subroutines). If this leads to recursive calls, treat the whole thing as a recursive routine. If it doesn't lead to recursive calls, call the routines $A1, A2$, and $B1, B2$. Different paths must be taken or else there is a finite probability that there will be a recursive call.

6. One of the parameters of a subroutine call is a dynamically determined identifier of a subroutine which it calls, etc. possibly ad nauseam. Example:

CALL SUBROUTINEA (JUNK,JINK, SUBROUTINENAME)

Each instance of the call is replaced with a model in which the SUB-ROUTINENAME is constant:

SUBA1 (JUNK,JINK,SUB1),
SUBA2 (JUNK,JINK,SUB2), etc.

3.3 When All Else Fails

Assume that you have attempted all the above analytical substitutions and a few more of your own, to no avail—you still can't model the beast. There is one more thing you can do before you throw your hands up and invoke simulation; ask yourself if it could be programmed another way. Preferably a way which is analytically reasonable. In doing this, you can ignore how much additional space in the form of redundant code is needed. You are not counting space at the moment. There is almost always another way of writing the routine. The difficulties are usually related to control structures and not the honest work that the routine is doing. The control structure itself typically accounts for a small portion of the instructions executed. Modifying the control structure in the interest of analytical simplification will usually lead to longer processing time. After all, we can assume that the design had a difficult control structure for reasons of economy. If space economy was the issue, the routine can usually be made feasible by use of the analytical equivalences of Section 3.2 above. If time economy was the issue, the analytically simpler, equivalent model will probably be (slightly) more time-consuming. The error, if any, is conservative.

If it is not your own routine that you are analyzing, discuss your analytical equivalence with the designer, taking pains to explain that you are not suggesting a new design, but that you are trying to model his beautifully intricate code. Admitting defeat to the designer, along the lines of: "Willy! You've got me stumped. I just can't analyze your routine," can be a great ego booster to the designer, especially one who delights in intricate, convoluted, elegant code. You will occasionally be rewarded by having the designer adopt your "equivalent" model because it is not merely analytically simpler, but because it really is better. Whatever else you may say about the subject, structured code is easier to model, [MAYN72, DAHL72].

4. TESTING FOR SIGNIFICANCE

4.1. What?

At various points in earlier sections I alluded to the principle of only modeling that which is significant without, however, being explicit about how one determines what is significant. Reasonably accurate models of most systems can be achieved by modeling about 10–15% of the code. This percentage can vary within broad limits. Generally, the more complicated a system is, the more its programs are concerned with low probability events, and consequently, the smaller the percentage of the code that must be modeled for accuracy. Extremely simple systems may require modeling almost all of the code. The purpose of this section is to provide guidance in the determination of what is and what is not significant.

4.2. The Principle

Recall that in principle we could determine the mean resource usage of a routine by tracing every path (potentially infinite number), and determining for each such path the probability of its occurrence and the resource usage along that path. The mean, then, is simply the sum of the products of the path probabilities and the resource usages. We could then consider all such paths and order them in decreasing probability–resource usage product order. The path with the highest product is clearly the major contributor to the mean resource usage. The lowest product is the least significant. If you know the mean, then you could tell how close to the mean you had gotten after considering the largest contributor, the next largest, etc., and you could stop after, say 99% of the contribution has been reached. This would of course require that you model everything, which would obviate what you set out to do. There is no known theoretical procedure that will allow you to examine a model and determine which paths to include or exclude, that does not require you to model that path. Therefore, every elimination of a path, a branch, etc., is an act of faith and intuition, rather than a formal, rigorous procedure.

4.3. Where to Start

There are usually one or more individuals on the design team who have an intuitive idea of what is or is not significant. This serves as a first rough guide to what to take into account and what to leave out.

1. If the designer says it is important, leave it in, unless you prove otherwise. If you leave it in, at worst it means extra work. If you take it out, the model is subject to criticism: "See, the model is no good. You left out. . . ."
2. If the designer says it is unimportant, caution is advised. Common subroutines are especially prone to error. The routine may itself be trivial, but no one has a clear idea of how often it is called.
3. Paths concerned with illogical conditions that can come about only through a hardware or software malfunction can almost always be left out.
4. Paths concerned with catastrophic conditions and recovery actions can almost always be left out.

5. Paths concerned with input data error processing can usually be left out, except if such error processing is considered part of the load. The specifier's concurrence is usually required. The boundary between input error processing and "normal" processing is fuzzy and arbitrary. Some systems are almost totally devoted to error processing.

4.4 Functional Probabilities

When the probabilities are functions (as is often the case) there is a real payoff to simplifying the model, even if you cannot avoid analyzing the routine. That is, you do not know whether or not a certain path or program segment can be safely left out. You do the analysis incorporating that segment. There are several probabilities that are nasty functions of all sorts of other things. You have an exact expression for the mean resource usage but realize that if you use it as is, the overall model will be unmanageable. How, when, and where can you simplify such expressions?

1. Set the probability to 0, 0.5, and 1, and evaluate the resulting resource usages. If it varies by only a small amount, and the value is small compared to the other contributions, use the worst case probability—typically 0 or 1. This in effect cuts off one leg of the decision, obviating all the code that follows along that leg and (more important) all the subroutines that are called along that leg.
2. Alternatively, find the derivative of the mean with respect to the probability of interest, set it to zero, and solve for the probability that will maximize the mean. Use that probability as a worst case. Its value will usually be zero or unity, which is why you should try step 1 above first. Similarly, determine the probability which minimizes the mean resource usage. If the difference between the maximum and minimum values is not significant, use the maximizing value as a worst case approximation.
3. When probabilities are nasty, there will be fractional terms in most routines involving loops. Maximize the mean resource usage by minimizing the denominator without modifying the numerator. Use that as a worst case estimate if it is not significantly different from the actual mean.
4. An expression may contain negative terms. Eliminate such terms and see what the impact is.

4.5. Other Tricks for Simplifying Algebraic Expressions

The idea behind all such simplifications is to substitute a *slightly* pessimistic but simple expression for a complicated accurate expression for the mean resource usage. The following techniques are useful.

1. Expand a term of the form $A/(B - X)$ as a power series in X. If X contains a probability, the series will rapidly converge. Cut off at a positive term (the last term is to be positive rather than negative) as a pessimistic approximation. Use this approach with caution, since the resulting expressions may be worse than before.
2. Use synthetic division on ratios of polynomials and estimate the contribution of the remainder; discard it when it is insignificant.
3. Modify the expression by adding additional (small) terms so that it becomes factorable.
4. Design an alternative, but equivalent, routine which you know is not as efficient, but which is analytically simpler.*
5. Be willing to use an approximation which is overly pessimistic in low load ranges (where a pessimistic prediction won't hurt) if it is reasonably accurate in the high load range.
6. Do not be slavishly consistent with any given probability. A probability may appear in different places. In some places, the mean is maximized by setting the probability to unity, in others by setting it to zero, or possibly to some other value. In some cases, you may wish to simplify an expression by one method and another expression by a totally different method that requires contradictory assumptions about the probability. If you are always slightly pessimistic, there is no need to be consistent regarding your opportunities for simplification.

Performance analysis is centered on the construction of mathematical models. The means by which such models are constructed are in principle complete and rigorous. Truly rigorous models, however, are almost useless because of their complexity. Modeling, then, is to a great extent an art. The essence of that art consists of exchanging the rigorous expressions for simpler, clearer, more intuitive expressions that are slightly pessimistic, but not overly so. The whole being sufficiently accurate to the needs of the model.

5. SUBMODEL VALIDATION

5.1. Why?

I shall have more to say about validating the entire model in Chapter 15. This section concerns mostly the kind of routine validation that you should do as you go along. Just as it is not effective to test a program only at the highest functional level, it is not effective to leave the testing of the model until the last. In programming we have generally adopted the principle of unit testing, whereby a

---

*All of the above procedures come down to this if you think about it.

unit, say, a subroutine or subprogram, is tested at the lowest possible level. This way bugs are eliminated early in the game. If unit program testing is not done, the bugs still show up, but they become extremely difficult to identify. Similarly, if model testing is only conducted at the topmost level, it may become difficult, if not impossible, to find the source of the bug.

5.2. Principles and Practices

The basic principle in all model testing is: "Is the model sensible?" Unlike program testing, in which there is usually a definite, readily recognizable criterion for workability, model testing can provide fuzzy results which are not so readily verified. The following practices are effective for submodel testing.

1. There is almost never a bug in the resource usage of a link. If there is, the error is usually small. The most common bug in resource usage is a scaling error, e.g., milliseconds instead of microseconds, failing to convert from instructions per second to microseconds, etc.

2. The model consists of a sum of terms (typically). It expresses resource units (e.g., seconds, transfers, instructions per second, etc.). Every term of that sum must be dimensionally identical and correct. Dimensionality errors creep in as a result of simplifications. Check the expression dimensionally and make appropriate corrections.

3. If the routine contains no loops, then every value of the probabilities in every combination must yield a finite result. Furthermore, the result must be positive and nonzero. Play around with probabilities to minimize and maximize the resource usage for the submodel. If a negative, zero, or infinite resource usage is possible for some combination of probabilities, there is a bug in the model.

4. Loops have expressions that are linear with load. If the loop probability is P, and P is interpreted as a "count" of the form $N/(N+1)$ (whether in fact it is or is not a true count), the resulting expression should be linear in N. Nested loops give rise to expressions in N^2. If the routine consists of an outer loop, with two sets of inner loops, one which is nested three deep and the other two deep, an expression of the form: $AN(BN^3 + CN^2 + D)$ should result. If the form of the polynomial that expresses the resource usage does not match the structure of the routine, check the discrepancy.

5. Routines with loops whose probabilities are load-dependent generally increase with increasing load. I say "generally" because it is not always true. It is possible to design routines whose absolute processing *decreases* with increasing load. These are rare and should always be treated with

suspicion; confirm the mechanism with the designer. There must be an explanation.

6. Routines that process tasks in a batch generally have decreased per task processing with increased batch size. Check at zero batch size and at large batch size. No matter how clever the programmer is, the total resource usage will never become negative (even if the model does predict it).

7. Try $0, 0.5$, and 1 values for all probabilities and check for sensibility.

8. If the routine has N inways and M outways, assign probabilities of unity to one inway and zero to the others. The sum of the outway probabilities should be unity. Set all the link resource usage to zero to do this.

9. Similarly, if the sum of the probabilities assigned to the inways is P, the sum of the outway probabilities should equal P.

10. If you have kept a parameter in the resource usage of the links (i.e., memory speed, but a dummy parameter will do), set it equal to zero for every path and every probability. (This catches a few bugs.)

11. If you have expressed all resource usages in terms of a parameter (a good idea), such as memory speed, it should always be possible to factor that parameter out of the expression. If not, find out why not; it's probably a bug.

12. Plot the growth curve of the routine with respect to important parameters such as load-dependent probabilities. Anything other than a simple linear expression must be explainable in terms of a program's structure (nested loop, queue scan, etc.). Extract the dominant nonlinear terms and find the corresponding program segments and/or paths. That is, discard all parts of the model that do not contribute to the nonlinearity. The resulting test model should be easily analyzed. Does it really behave that way? Why? Check with the designer to make sure your interpretation is correct.

6. OF HIGHER MOMENTS

6.1. General

This book is concerned primarily with determining the mean values of performance parameters and resource utilizations. Remember, however, that we are dealing with probability distributions that describe the performance or the resource. It is natural to wonder, therefore, about the higher moments, particularly the second moment (the standard deviation, or more often its square, the variance) or the third moment (skewness). Can the same analytical techniques be used to derive these higher moments? Under very broad assumptions, the answer is "yes." If the resource described by a link is itself distributed with defined higher moments[*] then the entire model has a distribution and all higher moments are defined and derivable.

The higher moments, especially the variance, can be used in two sets of circumstances. The most important of these is in conjunction with the solution of queueing theory problems. Closed form formulas and bounding approximations in queueing theory almost always require a knowledge of the variance of the resource usage. The second use occurs in systems in which not only is the mean performance specified, but the standard deviation of the performance must be met as well. For example, it is not only desirable that the output occur at a specified rate, but also that the output rate be relatively jitter-free. Alternatively, not only must the mean performance be met, but the mean plus four standard deviations must be met with a specified probability.

6.2. Rules for the Standard Deviation

6.2.1. The Series Rule

The series reduction involves the elimination of node k, so that there is a direct connection between nodes i and j, which previously had been a path from i to k and from k to j. The expression for the standard deviation is

$$\sigma_{ij} = \sqrt{\sigma_{ik}^2 + \sigma_{kj}^2} \; .$$

6.2.2. The Parallel Rule

There are n links in parallel between two nodes, indexed by i:

$$\sigma^2 = \frac{\sum\limits_{i=1}^{n} P_i \sigma_i^2}{\sum\limits_{i=1}^{n} P_i} + \frac{\sum\limits_{i=1}^{n} P_i \mu_i^2}{\sum\limits_{i=1}^{n} P_i} - \left[\frac{\sum\limits_{i=1}^{n} P_i \mu_i}{\sum\limits_{i=1}^{n} P_i} \right]^2 .$$

6.2.3. The Loop Rule

For a loop with looping probability P, and a mean for the forward link of μ_A and for the loopback link of μ_B, the expression is

$$\sigma^2 = \left[\frac{P(\mu_A + \mu_B)^2}{(1 - P)^2} \right] + \frac{\sigma_A^2 + P\sigma_B^2}{1 - P} \; .$$

---

[*]Actually, it must have a defined moment-generating function; see [ARMS71] for details and derivation.

The term in brackets is used or not used depending upon the nature of the looping probability. If the looping probability is merely an artifice that indicates how many times the loop is to be taken [i.e., it is of the form $N/(N+1)$ and not really a random variable], then the term in brackets is left out. If the looping probability does represent a random variable, the term is incorporated. Note that if the loop is deterministic and the process variances (σ_A^2 and σ_B^2) are zero, the overall variance is zero, as would be expected.

6.3. The Nature of the Resulting Distribution

The resulting distribution of a resource (say, processing time) is not normal. More often it is geometric, and in a complex routine, tends toward a hyperexponential distribution. The standard deviation, should you care to calculate it, will be larger than the mean (10 to 15 times is not unusual). The distribution is, by nature, considerably skewed.

We should expect the distribution of resource usage to be broad; narrow distributions are exceptional. Consider the following observations.

1. Characteristics of transactions are distributed—e.g., transaction length may be exponentially distributed.
2. The system processes several different kinds of transactions with widely varying resource usages.
3. Processing efficiency increases with batch size because of a routine's call-startup–return overhead. Transaction interarrival time is distributed, leading to variations in batch size.
4. Programs have many paths and the resource usages along those different paths differ considerably.
5. As more and more subsidiary processes are cascaded in series, the dispersion increases, as does the mean resource usage.
6. Designers consciously strive to trade off processing by decreasing the resource use on high probability paths at the expense of lower probability paths.
7. Switches are not really probabilistic. Similarly for many loops (i.e., the looping probability is really a shorthand for multiplying the processing time per loop by the number of times looped). Unless care is taken (e.g., by "unfolding" all such loops and switches), the calculated higher moments will be artificially high.

The last reason is not really a good one, since it expresses a limitation of analytical techniques and/or the analyst, rather than a characteristic of the system. However, disentangling just what loops and switches are to be treated as deterministic rather than probabilistic takes a lot of effort and it can be easier to simply treat them as probabilistic and accept the artificially higher standard deviation.

6.4. A Word of Warning

Beware of specifications that require proof of adequate standard deviation in addition to adequate mean performance. I give this advice to both specifiers and implementers. It only takes one sentence to add this to a specification. If the implementer takes it seriously, there will be a significantly higher cost, certainly for analysis, simulation and measurement, if not for design. It is difficult to demonstrate one way or the other.

If the intention is to be sure that the system meets the specification, then it would be better to say something like, "The delay at such and such a throughput shall not exceed X, and the probability that the delay will exceed $X + Y$ will be less than 10^{-z}." The designer has then the option of designing to meet some lower delay, such as X/M, or to use a worst case analysis to show that the delay will be within specifications.

7. EXERCISES

1. If A and B are two mutually exclusive events with probabilities P_A and P_B, respectively, what is the probability that one or the other or both will occur?
2. If A and B are two events with probabilities P_A and P_B, respectively, what is the probability that one or the other or both will occur?
3. If A and B are two events with probabilities P_A and P_B, respectively, what is the probability that they will occur simultaneously? What is the probability that they will not occur simultaneously? What is the probability that they will not occur?
4. Karelian Kraps is played with tetrahedral dice. A 2 or 8 on the first throw is kraps: you lose and pass the dice to the next player. A 5 on the first throw is a win and you keep the dice. With a 7 you neither win nor lose and you hold the dice. On a 3, 4, or 6, you roll again until you either get a 5 in which case you lose and pass the dice, or you roll your number (3, 4, or 6), in which case you win and continue to play. What is the probability of winning on the first roll? What is the probability of losing on the first roll? What is the probability of holding on to the dice on the first roll?
5. *Continuation.* Jugagug has made eight throws without getting his point; what is the probability that he will get it on this throw? Given that his point is 4, what is the probability that he will get it on this throw?
6. *Continuation.* Assume that the point is 3, 4, or 6 (one at a time); what is the mean number of throws to a win? What is the mean number of throws to a loss?

7. *Continuation.* Qualudia has a more pragmatic approach to the game. Her dice are loaded and cannot throw 1's. Do Exercises 4, 5, and 6 for Qualudia's game.

8. *Continuation.* Phlogiston's dice are even more clever: they get progressively more honest on each throw. One die throws only 1's on the first throw, 1's and 2's on the second throw, all but 4's on the third throw, and are honest on the fourth throw. The other die does the same in reverse, starting with 4, then 4 and 3, etc. On the fifth throw the dice are reset and are dishonest again. Diagram Phlogiston's game and determine the mean number of wins for any resetting of his dice.

9. *Continuation.* Qualudia, realizing that Phlogiston is cheating, engages her disrupter. It sends out a random stream of 1's and 0's, which reset his dice on a value of 1. She can direct the disrupter at neither, either, or both dice, but cannot otherwise control when it will or will not reset. How should she best use the disrupter (i.e., not use it, use it on both dice, reset the 1-4 die, reset the 4-1 die)?

10. Unfold the following models:

(a) A41
(b) A5
(c) A42(N1-N5)

(d) T004(A1-B3)
(e) T006(Z1-A1)
(f) T006(LAM-LU)

(g) T008
(h) T016(A1-I)

11. Use the unfolding procedure on a simple model with a loop to prove the validity of the loop equation. (Hint: some clever work with infinite series, convolutions of distributions).

12. Replace the following models with simpler, analytically equivalent, single inway-single outway models. That is, replace the original flowchart with $N \times M$ equivalent flowcharts, where N and M are the number of inways and outways, respectively.

(a) A42   (c) T006   (e) T010   (g) T016
(b) A37   (d) T003   (f) T012

13. In model A36, let the process whose value is 180.1 be replaced by model A44 modified as described in the next sentence. In model A44, let the process whose value is 23 be replaced by model A36 modified as described in the preceding sentence. Let N be the number of times model A36 is called, using A36 as the outermost model. Express the mean resource usage value as a function of N. Now simplify that expression so that it is valid to three significant figures. Alternatively, simplify the expression so that 99% of all cases have been considered (i.e. the exit probability is at least 0.99).

14. In the following models, assume that the probability of each named node is parametric rather than numerical. Derive the appropriate algebraic expres-

sion for the mean resource usage and determine the probability value that will minimize that mean, and the probability value that will maximize the mean.

(a) A36, D1

(b) A36, D1, D2 with $P(D1, D2) = P(D2, N2)$ lower link.

(c) A5, D01, D03 with $P(D01, A761) = P(D03, ABDX)$

16. Calculate the standard deviations for the following models.

(a) A5	(d) T006	(g) T010
(b) T003	(e) T008	(h) T012
(c) T004	(f) T009	(i) T016

8
Analysis Without Agony

1. SYNOPSIS

While the graphical reduction techniques of Chapter 5 are correct, they can be cumbersome because of needless drawing and redrawing of the flows. Furthermore, the transformation required to make the reduction possible is not always obvious. A representation of flowcharts as matrices is presented here. A matrix reduction technique is provided that is equivalent to the graphical techniques of Chapter 5. Both approaches are useful and sometimes it is convenient to switch between them.

2. MATRIX REPRESENTATION OF FLOWCHARTS

This section introduces another representation of flowcharts. It does not have processes in boxes, (since only the value of the resource associated with the process is of interest) and junctions are merged with decisions. This can be done by associating the value of resources at the decision (say processing time) with every process (link) either immediately preceding or immediately succeeding the decision. A section of a flowchart in this representation now looks like the following:

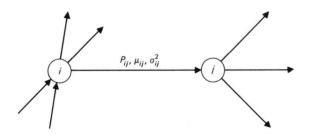

There are two nodes, i and j, joined by a link (i, j) to which is associated probability P_{ij}, a mean value of the resource μ_{ij}, and a variance for the resource σ_{ij}^2.

Using this notation for the example of Chapter 5 produces

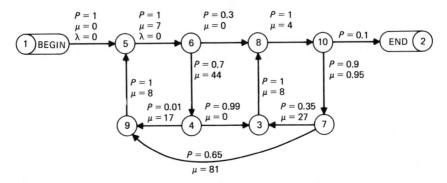

Do not bother to put down probabilities that are equal to 1.0 or means and variances that are equal to 0.0. The numbering and naming of the nodes is arbitrary since the same answer will result no matter how they are named. However, it is good practice to label the entrances and exits first.

The new model, then, instead of consisting of junctions, processes, decisions, and annotations, consists of nodes, links, and annotations.

While the above representation is more convenient than the original flowchart, since it is simpler, there would still be a lot of drawing and redrawing. Therefore, a more convenient matrix representation of the above flowchart will be used, as follows.

1. There is one row and one column for every node of the flowchart.
2. In each box of the matrix, corresponding to a hypothetical link (i, j) of the flowchart, place the resource usage numbers, (mean, variance, and probability). Note that the links are **directed**: (i, j) goes from i to j, while (j, i) goes from j to i.

Applying this conversion to the example yields:

	1	2	3	4	5	6	7	8	9	10
1					1 0					
2										
3								1 8		
4			0.99 0						0.01 17	
5						1 7				
6				0.7 44				0.3 0		
7			0.35 27						0.65 81	
8										1 4
9					1 8					
10		0.1 0					0.9 0.95			

Do not write entries for links that have zero probabilities. However, do put down mean values of zero for links that have a positive probability. A quick check shows the following.

1. A column depicts everything coming into a node.
2. A row depicts everything going out of a node.
3. Node *1* is an entrance, since nothing comes into it.
4. Node *2* is an exit, since it leads to nowhere.
5. Except for the exits, the sum of the probabilities for each row is equal to 1.0; if not, there is an error.

3. THE ALGORITHM

3.1. Overview

The procedure is a node-by-node elimination process consisting of the following steps.

1. Select a node for removal (the last row/column of the matrix).
2. Remove it and form an equivalent flowchart.
3. Combine any parallel links that may have been formed.
4. Eliminate any loops that may have been formed.
5. Repeat until only entrance and exit nodes remain.

I shall first show the equivalent processes in terms of flowchart elements and then illustrate it with the matrix.

3.2. Elimination of a Node—The Cross Term Equations

Consider the following situation:

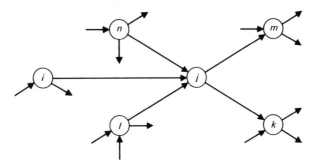

Eliminating node j, will result in the following:

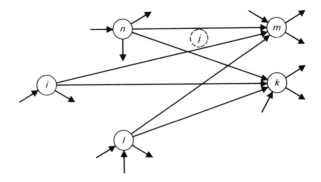

To eliminate node j, we had to replace the links that came into it and those that came out of it with equivalent links that bypassed node j, but properly accounted for everything that node j represented. We started with the following links:

$$(n, j) \quad (j, m)$$
$$(i, j) \quad (j, k)$$
$$(l, j)$$

We must now have a new link for every combination of incoming and outgoing links, which is to say:

$$(n, j, m) \Rightarrow (n, m)$$
$$(n, j, k) \Rightarrow (n, k)$$
$$(i, j, m) \Rightarrow (i, m)$$
$$(i, j, k) \Rightarrow (i, k)$$
$$(l, j, m) \Rightarrow (l, m)$$
$$(l, j, k) \Rightarrow (l, k)$$

This would seem to result in a net complication in the structure of the flow-chart, since we have increased rather than decreased the number of links. However, this will increase the possibilities for combining parallel links and replacing loops. The net effect is a steady progression to fewer and fewer links as the analysis proceeds.

Given the probabilities of the links and the resource usage prior to the elimination of the node, we must define the values of these properties after the elimination of the node and the replacements of the original links by the equivalent links. This transformation is expressed by the following:

Let

P_{ij} = the probability for link (i, j);
μ_{ij} = the mean for link (i, j);
σ_{ij}^2 = the variance for link (i, j);

- Probability: $P_{ik} = P_{ij} P_{jk}$;

- Mean: $\mu_{ik} = \mu_{ij} + \mu_{jk}$;

- Variance: $\sigma_{ik}^2 = \sigma_{ij}^2 + \sigma_{jk}^2$;

which is to say that the probabilities are obtained as the products of the probabilities of the original links, and that the means and variances of the resources are obtained as the sums of the component means and variances, respectively. If there had been several different resources of interest, there would have been an expression like the above for each one.

Consider now the matrix representation of the example, and the elimination of node *10*. There is a connection from node *10* to nodes *2* and *7*; only one link goes into node *10*, that coming from node *8*. This is readily seen since the column displays the links going into the given node and the row displays the links going out of the given node. We started with three links (*10, 2*), (*10, 7*) and (*8, 10*) and we will replace them with two links (*8, 2*) and (*8, 7*). This is shown in the following matrix:

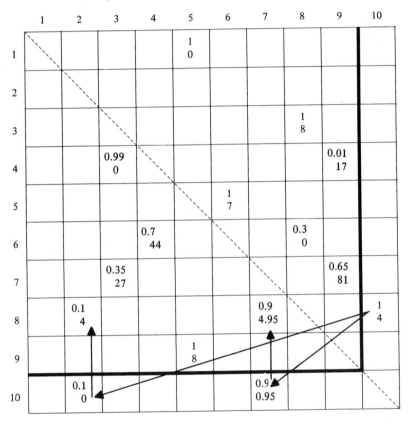

Using the equations as specified obtain the new entries at (*8, 2*) and (*8, 7*) with the following values:

$$P_{82} = 1.0 \times 0.1 = 0.1 \qquad \mu_{82} = 4 + 0 = 4.0$$
$$P_{87} = 1.0 \times 0.9 = 0.9 \qquad \mu_{87} = 4 + 0.95 = 4.95$$

An examination of the effects of eliminating node *10* on the original flowchart should confirm the equivalence of the matrix operation. Now proceed in the same manner to eliminate node *9*, resulting in:

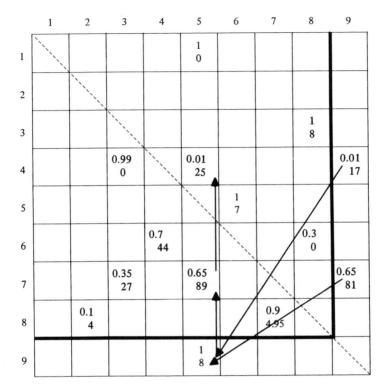

Eliminating node 8,

	1	2	3	4	5	6	7	8
1					1 / 0			
2								
3		0.1 / 12					0.9 / 12.95	1 / 8
4			0.99 / 0		0.01 / 25			
5						1 / 7		
6		0.03 / 4		0.7 / 44			0.27 / 4.95	0.3 / 0
7			0.35 / 27		0.65 / 89			
8		0.1 / 4					0.9 / 4.95	

Eliminating node 7 yields:

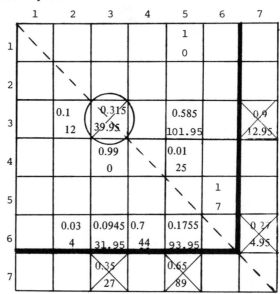

	1	2	3	4	5	6	7
1					1 / 0		
2							
3		0.1 / 12	0.315 / 39.95		0.585 / 101.95		0.9 / 12.95
4			0.99 / 0		0.01 / 25		
5						1 / 7	
6		0.03 / 4	0.0945 / 31.95	0.7 / 44	0.1755 / 93.95		0.27 / 4.95
7			0.35 / 27		0.65 / 89		

Something different has happened; there is an entry for node $(3, 3)$, which is to say that there is a loop. This is the reason that the dashed line was drawn through the diagonal. Any entry on the diagonal is a loop entry and must be eliminated using the loop equations. At this point it is worth checking the sums of the row probabilities; they are all equal to 1.0 as they should be.

3.3. Combination of Parallel Links

Assume that there are several parallel links between nodes i and j, as well as some other links emanating from i which do not go to node j.

Let

$P_{ij;n}$ = be the probability associated with the nth parallel link between node i and j;

$\mu_{ij;n}$ = be the mean of the nth parallel link;

$\sigma^2_{ij;n}$ = be the variance of the nth parallel link.

We have then:

- probability:

$$P_{ij} = \sum_n P_{ij;n};$$

- mean:

$$\mu_{ij} = \frac{\sum\limits_n \mu_{ij;n} P_{ij;n}}{\sum\limits_n P_{ij;n}} = \frac{\sum\limits_n \mu_{ij;n} P_{ij;n}}{P_{ij}};$$

- variance:

$$\sigma^2_{ij} = \frac{\sum\limits_n \sigma^2_{ij;n} P_{ij;n}}{P_{ij}} + \frac{\sum\limits_n \mu^2_{ij;n} P_{ij;n}}{P_{ij}} - \left[\frac{\sum\limits_n \mu_{ij;n} P_{ij;n}}{P_{ij}} \right]^2.$$

3.4. Reduction of Loops

The loops are eliminated by taking the contribution of the loop and distributing it amongst the outgoing links in proportion to the original outgoing probability. The outgoing probabilities will be readjusted so that they again sum to 1.0. In the following expressions the primed quantities indicate the values prior to the reduction and the unprimed quantities indicate the values after the reduction:

- probability:

$$P_{ij} = \frac{P'_{ij}}{1 - P'_{ii}};$$

- mean:

$$\mu_{ij} = \mu'_{ij} + \frac{\mu'_{ii}P'_{ii}}{1 - P'_{ii}};$$

- variance:

$$\sigma^2_{ij} = \sigma^{2'}_{ij} + \frac{\sigma^{2'}_{ii}P'_{ii}}{1 - P'_{ii}} + \frac{\mu'^2_{ii}P'_{ii}}{(1 - P'_{ii})^2}.$$

Applying this to the reduction of the loop at $(3, 3)$ yields:

$$P'_{33} = 0.315 \quad P'_{32} = 0.1 \quad P'_{35} = 0.585$$
$$\mu'_{33} = 39.95 \quad \mu'_{32} = 12 \quad \mu'_{35} = 101.95.$$

$$P_{32} = \frac{P'_{32}}{1 - P'_{33}} = \frac{0.1}{0.685} = 0.1460$$

$$P_{35} = \frac{P'_{35}}{1 - P'_{33}} = \frac{0.585}{0.685} = 0.8540$$

$$\mu_{32} = \mu'_{32} + \frac{\mu'_{33}P'_{33}}{1 - P'_{33}} = 12 + \frac{(39.95)\,(0.315)}{0.685} = 30.3712$$

$$\mu_{35} = 101.95 + \frac{(39.95)\,(.315)}{0.685} = 120.3212$$

3.5. Finishing Up

The elimination of the loop about node 3 resulted in following matrix:

	1	2	3	4	5	6
1					1 0	
2						
3		0.1460 30.3712			0.8540 120.3212	
4			0.99 0		0.01 25	
5						1 7
6		0.03 4	0.0945 31.95	0.7 44	0.1755 93.95	

which is equivalent to the following flowchart.

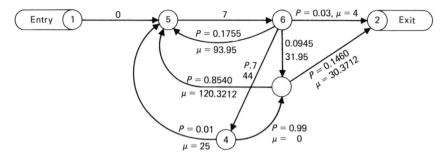

Eliminating node *6* results in a loop at node *5*, which after reduction produces

	1	2	3	4	5
1					1 0
2					
3		0.1460 30.3712			0.8540 120.3212
4			0.99 0		0.01 25
5		0.0364 32.4878	0.1146 60.4378	0.8490 72.4878	

Eliminating node *5* produces a loop at nodes *3* and *4* and parallels at links (*3, 2*) and (*4, 3*).

	1	2	3	4
1		0.0364 32.4878	0.1146 60.4378	0.8490 72.4878
2				
3		0.1460 | 0.311 30.3712 |152.809	0.0979 180.7590	0.7250 192.8090
4		0.004 57.4878	0.99 | 0.0011 0 |85.4378	0.0085 97.4878

The parallels are combined first to yield:

	1	2	3	4
1		0.0364 32.4878	0.1146 60.4378	0.8490 72.4878
2				
3		0.1771 51.8721	0.0979 180.759	0.7250 192.809
4		0.0004 57.4878	0.9911 0.0948	0.0085 97.4878

Removing the loop at $(4, 4)$,

	1	2	3	4
1		0.0364 32.4878	0.1146 60.4378	0.8490 72.4878
2				
3		0.1771 51.8721	0.0979 180.759	0.7250 192.809
4		0.0004 58.3236	0.9996 0.9306	

Removing the loop at $(3, 3)$ produces

	1	2	3	4
1		0.0364 32.4878	0.1146 60.4378	0.8490 72.4878
2				
3		0.1963 71.4889		0.8037 212.4258
4		0.0004 58.3236	0.9996 0.9306	

Removing node *4* we obtain:

	1	2		3	
1		0.0364 32.4878	0.0003 130.8114	0.1146 60.4378	0.8487 73.4184
2					
3		0.1963 71.4889	0.0003 270.7494	0.8034 213.3564	

Combining parallels:

	1	2	3
1		0.0367 33.2915	0.9633 71.8741
2			
3		0.1966 71.7930	0.8034 213.3564

Removing the loop at $(3, 3)$:

	1	2	3
1		0.0367 33.2915	0.9633 71.8741
2			
3		1. 943.6675	

Removing the last node, 3:

	1	2
1		0.0367 0.9633 33.2915 1015.3416
2		

yields $\mu_{12} = 979.4930$.

4. SOME PRACTICAL TIPS

If we had to constantly redraw the matrix as in the above exposition, we would not be much better off than if we were redrawing the flowchart. However, in practice, the original matrix is used as a work sheet; old results are crossed out and replaced as appropriate. For this reason it is convenient to make the lower order boxes larger than the higher order ones. Make row 2 smaller as well to save space. As each node is eliminated mark that row and column with a heavy line to indicate that it is to be removed. The work sheet for the above example is shown on page 148. While it may seem confusing at first, following through with the example, step by step, should make things clear.

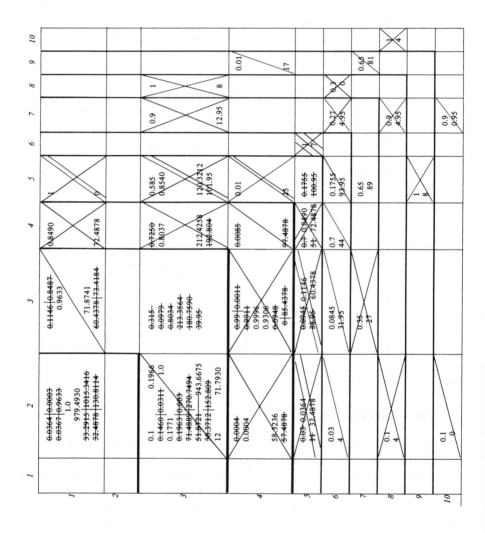

A high quality scientific calculator with several storage registers or a small programmable calculator is indispensable for hand work. Alternatively, the entire algorithm can be programmed. While the matrix reduction procedure is more straightforward, knowledge and practice with the flowchart reduction is useful, since it enables one to number the nodes in a manner which will result in less work. For example, had I labeled the nodes as in the flowchart reduction, in order to reduce them in the same order, the work sheet would have appeared as on page 150.

A comparison of the two work sheets shows that the second required less work and suffered less from round-off errors. A little strategy in numbering the nodes, and hence in directing the course of the reduction, can significantly reduce the labor. The order in which the nodes are numbered is opposite to the order in which they will be removed; e.g., node *10* is removed before node *9*. Count up the total number of nodes in the flowchart and number the nodes in reverse, from the highest number to the lowest, in accordance to the following procedure:

1. Number all inways and outways first (*1*, *2*, *3*, . . .) since they will not be eliminated at all.
2. Number all nodes with one incoming and one outgoing link with the highest remaining numbers in reversed order, since these will be the first to be eliminated.
3. Number (in reverse numerical order) all nodes with either one incoming and two outgoing links or two incoming and one outgoing links, with the following preferences:
   a. Nodes whose removal forms neither loops not parallel (highest remaining node numbers).
   b. Nodes whose removal forms parallels.
   c. Nodes whose removal forms loops.
4. Number all remaining $1 \times N$ and $N \times 1$ nodes (in decreasing numerical order) according to step 3 above.
5. Number all 2×2 nodes as above.
6. Number the remaining nodes (in decreasing node numbers) in the order of increasing total number of links.

I find it convenient to sketch the flowchart, stripped of all detail, and follow through to see if I have a reasonable ordering. While this is not terribly important if most of the matrix entries are numerical, it is indispensable if there are many functions and algebraic expressions for the probabilities. The steps for our perennial example are shown on page 151.

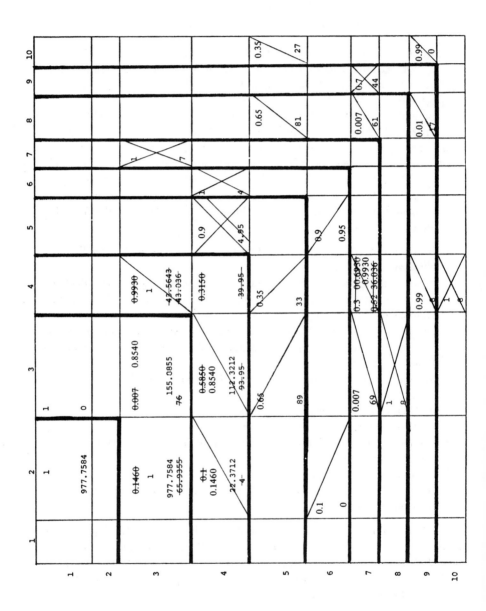

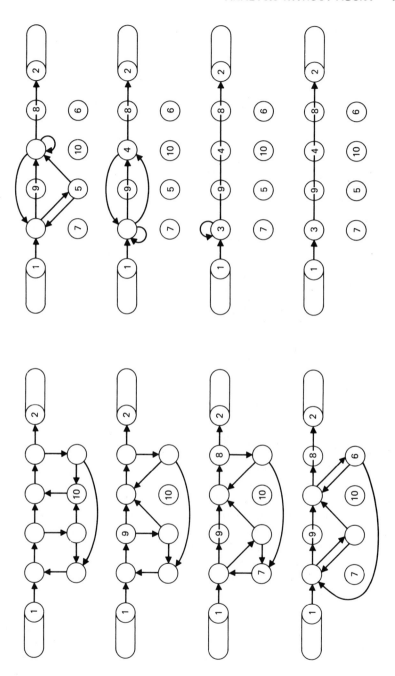

5. LINKS WITH FUNCTIONS

In many cases, a flowchart will not consist solely of numerical annotations, but may contain algebraic expressions for resource values or probabilities. The procedure is identical to that used for solely numerical entries; however, a slight modification of ordering should be made to reduce the work. The following modification to the numbering procedure is effective:

1. Reduce by removing all purely numerical nodes using the preferences for numerical nodes given in Section 4.
2. Remove nodes whose probabilities are numerical next.
3. Next, remove nodes whose resources are numerical and probabilities are functions.
4. Remove all other nodes.
5. In each of the above steps, follow the general rules of Section 4.
6. Try to leave non-numerical loops till last; i.e., try to let the last few nodes be a set of nested loops such that each successive node removed adds another loop term.

You may find that after the removal of all numerical nodes that the flowchart is easier to analyze by flowchart reduction, since the matrix may prove to be overly crowded and hence cumbersome. You may also find the index card algorithm of Appendix II convenient.

6. ANALYTICAL BASIS

The matrix procedure of this chapter and the node-by-node elimination procedure of Chapters 5 and 6, as well as similar procedures used to do other kinds of graph reductions are an example of a signal flow graph reduction process. It can be shown under very general conditions and interpretations of the operations that these procedures are exactly equivalent to solving a set of simultaneous linear equations—but how much nicer! [MAYE72]

The entire process then, is nothing more than a formalized approach to the solution of simultaneous linear equations by solving for a variable in terms of the others, substituting them in the remaining expressions, simplifying, and ending with one less equation than we started with. The cross term rule is the substitution step; the parallel rule is the simplification step; and the loop rule is equivalent to the solution step. The advantage of these procedures over the more direct linear equation solution using, say, matrices, is that it gives us a numerical answer only for the pair of nodes of interest, rather than, say, the mean time to every node. When the mean time to every node *is* needed, then the matrix inversion techniques are decidedly more efficient. You can set up the appropriate set of linear equations by simply starting at the exit and expressing each time in terms of the previous and unknown time. The time at the entry is of course, zero.

The same general approach can be used to analyze electrical networks, traffic networks, switching networks—in fact, any type of network whose properties can be represented by suitably defined operators whose behavior is linear. For more information on this versatile technique, I suggest Wataru Mayeda's book [MAYE 72].

7. EXERCISES

1. Repeat Exercise 1, Chapter 5, using the matrix method.
2. Repeat Exercises 2(a) and 2(b), Chapter 5, using the matrix method.
3. Repeat Exercise 3, Chapter 5, using the matrix method.
4. Repeat Exercise 4, Chapter 5, using the matrix method.
5. Repeat Exercise 7, Chapter 6, using the matrix method.
6. Modify the matrix method to work with activity flows and repeat Exercises 8, 9, and 10 of Chapter 6.
7. Calculate the standard deviations for the following models using the matrix method.

(a) A5   (c) T004   (e) T010   (g) T016
(b) T003   (d) T006   (f) T012

9

Interrupts, DMA, and Stretch

1. SYNOPSIS

Most systems operate at several priority levels, mechanized either as hardware or software, the most prevalent examples being interrupts and DMA transfers. Higher priority activities stretch the execution time of lower priority activities. This is one of the sources of differences between processing time and processing delay.

2. STRETCH—WHAT IS IT AND FROM WHENCE DOES IT COME?

Almost any system worth analyzing performs *quasi*-concurrent operations. I have to emphasize "quasi" because it is only in the larger multi-computer complexes or in CPUs with multiple ALUs that truly concurrent operations are possible. In most other computers true concurrency does not occur. Rather, the resources are shared between several "users," who contend for them. Thus, while the ALU may make the most demands on memory accesses or bus transfers, it must share the bus and the memory with other devices, predominant among them being the DMA hardware, and associated channels.

Assume for the moment that there are only two parties contending for the use of, say, memory—the ALU and a channel. Every memory cycle "stolen" by the channel is a cycle that cannot be used by the ALU. If in the absence of the channel's activity, a process took N microseconds to execute, what would be the elapsed execution time if the channel consumed K memory accesses? The number of memory cycles required to execute the process is the same regardless of the channel's activity; however, the elapsed time over which those memory cycles are taken is increased by the channel's activity. If the channel is not active, the elapsed time and the execution time will be the same. If the channel demands memory cycles at the maximum memory cycle rate, then the elapsed time is clearly infinite. The action of the channel is said to **stretch** the elapsed time for the execution of the process.

If higher priority functions demand service at a *rate R*, and the memory's access rate is M, the demand of the memory by the higher priority functions will be $\rho = R/M$. If the processing time for the routine in the absence of high priority functions is T, the elapsed time E is given by

$$E = \frac{T}{1 - \rho} \ .$$

The term $1/(1 - \rho)$ is called the **stretch factor**.

Stretch will occur under the following conditions:

1. The resource is characterized by a rate parameter (e.g., instructions per second) and the maximum rate is a fixed hardware characteristic (or if the resource is synthetic, directly related to fixed hardware characteristics).
2. The resource can be utilized by more than one process or in the processing of more than one transaction simultaneously and there is at least one process which can preempt the others that contend for the resource.

3. A CATALOG OF STRETCHES

3.1. General

It is not possible to exhaustively list all the sources of and mechanisms for stretch. These are as variegated as hardware. The more common sources, typical to most hardware configurations, are discussed below. Most actual mechanisms are variations or combinations of these.

3.2. Memory Contention

This is probably the single most common type of stretch. Memory is shared by several elements, including, but not limited to, the CPU, DMA channels, and other channels.

Contention for memory may have stretch associated with other resources. For example, in the case of interrupts a memory contention is typically associated with CPU contention as well. It is important to clarify the difference between memory contention and CPU contention. This distinction is not always obvious because the CPU's speed may be closely matched to the memory's speed. For example, the CPU may be capable of executing a million instructions per second, and be matched with a memory capable of executing two million transfers per second. The following hardware characteristics lead to differences between CPU contention and memory contention.

1. The CPU has generalized registers in sufficient quantities that many explicit memory accesses can be avoided; i.e., processing is dominated by inter-register operations. While the CPU and memory may be exactly matched for the most adverse instruction sequence, in the typical operation the CPU does not consume all of the available memory accesses in the absence of contention.

2. The CPU uses split cycle operations for some instructions (i.e., read-modify–write) during which time it locks out other accesses.

3. The memory is physically organized about a character length field, say. The CPU fetches instructions and manipulates operands that are several characters in length. The CPU could be limited by the memory and the other processes which contend for it.

4. The memory is organized into independent banks, with addressing arranged so that logically sequential characters are in physically separate memory modules. This is done, for example, by taking the two lower order bits of the address (logically) and using them as the physical two higher order bits. The memory (actually memories) are now significantly faster than the CPU and it is possible with an advantageous instruction stream, operand stream, and access contention pattern to allow full rate fetches on all memories simultaneously without contention, and therefore without stretch.

5. There are multiple CPUs in the system working out of shared memories that operate independently. The access pattern is such that they do not usually interfere. However, occasionally the access pattern is such that they do.

Given any one or two of the above situations, assuming reasonably simple access patterns, it is possible to evaluate stretch factors with fair accuracy. If however, the memory access environment becomes sophisticated, as in a typical large scale multi-computer complex with shared memory, etc., then simple analytical procedures are only approximate and accuracy demands the use of simulation.

3.3. CPU Contention

The primary sources of CPU contention are interrupts, traps, and multiple program states or operating levels. CPU contention invariably involves memory contention as well, as discussed above. The three concepts, interrupts, traps, and program states, are often confused, possibly because they are closely linked in many hardware implementations. However, they are independent concepts and the impact of stretch can be different in each case.

A computer is said to have multiple **program states**, if at the very least it has a means for recording the state, and for retaining the program counter for each state it can operate in. Such facilities may be primitive, consisting only of a state flip-flop to indicate "foreground" and "background" and an instruction that allows the storage of the program counter (say on a stack). At the other extreme, there may be a complete set of hardware registers for each program state. Program state changes may occur as a result of an interrupt, a detected condition, or an instruction issued to change the program state. A program state change consumes the resources required to completely store the old state and to establish the new state (i.e., all registers and condition flip-flops). Typically, processing is locked out during state changes. In a rudimentary micro-computer with barely minimal program state change facilities, a program state change could consume several hundred memory cycles and several hundred instruction execution periods. If the time period spent in the high priority states is short compared to that spent in the low priority states (say, under 5%) then the simple stretch analysis approach is feasible. If, however, program state changes are frequent (e.g., several thousand per second) and/or the time spent in such states is long (e.g., tens of milliseconds) simplistic analytical approaches will not work, nor perhaps will sophisticated analytical procedures. This leaves us again with simulation or measurement as the tool of choice.

Interrupts are responses by the CPU to externally detected events, usually resulting in a program state change. Directly or indirectly, an interrupt results in a transfer of control to a new state, the storage of the old state, and the initiation of a routine at a location dictated by the identity and nature of the interrupt. Interrupt mechanisms may be elegant: the interrupt causes a state change and a direct jump to a predetermined routine which is unique to that interrupt. Interrupt mechanisms may be rudimentary: storage of the old program counter followed a jump to a fixed universal interrupt handler with interrupt software required to particularize the interrupt. Since the state change is part of the interrupt processing sequence, the comments regarding analysis of program state change stretch effects apply to interrupts also. Since, however, interrupts imply additional processing, it is less likely that interrupts will be amenable to simple analytical treatment.

The term "trap" is often used synonymously with "interrupt." In some computers, however, there may be both interrupts and traps. In such cases, **traps** are interrupts that respond to internally detected conditions, such as overflow, underflow, arithmetic unit errors, internally sensed alarm conditions, protection area violations, etc. Machines that have both interrupts and traps are actually machines with two distinct interrupt mechanisms. The analytical issue here is that a computer may have several different ways of handling interrupts, and each such way will consume different resources. Each interrupt or trap mechanism must be identified and analyzed; it would be erroneous to assume that all interrupts or traps behave the same way.

3.4. Bus Contention

A bus is merely the most rudimentary kind of internal communication facility. The analysis of bus contention problems is best done by considering the bus as an internal switch facility that provided paths between the various units of which the system is composed. Thus, the computer can be viewed as an agglomeration of memories, CPUs, channels, devices, etc., tied to each other by a communication facility. The bus, as usually implemented, is a rudimentary $1 \times N$ time division switch. More elaborate internal communication topologies are available, including multiple buses, matrices, and multi-stage matrices.

When topology is complicated (e.g., a multi-stage switch rather than a simple bus), analytical methods are severely limited, and where available, require much exotic mathematics. Such topologies take us out of the realm of microanalysis. In most small systems, the internal communication facilities consist of one or two simple buses, which can be adequately treated by analytical methods.

Bus contention does not generally lead to stretch because the bus is usually sized to handle a far higher transfer rate than any pair of units are likely to require. The bus will typically have a priority scheme that will give access preference to high speed, synchronous transfer devices such as discs, drums, tapes, and high speed (50 kbs) telecommunications channels. The transfers involving these devices will not be stretched; i.e., transfer time will be independent of bus loading. Should a bus overload occur, through the simultaneous attempt to transfer from, say, several discs, at least one of these transfers will be aborted as a result of a detected transfer failure. This anomalous condition need not be considered in most analyses. That is, the bus will handle the high speed transfers at a cumulative rate up to and including the maximum bus rate without stretch. Lower priority functions such as CPU memory accesses, or memory to memory transfers will be stretched.

The major complication in analyzing the stretch depends on when things are happening. From the point of view CPU and memory stretch, it is often reasonable to assume that the high priority functions occur randomly and uniformly with respect to the low priority functions. Thus, we can think in terms of N interrupts per second and assume that these are evenly distributed across other functions.

Bus contention, however, may require a more detailed analysis. For example, if we had two high speed synchronous devices such as discs, each one of which consumed 25% of the buses' available bandwidth, we might be tempted to say that the bus utilization was 50%, leading to a twofold increase in delay for all processes that used the bus. This might be correct as a first approximation, but could well be wrong, as the following examples illustrate.

1. The transfers do not occur simultaneously, but rather sequentially. The stretch factor is not 2, but rather 1.33.
2. The instantaneous consumption is 25% per disc, but the duty cycle is only 5%. When one disc is in operation, the stretch is 1.33; if both are operating simultaneously, the stretch is 2. The average stretch however, is only 1.03.
3. The transfer consumes the entire bus's bandwidth. All other bus-utilizing operations are suspended for the duration of the transfer.

The stretch factor equation given on page 155 assumes a random relation between stretcher and stretchee. If this assumption is not valid, a more careful examination of the actual situation, perhaps as depicted in the activity flow, might be necessary. The need to carefully consider the point in time at which various processes are contending for a resource is not limited to the analysis of the bus; this situation can occur for almost any resource. However, it most often occurs in bus evaluation, and to a lesser extent in CPU evaluation.

3.5. Channel Contention

Channels may be dedicated to a single device, in which case there cannot be a channel contention problem. Some channels, particularly those used to terminate multiple, low speed, asynchronous devices, will have a contention problem. The analysis of channel contention stretch is similar to the analysis of bus contention-induced stretch. The principal differences are quantitative rather than qualitative. Bus accesses are usually granted a character or word at a time. Consequently, it is possible to have several activities going on quasi-simultaneously; if they contend for the bus, this situation can result in a true stretch, i.e., independence and simultaneity are valid assumptions. The channel, by contrast, is most often allocated to the device for the exclusive use of the device for the duration of the transfer.

Thus, the printer may be given the channel for the time it takes to transfer one line of type, the card reader for the time it takes to read one card, etc., whatever the instantaneous transfer rate might be. Hence, a channel capable of transferring 50,000 characters per second, when (momentarily) connected to the card reader may be tied up handling, say, 80 characters per second. Other processes must wait for the transfer to complete and are delayed for the duration of the ongoing transfer. The resulting delay is clearly far greater than would be expected on a random basis. A simplistic stretch analysis would yield a factor of 1.0016, while in practice, the additional delay would be 1 second.

A further complication in channel contention stems from the fact that such shared channels usually handle transfers in packet lengths which differ from device to device. For the high speed printer, it's a line; for the card reader or punch, a card; for the teleprinter, a character; for the VDU, a screen; etc. A clear idea of just how the channel handles these transfers is essential to their proper analysis.

4. STRETCH AND CONTENTION AT THE CHARACTER LEVEL

4.1 Conditions

This subsection concerns the treatment of stretch as it occurs for a shared resource such as a channel or a bus, in which it is possible to interlace the requests from several different sources and in which no one source is capable of operating at the maximum possible rate for the resource.

4.2. Buffering

Most devices attached to a shared resource such as a bus or a channel are capable of limited buffering, typically one or two characters or words (or whatever transfer unit is appropriate). This buffering allows two users to share the resource whatever the phase relation between them might be. Consider what would happen in the absence of buffering. A channel, say, capable of 100,000 transfers per second is connected to two devices, each of which require service at 50,000 transfers per second. If neither is buffered, there is a high probability that their instantaneous requests will clash. If one is buffered, then it can adapt by changing its phase with respect to the other, so that its transfers occur between those of the unbuffered device. In principle, unbuffered devices can share a resource if and only if (1) one rate is an integral multiple of the other, and (2) they are out of phase. Buffering, of at least one transfer unit, allows the absolute phase relation to be arbitrary and to a great extent eliminates the requirement that the two transfer rates be multiples of each other.

4.3. Synchronous Sources

Assume several processes share a resource and that the requests for service are synchronized with respect to each other, but that the phase relation between requests is random. If there is buffering, then as long as all the request rates are integral multiples of each other and their sum is less than the maximum transfer rate, they will be able to share the resource without interference and without any practically noticeable stretch. There is some stretch, or rather delay, of a character period or so, but in the context of a transfer of several hundred characters this is not noticeable. If you want to be terribly conservative and meticulous, add to each transfer time (time to transfer the block of data, say) as many character times as there are other devices in simultaneous operation. For example, the channel has a transfer rate of 100,000 characters per second. Three devices, operating respectively at 5,000, 25,000, and 50,000 characters per second use the channel simultaneously. The transfers are all of 1,000 characters. The per character time is 10 microseconds. The slowest transfer by this worst case analysis will require 5 milliseconds + 20 microseconds; the next transfer will require 40.02 milliseconds; and the last, 20.2 milliseconds. In most practical analyses, this can be safely ignored.

4.4. Incommensurable Sources

Consider now, the same situation, except that the various request rates are not multiples of each other but nevertheless still occur at fixed synchronized rates, say 7,000 characters per second and 7,100 characters per second. Since the difference in transfer rates is 100 characters per second, requests will clash at a rate of 100 per second. If there are several sources, then each pair will clash at a rate equal to their transfer rate differences. Note, however, that no matter how often requests for service clash, if there is sufficient buffering there will be little or no stretch beyond the worst case elongation of the transfer of one character per source, as in Section 4.3 above.

Generally, synchronized sources do not suffer stretch because if the delay caused by contention gets beyond N character times (where N is the number of characters the device can buffer and the time is determined by the device's transfer rate) a transfer fault will occur (e.g., lost character). The designer will avoid loading a channel this way. Since N is small—usually 1 or 2—the total number of devices which statistically make simultaneous requests on the shared resource is kept well below the point where missed transfers could occur.

4.5. Asynchronous Requests

Asynchronous devices such as teleprinters, manual keyboards, and low speed devices do not usually cause stretch on a channel or bus because the probability of simultaneous requests is typically designed to be low, and the individual transfer rates are much lower than the channel's capacity. Multiplying the transfer time by

$$S_j = \frac{1}{1 - \sum_{i \neq j} \rho_i}$$

where ρ_i is the demand of the resource by device i gives a worst case estimate to the stretch under these conditions.

5. STRETCH FOR SATURATING USERS

5.1. Principles

Assume that there is a user of a resource which is capable of demanding the resource to 100% and which will do so in the absence of other users. For example, a CPU may demand the memory or bus in this way; a memory engaged in a memory to memory transfer may demand the other memory or bus in this way also. Any **saturating user** of a resource is perforce delayed by the activity of other users of the same resource, be they saturating or not. The effect of the other users is to stretch the user of interest by

$$S_j = \frac{1}{1 - \sum_{i \neq j} \rho_i}$$

Where

S_j is the stretch factor for processes of priority j, i.e., the factor by which to multiply the activity time in the absence of stretch to obtain the elapsed time; and

$\Sigma\rho_i$ is the combined demands of all sources whose access priority to the resource is equal or higher* than j's.

5.2. The Priority Hierarchy

It is intuitively obvious that if two users of a resource make equal demands upon it, but one obtains service with a higher priority than the other, then the low priority user will be stretched, but the high priority user will not be. "Priority" as used in this context cannot be limited to program state priority or interrupt priority. The priority I am referring to here includes those mentioned, but does not necessarily correspond directly. The resource is shared by a number of (to a first approximation independent) "users" or processes. User A has priority over user B if that which allocates the resource will next grant service to A when both A and B have an outstanding request for service. For our purpose, it does not matter what the mechanism might be. It could be the built-in priority control hardware for bus service or memory access. It could be a consequence of the way the pieces of the system play with each other. It could be a software

---

*This is slightly pessimistic. For an optimistic analysis, include only the higher priority contributions. Exactitude is difficult here.

issue. Whatever it is, it is not always clear from a casual examination of the computer's reference manual.

- Do not assume that the effective priority hierarchy is the same for all resources. Just because the disc interrupt has a higher CPU priority than the printer interrupt does not mean that the DMA priorities are ordered similarly, or that bus priorities, channel priorities, etc., are similarly arranged.
- Do not confuse priority with importance or with the consequences of not being granted service. If the priorities are established by hardware, it is entirely possible the computer's designer had a different set of applications in mind or a different concept of what is or is not important.
- Distinguish carefully between preemptive and nonpreemptive service. In preemptive service, the higher priority user actually disrupts the operation. At the level at which stretch is a useful concept (i.e., the microscopic level of single memory accesses and one character transfers), preemptive service is rare.
- Do not assume that priorities, for a given set of users and a specific resource, are necessarily fixed, though they usually are. There are systems in which it is possible to modify this level of priority; if too much of that sort of thing is going on, you may be beyond the scope of microanalysis.

5.3. Typical Priority Structures

The typical computer has a simple priority relation between various users. The structure tends to be the same or similar for all resources, and is not changeable under program control, although the computer can be wired up for different priorities. Where the priorities are changeable by instructions, the changes are infrequent and tend not to occur in the normal course of running. The following list gives for various resources the typical order in which requests (or users) will be served.

Memory access:

1. High speed synchronous devices such as discs, drums, and bubble or CCD memories.
2. lower to moderate speed unbuffered synchronous devices such as tapes (paper and magnetic), card readers, punches, printers;
3. low to moderate speed buffered devices and asynchronous devices;
4. interrupt lines that require a memory access, e.g., where the target location for the interrupt is contained in a memory location;
5. computer-to-computer channels, where done via memory;
6. all other channels that require memory access;
7. CPU registers, where actually mechanized in memory;

8. CPU microroutines, for microprogrammed CPUs where the microroutines reside in the main memory rather than in a special memory such as a ROM;
9. CPU accesses in multiple access instruction, such as an indirect mode instruction;
10. CPU instruction fetches;
11. CPU operand fetches.

Channel priorities: These are typically assigned in the following order.

1. High bandwidth is given precedence over low bandwidth devices that share the same channel.
2. Synchronous devices are given precedence over asynchronous devices.
3. Unbuffered devices are given precedence over buffered devices.

Bus priorities: The order tends to be the same as for memory accesses, except that transfers on the bus associated with bus control and access assignment are given the highest priority.

CPU priorities: CPU priorities are generally closely associated with interrupt priorities. However, the behavior of interrupts is not the same as stretch, since the CPU is not allocated (in most architectures) on an instruction-by-instruction basis. The following order is typical:

1. alarm conditions internal to the CPU which result in a shutdown without an interrupt;
2. internally detected alarm conditions and traps;
3. interrupts in the order assigned;
4. program states in order.

Most resources in general: Where a resource is shared by several users of the same type (e.g., several discs on one channel) assignment of service is given in a fixed order, typically corresponding to some physical identity, i.e., every device is physically wired in.* The order of resource use priority is typically in increasing numerical order by physical identity. Watch out for the following possibilities.

1. The order need not be the same for all resources (e.g., disc 1 is physical unit 17 on the bus, but physical unit 8 with respect to a memory module).
2. The ordering may not be in physical numerical ascending order. Other orders are descending and unit distance code (i.e., a code in which only one bit of the identity changes at a time, e.g., 0, 1, 3, 2, 6, 7, 5, 4).
3. The typical reference manuals will probably not cover these fine points.

---

*In advanced architectures where such identities are controllable by software, changes are usually made in response to failures, malfunctions, and equipment repair, and are consequently statistically insignificant from the point of view of performance analysis.

Direct contact with the hardware's logic designers may be necessary. Sometimes they don't know either.

6. HIGHER ORDER STRETCH

6.1. Characteristics and Examples

So far, the discussion of stretch has been aimed at a relatively microscopic level such as character by character stretch, or memory reference stretch. What of higher orders of resource usage where the unit is not a single character or word, but a block or a group of words? A stretch analysis is appropriate if the following characteristics hold:

1. All (or most) users request the same kind of service (i.e., character, word, block, etc.).
2. The allocation unit (block, say) is constant or has a very narrow distribution (e.g., blocks are narrowly bounded between 120 and 128 characters).
3. A user is given unique unshared access to the resource for the duration of the allocation unit. It is not preempted by, or interlaced with, another user.

EXAMPLES

1. A card reader and punch share a channel. The reader has priority over the punch. The unit of transfer on the channel is a card. When the reader is active, the punch is not and vice versa. No other devices share the channel. One could analyse the elapsed time for punching cards by a stretch factor analysis.
2. Magnetic tape units share a common controller, capable of reading or writing one block at a time on one transport with a priority, say, between the transports or between read and write.

6.2. Mixing Up the Stretch

Say that we have several processes which are individually long, and which are interrupted by higher priority functions. The interrupts cause a state change to an interrupt state or level where the CPU spends several (perhaps several hundred) instructions to take care of the interrupt. Can the interrupts be treated as a stretch factor over the lower level processing? In general, the answer is yes, but caution is advised.

If the interrupts occur at random and at a relatively constant mean rate, and if the time spent in interrupt processing is small compared to the time spent in lower priority processing, and if the occurrence of the interrupt is not tied directly to the lower level processing, then a stretch analysis is probably valid. The key to the validity of treating any higher priority function (not just interrupts) by a stretch analysis is whether or not transactions are delayed by that process. Some examples follows.

1. A clock interrupt requires 100 microseconds of CPU and memory. It occurs every millisecond, independent of the load. Transactions are not delayed (except by the stretch) by the clock interrupt processing. A stretch analysis is valid. Incorporate the interrupt processing into the stretch analysis.

2. I/O operations entail channel and memory contention. They are terminated in an interrupt with an associated state change. Add the interrupt processing time to the elapsed time for the I/O operation and add the processing time for the interrupt to the contribution to stretch caused by the DMA of I/O transfer.

3. The program operates on several levels. Most of the processing occurs at the lowest priority level. A higher priority level is used to process some other transactions, whose total contribution to resource utilization is less than 5-10%. The main interest is in the delay of the low priority functions. Use a stretch analysis.

4. The program operates on several levels. Most of the processing occurs at the lowest priority level. A higher priority level is used to do part of the transaction's processing, so that a given transaction will spend time in each level. A stretch analysis may or may not be valid. It will at best tell you how much the elapsed time has been increased by the high priority functions, but it does not tell you how long the transaction might have spent in the high priority states.

7. LOCAL AND GLOBAL STRETCH

7.1 General

Consider a simple situation in which there are two processes contending for a resource. You have calculated the processing time for the low priority process and you know the demand for the high priority process or processes. If the high priority demand is constant and independent of the low priority demand, then the elapsed time (with respect to that resource) for the low priority process is obtained by multiplying the appropriate stretch factor. Suppose these assumptions are not valid; is there still a simple approach? The answer, as usual, is "it depends."

7.2. Local versus Global Stretch

Let us go back to the transaction flow. Assume that it is reasonably complex, with several things going on simultaneously, so that it is better represented as an activity flow. For the moment assume that there are two activities, processing and some I/O operation. Furthermore, assume that all stretch factors, except that due to I/O operations, have been taken care of. The following model will do:

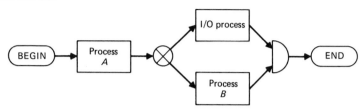

The elapsed time for process A, including any stretch, is assumed known, as is the expected duration of the I/O operation, and the processing time for process B including all the stretch, except that which is caused by the I/O operation. If the I/O operation is clearly longer, or clearly shorter, than process B, throughout all conditions of interest, then there is not much to analyze. Suppose however, that the I/O operation and process B are close in duration. Assume that the resource of interest is the memory. The I/O operation, because it is transfering data, induces a stretch on process B which could make B take longer than the I/O, even if it had been shorter in the absence of the I/O operation. As a first approximation, since we know that rate at which the I/O operation is consuming the resource, we can apply the stretch to all operations which it spans. This is what I mean by **local stretch**. It is local in the sense that it applies only to some processes—those that are concurrent with it.

A stretch factor which applies to all processes is said to be **global**. The activity flow might be complicated, such as the following:

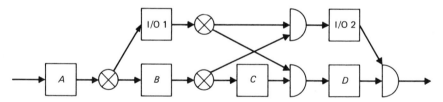

It is no longer clear as to how to assign the stretch factor. I/O operation 2 spans C and D. If I/O 1 finishes before B, it cannot stretch C, but I/O 2 can impact both C and D. It is obvious that it is not obvious just how the stretch factors are to be allocated.

Stretch factors caused by I/O operations are usually small. Consequently, we can make some worst case assumptions, the easiest of which is to assume that all stretches are global, rather than local. This is a worst case assumption: recall that we are dealing with resource demand rates, and to add all rates and assume that they occur at all times is a worst case assumption.

7.3. The Stretch Allocation Problem

Let's go back to the simple, two process model of the preceding section. The analysis is really more complicated than appears at first. In fact, you may have to solve an equation to find out just how much the I/O operation stretches the process.

Let

r be the resource rate (e.g., transfers per second);
u be the rate at which the I/O operation uses the resource;
t_u be the elapsed time for the I/O operation;
n_v be the number of resource units required to accomplish the process;
t_v be the elapsed time for the process in the absence of stretch;
T_v be the elapsed time for the process with stretch.

The way to analyze this is to compare the I/O time with the process time after the stretch. Yes, I know that is what we are trying to get by this analysis, but it is much easier to assume it to be known and to work backwards. There are two cases of interest: (1) the I/O time is greater than the elapsed process time; and (2) the I/O time is less than the elapsed process time.

CASE 1. I/O time greater than process time $(t_u > T_v)$

If the I/O time is greater than the process time after stretch, then the I/O operation induces a stretch throughout the duration of the process. Consequently it can be treated as a global stretch, and

$$T_v = \frac{t_v}{1 - (u/r)}.$$

Since by assumption

$$t_u \geq T_v = \frac{t_v}{1 - (u/r)},$$

we get

$$t_u \left(1 - \frac{u}{r}\right) \geq t_v.$$

as the condition for this case to hold.

CASE 2. I/O time less than process time $(t_u < T_v)$

In this case the process was not stretched throughout its duration, but only for a part of the time. There are two ways we can look at this: (1) the I/O operation added a delay exactly equal to the number of transfer periods it consumed;

or (2) a stretch was induced for some part X of the process, and the rest of the process occurred at the normal rate. Both approaches lead to the same answer.

First approach: Add the contribution of the I/O. The total number of I/O transfers is ut_u, and the time added to the process is ut_u/r, whence

$$T_v = t_v + \frac{ut_u}{r}.$$

Second approach: Figure out the period X over which the stretch does occur. For an unknown part X of the process, it was stretched as with a global stretch. The result was equal to the I/O time. Therefore,

$$t_u = \frac{X}{1 - (u/r)}.$$

The unstretched part is $t_v - X$; consequently,

$$T_v = \frac{X}{1 - (u/r)} + t_v - X.$$

but

$$X = t_u \left(1 - \frac{u}{r}\right),$$

whence

$$T_v = t_u + t_v - t_u \left(1 - \frac{u}{r}\right)$$

$$= t_v + \frac{ut_u}{r}$$

as before. Since by hypothesis

$$t_u \leq T_v = t_v + \frac{ut_u}{r},$$

we get

$$t_u - \frac{ut_u}{r} \leq t_v,$$

or

$$t_u \left(1 - \frac{u}{r}\right) \leq t_v.$$

as the condition for this case to hold: and lo and behold, it is complementary to the condition for the alternative assumption.

As long as we have only two users contending for a resource, and the situation (locally) is simple, as in the example, this sort of algebraic machination is acceptable. In principle, it is possible to extend this kind of analysis to more complicated cases, and occasionally it may be worth doing. The result will be a set of simultaneous inequalities, which in general are more difficult to solve than a set of simultaneous equations. Things get difficult very quickly. Well what's the fuss? We're all computer people—use the computer. Not so simple! You could set up an iterative scheme with numerous conditional branches, trying this assumption and then that assumption, calculating a tentative stretch allocation, seeing if it fits, etc. The trouble is that such procedures (for deep reasons imbedded in numerical analysis*) do not necessarily converge, but may rather cycle around the answer—never getting to it. Caution is advised.

7.4. What to Do about the Stretch Allocation Problem

The situation is—you have a bunch of quasi-concurrent operations that interact and stretch each other in a non-simple way. You set up the equations (inequalities) with numerous unknowns that describe just what parts of what process was stretched by what higher priority operation. The resulting expressions look like the basis of a Master's thesis in numerical analysis. Should you solve the equations? Cop out and opt for simulation? Ignore the whole problem? Or try for a reasonable approximation? A good, slightly pessimistic approximation can be obtained in most cases by means of the following observations and procedures:

1. The total contribution of the stretch, even if it is all global, is small—of the order of 5–10% in most systems.
2. If you assume that all stretches are global and at the rate appropriate to the devices that caused them, you might get a very pessimistic approximation.
3. Look at the stretch-causing operations and their sequence. Pick the worst simultaneous rate and use it for a global stretch. Still pessimistic, but better.
4. Examine all the resource demands over the time period of interest. Assume that the sum of the processing time exceeds the sum of the I/O time (whether or not it does) and add the I/O's stretch contribution to the processing time. This is optimistic.
5. Compare the results of 3 and 4 above. If they are close enough, quit—otherwise, go on.

---

*There is no assurance that we have a contraction mapping [RALL69].

6. Find the worst contributor to the stretch. Simplify the model by use of the procedure above (2-5) and do an exact analysis with respect to the worst stretch. The result should be someplace between 3 and 4 above.
7. Break down the activity graph further, into regions which do not interact, and repeat 6 for those regions.
8. Continue until you have reasonable convergence or have run out of time, money, and/or frustration quotient.

8. RETROSPECTIVE VIEW ON STRETCH

The following are preconditions to the treatment of resource contention by a stretch analysis.

1. The resource parameter is a rate which is a fixed hardware characteristic.
2. The resource can be utilized by more than one process quasi-simultaneously.
3. There is a priority hierarchy for the utilization of the resource and the priority is fixed over the period of time treated by the analysis.
4. Resource utilization requests occur randomly with respect to each other and with respect to priority levels.
5. The instantaneous request rate for a user of the resource and the mean rate do not differ significantly—i.e., it makes sense to talk about mean demand of the resource by a process, rather than having to treat burst or block transfers.
6. The partial demand of the resource by one process leaves the uncommitted remainder, up to the maximum rate, available for use by other processes.
7. Local versus global: use simple allocation. Avoid the rough allocation problems.

9. EXERCISES

1. A computer has four priority levels with 1 the highest and 4 the lowest. It has a complete set of registers at each level. It is capable of executing 10^6 instructions per second which it gets out of an instruction memory. A priority level or program state change requires 10 μsecs. Assume that interrupts are handled at the highest level and require T microseconds to process. Determine the stretch to the lower levels when the interrupt rate is N interrupts per second. Assume a state change for every interrupt. Did you forget a factor of 2?
2. As above, but assume that if an interrupt occurs while the computer is in the interrupt processing state, that it will service that interrupt also, thereby avoiding spurious level changes. Hint: do it approximately and assume that

T is small, but not too small. Compare the results of problem 1 and 2 as a function of T and N.

3. *Continuation.* The demand for level 1 is NT. Under the assumptions of problem 1, further assume that the rest of the available CPU cycles are distributed in proportions P_2, P_3, and P_4, with $P_2 + P_3 + P_4 = 1.0$ and $0 \leq P_2, P_3, P_4 \leq 1$. Determine the stretch factors for each level. Show that the stretch on level 4 is unaffected by the way the processing is distributed among levels 2 and 3.

4. A CPU and a channel have access to the same memory, capable of M operations per second. Every CPU instruction takes one memory cycle and K percent of the instructions take an additional memory cycle. The channel is asynchronous and operates at a transfer rate equivalent to C cycles per second. The channel has priority over the CPU. How does the channel stretch the CPU elapsed execution time.

5. Assume in problem 4 above that the channel is synchronous and buffered but that the CPU has priority over the channel. How does the CPU stretch the channel? Tricky.

6. Consider an unbuffered I/O channel with a maximum transfer rate of 100,000 characters per second. Let the time required to transfer a character be T microseconds where T is less than 10. Consider two synchronous devices sharing the channel with transfer rates A and B respectively, such that $A + B \leq 100,000$ cps. For arbitrary values of T, A, and B, determine the probability that there will be interference between the two devices.

7. *Continuation.* As in problem 6 above, but assume that the two devices are buffered and synchronous. Be careful.

8. Assume the demand at any of n priority levels is ρ_i and that such demands occur randomly and independently for each level. Within any one level, however, part of the stretch may be local or global. Is a global assumption always pessimistic? Prove your contention.

9. Set up and solve the stretch allocation problem for the four process model of section 7.2. Use specific numbers and do it numerically.

10. *Continuation.* Redo problem 9 above with all values parametric. Set up and solve by cases.

11. Modify the result of problem 10 above by the addition of a yet higher level global stretch.

12. *Continuation.* Redo problems 9 and 10 under the assumption that all stretch factors are small.

13. Refer to chapter 6, problem 8. Let the (D1, N2) link be a local stretch over the other processes and find the expected delay.

14. Refer to chapter 6, problem 9. Let the (D1, N2) link be a local stretch over the other processes and determine the expected delay.
15. Redo problems 13 and 14 above assuming that value of the (D1, N2) link is not an absolute expenditure of resources but is a rate at which resources are expended. Assume all figures to be given in microseconds, with the rate (13) replaced by a parameter.

10
Devices, Latency, and Scheduling

1. SYNOPSIS

Some peripheral devices, particularly mass memories such as discs, drums, and bubble memories, exhibit marked delays between the initiation of an operation and its completion. These delays can contribute to the overall transaction delay, and in some cases can be the binding factor. For some devices it is possible to arrange the task order so that the delay is minimized. Various models of device delays under different optimization strategies are presented in this chapter.

2. BASIC CONCEPTS

2.1. Physics, Economics, and Latency

The term "latency delay," or simply **latency*** is used to describe delays exhibited by devices connected to the system; delays which the system cannot control. Latency is inherent in the device and is usually a consequence of a trade between cost and performance. The behavior of the device, vis-à-vis latency, is tied to its physical structure and dynamics, i.e., its physics. There can be no understanding latency without understanding the device's operation in detail. This may mean getting details that are not normally included in the device's specification, or manuals not usually released to the buyer. To assume that one device, such as a tape unit, has the same latency characteristics as another, similar, competitive device, is often a source of gross error. It is worth finding out just how the thing works.

It is fallacious to assume that a device with a high transfer rate has a low latency, or that a low transfer rate implies a high latency. Just as a system has a specific throughput–delay characteristic, so has the device. Within

---

*The term "rotational latency" is also used because these delays are usually associated with physically rotating devices.

broad limits, latency and transfer rates are independent. Just as increased transfer rates imply increased cost, reduced latency is generally associated with higher costs, as the following examples show.

- A tape unit has to move wheels and tape before it actually starts to read or write. The delay can be reduced only by increasing the drive motor's power or the control system's finesse.
- A disc unit records data around a track on the disc's surface. To reduce its delay requires a faster motor, better head motion servos, or several sets of read heads.
- A remote terminal is reached by a satellite link. The satellite is in a stationary orbit at 28,000 miles. To reduce the delay the satellite must be placed in a lower orbit which is no longer stationary, necessitating the addition of satellites to provide the same coverage.
- The "device" is another system with specific throughput–delay characteristics. Decreasing the delay necessitates either a reduced throughput (which means more systems for the same load) or faster, and therefore more expensive hardware.

2.2. How to Beat the Latency

The worst* latency occurs when the tasks are served one at a time, in the order of arrival. This procedure effectively slows the device to a rate which is the inverse of the latency. Things can be improved by not insisting that the tasks be processed in that order. For example, you could keep track of the disc's position (i.e., the next sector to come under the read head) and order the tasks by sector number in the direction of rotation. Now you might be able to get several tasks done per revolution and the latency will be considerably reduced. While the delay for this approach is higher for any one task when compared to the one-at-a-time approach, the delay for the batch is not much higher than that of the single task, and far lower than N times the single task delay.

The above approach to the reduction of latency is an example of **scheduling**; the tasks are reordered to improve the throughput at the expense of individual delays and task order. The specifics of the optimization strategy are device-dependent, and it is not possible to generalize beyond saying that one or more of the following tactics are used:

1. service out of order;
2. buffering and batching;
3. initiation of a new task prior to the completion of an old one;
4. setting things up in advance.

---

*You can do worse, but you have to work at it.

Whatever combination of approaches is used, the combinations are collectively called "optimization strategies," "task scheduling," or "device scheduling." A device is said to be a **scheduled device** if some scheduling algorithm is used. Conversely, if no such algorithm is used, it is said to be an **unscheduled device**. A scheduled disc, then is not physically different from an unscheduled disc; it is only used differently.

2.3. Access Coordinates and Behavior

2.3.1. General Note

I will use three terms, "tape," "drum," and "disc," to cover a lot of different devices that may or may not physically correspond to these units. I could have just as easily called them one, two, and three dimensional systems, rather than by their more common names. The three terms are used because these devices are archetypes. For example, a single shift register, a magnetic tape, or a deck of punched cards are examples of "tapes;" while drums, fixed head discs, and acoustic delay lines are examples of "drums." Whatever engineering reasons may favor the choice of one physical device or another is not germane to the analytical problem—it is behavior that counts. Thus, you might find a "drum" or "disc" simulated in a main memory by a combination of software and operating procedures. Another computer system, to which yours is connected, and upon which its performance depends, might operationally behave as a "tape."

2.3.2. Access Geometry

The simplest geometry is that of a tape. The access coordinate system (the means by which a location is accessed) is one dimensional and sequential. That means, to get from record A to record B, you must traverse all records between A and B. (See Figure 10-1a.)

A drum has a two dimensional access coordinate system, one which is random and the other which is rotary. By "random" I mean that any record (actually set of records) along the "random" address axis is accessible in the same amount of time. The set of locations corresponding to a random coordinate address is called a **track**. The track is subdivided into sequentially accessible elements called **sectors**. The complete address of a location on a drum is given by its track/sector number combination. The time taken to go from one sector back to that sector is called the **rotation time** and its reciprocal is called the **rotation rate**. In reality, it is not possible to have truly random access to different tracks. A drum, even an ideal drum, is an approximation, as it may take some time to shift from track to track. If that time is negligible compared to the rotation time, then the device is generally treated as if it were a drum. If however, the

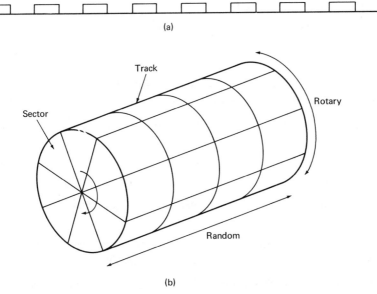

(a)

(b)

Figure 10-1. TAPE and DRUM access schemes. (a) Sequential access–TAPE; (b) random plus rotary access–DRUM.

track-to-track switching time is not negligible, and/or it is variable, then it is best to treat the device as if it were a disc.

A **disc** has three access coordinates—cylinder, track, and sector. For any given cylinder, the disc behaves exactly like a drum. Time is required to move the read/write mechanism—the heads*—from cylinder to cylinder. The cylinders are arrayed in a logically linear order just like the tape.

Reviewing the three kinds of coordinates, we have:

LINEAR—sequential access with no constraints on order except that all records between two points must be traversed to get from one point to the other;

RANDOM—all elements or groups of records are equally accessible in arbitrary order without (significant) constraints;

ROTARY—successive elements are available for access in a pre-determined, repetitive order, which is not controllable;

TAPE = LINEAR;

---

*The heads are on an arm and the arm moves from cylinder to cylinder.

DRUM = RANDOM + ROTARY;

DISC = RANDOM + ROTARY + LINEAR.

2.3.3. Combinations

Various devices can be classified by their access schemes. Consider all possible combinations of these three coordinate types, two at a time. (See Figure 10-2.)

Linear/Linear—this is just linear access and there is not much to the analysis of such devices.

Linear/Random—An example of this was a magnetic card file in which successive cards were brought to the read mechanism then read.

Linear/Rotary—A low cost floppy disc with a moving head is a good example—any single cylinder disc, for that matter.

Random/Linear—There was once a huge file consisting of 500 tape units (RCA-BIZMAC). Some bubble memories behave this way.

Random/Random—This is just random access like any common main memory.

Random/Rotary—This is a drum.

Rotary/Linear—This was a "juke box" memory that brought different reels of tape to a common read/write mechanism. The tapes were accessible only in rotational order.

Rotary/Random—This is a circular magnetic card file.

Rotary/Rotary—This is a juke box with tape loops.

Having succumbed to the temptation of treating these coordinates two at a time, one could go on to treating all 27 combinations of three access coordinates at a time—leading to a discussion of numerous past, present, and future exotic memories, only a few of which are familiar or practical. It is important to note, however, that solid state devices such as magnetic bubble memories and charge coupled device (CCD) memories lend themselves to the construction of access geometries of numerous dimensions and access schemes, most of which have no models.

2.4. Parameters of the Latency Problem

2.4.1. Physical and Geometric

Any analysis will require the accumulation of all pertinent size (number of tracks, sectors, etc.) and timing parameters and the aggregation of these in accordance to a perceived access geometry (i.e., it is a drum, disc, tape, etc.).

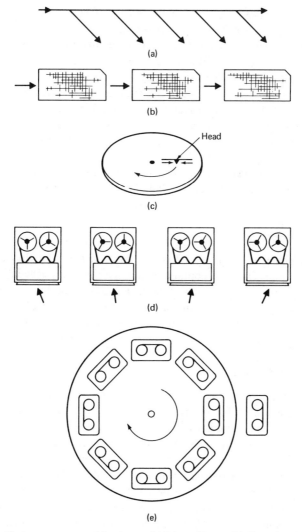

Figure 10-2. Various access combinations. (a) Linear/linear; (b) linear/random−magnetic card file; (c) linear/rotary−floppy disc; (d) random/linear−tape transport file; (e) rotary/linear−cassette juke box.

2.4.2. How the Tasks Arrive

Tasks can arrive continually or in a batch. If they arrive continually, the system employs whatever latency minimization techniques it has available on each task as it arrives; possibly rearranging the tasks previously scheduled but not yet processed.

Alternatively, the tasks can be accumulated into a batch, scheduling done for the entire batch, and the batch not revised until it has been processed. One approach is not better than the other, but there are circumstances where one might be preferred over the other. Batch operation requires buffers to store the task request, and entail a higher initial delay, but the batch is cleared in a shorter period of time than it would take a continual arrival mechanism to clear the transactions. That is, the batch system has a long initial delay followed by an intensive activity period. During the accumulation period, the unit is free for use by some other process. The continual arrival system delays each task less, but the unit is busy all the time.

In practice, a real system may use a combination of both, allowing some stragglers to be added to the batch, and the continual arrival system may do some minor batching in the interest of efficiency.

2.4.3. Scheduling Policies

The simplest policy is no policy. Take the tasks in the order they arrive (i.e., FIFO—First In First Out). A common component of many scheduling systems is ordering the task in linear order for a linear access coordinate or in rotation order for a rotational access coordinate. As the number of dimensions is increased, say to three, further strategies can be employed leading to a wide diversity of scheduling policies, each of which requires its own model.

2.4.4. Nature of the Records

Records can be of either fixed or variable length. If the records are of fixed length, the system is called a "paging" system (e.g., a **paging drum** or **paging disc**). Conversely, the records can be variable length, with the length specified by a probability distribution. Such systems are called "file" systems (e.g., a **file drum** or **file disc**). The paging drum is more common than the file drum. Furthermore, a file drum typically forces the beginning of a record to a sector boundary, and requires that records be written as a discrete number of (small) sectors. The models treated here will be mostly of paging systems because they are more common than file systems, have been more completely studied, and are easier to analyze.

2.4.5. Distribution of Tasks

Most latency models are based on the assumption that tasks are uniformly distributed throughout the access coordinate space, e.g., every sector is equiprobable. Most systems do not behave in precisely that way, exponential distributions being common. In tapes and drums, the distribution of tasks is not generally significant. The distribution of tasks across the cylinders of a disc unit, however, may be an important parameter of the problem. Of the many distributions possible, only the uniform has been treated in depth.

2.4.6. Restrictions and Concessions to Reality

Almost every device has some kind of restrictions that tend to corrupt the simplistic models we are able to solve. For example, it may not be possible to do a read immediately followed by a write; there may be a bias favoring one direction or another in a linear access system; there may be other physical restrictions that do not permit certain sequences of operations or that may impose additional delays for certain sequences of operations. The restrictions are not generic and depend on specifics of the unit.

3. TAPE UNITS—LINEAR UNITS

3.1. Mechanics

Tape (physical tape) units are much alike analytically. The main difference between expensive tape units and inexpensive cassette units are reflected in performance parameter values.

A tape unit has two motors—a precise, speed-regulated, small motor (the capstan motor) that controls the speed of the tape past the read/write heads; and a larger, imprecise motor that provides the power for winding and rewinding. Expensive transports may have two rewind motors, and low cost cassette units may have one motor doing all three jobs.

Tape is written in blocks whose length may be constant or variable, but which are written at a known density. The first component of latency is the time required to read the block. Given the density and the tape speed this time is readily determined. The tape itself has inertia, as have the guide wheels, the capstan motor, and the control system. Consequently, when the tape is commanded to stop, it coasts a centimeter or so. Similarly, when started, the inertia of the system imposes a delay before the tape is up to speed and reading or writing can begin. The inertia, therefore, forces a gap. When a sequence of records are written, there will be inter-record gaps interspersed. The space taken up by these gaps is often much longer than the records. For example, a 700 bits/cm (actually characters per cm) tape will have a 2 cm inter-record gap. If the average record is 256 characters long, the tape is mostly gaps. There is no simple way to determine the length of the inter-record gap. It is usually specified by the manufacturer. A common analytical error is to ignore the gap in calculating how long it will take a tape unit to do something. While the manufacturer may readily give you the gap length, you may find it more difficult to obtain accurate data on the start and stop times (which, of course, could contribute to latency). There is no simple way to analyze these either, since their value depends on physical characteristics which are more technical than the start and stop times. The start and stop time, particularly for a small, inexpensive cassette transport, may depend upon how much tape is wound up on each reel, as well as the total amount of tape. While this variation is small, it might not be negligible. It pays to check.

Some tape units, particularly expensive ones, employ what is called a **hot start**. If a new start command is given before the tape has stopped, it will again accelerate. This results in a shorter inter-record time than would have been obtained had the tape been allowed to come to a full stop.

3.2. The Tape Latency Problem

The latency problem for a tape is usually the following:

The tape is at position X. Move the unit N blocks to position Y, read or write a record, and stop. This is conceptually a trivial exercise, but keep the following in mind.

1. Does the start and stop time depend on X? If so, what is the relation and how does it change as you approach Y?
2. Does the tape employ a hot start? If so, you must use the hot start inter-record time rather than the cold start time.
3. Does the tape actually have to stop at every record, or can it count records without reading them while moving at rewind speed? If so, use the rewind characteristics discussed in the next section.
4. What is the average record length and inter-record gap size?
5. Can the tape be read in both directions, or does reverse reading actually require a backward skip (rewind) followed by a forward read?

3.3. Rewind Problems

During rewind or fast-forward operations, no attempt is made to keep the tape moving at a constant speed past the read/write heads. In fact, the tape or head is often moved aside to avoid excessive head wear. It should be obvious that the time it takes to rewind or move forward a fixed distance should *not* be constant. Suppose there is only one motor, used either for rewinding or for fast forward (as in a home tape recorder). If the motor is a constant speed motor and accelerates instantaneously to its rated speed, the tape will have a constant acceleration. The tape reel is moving at a constant angular rate, and as tape is wound up on it, the diameter increases, providing a constant acceleration to the tape. We are interested in reaching a certain *linear* position along the tape. The time it takes to reach that position clearly depends on the initial and final position. If you know the hub diameter, the length of the leader, the thickness of the tape, the linear position for the start point, the linear position for the stop point, and the rotation rate, it is not difficult to determine the time it takes to get from A to B.

If the tape is at initial position L, the true initial position is $L + l$, where l is the length of the leader. Let

$L_i = L + l$ true initial position;
t = tape thickness;
r_h = hub diameter;
r_i = initial radius, corresponding to L_i;
r_f = final radius.

then N, the number of wraps at the initial position is

$$N = \frac{r_i - r_h}{t},$$

and

$$L_i \cong \frac{r_i - r_h}{t} \cdot \frac{2\pi r_i + 2\pi r_h}{2} \tag{10.1a}$$

$$= \frac{r_i - r_h}{t} (r_i + r_h)\pi, \tag{10.1b}$$

whence,

$$r_i = \sqrt{r_h^2 + tL_i/\pi}. \tag{10.1c}$$

Similarly, you can determine the final radius. Given the two radii, and rotation rate for the take-up reel, you can determine the mean linear velocity as the average of the velocity at r_i and r_f. Knowing the full length of the tape between the start and the stop points you can determine the time taken to traverse it. Watch out for units, though—scaling errors (inches for feet, rpm, etc.) are common.

There are several complications ranging from negligible to major.

1. The effective thickness of the tape and actual thickness are not the same. The tape may stretch a little, or may be loosely packed. While negligible on a short length of tape it can be significant for a long reel. There is no easy way to calculate this. It is better to depend on the manufacturer for data.
2. The take-up reel may use a dc motor rather than a constant speed motor, in which case the angular velocity of the motor will slowly accelerate up to a maximum value. This value may be a function of time or of the amount of tape on a reel. The acceleration characteristics may have to be gotten from the manufacturer.

3. Some tape units control two independent motors to provide constant linear speed for the tape during rewind or wind. There is nevertheless at least an initial acceleration and a stop time.

I have not found manufacturers overly eager to supply the necessary data to determine the exact rewind time. As a rule, they do not have the appropriate curves. What they will give you is the time it takes to rewind a full reel, say 750 meters long, of a standard thickness tape. Knowing the mechanics of the tape unit, tape thickness, reel hub diameter, etc., I can set up a tentative model. Given the rewind time at two other points, such as rewinding a 365 meter reel and a 550 meter reel (with the same hub size, onto the same hub size) I can get the rest of the parameters, and so be able to figure out the rewind time for 10 meters of tape, mid-reel, if that's what I'm after.

3.4. Other Linear Access Devices

The magnetic tape unit is one of the more complex linear access devices, since its forward and reverse characteristics may be markedly different, and since it has two different modes of operation (read/write and rewind/fast-forward). The typical nonlinear characteristic of the rewind mode also complicates things. Most other linear access devices are simpler. Typically, the time required to get from A to B depends only on the number of records between A and B. This is the case for a card reader and punch, a paper tape reader or punch, magnetic card files, etc.

A long circular shift register can be treated as linear access device for a single task. If the present position and desired position are known, then the latency is simply determined from the shift rate and the distance between the two positions. If the present position is unknown, and is assumed to be random, then the latency is simply the time required to traverse half the register plus the time for one task. Many linear access devices are actually rotary in this sense, since there is no rewind as such.

4. THE DRUM

4.1. General Considerations and the State of the Art

The drum is the archetype of a rotary device. Consequently, it is important of itself and because its analysis is a major component of the analysis of discs. Closed-form analytical models amenable to simple calculations are few. Most models can only be evaluated (practically) on a computer. In addition to the few analytical models, there are several empirical models based either on simulation or a combination of simulation and analysis.

A detailed discussion of drum (and by extention, disc) latency models is beyond the scope of this book—beyond the scope of what I have been calling micro-analysis. Therefore, only useful results and references to previously published models will be presented. Derivation of these models requires advanced queueing theory and related mathematics.

4.2. The Sequential Drum (Paged or File)

The simplest latency problem for drums concerns drums used in a linear rather than rotary access mode. The drum has S sectors per track (paging drum). The record is N sectors long, and the rotation time is r. The delay is obviously

$$D = r\left(\frac{N}{S} + \frac{1}{2}\right) . \tag{10.2a}$$

The analogous model for a file drum with a mean record length of L characters, with M characters along the track is:

$$D = r\left(\frac{L}{M} + \frac{1}{2}\right) \tag{10.2b}$$

The half revolution term comes about because it is assumed that the drum's angular position is random with respect to the time at which the sequential operation is begun; the starting point is an average of one-half revolution away. This half revolution term is an infamous part of many drum or disc manufacturer's literature. You may look in vain for the rotation rate or rotation time, but you are sure to find a number called "average latency" or some such thing. It is usually one-half the revolution time.

The sequential drum, while analytically trivial (it's the only such model, by the way), is important because of its prevalence. One can analyze complicated systems with discs and drums, using exotic optimization techniques, and willy-nilly apply those models to a data transfer which is in reality sequential, thereby grossly overestimating the latency contribution for that data transfer.

As examples of sequential transfers, consider the following.

1. Records are written at random with respect to the sector, but are read back sequentially. The write operation requires a latency analysis, but the read operation is sequential.
2. Programs and/or table overlays are used extensively to conserve main memory. These are usually sequential.
3. Sections of the main memory data base are periodically written to disc or drum to protect the data base against main memory or CPU failures. These records are usually written sequentially.

4. The typical record is many sectors long and is completely buffered before being read—while the start point of a record may be random, the transfer is best treated as a sequential operation.
5. It is obvious that nothing can be faster than a sequential operation. If a best case analysis is indicated (where is the farthest brick wall?), saying that all accesses are sequential is the most optimistic assumption you can make.

4.3. The Unscheduled Paging Batch Drum

The time to complete one task (a one-sector read or write) is the expected time to reach the desired sector, plus the time required to traverse that sector, or

$$r \left(\frac{1}{S} + \frac{1}{2} \right),$$
(10.3)

which of course is just a special case of the sequential access with a one-sector-long record. The time required to process N tasks is simply N times this, or

$$Nr \left(\frac{1}{S} + \frac{1}{2} \right)$$
(10.3a)

The unscheduled or FIFO batch drum is just about the worst performer possible. It is not the actual worst, since the tasks could be reordered so that every task would have almost one revolution of latency. Therefore, the FIFO drum is a worst case batch model.

4.4. The Scheduled Paging Batch Drum

4.4.1. The Scheduling Algorithm

Tasks are accumulated over a known period of time. They are reordered in accordance with increasing sector number. The specifics of the reordering process are rarely significant for analytical purposes because the reordering processing time is typically small compared to the latency delay. The reordering can be done by several methods.

1. The sector number is transformed to an index used to access a table into which the task details are stored—typically the I/O instruction that will actually execute the task. In a small system, there could be a separate table entry for every sector–track combination.
2. The same procedure as above may be used in a large system. However, because the total number of track–sector combinations is large, a set of tables (each corresponding to one revolution) is maintained instead.

3. A set of linked lists, one per sector, is maintained. Orders are executed from the tops of all lists in sector order.
4. A doubly linked list may be used by sector and by successive tracks for each sector. This is used when the number of sectors is very large, or in discs.

Tasks are placed, within sector order, in FIFO order. Note that none of the above approaches requires actual sorting of tasks into sector order; it is all done implicitly, based on the sector identity. If a sort is used, the typical sparsity of tasks makes the sorting process quick, and again negligible compared to rotation time.

4.4.2. Some Batch Models

The first model is an optimistic model by Denning [DENN67]. The delay to complete *the last of N tasks is*

$$\frac{N}{S} + \left(\frac{1}{2} + \frac{1}{S}\right) r \tag{10.4}$$

where

N = number of tasks in the batch;
S = number of sectors;
r = rotation time.

Denning, in the same paper, provides a model for the expected delay to the beginning of the first task:

$$D \text{ (begin first task)} = \frac{r}{N+1} \left(1 - \frac{1}{2S}\right)^{N+1} \tag{10.5a}$$

Using this formula, and considering the entire sequence of tasks as a succession of beginnings to the next "first" task (with N reduced each time), and furthermore, using the defining series for $\ln X$, it is relatively easy to obtain the following model, which is generally pessimistic:

$$D = \left[\frac{N}{S} + \ln 2S - 1 + \frac{1}{2S}\right] r. \tag{10.5b}$$

Using the same approach, but starting with the mean delay for the first task of

$$D \text{ (begin first task)} = \frac{r}{N+1} \tag{10.6}$$

We obtain the following, fairly sharp, pessimistic model[*]

$$D = \left[\frac{N}{S} + \ln (N + 1) - 1 + \gamma + \frac{1}{2(N + 1)} \right] r + rR_N \qquad (10.6a)$$

where

$$\gamma = \text{Euler's number} = 0.577215665$$

$$0 < R_N < \frac{1}{8N^2} .$$

The R_N is a remainder term which can be safely discarded for $N > 2$.
A more precise approximation is given by Rosenberg [ROSE74]

$$D = r \left[N + \frac{1}{2S} - \frac{1}{S} \sum_{k=0}^{N-1} F(k) \frac{H(k)^S - 1}{H(k) - 1} \right] \qquad (10.7)$$

where

$$F(k) = \left[e^{-\rho} \sum_{J=0}^{k} \frac{\rho^J}{J!} \right]^S \qquad (10.7a)$$

$$H(k) = \sum_{J=0}^{k+1} \frac{\rho^J}{J!} \bigg/ \sum_{J=0}^{k} \frac{\rho^J}{J!} \qquad (10.7b)$$

$$\rho = \frac{N}{S}$$

Despite it's complexity, this formula is an approximation. It is good for more than four transactions and four sectors. Figure 10-3 shows typical values. Because of the computational complexity of the above formula, Rosenberg has developed a further approximation of the form

$$D = r \left[\frac{N}{S} + \frac{1}{2S} + \frac{S-1}{2S} N^{(A + B \log S)} + (E_1 + E_2 \log N) \log N (\log N + C) \right] ,$$

$$(10.8)$$

with

$$E_i = F_i + G_i \log S + H_i \log^2 S + J_i \log^3 S \qquad (10.8a)$$

where $F_i, G_i, H_i,$ and J_i are constants.

---

[*]After playing around with an approximate formula for $\sum_{j=1}^{N} 1/j$, see V. Mangulis [MANG65] page 59, #16.

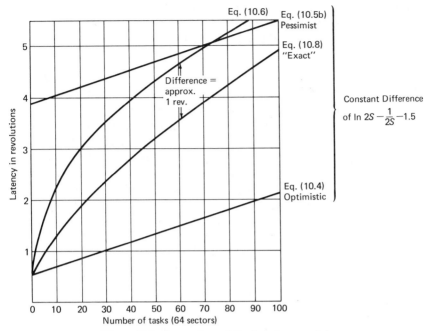

Figure 10-3. Comparison of the four drum models.

A FORTRAN subroutine that incorporates the appropriate constants is given in Appendix I. This approximation is good to within a few percent from 4 tasks and 4 sectors to 256 tasks and 256 sectors. It is reasonably accurate beyond that point, but falls off to about a 7% error beyond 512 sectors and tasks, and becomes rapidly incorrect beyond that point. For a comparison of these four models, at 64 sectors, see Figure 10-3.

For 1, 2, and 3 tasks, Rosenberg has exact formulas:

Tasks	Delay	
1	$$\frac{(S+1)}{2S} r$$	(10.9a)
2	$$\left(\frac{4S^2 + 9S - 1}{6S^2}\right) r$$	(10.9b)
3	$$\left(\frac{3S^3 + 12S^2 - 5S + 2}{4S^3}\right) r$$	(10.9c)

The program corresponding to Eq. (10.8) can fit in a small programmable calculator with approximately 200 memory locations. The exact amount will depend on how the calculator stores constants. The program is divided into two ranges corresponding (approximately) to 64 or more sectors, or 64 or less sectors. The actual logic is more complicated, as can be seen from the program listing in the Appendix.

4.4.3. A Semi-Batch Model

Burge and Konheim [BURG71] treat a semi-batch model. There is a buffer or table capable of holding N tasks. As a task is serviced, another task immediately replaces it in the buffer. The tasks are served in rotation order. The tasks are uniformly distributed over all sectors. This model corresponds to batch situations in which task arrival rates are sufficiently high to assure a full task buffer, or in situations in which the completion of a task generates a new task through feedback or a similar mechanism. They obtain, not the wait time for the batch, but the expected number of tasks serviced per revolution:

$$N_t = \frac{2NS}{2N + S - 1},\qquad(10.10)$$

where

N is the buffer size
N_t is the expected number of tasks serviced in one revolution.

4.4.4. Positional Knowledge

It is possible to sense the current sector on some drums and discs. Given this knowledge, instead of starting the batch from an arbitrary sector 0, it can be started from the next sector to come under the read/write heads. If a table structure is used to set up and store the tasks, the first I/O operation is issued for that point in the table which corresponds to the next sector; in practice, several sectors are anticipated to allow for processing time and such. If the task list is set up as a set of queues (with one queue per sector), then it is a matter of starting off with the right queue. Whatever mechanism is used, positional knowledge can reduce the mean delay of the batch by one-half revolution. If the drum has positional knowledge and the system has software which takes advantage of it, any of the previous models may be corrected by subtracting the half revolution time.

4.4.5. Read/Write and Head Switching Restrictions

Some drums force a delay of one or more sectors when switching tracks. As a worst case approximation, assume that a track switch must be done for every task and treat the drum as if it had only half the actual number of sectors. In some drums, the restriction is not on switching tracks, but on changing from a read to a write operation. This can be modeled by treating the two operations as separate batches. This treatment clearly provides an upper bound because you could always arrange to process the tasks that way. You can be a little more clever and eliminate the second half revolution latency by the following argument. In setting up the schedule, you would know which sector had the greatest number of read or write requests. Say the first batch was a read batch, then the second batch would be a write batch, which could be optimized starting with that sector that had the most reads. You could do this with or without positional knowledge. Therefore, the total time for read/write switching intermixed must be less than the sum of the time for separate read and write switching, less a half revolution, plus the read/write switching time. If the read/write switching time is very large, then you certainly would design the system to have separate reads and writes.

4.4.6. Other Batch Models

Denning [DENN67] also considers drum models in which there is a delay corresponding to several sector times for switching from read to write operations. A complete formula is given for the time to the beginning of the first transfer, but comparable expressions for the expected waiting time for the batch are not provided. This case is far more complicated and simple approximations are probably not forthcoming.

4.5. The Continual Arrival Drum

4.5.1. General

Far more research has been published on the continual arrival drum than on the batch drum. There are two reasons for this:

1. The batch drum models involve a lot of combinatorics, do not lead to nice closed formulas, and are in general messy to work with.
2. Large scale commercial and scientific computer installations, time shared systems, and commercial operating systems, tend to use continual scheduling rather than batch scheduling. Small and special purpose systems tend to the opposite. The former, being the more prevalent, have attracted the most attention.

While the continual arrival drum models are simpler than the corresponding batch models, you should not be tempted to substitute one for the other. Not only are the values not close, but the behavior is totally different. The batch drum can never lead to a nonfinite answer because the batch is always finite. The continual arrival drum, conversely, since there are always new tasks arriving, can exhibit saturation and blow up to infinity as the arrival rate of tasks approaches the rate at which they can be serviced.

4.5.2. The FIFO Paging Drum

The simplest drum model in this class is FIFO drum model. Tasks arrive at a mean rate λ. It is common to assume that the arrivals are random and that the interarrival time is exponentially distributed. This is done for several reasons explained in Chapter 11. This assumption also leads to nice* analytical results. Fuller [FULL75A] gives an exact model for a FIFO paging drum:

$$D = r\left\{\frac{1}{2} + \frac{1}{S} + \frac{\lambda\left(\frac{1}{2} + \frac{1}{2S}\right)\left(1 + \frac{1}{2S}\right)r}{3\left[1 - \lambda\left(\frac{1}{2} + \frac{1}{2S}\right)r\right]}\right\}, \tag{10.11}$$

where

λ = arrival rate in tasks per second;
r = rotation rate in seconds;
S = number of sectors;
D = mean delay to the completion of transfer.

4.5.3. The FIFO File Drum

Fuller discusses a model of a file drum in which the exponential record length assumption is not made:

$$D = \left[1 + \frac{X(1 + C^2)}{2(1 - X)}\right]\frac{X}{\lambda}, \tag{10.12a}$$

where:

$$X = \lambda(\tfrac{1}{2} + L)r \tag{10.12b}$$

$$C^2 = \frac{(r^2/12) + \sigma^2}{(\tfrac{1}{2} + L)^2 r^2} \tag{10.12c}$$

where

D, λ, r, are defined as before;
L is the mean record length in circumferences;
σ is the standard deviation of the record length for the distribution of interest.

---

*"Nice" is relative—the formula is "nice" since it can be whipped out in a few minutes on a calculator. Other formulas are not nearly so nice.

He also discusses another FIFO file drum in which records are constrained to be multiples of sector size in length. The simpler FIFO file drum model above will suffice in most cases. As the number of sectors per track increases the models converge as expected.

4.5.4. The Scheduled Paging Drum

There is only one scheduling algorithm of interest—transaction sector order and FIFO within sectors. This case is commonly called the "Shortest Latency Time First" or SLTF model. This model leads to a simple expression,

$$D = \left[\left(\frac{1}{2} + \frac{1}{S} \right) + \frac{\rho}{2(1 - \rho)} \right] r, \qquad (10.13a)$$

where

$$\rho = \frac{\lambda r}{S} = \text{drum demand factor.} \qquad (10.13b)$$

This model and variations thereof are also discussed in Coffman [COFF69], but the derivation may prove difficult and it takes a little work to get the answer in usable form.

4.5.5. The Scheduled File Drum

Fuller derives an exact model for the scheduled file drum, which is computationally nasty. He also provides an empirical model based on a combination of simulation and analysis:

$$D = \left[\frac{1}{2} + L + \frac{\rho}{1 - \rho} + 0.368 \left(\frac{\rho}{1 - \rho} \right)^{1.5} \right] r, \qquad (10.14)$$

where ρ is defined as before.

4.5.6. Comparisons

Comparisons of various continual arrival drum models are given in Weingarten [WEIN66], Denning [DENN67], and Fuller [FULL75B]. The capabilities of these drums, ordered from worst to best, is: FIFO-file, FIFO-page, SLTF-file, SLTF-page. Comparison with batch models cannot be made directly because it may depend on what assumptions are made with respect to the time during which the tasks are accumulated for processing.

5. THE DISC

5.1. General Characteristics of the Problem

5.1.1. Source of Complications

The disc is a more complicated device than the drum, mainly through the additional effect of head motion from cylinder to cylinder. Each cylinder, once the heads are on it, behaves like a drum and is analytically treated as such. The usual scheduling policy within each subsidiary "drum" is SLTF, although FIFO may also occur. The disc is further complicated by the following.

1. Different discs have different head motion characteristics.
2. The distribution of records across cylinders may not be insignificant.
3. There are many possible optimization strategies.

5.1.2. Head Motion

Figure 10-4 shows some seek-time characteristics of discs. The simple model is linear. It is assumed that the total seek time is a linear function of the number cylinders traversed from the present head positions to the target head positions. This is the most common simplifying assumption made. Although real discs do not display this linear seek time behavior, it is not a terrible assumption to make,

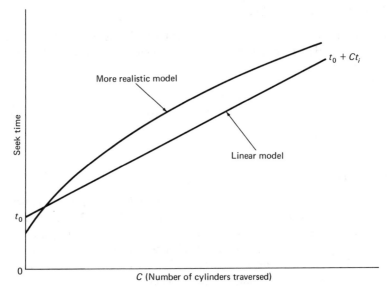

Figure 10-4. Disc seek models.

particularly if the problem concerns motion among adjacent cylinders rather than over the entire disc. This is an important assumption, because without it analytical models may not be possible.

The curve of Figure 10-4 is more typical. The disc unit with this characteristic would appear to have noticeable inertia, but once it gets moving it can traverse many cylinders in a short period of time. This "typical" may not be valid either, but may be representative of part of the head motion behavior. As an example, some discs use a set of mechanical devices whose motion is binary. It may take varying amounts of time to traverse M cylinders; depending on how many "bits" had to change in the mechanical linkage. A traversal from one cylinder to another that differed only by one bit, even if across the disc, might take less time than traversing to a cylinder three away, since fewer bit changes were required.

There are many models of discs; some of them differ only in the assumptions made about seek characteristics. To apply a model, you must first know your disc's seek characteristics. This may be difficult to obtain; keep the following in mind.

1. The seek function may be valid only from the innermost to the outermost cylinder. It may not apply to a traversal of intermediate cylinders.
2. The seek function may show seek time as a function of total cylinders traversed, but the function might or might not differ from cylinder to cylinder.
3. The time may not be the same in both directions.
4. You might be given an "average" seek time (comparable to "average latency" for drums) which presumes all sorts of things about scheduling, distribution of records, etc., which may or may not apply to your case.

5.1.3. The Subsidiary Problem

While most models treat the entire disc, the typical small system application demands an analysis of only a portion of the disc. That portion may or may not be the same for read and write operations. For example, a communication system writes incoming messages onto the disc over a relatively compact area determined by the incoming message transmission time and the total number of incoming messages. The disc, from the point of view of writing operations, has records uniformly distributed over several cylinders. Conversely, read operations are associated with message deliveries, which because of network congestion and other factors tend to be spread over a period of several hours. From the point of view of reading, the messages are exponentially distributed over several dozen cylinders, or perhaps the entire disc.

The typical problem, then, involves the analysis of a subdisc with only a few cylinders, and with the head seek characteristic corresponding to a segment of the seek curve. The limiting case is that of a single cylinder disc, i.e., a drum. Unfortunately, most of the published models employ simplifying assumptions that render their applicability to this situation marginal. Because in early discs, and in many present discs, the seek time is large compared to the rotation time, attention has been focused on the head motion aspect of the disc and scheduling the seek operations. Furthermore, if the tasks are spread over many cylinders, say, more than 50, the expected number of tasks per cylinder is small and the latency is of the order of a half revolution, whether scheduling is used within the cylinder or not. Consequently, most models make the simplifying assumption that tasks for a given cylinder will not be scheduled, but will be treated as a FIFO drum. It is clear, then, that if the number of tasks is large, and/or the number of cylinders over which they are distributed is small, these simplifying assumptions will lead to an overestimate of the disc latency.

5.2. The Sequential Disc

Most of the observations made in Section 4.2 (sequential drum) also apply to the sequential disc. The analysis is straightforward if we assume things are continuous rather than discrete. Let:

S = number of sectors per track;
T = number of tracks per cylinder;
ST = number of sectors per cylinder;
L = mean record length in sectors;
r = rotation time;
t_0 = initial seek time to the region of interest;
t_i = intercylinder seek time (for one cylinder) in the region of interest;

Then, assuming that a record can start at any point (i.e., record beginnings are uniformly distributed),

L/ST = the expected number of cylinders over which the record will lie; and
L/S = the expected number of tracks over which the record will lie.

Then,

$$D = t_0 + \frac{t_i L}{ST} + \frac{rL}{2ST} + \frac{rL}{S} + \left\lfloor \frac{rL}{S} \right\rfloor. \tag{10.15}$$

The t_0 term is the time required to get to the region of interest. The next term is the intercylinder seek time multiplied by the expected number of seeks. The third term is the half revolution latency term for each new cylinder, since it is assumed that seeks and rotation are not synchronized and that the effect of the seek is to force an effectively random start with respect to the first track on the next cylinder. The fourth term is simply the time required to write or read the entire record. The last term requires some explanation. The symbol $\lfloor X \rfloor$ denotes the integral part of X. This is an additional revolution for each track. Such a term could have been added to the sequential drum expression too. In some drums and discs, where the track switching time is not negligible, a track switching guard band one or two sectors long is provided. If the number of sectors used in the above expression is the logical rather than physical number of sectors, the expression is still valid. If a track switching guard band is not provided, then the additional revolution must be paid for; note that it is a full rather than a half revolution.

5.3. The Unscheduled Paged Batch Disc

Let the intercylinder seek time be linear, with some initial value t_0 and a term which is proportional to the number of cylinders traversed. That is, the seek function is of the form $t_0 + kt_i$, where k is the number of cylinders traversed. Let this function apply for all initial head positions. Furthermore, assume that the records are uniformly distributed over the entire disc. Then, with C cylinders:

$$D_{\text{seek}} = \left[\frac{t_i(C-1)^2}{3C} + \frac{t_0(C-1)}{C} \right] N \qquad (10.16)$$

If the rotation latency is significant compared to this, then the right-hand side of Eq. (10.2a) must be added, yielding

$$D = \left[\frac{t_i(C-1)^2}{3C} + \frac{t_0(C-1)}{C} + r\left(\frac{1}{S} + \frac{1}{2}\right) \right] N. \qquad (10.16a)$$

This analysis is a simplified version of Weingarten [WEIN69]. Weingarten also shows that the expected number of cylinders traversed is approximately* $\frac{1}{3}$ rather than $\frac{1}{2}$, as might naively be extrapolated from a consideration of the drum. The reason for this can be intuitively understood by considering the fact that the initial head position can be on any cylinder with equal probability, and unlike the drum, the disc allows movement in two directions. Frank [FRAN69] provides a more general analysis yet, but it does not lead to closed numerical forms without making assumptions similar to the ones made above. Both models, if followed to the bitter end, will allow the assumption of any seek-time characteristic curve, although the derivation of a closed expression could be brutal for a complicated seek function.

---

*Actually $(C^2 - 1)/3C$. $\hfill$ (10.16b)

5.4. The Scheduled Paging Batch Disc

5.4.1. General Assumptions

There are two components to the scheduling algorithm, the seek component and the cylinder (drum component). The drum component can either be based on an optimum schedule as in Section 4.4, or be a FIFO model as in Section 4.3. The scheduling is assumed to be an extension of the sector ordering. That is, tasks are ordered in cylinder order and sector order within cylinder order, relative to an initial "home" cylinder, such as the first or last of a set of contiguous cylinders. This is a reasonable assumption for the batch model because the seek to the home position can be done while the batch is being accumulated. In most batch models, the initial position of the head tends not to be random, since the disc was being used to serve some other batch in another segment of the disc. The operation consists of starting with the home cylinder and moving to the first cylinder that has tasks, servicing them in sector order, and then proceeding to the next (numerically higher, say) cylinder that has tasks, and so forth until the entire batch is cleared. Tasks are assumed to be distributed with equal probability across all cylinders and sectors.

5.4.2. The Basic Model

The basic model is given by Rosenberg [ROSE 74]:

$$D = CPr + C't_0 + \frac{C'(C - C')(Ct_i - t_0)}{(C' + 1)(C - 1)}, \qquad (10.17)$$

where

$$C' = C - \frac{(C - 1)^N}{C^{N-1}} \qquad (10.17a)$$

and

$$P = \sum_{j=1}^{N} P_j \binom{N}{j} \left(\frac{1}{C}\right)^j \left(1 - \frac{1}{C}\right)^{N-j}, \qquad (10.17b)$$

where P_j is the drum latency model for j tasks [Eq. (10.3), (10.4), (10.6a), or (10.7)].

Furthermore, the expected position of the furthest cylinder is

$$\frac{C'(C + 1)}{C' + 1}. \qquad (10.17c)$$

This is without a doubt an ugly expression beyond the power of manual calculation or small stored-program calculators. A program for this is not, however, overly long (see Appendix I).

5.4.3. Some Approximations

By using the FIFO drum model [Eq. (10.3)] instead of the more precise Eq. (10.7) we have

$$P = \sum_{j=1}^{N} j \left(\frac{1}{S} + \frac{1}{2} \right) \binom{N}{j} \left(\frac{1}{C} \right)^{j} \left(1 - \frac{1}{C} \right)^{N-j}, \tag{10.18}$$

which after a bit of sweaty algebra boils down to

$$P = \frac{N}{C} \left(\frac{1}{S} + \frac{1}{2} \right). \tag{10.19}$$

Hence the mean latency is

$$D = Nr \left(\frac{1}{2} + \frac{1}{S} \right) + C't_0 + \frac{C'(C - C')(Ct_i - t_0)}{(C' + 1)(C - 1)}, \tag{10.20}$$

which you will note is equivalent to saying that every task is on a different cylinder.

By using Eq. (10.4) for the optimistic embedded drum model, we obtain

$$P = \sum_{j=1}^{N} \left(\frac{j}{S} + \frac{1}{2} + \frac{1}{S} \right) \binom{N}{j} \left(\frac{1}{C} \right)^{j} \left(1 - \frac{1}{C} \right)^{N-j}. \tag{10.21}$$

Some more algebra yields

$$P = \frac{N}{CS} + \left(\frac{1}{2} + \frac{1}{S} \right) \left[1 - \left(1 - \frac{1}{C} \right)^{N} \right]. \tag{10.22}$$

Therefore, the delay is

$$D = \frac{Nr}{S} + Cr \left(\frac{1}{2} + \frac{1}{S} \right) \left[1 - \left(1 - \frac{1}{C} \right)^{N} \right] + C't_0 + \frac{C'(C - C')(Ct_i - t_0)}{(C' + 1)(C - 1)}. \tag{10.23}$$

Using the model of Eq. (10.5b) we obtain, by similar means,

$$D = \frac{Nr}{S} + Cr \left(\ln 2S - 1 - \frac{1}{2S} \right) \left[1 - \left(1 - \frac{1}{C} \right)^{N} \right] + C't_0 + \frac{C'(C - C')(Ct_i - t_0)}{(C' + 1)(C - 1)} \tag{10.24}$$

The Nr/S term, which corresponds to the transfer time for N tasks, appears in all three approximations. Equation (10.20) charges each task with a half rotation additional delay. In Eq. (10.23) and (10.24), the half rotation term depends upon the number of cylinders and the number of tasks. As the number of tasks are increased, the number of cylinders getting stuck with the half cycle initial latency effectively decreases.

5.4.4. The Scheduled Batch Disc Without Home Position

An approximate model of the batch disc without a home position is given in Oney [ONEY75]. Oney assumes that all requests are for different cylinders (pessimistic) and that FIFO is used within the cylinder. The head is assumed to be on any cylinder with equal probability. If all requests are to one side of the initial head position, then the operation is identical to that of the batch disc with a home position. If the requests lie to either side of the initial position, the disc will start in one direction (that having the most requests) clear all those tasks, reverse direction, and pick up the residue. As usual, the seek time is assumed to be a linear function of the number of cylinders traversed. With these assumptions, we have

$$D = N\left(t_0 + \frac{r}{S} + \frac{r}{2}\right) + \frac{t_i(5N^3 + 10N^2 - 2N - 1)}{3(N + 1)^2(N + 2)}. \tag{10.25}$$

5.5. The Continual Arrival Disc

5.5.1. General

Unlike the drum or the batch disc in which there are limited numbers of scheduling algorithms, the continual arrival disc can be scheduled in many different ways. The scheduling of tasks within a cylinder and across the cylinders are not necessarily the same. Most models assume FIFO within the cylinder. When the intracylinder (drum) and intercylinder (seek) terms are separable, it is relatively easy to substitute the appropriate drum function. In most continual discs, because of the large spread of tasks across cylinders and the long seek time compared to rotation time, the FIFO assumption is reasonable. Therefore, a FIFO model will be used. Generally, this is a slightly pessimistic assumption. All models presented here are paging models. The main differences between the models arise from the seek scheduling policy used.

5.5.2. The FIFO Continual Arrival Paged Disc

The expected delay is given by Coffman and Denning [DENN73] and Weingarten [WEIN69]:

$$D = \frac{\rho^2 + \lambda^2 \sigma^2}{2\lambda(1 - \rho)} + \frac{1}{V}; \tag{10.26}$$

where

$$\rho = \frac{\lambda}{S}$$

$$V = \frac{t_0(C-1)}{C} + \frac{t_i C(C-2)}{3(C-1)} + r\left(\frac{1}{S} + \frac{1}{2}\right) \qquad (10.26a)*$$

$$\sigma^2 = \frac{\mu^2(C-1)}{C} + \frac{2t_i \mu C(C-2)}{3(C-1)} + \frac{t_i^2(C-1)(C+1)}{6} \qquad (10.26b)*$$

$$\mu = \frac{3t_0(C-1) - t_i^2 C^2(C-2)}{3C(C-1)}, \qquad (10.26c)*$$

where λ, C, t_0, t_i, and S are defined as before. Furthermore, the number of tasks queued (including the one being processed) is given by

$$\rho + \frac{\rho^2 + \lambda^2 \sigma^2}{2(1-\rho)}. \qquad (10.26d)*$$

Despite the complexity, this model is only an approximation. It is pessimistic** because it assumes that all tasks will be on different cylinders. The error in most applications should be small.

5.5.3. The SCAN Model

The SCAN policy serves tasks in increasing or decreasing cylinder order. The heads start at some point, in some direction, and serve all cylinders ahead for which there are tasks. When there are no more tasks ahead, it reverses direction and serves all tasks that have accumulated "behind" it. An earlier version of this algorithm which forced all cylinders, from rim to hub, to be traversed whether or not there were tasks, is also called SCAN. The present SCAN algorithm is clearly more practical and is one that is typically implemented. SCAN is important because most other scheduling policies are not as good. SCAN,

---

*Sorry about that.
**Actually, there is a slight optimistic component. However, it is totally outweighed by the general pessimism of the model. The model is a straightforward application of the $(M/G/1)$ queueing model (see Chapter 11), which depends, among other things on the standard deviation of the service time distribution. The service time distribution contains the constant term of the seek time function and the rotational latency term. The standard deviation of that distribution would have to contain components that included latency effects as well as seek variation effects. Because the rotational terms are typically small compared to the seek terms, we have left out that part in deriving the standard deviation of the service time distribution—hence the optimistic component.

while efficient, is unfair, since it discriminates against tasks on the innermost tracks.*

Oney [ONEY75] has several models for the SCAN policy. The most accurate (and most complicated) does not have a closed form solution; only a numerical/ iterative procedure is given. The discussion of that model is beyond the scope of this book. He also provides a pessimistic approximate model, and two other approximations derived from the accurate model, one for high loadings, and the other for low loadings. We have, then, good accuracy at the low and high end, and slight pessimism in the middle which should be adequate for most practical purposes.

The pessimistic model is

$$D = \frac{\lambda r^2 \left(1 + \frac{\lambda T_s}{C}\right)}{24(C - \lambda^2 T_s^2)} + \frac{kCt_i \left(1 - \frac{\lambda T_s}{C}\right)}{1 - \lambda T_s}, \tag{10.27}$$

where

$$T_s = t_0 + \frac{r}{2} + \frac{r}{S} \tag{10.27a}$$

$$k = \frac{1}{C(C-1)} \sum_{i=0}^{C-1} \frac{[(C-1-i)^3 + i^3]}{[(C-1-i)^2 + i^2]}. \tag{10.27b}$$

Fortunately, k converges rapidly for large values of C, as Figure 10-5 shows. The limiting value is ~ 0.71.

For very light loads ($\lambda T_s \ll 1$) no significant queue is formed and the delay is dominated by the seek (for one third of the cylinders) and the time to process one task, or

$$D(\text{very light load}) \simeq T_s + \frac{Ct_i}{3} \tag{10.28}$$

for near saturation loads, with $\lambda T_s \simeq 1$, we have

$$D(\text{heavy load}) \simeq \frac{\lambda r^2}{24(1 - \lambda T_s)} + \frac{Ct_i}{1 - \lambda T_s} + \frac{1}{\lambda}. \tag{10.29}$$

---

*SCAN must go back and forth, and cannot continue in the same direction as in a drum. To have a drumlike lack of bias, one would have to come up with a "disc" access geometry that had two rotary components—effectively a torus. If someone can figure out how to pack bits on bagel, then we shall have to analyze that memory also.

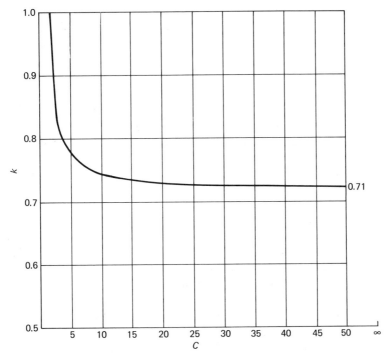

Figure 10-5. The k factor of Eq. (10.27) as a function of the number of cylinders.

5.5.4. Other Models

The most common model treated in the literature, other than the above two, is the SSFT (Shortest Seek Time First) model, which is analogous to the drum policy. That task whose seek time is least is chosen for service. This means that the heads will peregrinate about the disc. Generally, the SSTF policy provices a service which is midway between FIFO and SCAN, generally being closer to SCAN. There are models for SSTF, as well as other versions of SCAN; however, they are not closed-form models, requiring either the solution of equations, or an iterative procedure of some kind. To explain these models and the computational procedure would take us beyond the scope of this book.

While simulation has been the mainstay of the disc and drum analysis, many have come to realize that the cost of such simulations, especially when they represent only a fraction of the system analysis, is often excessive. Of late, there has been an encouraging trend toward the development of useful, sharp approximations and empirical formulas.

6. EXERCISES

NOTE: Use representative numerical values in all of the following problems unless numbers have been given or unless the problem specifies that the value be kept parametric.

1. Plot the effective recording density of a tape (i.e., net number of characters per centimeter including gaps) as a function of local density and mean record length parametric with gap size over a range of 1 mm to 5 cm and densities from 50 characters per cm to 10,000 characters per cm. Given the existence of an industry standard (read "IBM compatible") gap of approximately 2 cm, describe some approaches you might take to improve the unit's performance without modifying it physically. Identify the resources that would have to be increased to accomplish this.

2. The angular acceleration of the rewind motor of a tape unit is of the form $k/(a + w)$, where k and a are constants and w is the angular velocity. The inner and outer hub diameters are 10 and 30 cm respectively. The effective tape thickness is 0.02 cm. Derive an expression that gives the expected time to rewind the rest of the reel given that there are already N meters on the reel.

3. A tape unit is used to store records whose effective length including the inter-record gap is 2.0 cm. The unit can read in the forward or backward direction at 200 records per second. The reel can hold 650 meters of tape. Records are written at a mean rate of one per second. Uniformly distributed (with respect to the record's position along the tape) read requests occur at a rate of 0.05 per second. The tape is to be used (simultaneously) for read and write operations. Show how you can arrange things so that the mean delay for a read request is approximately 81 seconds. Derive an exact expression for the mean read request delay. Compare with a FIFO service approach. (Hint: It's scandalous how easy this is).

4. *Continuation.* Redo exercise 3 under the assumption that the read requests are exponentially distributed from the most recently written record with a mean elapsed time between write and subsequent read of 200 seconds. Compare with the result of exercise 3. Compare the optimum approach with a FIFO approach. Do not do this exactly—approximations will suffice.

5. *Continuation.* For exercises 3 and 4 above, what is the expected write request delay?

6. The mean read or write access time for a single transaction to a drum is approximately 0.5 revolutions and this approximation gets better as the number of sectors is increased. Consider N drums. You are to write a copy of a record to each drum at the same sector/track location for each drum. Show

that the expected time to complete the writing of all the copies is proportional to $N/(N + 1)$. (Difficult).

7. *Continuation.* Assume that you initiate a read request to all N drums and stop as soon as the first copy arrives. Show that the expected time to read a request is proportional to $1/(N + 1)$. (No worse than problem 6).

8. *Continuation.* If the mean read and write request rates are equal, show that there is nothing to be gained by writing multiple copies to reduce the expected read time. (Trivial) Assume that the read request rate is k times the write rate (i.e., k copies of each record are to be read). For what values of k does it pay to employ multiple writes? Examine the mean transaction time (averaged over the total read and write transactions) as a function of k and n, for k positive and greater than zero.

9. *Continuation.* Describe qualitatively how your answers to exercises 6, 7, and 8 change when the same procedure is used to handle a batch of transactions rather than a single transaction.

10. Derive equations (10.5b) and (10.6a).

11. A tape-drum consists of a wide sheet of magnetic tape draped over a rotating cylinder that contains read/write heads. The part of the tape that drapes over the cylinder is called a page. The tape is 40 cm wide and has 500 tracks across it, with 64 sectors per track per page. A new page can be brought to the heads by allowing the tape to move with the drum surface. The cylinder contains two complete sets of read/write heads and rotates at 3600 RPM. Describe the coordinate geometry of this device. Sketch the optimization procedure. What is the mean access time to a record on a given page which is already in position? Wrong! Try again. What is the mean access time to a record on a given page which is already in position if the cylinder contains $2N$ sets of heads? Modify and/or combine models from this chapter to obtain an approximate batch model for this nonfictitious device.

12. A batch scheduled drum is required to process N transactions of which 30% are write operations and 70% are read operations. The drum has 512 tracks, 128 sectors per track, and a rotation time of 25 msec. There is a k sector time gap to switch between read and write operations. Calculate the latency for 1–100 transactions using the drum latency model in the appendix, parametric with k over the range 0 to 32 by powers of 2. Compare the following modeling approaches:

   a. Ignore the read/write gap time.
   b. Do the problem by separating the reads and writes.
   c. Fudge the model by adding the correct number of expected read/write switchings.

13. *Continuation.* Be clever—modify the scheduling algorithm so that you can ignore the switching time. Relate the efficacy of this new algorithm to the gap size and the expected number of transactions in the batch. Describe qualitatively how this new algorithm fares with varying number of tracks and sectors; with varying ratios between read and write operations.

14. Derive equation (10.19).

15. Derive equations (10.21) through (10.23).

16. Derive equation (10.24).

17. A batch disc unit has many cylinders; say a thousand. The distribution of tasks across cylinders is known but arbitrary. Using only the information found in this book, describe how to model this unit with fair accuracy. Why won't this modeling approach work with a continual arrival disc under one of the SCAN policies?

18. A moving head disc is used to store records whose length can be taken as one sector. Records arrive at a specified rate and are written sequentially. Read requests are uniformly distributed over the k tracks following the most recently written track. Requests for read operations occur at a rate r which is a multiple of the write request rate. What is the expected delay for a read and write request assuming no scheduling.

19. *Continuation.* Compare the above to a system in which you separately batch the read and write requests, optimizing each batch. Determine the mean delay for a read and write request.

20. *Continuation.* Minimize the mean request delay (averaged over the read and write request rates) by selecting the optimum write batch accumulation time as a function of k and r.

11
Queueing Theory and All That

1. SYNOPSIS

Being a cursory introduction to that pit of arcana—queueing theory.

2. AN APOLOGY

I think that only queueing theorists don't get intimidated by queueing theory. I for one can blame it on my maternal grandfather. He was a mathematican. He unwittingly frightened my mother (an infant at the time) with a moment generating function rampant on a field of complex variables; I never got over it.

Here's the problem: queueing theory is good for you, but it can taste awful. A fair introduction takes a whole book [GROS74], so this introduction is not fair; hopefully it's adequate. If you want to go beyond microanalysis and into macroanalysis, queueing theory, advanced queueing theory at that, is indispensable. Since this is a book on microanalysis with only limited space, the only thing to be done is to provide a summary of some of the more important concepts and formulas and some guidance as to when and where they are applicable.

Queueing theory is still a relatively new field, and as of now no handbook has been published. Some of the best books on the subject are concerned with queueing theory problem-solving methodology (i.e., *doing* queueing theory rather than *using* it). Consequently, they leave solutions of specific cases as "exercises for the reader." Unfortunately, that's the best we have today.

I have restricted the presentation of solutions to those that can be expressed by relatively simple* closed-form expressions, or in terms of tabulated functions. Many queueing theory problems that have been solved are not presented because the solution involves one or more of the following: (1) solution of a nonlinear

---

*You might argue that some of the formulas are hardly simple. However complicated it might look, a formula that can be programmed in 20 lines of FORTRAN with no more than two nested loops is, in some sense, simple.

equation: (2) inversion of a Laplace transform; or (3) numerical analysis. All of these would consume too much space and be beyond the scope of this book.

3. CONCEPTS AND NOTATION

3.1. General Concepts

A queueing system consists of customers (tasks), servers (processors or resources), and a queue. Customers arrive at the system at a rate with defined statistical properties. A queue forms because the customer arrival rate is not controlled and/or because the service time is not constant. A naive intuition might lead one to believe that if the mean arrival rate was less than or equal to the mean service rate, then no queue would form. Such intuition is incorrect; if the mean arrival rate equals the mean service rate, not only will a queue be formed, but it will be infinite. If the mean arrival rate exceeds the mean service rate the queue will grow without bounds. It is then interesting to determine the rate at which it will grow. Unfortunately, this requires transient analysis of queues, which is also beyond the scope of this book.

If the mean arrival rate is less than the mean service rate a finite length queue will be formed. A customer is "in the queue" if he has entered the system, but has not yet been served. A customer is "in the system" if he is in the queue or is being served. The objectives of queueing theory are the following.
Given the statistical characteristics of the servers and the customers, find

- the expected number of customers in the queue (N_q);
- the expected number of customers in the system (N_s);
- the expected waiting time while in the queue (T_q);
- the expected total time in the system (T_s);
- the probability that the queue length is of a given size or greater;
- the probability that the waiting time exceeds or equals a given time.

3.2 Notation

Queueing theorists have developed a convenient shorthand for describing queueing problems. The notation has the following form: $(A/B/C):(D/E/F)$, where:

    A represents the statistical characteristics of the customer, ie., the probability density function (pdf)* that describes their arrival rate.**

---

*The probability distribution is often confused with its derivative, the probability density function. The probability distribution, or as it is sometimes more revealingly described, the cumulative distribution, specifies the probability that a given value or less will be achieved. In discrete distributions, the equivalent of the probability density function (the point probability function) does give the probability that the specified value will be achieved. This is

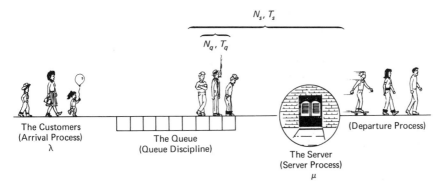

Figure 11-1. Queueing systems.

B represents the statistical characteristics of the server—the probability density function that describes the service time.

C represents the number of servers, typically one, finite, or infinite.

D represents an acronym that describes the rule that will be used to select the next customer to be served.

E represents a restriction, if any, on the maximum size of the system (in the queue plus in service).

F represents the size of the population from which the customers are drawn, typically finite or infinite.

The second set of three terms is often left out. This usually (but not always) means that the service discipline is FIFO, the queue length is unrestricted, and the customer population is infinite. For example, M/M/1 really means $(M/M/1)$: (FIFO/∞/∞). Additional terms may be added to the notation to denote things like bulk service, bulk arrival, and other variations on the characteristics of the customers and/or servers. A queue in which the customer's arrival rate is characterized by an exponential **interarrival time** pdf (M), with an unspecified but reasonable service time distribution (G), with three servers, not allowing more than 100 customers in the system who are being served in Last-In-First-Out (LIFO) order, with customers drawn from an infinite population, is denoted by $(M/G/3):(\text{LIFO}/100/\infty)$.

---

not the case for continuous distribution. The probability density function will be referred to as the pdf and will be denoted by a lower case letter, as in $p(x)$. Its integral, the cumulative distribution, will be denoted by an upper case letter, as in $P(x)$. Where there is no point in being punctilious and either the pdf or the cumulative distribution is appropriate, the term "distribution" will be used.

The distributions actually describe the **interarrival time, which is the reciprocal of the arrival **rate.** However, the arrival **rate** is more convenient to work with.

3.3. Interarrival Time Probability Density Functions and Distributions

3.3.1. General

Customers arrive at arbitrary intervals of time. Measure the successive arrivals, accumulate data, and eventually you obtain a probability density function for the interarrival times. The arithmetic mean or expected value of that function is what we mean by the "mean interarrival time." Its reciprocal is defined as the mean arrival *rate* and is denoted by λ. Where there is no possibility of confusion, the term "arrival rate" will mean "mean arrival rate."

3.3.2. Exponential pdf (M)

The exponential pdf is the most important one in queueing theory. It is denoted by M and defined as:

$$p(t) = \lambda e^{-\lambda t}.$$

It is important because

- assuming it leads to reasonable expressions for the queueing parameters;
- it is a good approximation to many distributions that are otherwise too difficult to handle;
- assuming it is usually (but not always) pessimistic;
- assuming this distribution is equivalent to saying that the arriving customers individually and collectively behave as if they are not aware of each other's existence.

To say that the arrivals occur individually and collectively at random is equivalent to saying that the customers are not aware of each other's presence nor of the past history of arrivals. That is, considering the arrival pattern as a process, it is a process without memory. Hence the use of M for "memoryless."* Systems with an exponential interarrival distribution are said to "satisfy the Poisson assumption" (so why not P for Poisson instead of M for memoryless?). It can be shown that an exponential interarrival time distribution will lead to a Poisson arrival rate distribution. The probability that exactly n customers will arrive in a period of time t is given by

$$p(n, t) = \frac{(\lambda t)^n e^{-\lambda t}}{n!},$$

which you undoubtedly recognized as the Poisson probability function. To recapitulate the notational morass surrounding the specification of the arrival

---

*M really stands for "markovian," after the Russian mathematician A. A. Markov, who made many of the basic contributions to the theory of such systems. I prefer "M for memoryless" to "M for markovian," even if it is wrong.

process: an exponential interarrival time distribution, denoted by M, is generated by a Poisson process, in which the arrival of any customer is independent of previous arrivals; it is a memoryless/markovian process.

3.3.3. General Interarrival Distributions (GI)

The second most important interarrival distribution is the general distribution, denoted, surprisingly by G. This is not a specific distribution, but an unspecified distribution characterized by the mean, the variance, and possibly other information.   An important subclass of the general interarrival distribution is the General Independent (GI) distribution. This restricts the arrival pattern to those processes in which the customers' arrivals are independent of one another and of the state of system (number on queue). Many queueing theory references do not distinguish between G and GI.   If GI does not appear in a reference, it is probably safe to assume that G really means GI.

3.3.4. Deterministic Arrivals (D)

When the interarrival time distribution is not a distribution at all, but is constant, it is denoted by D, not for constant, but for deterministic.

3.3.5. Erlang Arrivals (E_k)

This is named after Agner Krarup Erlang (1878–1924) and is denoted by E_k. The k does not stand for Erlang's middle initial, but rather to remind us that the Erlang distribution is really a family of probability functions defined by

$$p(k, t) = \frac{\lambda(\lambda t)^{k-1} e^{-\lambda t}}{(k - 1)!}.$$

Note that for $k = 1$, the expression is identical to the exponential interarrival time pdf, which is indeed the first member of the family. As k is increased toward infinity, this pdf approaches the deterministic case.   Therefore, the Erlang pdf spans the entire range from exponential (random arrival) to deterministic arrivals.

3.3.6. Gamma Distributions (Γ)

The Erlang distribution, by definition, exists only for integer values of k.   The Gamma distribution is closely related and is defined for noninteger values as well.   It is identical to the Erlang for integers.   It is a useful approximation to the Erlang and will sometimes yield more tractable results than a more precise formulation in terms of the Erlang.   It is defined as

$$p(t) = \frac{\lambda^n t^{n-1} e^{-\lambda t}}{\Gamma(n)},$$

where

$$\Gamma(n) = \int_0^\infty x^{n-1} e^{-x}\, dx$$

$$= (n - 1)! \quad \text{for } n \text{ an integer.}$$

3.3.7. The Hyperexponential Distribution (H_k)

The hyperexponential distribution family is defined as

$$p(t) = \sum_{i=1}^{R} \frac{\alpha_i}{m_i} e^{-t/m_i}, \quad \text{with } \sum_{i=1}^{R} \alpha_i = 1.$$

Note that for one factor, $R = 1$, this is identical to the exponential, which indeed is the first member of this family.

3.4. The Server's Distribution

3.4.1. General

Each customer's service is variable. This may be because the customer does require varying amounts of service (as in a supermarket checkout), or because the server is arbitrary (as in a bureaucracy): queueing theory does not distinguish. The server's behavior is described by the service time distribution. The arithmetic mean of that distribution is what we mean by the mean service time. Its reciprocal is defined as the mean service *rate* and is denoted by μ. The same notation is used for the server's distribution. That is, M, D, G, E_k, Γ, H_k, describing respectively the exponential, deterministic, general, Erlang-k, Gamma, and hyperexponential behavior.

3.4.2. The Exponential Service Time Distribution

A server whose behavior is described by an exponential service time is not aware of the state of the system (i.e., the number of customers on the queue). He is not flustered by long queues and never gets tired. Therefore, such servers are also memoryless, hence the *M*. A process which requires buzzing up and down a queue to find an entry, or say, to sort the entries, does not have this property.

3.4.3. General Service

General service in the context of service time distribution is truly general, and no special annotation such as *GI* need be made.

3.4.4. Erlang Service, Gamma Service, Hyperexponential Service

Just as the Erlang arrival distribution spanned the range from exponential to deterministic arrivals, the Erlang service distribution does also. The Erlang-k distribution can also be profitably interpreted as the distribution corresponding to the behavior of a succession of k stages of exponential service. Again the Gamma distribution can prove to be a useful approximation. The hyperexponential distribution can be interpreted as the distribution corresponding to k stages in parallel.

3.5 Queue Discipline

The following are common.

FIFO First in First Out.
LIFO Last In First Out.
SIRO Service in Random Order.
GD   General Discipline. This usually means a general discipline in which selection is independent of service time. However, not all sources are clear on this. *GI* will be used in this book to denote disciplines that do not depend on service time.

3.6. Continuous versus Discrete

1. The overwhelming majority of queueing theory problems that come up in system analysis, if treated rigorously, involve discrete variables. A computer cannot execute 3.4 instructions; 1998.345 bits cannot be allocated for buffers. Neither time, nor space, nor any other resource is truly continuous.
2. The overwhelming majority of workable results in queueing theory apply to continuous systems rather than to discrete systems. Discrete systems are difficult to analyze.
3. Therefore, the greatest part of queueing theory does not apply to computer problems.

A more productive way of interpreting this situation is to recognize that to some extent or another, most applications of queueing theory will be approximations—approximations, however, that will usually be good to within a bit or two, a buffer block or two, etc. The point is:

1. our data usually contain more error than the difference between a discrete problem and its closest continuous approximation;
2. a good approximation is better than no answer at all;
3. if it really matters, you can always simulate.

Table 11-1. Some Distributions and Their Moments

Name	Notation	Range	pdf Definition	Mean, m_1
General continuous	G, GI	$-\infty < x < \infty$	$f(x)$	$m_1 = \int_{-\infty}^{\infty} xf(x)\, dx$
General discrete	G, GI	$0 < n < \infty$	$p(n)$	$m_1 = \sum_{n=0}^{\infty} np(n)$
Deterministic	D	constant	$p = 1$	C
Uniform	U	$-\infty < a < b < \infty$	$f(x) = \begin{cases} \dfrac{1}{b-a} & a < x < b \\ 0 & \text{otherwise} \end{cases}$	$\dfrac{a+b}{2}$
Exponential	M	$m_1 > 0$	$f(x) = \begin{cases} \dfrac{1}{m_1} e^{-x/m_1} & x > 0 \\ 0 & \text{otherwise} \end{cases}$	m_1
Gamma, Erlang	Γ E_N, E_x	$N > 0$ N integer, $\Gamma(N) = (N-1)!$	$f(x) = \begin{cases} \dfrac{\left(\dfrac{x}{m_1}\right)^{N-1} e^{-x/m_1}}{m_1 \Gamma(N)} & x > 0 \\ 0 & \text{otherwise} \end{cases}$	Nm_1
Hyperexponential	H_R	$x > 0$ $\sum_{i=1}^{R} \alpha_i = 1$	$f(x) = \sum_{i=1}^{R} \dfrac{\alpha_i}{m_i} e^{-x/m_{1i}}$	$\sum_{i=1}^{R} \alpha_i m_{1i}$
Poisson	P	$m_1 > 0$	$P(n) = \begin{cases} \dfrac{e^{-m_1} (m_1)^n}{n!} & n = 1, 2, 3 \ldots \\ 0 & \text{otherwise} \end{cases}$	m_1
Geometric	g	$0 < P < 1$	$P(n) = \begin{cases} (1-P)^{n-1} & n = 1, 2, 3 \ldots \\ 0 & \text{otherwise} \end{cases}$	$\dfrac{1}{1-P}$
Normal	Q, P, G	$-\infty < m_1 < \infty$ $\sigma > 0$	$f(x) = \dfrac{\exp -\dfrac{1}{2}\left(\dfrac{x - m_1}{\sigma}\right)^2}{\sigma\sqrt{2\pi}}$	m_1

Table 11-1. Some Distributions and Their Moments (Continued)

Variance, $\sigma^2 = m_2 - m_1^2$	Second moment about origin, $m_2 = \sigma^2 + m_1^2$	Third central moment, $\tau = m_3 - 3m_1\sigma^2 - m_1^3$	Third moment about origin, $m_3 = \tau + 3m_1\sigma^2 + m_1^3$
$\sigma^2 = \displaystyle\int_{-\infty}^{\infty} (x - m_1)^2 f(x)\,dx$	$m_2 = \displaystyle\int_{-\infty}^{\infty} x^2 f(x)\,dx$	$\tau = \displaystyle\int_{-\infty}^{\infty} (x - m_1)^3 f(x)\,dx$	$m_3 = \displaystyle\int_{-\infty}^{\infty} x^3 f(x)\,dx$
$\sigma^2 = \displaystyle\sum_{n=0}^{\infty} (n - m_1)^2 p(n)$	$m_2 = \displaystyle\sum_{n=0}^{\infty} n^2 p(n)$	$\tau = \displaystyle\sum_{n=0}^{\infty} (n - m_1)^3 p(n)$	$m_3 = \displaystyle\sum_{n=0}^{\infty} n^3 p(n)$
0	C^2	0	C^3
$\dfrac{(b - a)^2}{12}$	$\dfrac{a^2 + ab + b^2}{3}$	0	$\dfrac{(a^2 + b^2)(a + b)}{4}$
m_1^2	$2m_1^2$	$2m_1^3$	$6m_1^3$
Nm_1^2	$N(N + 1)m_1^2$	$2Nm_1^3$	$(N + 2)(N + 1)Nm_1^3$
$2\displaystyle\sum_{i=1}^{R} \alpha_i m_{1i}^2 - \left[\sum_{i=1}^{R}\alpha_i m_{1i}\right]^2$	$2\displaystyle\sum_{i=1}^{R} \alpha_i m_{1i}^2$	easy but messy	$6\displaystyle\sum_{i=1}^{R} \alpha_i m_{1i}^3$
m_1	$m_1(m_1 + 1)$	m_1	$m_1 + 3m_1^2 + m_1^3$
$\dfrac{P}{(1 - P)^2}$	$\dfrac{P + 1}{(1 - P)^2}$	$\dfrac{P(P + 1)}{(1 - P)^3}$	$\dfrac{P^2 + 4P + 1}{(1 - P)^3}$
σ^2	$\sigma^2 + m_1^2$	0	$3m_1\sigma^2 + m_1^3$

3.7. Distribution Summary and Notation

Table 11-1 shows the distributions most likely to be met within computer analysis problems. The mean and variance are given in addition to the definition of the pdf. This table also shows the second and third moments about the origin and their relations to the ordinary moments. Many queueing theory expressions are considerably simplified through the use of moments about the origin rather than the ordinary moments (which are about the mean). If there is some confusion about the differences between the previous definitions of the exponential, Erlang, and Gamma distributions and those in the table, recall that the previous definitions were in terms of the mean arrival *rates* or mean service *rates*, while the distributions are formally defined for interarrival *time* and service *time*.

3.8. Generally Applicable Formulas and Notation

3.8.1. Notation and Definitions:

λ = mean arrival *rate* in tasks per unit time. $\hfill$ (D11.1)

σ_λ = standard deviation of the arrival *time* distribution [i.e., $\sigma(1/\lambda)$]. $\hfill$ (D11.2)

μ = mean service *rate* in tasks per unit time. $\hfill$ (D11.3)

σ_μ = standard deviation of the service *time* distribution [i.e., $\sigma(1/\mu)$]. $\hfill$ (D11.4)

c = number of servers in a multi-server system. $\hfill$ (D11.5)

$\rho = \dfrac{\lambda}{c\mu}$ = demand in erlangs, or traffic intensity for multi-server system. $\hfill$ (D11.6)

$\rho = \dfrac{\lambda}{\mu}$ = demand or traffic intensity for a single-server system. $\hfill$ (D11.6a)

N_q = expected number of customers (tasks) on the queue not yet being served. $\hfill$ (D11.7)

σ_{Nq} = standard deviation of number of customers on the queue. $\hfill$ (D11.8)

N_s = expected number of customers in the system (those on the queue plus those being served). $\hfill$ (D11.9)

σ_{Ns} = standard deviation of number of customers in the system. $\hfill$ (D11.10)

T_q = expected waiting time on the queue (excluding service time).   (D11.11)

σ_{Tq} = standard deviation of waiting time on queue.   (D11.12)

T_s = expected time in the system (queue time plus service time).   (D11.13)

σ_{Ts} = standard deviation of waiting time in the system.   (D11.14)

p_0 = probability that the system is empty (none on queue, none being served).   (D11.15)

$P_s(k)$ = probability that there are k or more customers in the system.   (D11.16)

$p_s(k)$ = probability that there are exactly k customers in the system.   (D11.16a)

$P_{tq}(t)$ = probability that the time waiting on queue equals or exceeds t.   (D11.17)

3.8.2. Relations That Hold for Most Queueing Systems–Little's Theorem

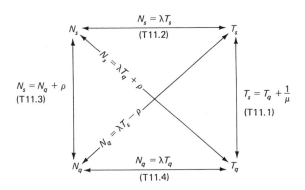

Equation (T11.1) holds for all queueing systems; (T11.2), (T11.3), and (T11.4) hold for all reasonable queueing systems that are not operating at or near saturation (i.e., near $\rho = 1$). The conditions under which these relations do not hold are not likely to be met with in practice. The importance of these relations is that you need only one of the four numbers (N_q, N_s, T_q, T_s) to get the other three. (T11.2) is called Little's theorem. Equations (T11.3) and (T11.4) hold whenever Little's theorem holds.

$$N_s = N_q + (1 - p_0) \qquad \text{(T11.5)}$$

holds for all single server queues.

$$p_0 = 1 - \rho \qquad \text{(T11.6)}$$

holds for all single server queues whenever Little's theorem holds.

3.8.3. Inequalities and Approximations

$$p\{|x - \bar{x}| \geqslant t\} \leqslant \frac{\sigma^2}{t^2}, \qquad \text{(T11.7)}$$

where

x is an arbitrary value;
$\bar{x}$ is the mean value of a distribution;
σ is the standard deviation of the distribution;
t is another arbitrary value.

This theorem is known as Chebyshev's inequality. It applies to all distributions. It is a useful tool for bounding the probability of an occurence when only the mean and standard deviation of the distribution are known. Unfortunately, despite its simplicity, lack of restrictions, and generality, the use of this inquality is often disappointing because it is not very sharp. If you want to determine the probability that the queue length is a certain size, say, because you want to see if it is possible to ignore a queue length dependent processing path, this inequality might be useful. It might predict a probability of 0.01, when the actual probability was 10^{-10}. For such purposes, this difference is not significant. As an example, if you had determined the mean time in the system to be 7 seconds (using one of the subsequent expressions), and wanted to know the probability that the time spent in the system was greater than 120 seconds, you would have

$$p\{|x - 7| \geqslant 120\} \leqslant \frac{\sigma_{T_s}^2}{(120)^2}.$$

If your interest is in "proving" that a given event will (almost) never occur, then Chebyshev's inequality is not likely to be useful; the bounding value will often be too large to be of help. To get sharper bounds on the probability of occurence you need the actual distribution or use sharper inequalities based on the higher moments of the distribution. Except for the mean and standard deviation of waiting time (and related expressions), there is no general information regarding the waiting time distribution, although the distribution is known for some very simple systems. Because of this information paucity, the higher moments are generally not available; consequently, sharper inequalities are not usable. In such cases, you can fit either an exponential, Gamma, or hyperexponential distribution.

The exponential, Erlang, Gamma, and hyperexponential distributions form a family that can be used to advantage to approximate the behavior of many queueing systems, either as a description of the server's behavior or as a description of the arrival behavior. To determine which distribution to use as an approximation, calculate the **coefficient of variation,** defined as the ratio of the standard deviation of the distribution to its mean:

$$C \stackrel{\triangle}{=} \text{coefficient of variation} \stackrel{\triangle}{=} \frac{\sigma}{m} = \frac{\text{standard deviation}}{\text{mean}}.$$

Table 11-1 gives the mean and variances (the standard deviation squared) for these distributions. The following characteristics are obvious:

Distribution	Coefficient of Variation
Gamma, Erlang	$C < 1$
Exponential	$C = 1$
Hyperexponential	$C > 1$

If you have obtained the mean and variance (typically of a service time distribution) perhaps by means of a timing analysis, or as a solution to a queueing problem, you can use the above criteria to decide on which form of distribution to use. For the Gamma, erlang, and exponential distributions, the relation between the mean and variance totally determine the parameters. For the hyperexponential distribution, there is more freedom of choice. Two factors (see Table 11-1) are usually sufficient for most purposes.

Once you have used the mean and variance to obtain an approximating distribution (Gamma, exponential, hyperexponential), use tabulated values of these distributions to obtain an estimate of the probability. This is not a rigorous procedure and it does not give you the actual probability—only an estimate thereof. Note that it is not a good idea to use a Gaussian (normal) distribution approximation to obtain the probability, since in general the conditions under which it would be valid are not met. It is not a bad approximation, however, for very heavy traffic conditions ($\rho \approx 1$).

4. THE SINGLE SERVER SYSTEMS

4.1. The $(M/G/1)$ System—$(M/G/1):(GI/\infty/\infty)$

4.1.1. General

While this is not the most general kind of queueing system, it is the set of systems for which the most is known. The arrival time distribution is assumed to be exponential. Further assumptions are not made about the service distribution or the service doctrine (FIFO, LIFO, etc.) except as noted. The results obtained apply to all specific cases of $(M/G/1)$, such as $(M/M/1)$ and $(M/D/1)$. The usefulness of the $(M/G/1)$ model is further enhanced because:

1. Variations in problems are more likely to involve different service distributions than different arrival distributions.
2. The $(M/G/1)$ results can be used to establish lower and upper bounds on queue behavior when the service distributions are unknown or hard to derive. Most systems lie between $(M/D/1)$ and $(M/M/1)$.
3. The general results, those that apply to all $(M/G/1)$ queues, are often all that is needed to solve a problem.

4.1.2. General Results

These results apply to all $(M/G/1$ queueing systems *in which the selection for service does not depend on the service time*, i.e., $(M/G/1):(GI/\infty/\infty)$. The various FIFO drum and disc models fit this criterion, but the scheduled drums and disc do not; consequently, the following relations do not necessarily hold for scheduled drums and discs.

The first set of relations are a generalization of Little's theorem (T11.2) for the standard deviations of the four queue parameters. Equation (T11.8) holds for all $(M/G/1)$ systems, while (T11.9) through (T11.11) hold for $(M/G/1):(GI/\infty/\infty)$ systems.

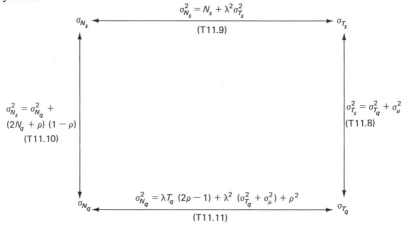

Furthermore,

$$N_q = \frac{\rho^2 + \lambda^2 \sigma_\mu^2}{2(1 - \rho)} \qquad \text{(T11.12)}$$

$$N_s = \frac{\rho^2 + \lambda^2 \sigma_\mu^2}{2(1 - \rho)} + \rho \qquad \text{(T11.13)}$$

$$T_q = \frac{\rho^2 + \lambda^2 \sigma_\mu^2}{2\lambda(1 - \rho)} \qquad \text{(T11.14)}$$

$$T_s = \frac{\rho^2 + \lambda^2 \sigma_\mu^2}{2\lambda(1 - \rho)} + \frac{1}{\mu}. \qquad \text{(T11.15)}$$

You may find it useful to apply (T11.2) through (T11.4) to these expressions to generate the others in the set in order to gain familiarity with the definitions and theorems. *The above expressions apply to all queue disciplines which do not depend on the service time.* This means that the mean wait on the queue is the same for a FIFO queue, a LIFO queue, or one which serves customers in random order. This is a surprising, but true result for $(M/G/1):(GI/\infty/\infty)$ queues.

4.1.3. The Standard Deviations of the Queue Parameters

The standard deviations of the four basic queue parameters depend on the service discipline, as do all higher moments. Expressions for the third and higher moments of the queue parameters have been derived, but they are even messier than the ones presented here. The first relation between the standard deviations of the queue parameters (see Kleinrock [KLEI76], Vol. II) relates the FIFO discipline with the LIFO discipline. Since FIFO is often the best case, and LIFO often a worst case, this expression can help bound the standard deviation for an unknown discipline. Note that FIFO and LIFO are not true extremes. For example, the drum and disc scheduling disciplines perform significantly better than FIFO. Conversely, if a discipline is chosen which next schedules the tasks so that each task will miss, the mean time per task would exceed one revolution, which would be worse than LIFO. If the discipline is not state-dependent, then FIFO and LIFO are reasonable bounds on queue discipline influence:

$$\sigma_{T_q}^2 \text{FIFO} = (1 - \rho) \sigma_{T_q}^2 \text{LIFO} - \rho T_q^2. \qquad \text{(T11.16)}$$

Since (T11.8) through (T11.11) relate the standard deviation of one of the four queue parameters to the other three, there is no need to present all four. The standard deviations are more conveniently expressed in terms of the moments about the origin of the service time distribution (m_2 and m_3):

$$\sigma^2_{T_q \text{FIFO}} = \frac{\lambda m_3}{3(1 - \rho)} + \frac{\lambda^2 m_2^2}{4(1 - \rho)^2} \tag{T11.17}$$

$$\sigma^2_{T_q \text{LIFO}} = \frac{\lambda m_3}{3(1 - \rho)^2} + \frac{\lambda^2 m_2^2 (1 + \rho)}{4(1 - \rho)^3} \tag{T11.18}$$

$$\sigma^2_{T_q \text{SIRO}} = \frac{2\lambda m_3}{3(1 - \rho)(2 - \rho)} + \frac{\lambda^2 m_2^2 (2 + \rho)}{4(1 - \rho)^2 (2 - \rho)}. \tag{T11.19}$$

4.2. The (M/M/1) Queue—(M/M/1): (GI/∞/∞)

The $(M/M/1)$ queue is the classical system and the one about which the most is known. There are several additional relations available for this system, in addition to those which apply to all systems and all $(M/G/1):(GI/\infty/\infty)$ systems:

$$P_s(k) = \rho^k \tag{T11.20}$$

$$p_s(k) = (1 - \rho)\rho^k \tag{T11.21}$$

$$P_{T_q}(t) = 1 - \rho e^{-\mu(1 - \rho)t}, \quad t \geqslant 0, \text{FIFO}. \tag{T11.22}$$

$$P_{T_q}(t) \cong \tfrac{1}{2}\alpha \exp\left[-\alpha(\mu - \lambda)t\right] + \tfrac{1}{2}\beta \exp\left[-\beta(\mu - \lambda)t\right] \tag{T11.23}$$

where

$$\alpha = 1 + \sqrt{\rho/2}$$
$$\beta = 1 - \sqrt{\rho/2},$$

valid for $\rho < 0.7$, SIRO.

Expressions for the basic queueing parameters can be readily derived from the $(M/G/1)$ expressions by substituting the appropriate values for σ_μ and $m_{3\mu}$, which you can get from Table 11-1 or a good handbook. For $(M/M/1)$ queues, $\sigma_\mu = 1/\mu^2$, $m_{3\mu} = 2/\mu^3$. Substituting these with a little algebra yields

$$N_q = \frac{\rho^2}{1 - \rho} \tag{T11.24}$$

$$N_s = \frac{\rho}{1 - \rho} \tag{T11.25}$$

$$T_q = \frac{\lambda}{\mu(\mu - \lambda)} \tag{T11.26}$$

$$T_s = \frac{1}{\mu - \lambda} \tag{T11.27}$$

$$\sigma^2_{N_s \text{FIFO}} = \frac{\rho}{(1-\rho)^2} \qquad \text{(T11.28)}$$

$$\sigma^2_{T_s \text{FIFO}} = \frac{1}{\mu^2(1-\rho)^2} \qquad \text{(T11.29)}$$

$$\sigma^2_{T_q \text{FIFO}} = \frac{\rho(2-\rho)}{\mu^2(1-\rho)^2}. \qquad \text{(T11.30)}$$

4.3. The $(GI/G/1):(GI/\infty/\infty)$ Queue

There are no exact, closed-form expressions for $(GI/G/1)$ queues. There are, however, several useful approximations. The relations of Section 3.8.2 that applied to (almost) all queues apply to $(GI/G/1)$ queues also. Furthermore, if the queue discipline and service time do not depend on the system state, then the values of the basic queue parameters will be independent of the queue discipline, as will the various approximations presented below. The same cannot be said of the variances of the queue parameters; since there are no closed-form expressions for these, this fact should not be of concern. The following approximations are given for T_q. Section 3.8.2 can be used to obtain corresponding approximations and bounds for T_s, N_q, and N_s.

$$T_q \cong \frac{\lambda(\sigma^2_\mu + \sigma^2_\lambda)}{2(1-\rho)}, \qquad \rho \approx 1. \qquad \text{(T11.31)}$$

This is called the "heavy traffic" approximation, since its validity improves as $\rho \to 1$. The error in this approximation is of the order of one mean interarrival time (i.e., error $\approx 1/\lambda$). Similarly, the error in the approximations for N_q obtained from (T11.31) by application of Little's theorem are of the order of one task. This is usually a tolerable error. It can also be shown that (T11.31) is a solid upper bound for T_q, or

$$T_q \leqslant \frac{\lambda(\sigma^2_\mu + \sigma^2_\lambda)}{2(1-\rho)}. \qquad \text{(T11.31a)}$$

A slightly sharper upper bound is given by

$$T_q \leqslant \frac{1 + \mu^2 \sigma^2_\mu}{(1/\rho)^2 + \mu^2 \sigma^2_\mu} \left[\frac{\lambda(\sigma^2_\mu + \sigma^2_\lambda)}{2(1-\rho)} \right]. \qquad \text{(T11.32)}$$

A lower bound which is not as sharp as the upper bound above is

$$\frac{\rho^2 \mu^2 \sigma^2_\mu + \rho(\rho - 2)}{2\lambda(1-\rho)} \leqslant T_q. \qquad \text{(T11.33)}$$

It is valid for

$$\mu^2 \sigma_\mu^2 \geq \frac{2 - \rho}{\rho}, \qquad \text{(T11.33a)}$$

error $\approx 1/\mu(1 - \rho)$.

Note that the error on this bound gets worse as traffic increases. This lower bound is therefore better at lower traffic rates. Similar upper and lower bounds for the variances of the queue time or system time are not available; development of such bounds is an area of continuing research and one should expect more of these in the future. There is, however, a useful upper bound to the queue time distribution which largely obviates the need for the variance:

$$P_{T_q}(t) \cong 1 - \exp \frac{-2(1 - \rho)t}{\lambda(\sigma_\mu^2 + \sigma_\lambda^2)}. \qquad \text{(T11.34)}$$

This bound may prove more useful than Chebyshev's inequality used with the variance of the queueing time. If you cannot find the actual queue time or system time distribution and are forced to work with approximations and bounds, try (T11.34) first, since it will usually require less work than using Chebyshev's inequality.

4.4. Other Simple Single Server Systems

The literature of queueing theory is vast, and closed form analytical expressions will only get you halfway. An excellent survey of the state of the art is to be found in Gross and Harris [GROS74]. Closed-form expressions can always be obtained for those queues that satisfy the non–state dependent service time $(M/G/1)$ requirements. Numerous single server queues with state-dependent service times are given in Kleinrock [KLEI76]. Many of these are derived from specific computer systems analysis problems.

A useful inequality for $(G/M/1)$ systems compares them to the dual $(M/G/1)$ system: that is, a system in which the service and arrival time distributions are interchanged. It can be shown [SPHI77] that if G is an erlang, hyper-exponential, deterministic, or uniform distribution, then the waiting time for the $(G/M/1)$ system is smaller than that of the equivalent $(M/G/1)$ system.

5. MULTI-SERVER QUEUES

5.1. General

All single server queueing systems are special cases of the more general multiserver queueing systems. A multi-server queueing system is not the same as c

single servers each handling one cth of the load.   The c single servers provide worse service than the multi-server with c servers.   It is instructive to compare three ways of handling a system load of λ:

1. a fast single server working at a rate of $c\mu$;
2. c servers each, handling an average load of λ/c at a rate μ per server, working as a multi-server.
3. c single servers each handling a load of λ/c at a rate of μ per server.

The demand $\rho = \lambda/\mu c$ is the same for all three cases.   In general, the fast server is best and the c single servers are worst from the point of view of expected time and total number of items in the queue(s).   Consequently, the fast single server can be used as an optimistic bound for the multi-server, while the c single servers can be used as a pessimistic bound.   Since there are no simple expressions for any but the $(M/M/c):(\text{FIFO}/\ /\ )$ systems, this form of bounding can be useful if you are interested in say, a $(M/G/c):(\text{LIFO}/\ /\ )$ system.

5.2. $(M/M/c):(GI/\infty/\infty)$

These systems have the same general properties as the $(M/M/1)$ systems.   That is, the mean values of N_s, N_q, T_s, T_q, are not affected by the discipline.   Furthermore, Little's theorem holds.   The expressions, however are not nice:

$$N_q = \frac{\rho(c\rho)^c p_0}{c!(1-\rho)^2} \tag{T11.35}$$

$$T_q = \frac{(c\rho)^c p_0}{c!c\mu(1-\rho)^2} \tag{T11.36}$$

$$p_0 = \left[\frac{(c\rho)^c}{c!(1-\rho)} + \sum_{n=0}^{c-1} \frac{(c\rho)^n}{n!}\right]^{-1} \tag{T11.37}$$

5.3. $(M/M/c):(GI/N/\infty)$

General formulas for this system have been developed, but they are truly awesome.   This system, recalling the notation, is one with exponential arrivals and servers, c servers, a general independent service doctrine and a total system size limited to N.   Two special cases are of interest: $(M/M/1):(GI/N/\infty)$, which is a single server with a restricted system size; and $(M/M/c):(GI/c/\infty)$, which is a multi-server in which no queue is allowed to form.   The latter case is treated in Chapter 14.

$$N_q = \frac{\rho^2[1 - \rho^N - N\rho^{N-1}(1-\rho)]}{(1-\rho)(1-\rho^{N+1})} \tag{T11.38}$$

$$T_q \ = \ \frac{\rho\,[1 - \rho^N - N\rho^{N-1}(1 - \rho)]}{\mu(1 - \rho)(1 - \rho^N)} \tag{T11.39}$$

$$P_{delay} = \frac{\rho\,(1 - \rho^{N-1})}{1 - \rho^{N+1}} \tag{T11.40}$$

$$p_0 \ = \ \frac{1 - \rho}{1 - \rho^{N+1}} \tag{T11.41}$$

6. PRIORITY QUEUES

6.1. General

Priority queueing systems differ from those previously discussed because their queue discipline does involve the state of the system. A priority scheme is a method for selecting which customer is to be served next. Customers arrive with inherent priorities that are not set by the system.* They are placed at the end of the queue corresponding to their priority. That is, service is FIFO within a priority class. If there are no customers of a higher priority in the system, the incoming customer will be given immediate service. Otherwise, service is given to the first-in, highest priority customer. Priority classes are numbered from 1 to n, with 1 having the highest priority and n the lowest. Each class is assumed to have its own arrival and service parameters. The following definitions are used.

λ_i $\qquad$ = mean arrival rate for ith priority class. $\qquad$ (D11.18)

$\lambda = \sum\limits_{i=1}^{n} \lambda_i$ = total arrival rate. $\qquad$ (D11.19)

μ_i $\qquad$ = mean service rate for ith priority class. $\qquad$ (D11.20)

$\rho_i \qquad = \dfrac{\lambda_i}{\mu_i}$ = demand for ith priority class. $\qquad$ (D11.21)

$\sigma_i = \sum\limits_{j=1}^{i} \rho_j$ = total demand for i'th level and higher. $\qquad$ (D11.22)

n $\qquad$ = number of priority levels. $\qquad$ (D11.23)

---

*In general, the system can set priorities, but that sort of thing is beyond the scope of this introduction.

$$\rho = \sigma_n \quad = \sum_{j=1}^{n} \rho_j = \text{total demand.} \tag{D11.24}$$

$m_{\mu 2i}$ = second moment about the origin of the service time distribution for priority level i.   (D11.25)

$$= \sigma_{\mu i}^2 - \left(\frac{1}{\mu_i}\right)^2.$$

$m_{\mu 3i}$ = third moment about the origin of the service time distribution for priority level i.   (D11.26)

6.2. $(M/G/1):(\text{NPRE}/\infty/\infty)$

This is a single server queueing system in which the service time for the individual priority levels are not specified. The priority scheme is non-preemptive (NPRE), which means that a customer in service will be allowed to finish before being interrupted by a higher priority request. Tasks handled by a central scheduler fit this model. Interrupt processing does not. However, the expressions for pre-emptive schemes are more complicated and less complete. In most cases, since the service time for any one service epoch is small, the error introduced is also small.

$$T_{qi} = \frac{\sum_{i=1}^{n} \lambda_i m_{\mu 2i}}{2(1 - \sigma_i)(1 - \sigma_{i-1})} \tag{T11.42}$$

$$T_s = \frac{1}{\lambda} \sum_{i=1}^{n} \lambda_i T_{si} \tag{T11.43}$$

$$T_q = \frac{1}{\lambda} \sum_{i=1}^{n} \lambda_i T_{qi} \tag{T11.44}$$

$$N_q = \sum_{i=1}^{n} N_{qi}, \quad N_s = N_q + \rho \tag{T11.45}$$

$$N_{qi} = \lambda_i T_{qi}, \quad T_{si} = T_{qi} + \frac{1}{\mu_i}, \quad N_{si} = \lambda_i T_{si}. \tag{T11.46}$$

Equation (T11.46) is just Little's theorem applied in the obvious way to the individual waiting times and queue size. (T11.42) is revealing. Note that the queue time (and hence the other parameters) can be finite for some priority level and higher, but infinite for lower levels. A priority level is influenced by what is happening above, rather than by what is happening below. The variance for level i (for the very hardy) is given in Saaty [SAAT 61] as

$$\sigma^2_{T_{qi}} = \frac{\sum\limits_{j=1}^{n} \lambda_j m_{\mu 3j}}{3(1 - \sigma_{i-1})^2 (1 - \sigma_i)} + \frac{\sum\limits_{j=1}^{n} \lambda_j m_{\mu 2i} \sum\limits_{k=1}^{i-1} \lambda_k m_{\mu 2k}}{2(1 - \sigma_{i-1})^2 (1 - \sigma_i)^2}$$
$$+ \frac{\sum\limits_{j=1}^{n} \lambda_j m_{\mu 2j} \sum\limits_{k=1}^{i-1} \lambda_k m_{\mu 2k}}{2(1 - \sigma_{i-1})^3 (1 - \sigma_i)} \quad . \tag{T11.47}$$

6.3. $(M/G/1):(PRER/\infty/\infty)$

This model uses a preemptive resume discipline. This means that the customer in service will be preempted by a higher priority customer, but no work will be lost:

$$T_{qi} = \frac{\sum\limits_{i=1}^{n} \lambda_i m_{\mu 2i}}{2(1 - \sigma_i)(1 - \sigma_{i-1})} + \frac{1/\mu_i}{1 - \sigma_{i-1}} . \tag{T11.48}$$

Little's theorem can be used to obtain the other parameters.

6.4. Comments

Notation, as always in queueing theory, can be confusing. Some author's number priorities with 1 highest and n lowest, while others do it the other way around. This is something to watch out for when looking up a formula. Solutions for multi-server priority systems, for systems with a continuum of priorities, with nonconservative priority schemes etc., have been derived and are available in the references.

The $(M/G/1)$ priority equations were given, rather than the simpler and more usual $(M/M/1)$ equations, because they allow you to model a system in which every level has its own parameters. Since the values of the four basic queue parameters are discipline-independent, you do not even have to assume FIFO within each level. Thus, a system with deterministic interrupt service, exponential at the second level, and erlang at the third could be modeled by these expressions. Where a given level uses a mix of different service pdf's, you can evaluate the mean of the mix and the variance of the mix (as the sums of the means and variances, respectively), fit a close Gamma or hyperexponential to the lot, and use Table 11-1 to particularize (T11.42) or (T11.43) as required.

7. NETWORKS OF QUEUES

7.1. General

This is another area in which semi-invalid but still useful procedures are available. The transaction flow can be looked upon as representing the flow of tasks through a network of independent single server queueing systems.* Furthermore, by considering only simpler cases, in which there are no MUST or AND nodes, but perhaps loops, a familiar and particularly simple kind of model emerges. (See Figure 11-2.) This is a network of interconnected queueing subsystems. A subsystem could be a CPU, an I/O device, a bus, or any other resource-limited device that can result in a queue buildup and, therefore, delay.

Tasks arrive at the network at a mean rate λ. It is reasonable (essential) to assume that tasks are neither created nor destroyed. Consequently, λ must also be the rate at which tasks eventually leave the network, as shown at the output of $S6$. We don't really know what the true arrival rate to $S1$ is because of the feedback from $S6$ via $S4$, which circulates some tasks through the network an undetermined number of times. Assume that rate to be known, calling it λ_1. Tasks arrive at subsystem 1, then, with rate λ_1. They are processed by subsystem 1 after some delay which is a function of the particulars of the subsystem and the arrival rate to that subsystem. At the conclusion of service, a decision node splits the tasks into two streams with probabilities P_{12} and P_{13}, respectively, with $P_{12} + P_{13} = 1$. Each queueing subsystem is now considered as a (new kind of) node. The flow from node 1 to node 2 is $P_{12}\lambda_1$. At $S3$, two task streams converge, each with their own arrival rates or flows, of $\lambda_1 P_{13}$ and $\lambda_2 P_{23}$, respectively. All of this should be familiar by virtue of its similarity to the analysis of processing time; indeed, with enough simplifying assumptions the analysis can be made similar.

The problem with this analysis is that it is valid only for $(M/M/c)$ servers. If this was the kind of simplifying assumption that had to be made I could well expect the reader to be antagonized after mucking about for n pages with numerous queueing models other than $(M/M/1)$. At least, an analytical procedure should apply to $(M/G/1)$ queues. Actually, the problem is more complicated than that. One has to consider the nature of the distribution that describe the *interdeparture time* from a queueing process. It turns out that the departure process is a Poisson process, and therefore an input Poisson process for the next queue in the network, if and only if the queue is a $(GI/M/c)$ queue. This means that even our assumptions of $(M/G/1)$ is not valid, but that we have to generalize to treating networks of $(GI/G/1)$ queues. At this point we have

---

*Actually, they can be multi-servers, but why complicate things.

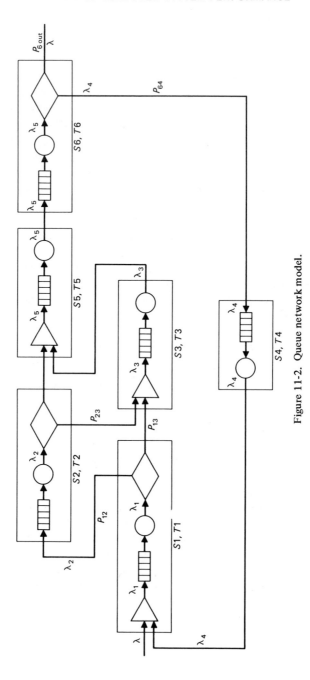

Figure 11-2. Queue network model.

three alternatives:

1. simulate;
2. be very erudite and solve the exact problem in all its glory;
3. be sophisticatedly naive, treat all servers as $(M/M/1)$ or $(GI/G/1)$ as convenience dictates, with suitable approximations.

Option 3 is the only one that fits the confines of this book. Two algorithms are presented. The first ignores the arrival distribution, but not the details of the individual queueing subsystem. This algorithm is then refined using a heavy traffic approximation similar to those used for the $(GI/G/1)$ queues. The first algorithm is generally pessimistic—although not necessarily so. Typically, the over-all error in the first algorithm should be of the order of 20%. The second algorithm is more precise and becomes increasingly so as load is increased. At high loads, the error is negligible. The error in the variance of the time in the system is comparable to the error of the mean. In either case, the time spent in the system is of interest. It is relatively less important to obtain the time spent in the queue. Furthermore, since main use of N_q is to determine how many queue blocks should be provided, and since in a practical system a queue block is held until the processing is done, the number of items in the system (N_s) is more useful than the number of items queued (N_q).

7.2. Rudimentary Models and Assumptions

7.2.1. Input and Output

Transactions enter queue subsystem i at a rate λ_i and leave it at the same average rate. Flow is conserved. The queue is an $(M/G/1)$ queue, or whatever model is appropriate and tractable. For example, use a disc latency model if the queue is waiting time for the disc. If it is a general processing model, determine the mean and variance of the processing time by the techniques of Chapters 5 or 8 and treat it as an $(M/G/1)$ queue. The output, theoretical considerations aside, is assumed to be a Poisson process. The time spent on the queue will be denoted by $T_i(\lambda_i)$ and the variance by $\sigma_i^2(\lambda_i)$, where the parentheses indicate that these numbers are functions of the yet unknown flow into that queue, λ_i.

7.2.2. Series Queues

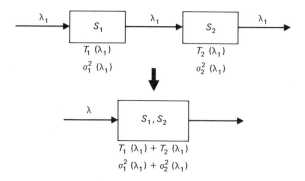

The two queues in series are replaced by an equivalent (not really, but what else can we do?) queueing subsystem whose mean time is equal to the sums of the means of its component systems; similarly for the variance. If they were actually $(M/M/1)$ queues, this procedure would not only be convenient, but correct.

7.2.3. Parallel Queues

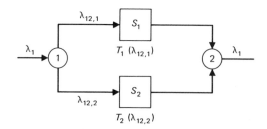

$$T_{12} = \frac{\lambda_{12,1} T_1(\lambda_{12,1}) + \lambda_{12,2} T_2(\lambda_{12,2})}{\lambda_{12,1} + \lambda_{12,2}} \qquad \text{(T11.49)}$$

$$\sigma_{12}^2 = \frac{\lambda_{12,1}\sigma_1^2(\lambda_{12,1}) + \lambda_{12,2}\sigma_2^2(\lambda_{12,2})}{\lambda_{12,1} + \lambda_{12,2}} + \frac{\lambda_{12,1} T_1^2(\lambda_{12,1}) + \lambda_{12,2} T_2^2(\lambda_{12,2})}{\lambda_{12,1} + \lambda_{12,2}}$$

$$- \left[\frac{\lambda_{12,1} T_1(\lambda_{12,1}) + \lambda_{12,2} T_2(\lambda_{12,2})}{\lambda_{12,1} + \lambda_{12,2}} \right]^2 \qquad \text{(T11.50)}$$

These expressions are not so gruesome as they appear at first glance. In fact, they are identical to the analogous processing time expressions of Chapters 5 or 8, with the flows replacing the probabilities. However, recognize that

$$\lambda_{12,1} = P_{12,1}\lambda_1$$

$$\lambda_{12,2} = P_{12,2}\lambda_1,$$

substitute these expressions into (T11.49) and (T11.50), and simplify. The flows all cancel, leaving

$$T_{12} = \frac{P_{12,1}T_1 + P_{12,2}T_2}{P_{12,1} + P_{12,2}},$$

and similarly for the variance, which is indeed identical to the timing equations.

7.2.4. Looping Queues

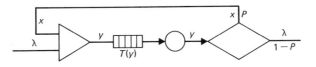

First of all, solve for the flow. The incoming flow is:

$$x + \lambda = y$$

but

$$y(1 - P) = \lambda$$

and

$$yP = x$$

and

$$\lambda + yP = y$$

or

$$y = \frac{\lambda}{1 - P}, \qquad x = \frac{\lambda P}{1 - P}.$$

Therefore, the time spent in the queueing subsystem is

$$T\left(\frac{\lambda}{1 - P}\right). \qquad\qquad *$$

But this is nothing more than a flowchart with a loop, a processing time $T(\lambda/(1 - P))$, and a looping probability P. Therefore, the mean and variances are simply

$$t = \frac{T\left(\dfrac{\lambda}{1 - P}\right)}{1 - P} \qquad\qquad *$$

---

*Recall that here $T(\lambda/1 - P)$ and $\sigma^2(\lambda/1 - P)$ do not mean multiplication but rather that T and σ are functions of $\lambda/(1 - P)$; see 7.2.1.

$$\sigma^2 = \frac{PT^2 \left(\frac{\lambda}{1-P}\right)}{(1-P)^2} + \frac{\sigma_{T_s}^2 \left(\frac{\lambda}{1-P}\right)}{1-P} , \qquad *$$

which again is identical to the timing equations.

7.2.5. Finding the Flows

This is not as bad as it seems. Flow must be conserved. Consequently, a set of balance equations exist for every node. The balance equations for Figure 11-2 are, by inspection,

$$\lambda_1 = \lambda + P_{41}\lambda_4$$

$$\lambda_2 = P_{12}\lambda_1$$

$$\lambda_3 = P_{13}\lambda_1 + P_{23}\lambda_2$$

$$\lambda_4 = P_{64}\lambda_5$$

$$\lambda_5 = P_{25}\lambda_2 + \lambda_3$$

$$\lambda_6 = \lambda = P_{6\,out}\lambda_5 .$$

Given numerical values for the probabilities, the solution of this bunch is straightforward; they can be solved almost by inspection. Since the equations are linear, λ can be factored out of all of the expressions, yielding a set of numbers which are only functions of the interconnection pattern and the probabilities. These are readily obtained by setting $\lambda = 1$ prior to solving the equations. Call these the **flow correction terms**, denoted by F_i: the flow term for node i of the network. The flow at any point in the network is then the flow into the network multiplied by the appropriate flow correction term for the node: i.e., $\lambda_i = \lambda F_i$.

7.2.6. The Algorithm Reviewed

The steps in the algorithm are as follows.
1. Derive a queueing model for each queueing subsystem of the network.
2. Set up and solve the flow balance equations for the correction terms for each queueing subsystem.
3. Substitute $\lambda_i = \lambda F_i$ into the queueing equations for each node to obtain T_{si} and σ_{si}^2.
4. You now have a model identical in every respect to a timing model, with

---

*Recall that here $T(\lambda/1 - P)$ and $\sigma^2(\lambda/1 - P)$ do not mean multiplication but rather that T and σ are functions of $\lambda/(1 - P)$; see 7.2.1.

specified timings, variances, and probabilities. Use the techniques of Chapter 5 and 8 to reduce it, thereby obtaining the mean time in the network. Note the shift in definition of nodes and links in going from the queueing model to the timing model.

5. Similarly, use the appropriate expressions for the number of items in each subsystem: their sum approximates the mean number of occupied queue blocks in the network.

7.3. A Refinement

7.3.1. General

As you might expect, refinements take more work. The main problem with the above algorithm is that it does not take into account the fact that the departure process is not Poisson. What is needed is something to nudge the arrival rates to the individual queues in a manner which compensates for this error. This is done by adjusting the demand ρ and using the heavy traffic approximation for $(GI/G/1)$ queues, (T11.31). As you might expect, this approximation will be better at higher loads. Unfortunately, it is not universally pessimistic when applied to a network of queues. The algorithm is based on a procedure developed by Reiser and Kobayashi [REIS74].

7.3.2. The Algorithm

1. Derive a queueing model for each queueing subsystem of the network. Include an inway and outway node to complete the model.
2. Set up and solve the flow balance equations to obtain the flow correction terms for each node, F_i.
3. Evaluate for every node*

$$C_i^2 = 1 + \sum_{j=1}^{M} (K_j^2 - 1)P_{ji}^2 \frac{F_j}{F_i} \qquad \text{(T11.51)}$$

where

$$K_j^2 = \sigma_{\mu j}^2 \mu_j^2 \qquad \text{(T11.52)}$$

4. Evaluate for every node:

$$\hat{\rho}_i = \exp \frac{2(\lambda F_i - \mu_i)}{C_i^2 \lambda F_i + K_i^2 \mu_i} \qquad \text{(T11.53)}$$

---

*I may have promised you a rose garden, but without thorns?

and

$$\rho_i = \frac{\lambda F_i}{\mu_i}.$$ (T11.54)

5. Evaluate (as required)

$$N_{Si} = \frac{\rho_i}{1 - \hat{\rho}_i}$$ (T11.55)

$$\sigma^2_{NSi} = \frac{\rho_i \, (1 - \rho_i + \hat{\rho}_i)}{(1 - \hat{\rho}_i)^2}$$ (T11.56)

$$T_{Si} = \frac{\rho_i}{(1 - \hat{\rho}_i)\lambda F_i}$$ (T11.57)

$$\sigma^2_{TSi} = \frac{\sigma^2_{NSi} - N_{Si}}{\lambda^2 F_i^2} = \frac{\rho(2\hat{\rho} - \rho)}{(1 - \hat{\rho})^2 \lambda^2 F_i^2}.$$ (T11.58)

6. The model is now trivially convertible to an ordinary timing analysis model. Proceed accordingly.

7.3.3. A Note on Accuracy

This model is most accurate for those nodes that have a high load. It improves as $\hat{\rho} \to 1$. Furthermore, accuracy is best when K_j is near 1. This corresponds to the $(M/M/1)$ system. The individual nodes are pessimistic for $K_j < 1$ and optimistic for $K_j > 1$. Generally, most realistic queueing models will have $K < 1$, and consequently the over-all model will tend to be pessimistic.

8. EXERCISES

1. Use standard queueing theory notation to describe the following queueing systems. Where the system has multiple queues, draw a diagram to show how they are interconnected.

   a. A chair-type ski lift (careful).
   b. A rope-type ski lift.
   c. The queue between the end of the ski lift and the ski slope for a and b above.
   d. A single-play juke box (more or less).
   e. A fast-food service counter.
   f. A movie theater that shows three movies but has only one ticket seller.
   g. A cafeteria counter on Main Street (beginning to end).

   h. The White House staff cafeteria.

   i. Users logged into a time-shared system waiting for service.

2. Describe a queueing system in which no queue will occur even when the arrival rate and the service rate are equal. (Determination will solve this one.) Prove your answer by using the appropriate queueing formula and parameter values.

3. Go to the local supermarket and gather statistics on arrival and service rates. Compare the observed N_s with the calculated N_s. Does the express line really work?

4. Why is a $(GI/G/c)$ queueing model of a supermarket checkout counter or bank tellers only approximate? Describer server and/or customer state dependencies that might apply.

5. Consider a computer system as a single-server system. Order N_q, N_s, T_q, and T_s, as well as λ, μ, and ρ in order of increasing difficulty with respect to measurement or observation. Difficulty is measured by code complexity and/or execution time, and the computer is to do its own measurements. List combinations of these parameters sufficient to determine the others.

6. Derive (T11.24) through (T11.27).

7. Using the appropriate definitions for first, second, and third moments of continuous and discrete distributions, derive the first, second, and third moments about the mean and origin for the following distributions: deterministic, uniform, exponential, hyperexponential, Poisson, geometric, and normal.

8. Your system is connected to another system that has an unknown service characteristic. You want to minimize the other system's delay to your transactions. The interdeparture time of your system is characterized by an exponential distribution. How should you modify your system to minimize the delay? Derive an algebraic expression for the best you can expect to do. Show that the relative improvement is indepent of the transaction rate. (Gee! Gosh! I think this is an easy one!)

9. Starting with (T11.2) for $(M/G/1)$ systems, derive (T11.13)-(T11.15) using (T11.2)-(T11.4).

10. Derive specific cases of (T11.8)-(T11.15) for $(M/G/1)$ systems with G the following distributions: D, U, M, E_k, H_R, P, g, and Q. Send the result to the author so he can include them as a handbook appendix in a subsequent edition of this book.

11. Consider an $(M/M/c)$ system. The cost of a server is $C_s = k_1 + k_2\sqrt{\mu}$. The cost of the system is given by $k_3 + k_4 N_s + SC_s$, where N_s is the total number of customers allowed in the system and S is the number of servers. For a given arrival rate and maximum possible mean delay D, find the number of servers and their service rates which minimize the system's cost. Ignore

the effect of a finite queue—that is, treat this as an $(M/M/c):(GI/\infty/\infty)$ system.

12. *Continuation.* Do Exercise 11 using a more precise $(M/M/c):(GI/N_s/\infty)$ model and compare the answer to exercise 11.

13. Show that the delay as averaged over all transactions in a single-server, multi-priority system is independent of how transactions are distributed among priorities. Assume an $(M/M/1):(NPRE/\infty/\infty)$ model.

14. Consider two $(M/M/1)$ queueing processes in series with parameters μ_a, μ_b, and λ. Let $\mu_a = k\mu_b$. Plot the subjective rate function parametric with λ, k and ρ.

15. Consider two $(M/M/1)$ queueing processes in parallel with parameters μ_a, μ_b, λ, ρ, with $\mu_a = k\mu_b$. Plot the subjective rate function parameteric with λ, ρ, and k.

16. Consider two $(M/M/1)$ queueing processes in a loop with forward service rate μ_a, feedback service rate μ_b, looping probability p, $\mu_a = k\mu_b$. Solve the flow balance equations and determine the mean delay of the two processes as a function of the parameters. Now find the mean delay of the system as a function of the parameters. Find the conditions under which the system will saturate. What should the relation between the two service rates be (i.e., k's value) so that both processes will saturate simultaneously? Select an arbitrary value of μ_a and several values of k. Plot the subjective rate functions parametric with p for each value of k.

17. Treat the following models as queueing networks. Interpret the given resource value as rate in some convenient unit. If no deviations is given assume an $(M/M/1)$ server. If a deviation is given assume a $(M/G/1)$ server.

   a. Calculate T_{si} and N_{si} for each queue i in the network.
   b. Calculate the mean delay of the network as a whole as a function of the network transaction arrival rate.
   c. Plot the subjective rate function.
   d. List the saturating resources in order of saturation.
   e. Assume that memory usage is proportional to $\sum_i N_{si}$. Plot the expected memory usage as a function of the transaction arrival rate.

1. A36	4. A5	7. T008
2. A44	5. A39	8. T016
3. A41	6. A38	

18. *Continuation.* Redo problem 17 using the more accurate procedure of section 7.2. Compare your results.

19. For the models analyzed in exercise 17 above, assume that the service rate is a measure of cost of the queueing subsystem and that one unit of mem-

ory and one unit of service have the same cost. The system cost is the sum of the service rates and the memory usage. Calculate the system cost for the original model at a specified arrival rate in the neighborhood of the first resource to saturate. Modify the model by moving service rates from nonsaturating resources to saturating resource with the intent of minimizing the system cost. Observe the effect on memory usage. Sketch a heuristic procedure that might lead to an optimum design. Is there only one minimum cost design, or are several possible?

12

Analysis of Cyclic Systems

1. SYNOPSIS

Cyclic structures are among the most common system software designs used in small or special purpose computers and applications. The inherent simplicity of the cyclic system leads to numerical performance results with relative ease.

2. CYCLIC SYSTEMS

2.1. What Are They?

The term "cyclic system" refers to the organization of the system's executive or controlling software. A cyclic system is a batch processor. It accumulates inputs over a period of time and stores them for subsequent processing. Once the collection phase has been completed it processes all pending transactions and produces the required outputs. In practice, things are organized so that input, output, and processing occur concurrently. Inputs are typically heralded by interrupts. They are processed in part at a high priority level, and queued or stacked for subsequent processing at a lower level. Cyclic systems operate at at least two functional priority levels, commonly called the "interrupt level" and the "base level." Things are arranged so that most of the processing is done at the lower priority base level. Consequently, most of the model is concerned with what happens at the base level.

Figure 12-1 shows the structure of an unrealistically simplified cyclic system. The software's structure is a loop since at the conclusion of all processes, the program will resume at the BEGIN point. A traversal of the base program from BEGIN back to BEGIN is called a **cycle**. The objective of the analysis is to determine the expected duration of that cycle (called the **cycle length**) as a function of the imposed load. Given the relation between load and cycle length, it is relatively easy to obtain the delay because it is usually a simple function of the cycle length, such as a multiple of it.

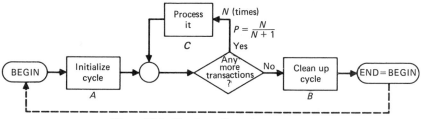

Figure 12-1. Simple cyclic system.

2.2. Operation and Behavior

It is obvious from Figure 12-1 that this is a batch processor. Some overhead processing is done to set up and later to clean up the cycle, but most of the time is spent processing transactions. As a further assumption, assume (for now) that only those transactions that arrive in the previous cycle are processed in the present cycle. Specific details of input and output processing are not important at the moment. It is sufficient to assume that inputs are on an input queue and outputs are handled from an output queue.

The program examines the input queue and processes any outstanding transactions. It continues doing this until the transactions are exhausted, at which time it does the cleanup and starts a new cycle. If the cycle length is L, the process execution times (ignoring stretch) are as in Figure 12-1, and N is the number of transactions in the batch, then

$$L = A + B + NC. \tag{12.1}$$

However, N is a function of the cycle length. The fundamental assumption in the analysis of cyclic systems is that every cycle is (statistically) the same. If transactions arrive at a rate R (transactions per second), and the cycle length is L seconds, then it is evident that*

$$N = RL. \tag{12.2}$$

Substituting into equation (12.1) and solving for L yields**

$$L = \frac{A + B}{1 - RC}. \tag{12.3}$$

Since the delay suffered by the transaction is a multiple of the cycle length, say K, the subjective rate is

$$\frac{1}{S} = D = KL = \frac{K(A + B)}{1 - RC} \tag{12.4}$$

---

*Compare to Little's theorem.
**Compare the RC term to ρ in an $M/G/1$ queueing system.

Combining parameters by setting $K_2 = K(A + B)$, with a little algebra,

$$K_2 S + RC = 1. \tag{12.5}$$

This is readily seen to be a quasi-ideal system. Equation (12.4) shows the throughput–delay behavior we have come to expect: a nonzero delay at zero load and an infinite delay at a load equal to $1/C$. Note that no assumptions were made about arrival rate or service rate distributions. The behavior, while similar to a queueing system, is not based on a queueing phenomenon. A cyclic system in which all components were deterministic would behave the same way.

2.3. Examples of Cyclic Systems

The following are examples of simple cyclic systems, or systems in which the cycle structure may be a dominant feature.

- A data logger scans sense points according to a periodic, preprogrammed order. It solicits the inputs, does some conversions, and prepares an output record. A cycle consists of a traversal of the entire scan list.
- A calculator waits in a loop for a key stroke. When the key stroke arrives, it is processed. The processing details depend upon the state of the calculator at the time the keystroke came in. The cycle length is variable, but statistically predictable. The cycle consists of processing exactly one transaction. The tough part of the analysis is predicting the probability of being in a given state.
- A process control system senses inputs, some of which are under a cyclic scanner control and some of which occur asynchronously and are uncontrolled. Inputs are accumulated and control parameter changes are calculated. Commands to change the control settings are transmitted asynchronously at a high priority level. The cycle consists of a scan/input/output process for all events that have accumulated during the previous cycle.
- A communications concentrator accumulates incoming characters on several lines by means of DMA channels. The incoming characters are cleared out of the input buffers and repackaged into an output buffer for synchronous transmission over a high speed line. The converse occurs for characters arriving on the high speed trunk; they must be distributed to low speed lines. The cycle is determined by the number of input and output characters that must be processed.

2.4. Cyclic and Noncyclic Systems Compared

The cyclic structure is common in small, special purpose, real-time systems which perform a narrow range of tasks. This structure is also used in large systems that also perform a narrowly defined set of tasks—process control and communications systems are primary examples. Almost all known systems (at least all those I know about) have a cyclic component, usually operating at the lowest priority level.

The operation of a noncyclic or asynchronous system is distinctly different. In such systems, it is the transaction that triggers the process. For example, an input event occurs; it triggers an input processing module. The input processing module queues its outputs to the next process to be performed, either directly or via a centralized dispatcher. The active process depends upon the sequence in which things have occurred. The order of process activation is random. If the asynchronous system has a central dispatcher, the dispatcher may operate as a cyclic program, the cycle consisting of examining all queues and dispatching tasks as appropriate. A cyclic system can be characterized as processes looking for tasks, while noncyclic systems can be characterized as tasks looking for processes.

It is not the purpose of this book to delve into the merits and deficiencies of either philosophy. One is not *better* than the other, merely more effective under certain circumstances. Some contrasting characteristics of the two types of systems are listed below.

1. Cyclic systems achieve higher ultimate throughput than asynchronous systems. They are more efficient at high loads, but have higher delays than equivalent noncyclic systems. (See Figure 12-2 for a typical comparison. Cyclic systems are designed for maximum throughput, while asynchronous systems are designed for minimum delay.

2. The asynchronous system tends to be self-tuning throughout its operating range. The cyclic system must be tuned, but is well tuned only over a small operating range (typically in the high load region).

3. The asynchronous system's performance is relatively insensitive to changes in the application program—such changes usually produce proportional changes in delay. The cyclic system's performance is more sensitive to changes, and becomes detuned as a result of such changes.

4. The cyclic system tends to require less buffer storage and queue storage space than the equivalent asynchronous system.

5. The cyclic system's efficiency increases with load; the asynchronous system becomes less efficient with increasing load and may exhibit many queue length processing dependencies.

6. Recovery from hardware and software malfunctions and the maintenance of data integrity and accountability is significantly simpler in cyclic systems than in asynchronous systems.

These characteristic differences dictate the applications in which each type will excel. For example, the relative uncertainty of the application programs in a commercial or time-shared environment forces a noncyclic structure on com-

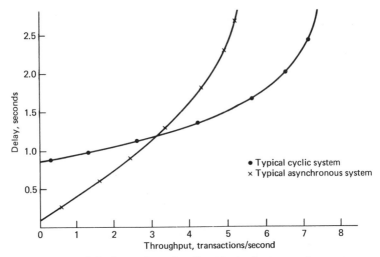

Figure 12-2. Comparison of cyclic and asynchronous systems.

mercial operating systems. Most generalized, off-the-shelf packages tend to be noncyclic; by contrast, special purpose technical programs tend to be cyclic. A more fundamental distinction is to be drawn between cyclic and asynchronous systems—the ease of analysis. Cyclic systems are almost totally amenable to analytical treatment using elementary algebra and only the simplest aspects of queueing theory. Asynchronous systems almost always require a queueing theory approach, and are often beyond the scope of microanalytical techniques. In other words, whatever other virtues or failings cyclic systems may have, they are (relatively) easy to analyze.

Unlike queueing systems in which delay (over and above the time required to process the transaction) is a result of the stochastic nature of the arrivals and servers, the cyclic system is primarily deterministic. Queueing effects, while they do exist, are secondary. A queueing system with input, output, and processing synchronized and deterministic will not form a queue. The delay will be constant up to the saturation point. A cyclic system's delay, by comparison, will always depend on load, even if all components are deterministic.

2.5. When Is a System Cyclic?

There is no such thing as a pure cyclic or pure asynchronous system. Every cyclic system worth analyzing has noncyclic processes, such as interrupt processing. Every asynchronous system has cyclic processes imbedded in them, such as task schedulers, and cleanup routines. Typically, asynchronous processes in both systems are done at higher priority levels, while synchronous (cyclic) processes are done at lower priority levels. Consequently, as a first order approximation, a system can be characterized as cyclic or noncyclic according to whether the bulk of the processing is cyclic at the lower levels, or asynchronous at the high levels.

1. If most (say, 75% or more) of the processing can be accounted for in cyclic processes over the range of throughput of interest, treat the system as cyclic. This will be slightly optimistic because you tend to underestimate the delay contributions of high priority queues. A little judicious worst-casing turns this into a slightly pessimistic model. The error decreases with decreasing noncyclic contributions.
2. If most of the processing (again 75% or more) is asynchronous, use asynchronous analysis (see Chapter 13), treating the cyclic portion as a low priority task. The model will be pessimistic, since it will overestimate the cycle length and the contribution thereof to the delay.
3. If you are in between, do it both ways. The cyclic analysis will be optimistic at high loads and pessimistic at low loads. The asynchronous analysis will behave in the opposite way.

3. ANALYSIS OF CYCLIC SYSTEMS—FIRST STEP

3.1. The Procedure

The ultimate objective is to obtain the throughput-delay function. The first step is to derive the throughput-cycle length function. That is gotten by solving the cycle equation, which is in turn obtained from the cycle diagram—the first step. Actually, there was a previous step, the place where most of the hard work was done—the analysis of all the components that go into the cycle equation: the processing time for all statistically significant routines (and similar expressions for any other resource that may affect cycle length), all device latencies, interrupts, DMA, etc.

3.2. The Cycle Diagram

The cycle diagram starts as a simplified flowchart of the base level processing. Usually, this is a loop with no intervening decisions:

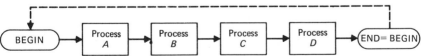

In practice there are several decisions, and at least one that will terminate the cycle, thereby shutting the system down. But since this event is statistically insignificant, it can be ignored. If there are decisions at the base level, simplify the flowchart until it is decision free. If, however, those decisions trigger high priority events, or I/O operations, do not simplify them. I'll get to that later.

Consequently a base level processing flowchart that looks like this:

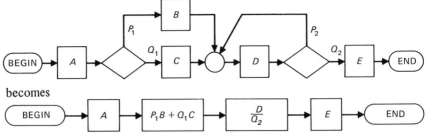

becomes

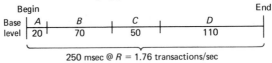

It is to be understood that A, B, C, etc. are functions of the load and/or the cycle length. Make a rough guess as to what the cycle length will be at a typical or interesting throughput, substitute that throughput and length into A, B, C, etc., and redraw the flowchart as a sequence of straight line segments whose length is proportional to the duration of the process. This step is not mathematically or procedurally required, but it will help you keep things straight. The cycle chart has the following appearance now:

	Begin			End
Base level	A	B	C	D
	20	70	50	110

250 msec @ R = 1.76 transactions/sec

3.3. Interrupts, DMA, and Stretch

Draw another series of lines above the base line, each one corresponding to a different priority level, remembering that DMA transfers are treated as a higher priority than interrupt processing. First fill in all interrupts and transfers that will take place independently of the cycle, e.g., clock interrupts, input interrupts, and (perhaps, but caution*) output interrupts. The result is:

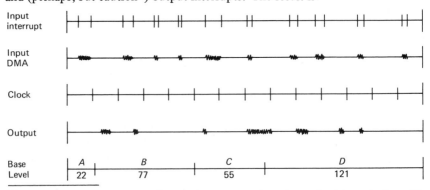

*Because these are not necessarily asynchronous events and may be triggered at specific points in the cycle.

It usually only pays to put down the clock interrupts and associated DMA transfers (if any) because most of the other activities occur asynchronously. But it may help to put these down as a reminder. At this point you should have accounted for all global stretch and you might want to redraw the base level times to take this into account.

3.4. I/O Latencies and Other Dependencies

If we keep crowding the cycle diagram with more lines it will become incomprehensible, so let's not continue to redraw the cycle-independent, high priority stuff and concentrate only on what affects the cycle length directly. The next step is to put in all cycle dependent/affecting transfers, such as disc operations, drums, tapes, other I/O devices, etc., which are initiated at the base level and whose completion is a condition for the cycle to continue. For example, say that process A kicked off an I/O transfer, and that process C could not continue until that transfer has been completed and that there was a second I/O transfer that requires the completion of process C and the first transfer. The modified cycle chart would have the following appearance:

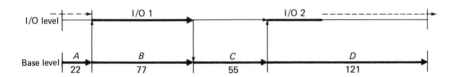

I admit to having slipped in a few notational changes here. There are heavy lines, light lines, and arrows. The light lines help the eye follow things. The heavy lines represent an activity. The arrows indicate that the subsequent activity cannot continue until it has completed. Thus, B's initiation requires the completion of A; C's initiation requires the completion of B and the first I/O transfer; while D only requires the completion of C. The second I/O transfer can be initiated only if the first I/O and C are done, but it does not impede any further part of the cycle. (Actually, it could impede the cycle because the first transfer of the next cycle cannot be initiated unless this transfer is done.) The elapsed times for the I/O transfers are obtained from the appropriate latency model. Every device which acts independently of (i.e., which can operate concurrently with) other devices should be given its own line on the chart. At this point you may want to have two sets of high priority lines: one corresponding to global stretch and one set corresponding to local stretch. The local stretch will usually be tied to an I/O operation of some kind.

3.5. Stretch Allocation

You may find that the conclusion of an I/O operation may cause a transfer of control not back to the base level, but to some higher priority level, during which time base level processing must be suspended.

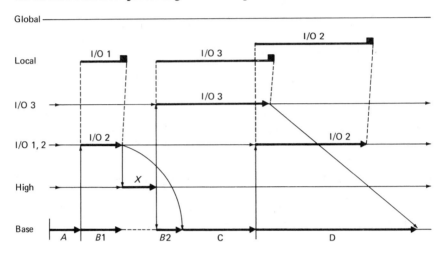

The high priority process X in this example is troublesome. It will act like a local stretch of process B. Since process C cannot continue until $B2$ is done, it cannot continue until X is done. Consequently, we can modify the cycle chart to the following, without introducing any error.

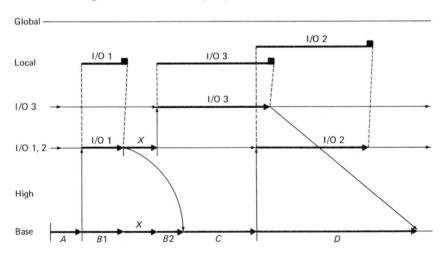

This last transformation is important. Process X now appears in two places: the base level and the I/O level. At the base level, it is a contributor to the cycle length because we were able to show by its logic that it exerted a purely local stretch and could not effect any other base process. It occurs also in the I/O level as an elapsed time to be added to I/O1, being a precondition to kicking off I/O3. We were lucky; it was possible to delimit the local stretch of X. Had X been in a position to potentially span more than one process, depending on the relative durations of the various transfers at that throughput, there would have been a stretch allocation problem, and the resulting cycle equations would have contained notations of the form: "IF . . . THEN . . . ELSE. . . ."

Looking at which stretches are local to a unique process, we see the following

- I/O1 must be local to $B + X$. Its contributing DMA and interrupt processing can be added directly to $B + X$.
- I/O2 is probably local to D, but could at high throughputs spill over into A. Compare the derivative with respect to throughput of the processing time for D to the derivative of the elapsed time with respect to throughput for I/O2. If I/O2 has a smaller derivative throughout the throughput range of interest, don't worry. If not, spillover could occur and must be included in your figuring.
- I/O3 could span B, C, or D and consequently there is a stretch allocation problem.

Go back to Chapter 9 to see how to fudge the stretch allocation problem. What I would do in this case is to examine the relative lengths of I/O3 and the affected processes at the zero load point, the throughput for which the system was designed, and the blow-up point. I would then see how much of I/O3's stretch contribution affected B, C, and D in all three cases. The ratios would be almost constant. I would reason as follows. If I allocate I/O3's stretch to D, I hold up the cycle, but nothing else. If I allocate it to C, (which is where most of it will go anyhow) it will have the worst possible effect on the cycle since it holds up both C and D. Therefore, I'll plot the allocation ratios that I found before and find that throughput at which C gets the maximum allocation. I multiply the stretch effect of I/O3 by the appropriate ratio and add it respectively to B, C, and D. Since the local stretch contribution is small anyhow, this slight worst-case is acceptable. The alternative to such approximations is to derive an exact conditional expression for the stretch and incorporate it into the cycle equation, which is no longer merely a nonlinear equation, but an algorithm. I adopted this attitude after I had several times meticulously derived expressions for the proper allocation of the stretch only to discover that all that painful work was wiped out in the roundoff errors of the procedure I used to solve the cycle equation.

4. DERIVE THE CYCLE EQUATION–SECOND STEP

4.1. Where to Start the Cycle

You have a cyclic program. There is a label such as BEGINDEBEGUINE and a statement someplace such as PLAYITAGAINSAM: GOTO BEGINDEBEGUINE. The programmer has told us where the cycle begins and where it ends, so what's the issue? The issue is that it's a cycle without beginning and without end, and anyplace you want to start is O.K. and should lead to exactly the same cycle equation although it might not look the same and could cause you a lot of grief before you found that out. The programmer's beginning and end are conventional and, analytically, non sequitors. It happens that, because they are likely to do initialization processing at the "beginning" of the cycle, things tend to be simple in that neighborhood. But this is not always the case. The place to begin the cycle (analytically) is at any point where there will be minimum spillover from the previous cycle. In the above example, the "beginning" is a good place to start; the only potential problem being the spillover of I/O2 into the next cycle. If you begin the cycle just after C, I/O3 would plague you and you would end up with an expression that involved the present and the previous cycle. Similarly for the end of X, and B. The end of A, though, would also be a good place to begin the cycle.

To set up and solve the cycle equation you must find at least one point at the base level over which no other arrows pass.* As to which point to choose:

1. Give preference to the programmer's beginning and end if it doesn't cost you anything–it will be easier to explain the analysis.
2. If two points are possible, choose the one for which things are simpler counterclockwise (i.e., the point for which the arrows and crossovers are fewer toward the left).
3. If criteria 1 and 2 above do not help you select the point, pick the point which keeps all analytically difficult areas as far away as possible in a counterclockwise direction. That is, pick the point which is just to the left of the toughest and nastiest expression.

The reason for these suggestions is that we start to derive the equations from the rightmost point and work backwards in time (towards the left). It's best to keep the bad stuff until last; this is known as constructive procrastination.

---

*One could get very exotic about the whole thing and get involved in graph theoretical considerations [MAYE72] along the lines of "there exists a cut which breaks all cycles and converts the graph into a partly ordered set," but why bother, you can always find such a point or fudge it by reasonable assumptions and judicious worst-casing.

4.2. The Cycle Equation

1. Label every arrow junction with a time variable, to yield:

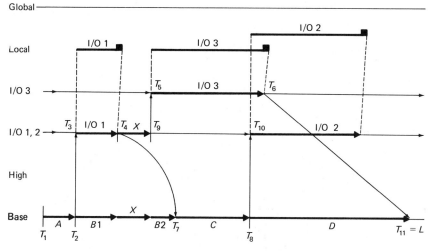

The completion of D is the "end" of the cycle.

2. Express the last time as a function of the previous time, starting with one cycle's end, as follows:

$$L = T_{11} =$$
$$T_{11} = \max(T_6, T_8 + D)$$
$$T_6 = T_5 + I/O3$$
$$T_8 = T_7 + C$$
$$T_5 = T_9$$
$$T_7 = \max(T_4, T_2 + B + X)$$
$$T_9 = T_4 + X$$
$$T_4 = T_3 + I/O1$$
$$T_3 = T_2$$
$$T_2 = T_1 + A$$
$$T_1 = 0.$$

Write a new equation if and only if it is needed for the definition of a previous term. T_{10} was not needed in the above example. Continue until the sequence of equations terminates. If there are more equations than there are points, then the cycle has spilled over and will actually take more than once through to complete.* You will then have a set of simultaneous

---

*Possibly an infinite number of times, which means you can't solve the cycle equation without assuming something.

equations to solve. It would be preferable to "break" the cycle at some point. Had we been more meticulous in the above example, the I/O2 arrow would have come around again to provide the following set of expressions, where the prime indicates the previous cycle.

$$L = T_{11}$$
$$T_{11} = \max (T_6, T_8 + D)$$
$$T_6 = T_5 + I/O3$$
$$T_8 = T_7 + C$$
$$T_5 = T_9$$
$$T_7 = \max (T_4, T_2 + B + A)$$
$$T_9 = T_4 + X$$
$$T_4 = T_3 + I/O1$$
$$T_3 = \max (T_2, T'_{10} + I/O2)$$
$$T_2 = T_1 + A$$
$$T_1 = T'_{11}$$
$$T'_{10} = \max (T'_8, T'_9)$$
$$T'_8 = T'_7 + C$$
$$T'_9 = T'_4 + X$$
$$\cdot$$
$$\cdot$$
$$\cdot$$
$$T_1 = 0$$

3. Simplify by successive substitutions:

$$T_1 = 0$$
$$T_2 = T_1 + A = A$$
$$T_3 = T_2 = A$$
$$T_4 = T_3 + I/O1 = A + I/O1$$
$$T_9 = T_4 + X = A + I/O1 + X$$
$$T_7 = \max (T_4, T_2 + B + X) = \max (A + I/O1, A + B + X)$$
$$\quad = A + \max (I/O1, B + X)$$
$$T_5 = T_9 = A + I/O1 + X$$
$$T_8 = T_7 + C = A + C + \max (I/O1, B + X)$$
$$T_6 = T_5 + I/O3 = A + X + I/O1 + I/O3$$
$$L = T_{11} = \max (T_6, T_8 + D) = \max [A + X + I/O1$$
$$\quad + I/O3, A + C + D + \max (I/O1, B + X)]$$

4. Examine the resulting expressions and eliminate as many max terms as you can.

There is not enough information in the above example to see if this is possible. However, in most cases you will be able to get rid of a few max terms by showing that one component must always be larger than another over the entire range of possible values. Common terms, such as A in T_7 above, can always be pulled out. The algebraic expressions for A, B, C, I/O1, etc., are all functions of the load and the cycle length. To remove a max you must be able to show that one term always exceeds the other for all combinations of values of load and cycle length. This sort of thing is often obvious by inspection, or after a little judicious maximization and minimization. If you suspect, say, that term T_3 is always greater than term T_4, in an expression of the form max (T_3, T_4), minimize T_3 by maximizing its denominator and minimizing its numerator; similarly, maximize T_4 by minimizing its denominator and minimizing its numerator. For example, let:

$$T_7 = \max (T_3, A + T_4)$$

with

$$T_3 = \frac{A - C}{C + D + E}$$

and

$$T_4 = A + \frac{3C - D}{C + D}$$

determine if:

$$T_3 \overset{?}{>} A + T_4$$

first minimize T_3,

$$\min T_3 = \frac{A - C}{C + D}$$

then maximize $(A + T_4)$

$$\max (A + T_4) = A + \frac{3C}{C + D} = \frac{A(C + D) + 3C}{C + D}$$

This now results in the simpler comparison:

$$A - C \overset{?}{>} A(C + D) + 3C$$

or

$$A \overset{?}{>} A(C + D) + 4C$$

It is not unusual to have all but one or two max terms eliminated this way.

4.3. Load Dependent Probabilities

There are many probabilities in the model that depend on the load. Since the program will process all tasks that arrive in a time equal to a cycle's duration, the number of times a routine will loop, say N, is equal to the number of tasks accumulated in a cycle—which is the cycle length multiplied by the transaction arrival rate: $N = LR$. If a process is activated twice per cycle, then each activation will have half as many tasks, or $N = LR/2$. Similarly if a process is activated every other cycle, $N = 2LR$; this term will then be multiplied by a probability of 0.5. Note that one cannot simply cancel such terms out because of possible nonlinearities in the routine or process that depends on N, that is, $0.5f(2N) \neq f(N)$. Actually, it does not matter whether a routine actually processes tasks that arrived in the previous cycle, the present cycle, or a combination thereof. Every cycle is statistically identical. Since it is only the number of tasks processed and not the particular tasks that is of interest, you can assume, without error, that all tasks arrived in the previous cycle.*

It is a good idea to express looping probabilities in terms of the cycle length right from the beginning. If the task arrival rate is R, and the cycle length is L, then the probability will be $RL/(RL + 1)$. If this occurs in a simple loop, the resulting expression will be of the form $A(RL) + B$, with A a function of RL. In more complicated loops and nested loops, the terms may not necessarily cancel; however, overall behavior is as if it had cancelled.

4.4. Appearance of the Cycle Equation

The general appearance of the cycle equation, ignoring max terms and similar complications is that of a polynomial in R and L, of the form

$$L = A + BRL + CR^2L^2 + \cdots$$

The effect of local and global stretch complicates things a bit, to give you

$$L = \frac{A}{1 - K_1R + K_2RL} + \frac{BRL}{1 - K_3R - K_4R^2L} + \frac{CRL^2}{1 - K_5RL} + \cdots \quad (12.6)$$

On a very simple model, you might have a simple quadratic to solve, or a rational polynomial in R and L. At this point it is a good idea to examine the entire equation for sensibility. Examine each term at zero traffic ($R = 0$). The resulting expression should be a constant. Individual terms of the equation may be negative as a result of simplifications carried out earlier. Try to relate such terms back to the cycle structure to make sure they make sense. It is judicious to examine the cycle equation this way, one part at a time, to make sure it is reasonable before investing vast effort in possibly meaningless solutions.

---

*For cycle length determination, but not necessarily for delay determinations.

5. SOLVING THE EQUATION

5.1. Outline of the Procedure

The solution is obtained by using the Newton-Raphson or similar method for solving polynomial equations [CARN69, KUOS65, MCCR64]. The overall process consists of the following steps.

1. Evaluate the cycle length at zero load.
2. Find all potential blow-up points and select the smallest.
3. Approximate the cycle function by an appropriately selected quasi-ideal or simplified model.
4. Substitute the load value of interest and use the simplified approximation as a starting point.
5. Use Newton-Raphson iteration to obtain the solution.
6. Correct the simplified model for the next value. Go back to 4 for the next solution.
7. Continue until you have the entire curve to a sufficient degree of accuracy.

In principle, it is possible to use Newton-Raphson iteration directly without an auxiliary simplified model. However, this can require you to perform many difficult auxiliary calculations. The above procedure takes advantage of what we know about the system's behavior to simplify the solution process.

5.2. The Zero Load Point

This is obtained by setting the load to zero. In almost all cases, the cycle equation falls apart and the cycle length can be obtained almost by inspection. Should you be so unlucky as to not have this happen, you will have to solve the cycle equation at zero load by using Newton-Raphson iteration as described below. I recommend checking the equation, though, since it it more likely that you made a mistake. The structure of the cyclic system is such that it is almost impossible to have a rational design in which there is a major term which is cycle length dependent and not simultaneously load dependent. There are exceptions, like clock interrupts that occur at a regular interval, independent of load. These will show up in the cycle equation and may lead to a quadratic for the zero load point. The zero load point is important because:

1. it is one point on which to hang our approximate, quasi-ideal model;
2. if the cycle length is not positive and sensible at this load level, it will not be positive and sensible at any other load level. Two or more real roots at zero load are always indicative of a model error; find it and fix it.

5.3. Blow-Up Points

Look at equation (12.6). Each denominator term can be solved individually for zero. Each such solution represents a potential blow-up point. Find the potential blow-up points by setting each denominator term to zero and solving it for the load at which this can occur. There will typically be several such solutions. These do not correspond to the actual blow-up point, but rather establish an upper bound for the actual blow-up point. That is, the least value of the load R which causes a term to be infinite (zero denominator) must equal or exceed the actual blow-up point.

5.4. Approximate Quasi-Ideal Model

You have the zero length cycle and the blow-up point. Fit an approximate quasi-ideal model as follows:

Let

$$L_0 = \text{cycle length at zero load.}$$
$$R_{MAX} = \text{the blow-up point.}$$

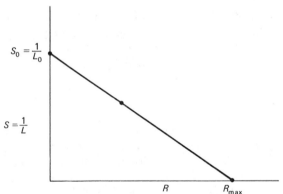

The model is:

$$\frac{S}{S_0} + \frac{R}{R_{max}} = 1,$$

or, solving for L,

$$\frac{1}{LS_0} + \frac{R}{R_{max}} = 1,$$

or

$$L = \frac{L_0 R_{max}}{(R_{max} - R)}. \tag{12.7}$$

5.5. Newton-Raphson Iterative Solution of Polynomial Equations

This is one of the oldest and best numerical procedures for finding roots of a polynomial or for that matter, almost any equation. You start with a guess and obtain a new guess by the following iteration:

$$L_{n+1} = L_n - \frac{f(L_n)}{f'(L_n)}. \tag{12.8}$$

That is, the next approximation is the previous approximation less the value of the function divided by its derivative at the previous approximation.

We are trying to find a root of a polynomial: $f(L_n) = 0$, at a specific value of $R = R_x$.

$$f(L_n) = L - \frac{A}{1 - K_1 R_x + K_2 R_x L} - \frac{B R_x L}{1 - K_3 R_x - K_4 R_x^2 L} - \cdots = 0, \tag{12.9}$$

where

$$f'(L_n) = \frac{d}{dL}\left(L - \frac{A}{1 - K_1 R_x + K_2 R_x L} - \cdots\right)$$

$$= 1 - \frac{d}{dL}\left(\frac{A}{1 - K_1 R_x - \cdots} + \frac{B R_x L}{1 - \cdots}\right) - \cdots$$

1. Use the value of L obtained from the quasi-ideal approximation as the starting point, or L_0, having substituted the value of R_x into (12.8) to obtain it.
2. Substitute that value of $L_n(R_x)$ into the cycle equation (12.9) to obtain $f(L_n)$.
3. It is rarely practical to analytically differentiate the cycle equation because of the presence of max terms and other nonlinearities. Use a numerical approximation for the derivative instead, by saying that the derivative is equal to

$$f' = \frac{df}{dL}$$

$$f'(L_n) = \frac{df(L_n)}{dL} \cong \frac{f(L_n + \Delta L) - f(L_n)}{\Delta L} \tag{12.10}$$

You have already calculated $f(L_n)$. Now calculate $f(L_n + \Delta L)$, a nearby value. ΔL is called the **mesh size**. It should not be larger than $0.1 L$. A value of $0.001 L$ is typically best. Doing this gives you

$$f'(L_n) = \frac{f(1.001 L_n) - f(L_n)}{0.001} \tag{12.11}$$

for the derivative, or

$$L_{n+1} = L_n - \frac{0.001\, f(L_n)}{f(1.001\, L_n) - f(L_n)}.$$ (12.12)

This is where the quasi-ideal model or an approximate model comes in. The approximate model gets you a fair starting point for the next throughput value. By correcting it as you go, you are adjusting your estimate of the next point. The crude cycle equation is used to obtain an analytical expresfor the derivative. This is generally easier than evaluating the entire cycle equation twice. The quasi-ideal model is useless for this purpose, since it has a constant derivative.

As you near the blow-up point, or in the neighborhood of load values where there is a contention between I/O binding and process binding, you may find it necessary to reduce the mesh size. Conversely, under low traffic conditions, a larger mesh size can lead to faster iterations. It is not necessary to reevaluate the derivative at every iteration. The first evaluation of the derivative is usually good for all iterations at a given load value, if the iterations are converging. If they are not converging, then you must reevaluate the derivative.

4. Find the new value of L, L_{n+1}, and return to step 2 for the next iteration. Continue until sufficient accuracy has been obtained.

For relatively simple polynomials and models of the type you are likely to do on a calculator or programmed calculator, this iteration procedure should give you between one and two digits of additional accuracy per iteration. For complex systems whose cycle equation consists of several hundred terms, more sophisticated iterative procedures can be employed (see (KUOS65, MCCR64, or CARN69)).

5.6. Finding the Whole Curve

You now have three points—the zero load point, an intermediate point, and a blow-up point. You should start the curve in the neighborhood of the zero traffic point, since this is the most reliable initial point. Proceed in small steps in the direction of increasing load. Having obtained an intermediate point, you pass a straight line through it from the zero load point to obtain a new approximate quasi-ideal model. This can be used to estimate the next initial trial value for the next load value. If your increments are small enough, you can simply use your old answer for the start.

For small models in which the cycle equation consists only of a half dozen to a dozen terms and in which it is easy to get a good expression for the derivative analytically, it will take five or six Newton–Raphson iterations per point. Ten to twenty points should suffice for the entire curve. Much caution must be exercised in solving for the blow-up point. The conditions under which Newton–Raphson iteration works do not necessarily hold in that neighborhood. I have found it effective to express everything in terms of the reciprocal of the cycle length (i.e., the cycle frequency), and solve for it. The greater regularity of this function tends to make solution faster and easier.

Complicated models have their own problems. By "complicated" I mean those in which the cycle equation has several hundred terms, many of them nonlinear. A pocket calculator is clearly out of the question. Beware of using packaged solution programs. They may not have adequate controls. It is essential to be able to vary the mesh size, particularly in the neighborhood of points where a selection is being made between two or more terms of a max function. It is also essential to be able to drop the present trial value and to come in from above (i.e., from a higher trial cycle length) rather than below. Furthermore, it must be possible to establish bounds on the solution and to have the program check for such bounds as it proceeds.

Another, and effective, approach to finding the blow-up point is to solve for the load that makes the cycle large. That is, treat the thing as a polynomial in R and solve for that R which makes $L = 10,000$, say. This same principle can be extended to solving always for R, rather than for L or S. Often the cycle equation viewed as polynomial in R is more tractable than one viewed as polynomial in L. The only disadvantage to this approach is that people expect to see neat values of R and resulting values of L. If that is the case, get a rough cut on the curve in terms of R. Use that to get your starting points (very accurate now) and do it over again iterating in L.

5.7. Spurious Solutions

These polynomials do not necessarily have a single real root. A complex model may exhibit several cycle lengths at a given load, and such behavior may be physical rather than merely analytical. Real systems never really blow-up, since all kinds of mechanisms are programmed into them to prevent such occurrences. Instead, they may exhibit quantum jumps in behavior corresponding to multiple throughput–delay curves of which the lowest represents normal behavior. The upper curvature curves represent stable behavior such as might occur following a long period of overload. Not much is known about this kind of behavior. Furthermore, so many simplifying assumptions must be made to get a tractable model that it is not clear if the spurious roots are really physical or merely analytical in origin. This is one of the virtues of solving for successive load levels starting from zero load point and working upwards, rather than the other way around; it guarantees staying on the proper track.

5.8. Stretch Allocation

Once you have the entire throughput–delay function, check it against your assumed local stretch assignments. This check should be made at several points. If an assignment is wrong, it will tend to stay wrong to the left or right of the throughput level at which the assumed allocation fell apart. Once wrong, it will only rarely become correct for some higher throughput level. In cyclic systems, where stretch is relatively small compared to base level processing (i.e., where local stretch tends to be miniscule), all stretch factors are only weakly coupled to the cycle length. It is sometimes advantageous to take a first cut by ignoring the local stretch problem altogether and treating all stretch as global. The resulting (simple) system is then solved and used to "prove" that the details of local versus assumed global allocation did not materially influence the solution.

If local stretch is significant, then the entire procedure must be looked upon as an iterative one. You guess at the initial allocation, solve the system, find corrected allocations, and resolve the system (i.e., get the entire curve). You do this until the assumed allocation and the subsequently derived allocation match. Two iterations are usually sufficient to tune up a model in this respect. The only other alternative is to set up a complicated set of simultaneous equations with all local stretches unknown. This is very difficult to do at all, harder to do right, and even harder to solve. There just aren't any good, reliable, equation solver routines for simultaneous nonlinear equations comparable to Newton-Raphson for a single equation. You can expect a relatively simple conditional stretch allocation to square the processing costs. If it is really important, you are transcending the scope of microanalysis and may be committed to simulation.

6. DELAY DETERMINATION

Delays in cyclic systems usually have a simple relation to cycle length. Most often it is a direct multiple (not necessarily an integer multiple) of the cycle length. The entire cycle can be treated as a rotating device. Therefore, since transactions are assumed to occur at random with respect to the current cycle "position" a rotational latency of one-half cycle can be assumed. This cannot be assumed for a system that controls the arrival of transactions by polling or some similar means unless the solicitation occurs uniformly or randomly throughout the cycle. If input can occur at only fixed points (do not confuse this with the point at which input proccessing starts) such points of the cycle must be identified. Delay is determined by the following steps.

1. Reexamine the transaction flow and label each point or event in it by a corresponding point in the cycle, say T_1, T_2, T_3, etc. You can use the same points and variables you used to develop the cycle equation.

2. Using the solution of the cycle length as a function of load, calculate the values of T_1, T_2, T_3, etc. This should not require additional calculations if you organized your solution correctly. These are intermediate terms in the cycle equation; it does not always pay to simplify expressions.

3. Assuming that you have labeled your points in increasing order, a complete transaction corresponds to a sequence of time periods—e.g., T_1, T_2, T_5, T_6, T_3, T_7, etc. If the sequence starts at T_i and ends at T_j and is monotonic from T_i to T_j, the delay is one-half cycle plus the time difference between T_i and T_j (i.e., $T_j - T_i$). The sequence T_1, T_2, T_5, T_{11} is monotonic. The sequence T_1, T_5, T_4 is not monotonic.

4. Every nonmonotonic break in the sequence of events implies an additional cycle or a fraction thereof. Example: the sequence is T_1, T_4, T_5; the delay is $\frac{1}{2} + T_5 - T_1$. The sequence is T_1, T_2, T_5, T_6, T_3, T_7; the delay is $\frac{1}{2} + T_6 - T_1 + T_3' - T_6 + T_7 - T_3 = 1\frac{1}{2} + T_7 - T_1$, because, $T_3' = T_3 + 1$.

It is not necessary to assume that tasks are processed only at the conclusion of the routine. This applies (typically) only to the first and last routine in the string, although it may apply every time an I/O operation occurs. The software might be arranged to allow a new input to be processed in the same cycle it arrives in, as long as it arrives before the input processing routine has completed. Analogously, an output might be activated as soon as its processing was through and not wait for the conclusion of the output routine. The affected routines can be assumed to have a latency as well. The probability of hitting the input routine is simply its length divided by the cycle length. Such tasks have only one-half the routine's length for delay. The rest of the inputs have a delay equal to half a cycle. Similar thinking can lead to further refinements of the delay expression.

Examination of a detailed delay expression, developed as above, is a prerequisite to tuning. Rearranging the order of processes can produce beneficial improvements in delay without affecting cycle lengths. Furthermore, there are instances when such rearrangements can result in a longer cycle but in a shorter delay. Delay is a simple multiple of cycle length only as a first order approximation. It is often a sufficient approximation.

7. OTHER RESOURCES

Determining the utilization of other rate resources is a simple arithmetic exercise once you have the cycle length as a function of load:

$$\text{CPU utilization} = \frac{\text{total CPU usage in cycle}}{\text{cycle length}}$$

$$\text{channel utilization} = \frac{\text{total usage of channel in cycle}}{\text{cycle length}}$$

etc.

262   MICRO-ANALYSIS OF COMPUTER SYSTEM PERFORMANCE

The CPU usage in a cycle must be carefully modeled. If the model is reasonably complete, then you will have included within it at least one expression or path corresponding to waiting for I/O transfers to complete, at every point in the cycle where such waits can occur. Cyclic systems are designed not to stop. If there is nothing to do, or if there is an enforced wait, the program cycles in a loop, or in a more sophisticated system performs overhead functions. In either case, such loops, beneficial or not, should have been included in the model. If you have not included wait loops like this (with cycle length dependent durations), then you must assume that processing is totally consumed during the wait periods. Similar considerations apply to other waiting situations.

The above resource utilization expressions lead to what may appear at first glance to be a paradox. In almost any system in which CPU or memory access is the binding resource, you will find that the utilization is 100% independent of the demand. This should not be surprising, because, as we saw above, the cycle makes work for itself when it has nothing to do. At the very least, it runs through the entire cycle looking for work, finds none, and starts a new cycle. This obviously consumes all available CPU resources leading to noticeable differences between utilizations and demand, especially at low load levels. If the cycle design actually does incorporate a HALT instruction, demand and utilizations will be closer. But such designs are patently poor since, at the very least, it is more effective to waste the time doing test and diagnostic functions rather then waste it altogether.

The number of resource units required per task is not constant (see Chapter 2) and decreases with increasing load. At zero load, because there is cycle overhead, the resource units per task are large. As load is increased, the resources consumed per task decrease (typically) and stabilize at some constant value (typically again) achieved only at an infinite cycle length. If you insist on specifying how many instructions it takes to process a task, then it must either be related to throughput or be unambigously identified as the limiting value achieved at maximum throughput.

It is interesting to examine resource utilization as a function of load for nonbinding resources or for components of binding resources:

1. The *resource usage* (e.g., instructions per second) is constant and independent of load or a cycle length. Therefore, the utilization for that component will decrease with increasing load.* Cycle overhead processing is an example of this.
2. The resource usage is proportional to cycle length. Therefore the utiliza-

---

*Do not confuse the utilization for a component of a process with the utilization for the entire system.

tion for that component will be constant for all loads. Example: clock interrupt processing.

3. The resource usage for a component is a function of the load. The utilization for that component will generally decrease with increasing load.

8. PSEUDO CYCLIC SYSTEMS

It is sometimes convenient when dealing with experimental data (see Chapter 15) to treat a system as if it were cyclic even if in fact it is not, or if its structure is unknown. Assume a very simple cyclic model of the form:

$$L = To + RLT$$

where

L is the cycle length,
To is the length of the no data cycle (zero throughput),
R is the throughput,
T is the time spent per transaction.

Solving for L and assuming that the delay is some multiple, K, of the cycle length, and further converting to subjective rate, we obtain:

$$S = \frac{1 - RT}{KTo}.$$

The reciprocal of T is recognized as the processing rate. Note that this does not lead to an ideal or quasi-ideal model. Rather, the subjective rate curve will typically exhibit an upward concavity. T is typically not constant but tends to start out large and to approach an asymptotic value at high throughputs. It is evident from the above that the reciprocal of T is the ultimate throughput—certainly an upper bound to the ultimate throughput. From this fact stems the usefulness of a pseudo-cyclic model. You can measure load and delay experimentally. A measurement of delay at very low loads and the general shape of the curve in the low load region allows you to extend the curve to the zero throughput point to obtain To with fair accuracy. You can now express T as a function of R and To. If T is converging to a fixed value (it will often, but not always do so), the reciprocal of that value gives you the ultimate throughput point. Consequently, even though you cannot set up measurements at the ultimate throughput, that point can be determined with reasonable accuracy. You can then draw the entire subjective rate curve from which the throughput delay curve is readily obtained. If T does not converge, then the system is exhibiting some strong queue dependencies or similar effects and this is not a particularly good modeling approach.

9. EXERCISES

NOTE: All of the following exercises are variations on the model described in exercise 1.

1. A cyclic system consists of five processes in series whose execution time is given by:

$$T_a = 0.05$$
$$T_b = 0.001 + 0.025N$$
$$T_c = 0.001L$$
$$T_d = 0.02 + 0.1N$$
$$T_e = 0.110.$$

   All terms are in seconds. L is the cycle length and N is the number of transactions that accumulated in the previous cycle. Transactions arrive at R per second. Derive the cycle equation and solve for the cycle length as a function of the imposed load R. What is the zero load cycle length? What is the load at the blow-up point?

2. *Continuation.* Only processes b and d are directly involved in processing a transaction. A transaction first passes through process d and then through process b, after which it leaves the system. Transactions that arrive while process d is still active will be processed during the same cycle in which they arrive. Show that the mean delay is given by: $D = L + (T_a + T_b - T_c - T_d)/2$. Is the system quasi-ideal?

3. Assume you can redesign the system by rearranging the order of the processes. With five processes, there are evidently $5! = 120$ different designs, each with a potentially different mean delay. A trivial argument reduces the number of cases to be considered to 24. Find the design with the minimum delay. Is there only one? If more than one design with the same minimum delay, how do they differ? There is no need to repeat the work of exercise 2 twenty-four times. Another argument cuts the cases down to 10. Some more thinking along the same line cuts it to five cases. (Hint: A cycle is a cycle is a cycle and if that doesn't do it, you might as well exchange this book for some other text.)

4. Repeat exercises 1 and 2 above with $T_b = 0.001 + 0.025N + 0.0003N^2$.

5. Repeat exercises 1 and 2 above with $T_b = 0.001 + 0.025N + 0.0007LN/(0.0009N + 1)$.

6. Repeat exercises 1 and 2 above with the following modifications. At the conclusion of process d, the system performs a write operation to a sched-

uled batch drum. It has 16 sectors and rotates at 1800 rpm. Each transaction is written on a single sector. Process b cannot be initiated until the write operations have finished.

7. Modify exercise 6 above by assuming that each transaction requires a 16 sector write. Assume the write requests are random so that you must optimize and cannot do them sequentially.

8. Modify exercises 1–7 above with the addition of a global stretch consisting of the following elements: 0.001 second per cycle plus 0.01 second per second plus 0.005 second per transaction.

9. Repeat exercise 7 above under the assumption that the write operations consume 0.00005 second per sector written and provides a stretch local to the I/O operation.

10. Repeat exercise 7 under the assumption that process b can be initiated prior to the completion of the write operation but cannot be concluded until the end of the write operation.

11. Repeat exercises 1 and 2 with the additional assumptions of exercises 5, 7, 8, 9, and 10.

12. Find the optimum design as in exercise 3 for the system described in exercise 11.

13. For exercises 4–11, resolve the cycle equation by finding the load that gives you a specified cycle length (i.e., a polynomial in R) and again using cycle frequency as the variable rather than cycle length. Compare ease of solution with direct solutions in terms of cycle length.

13

Analysis of Asynchronous Systems

1. SYNOPSIS

There are no truly satisfactory models of asynchronous (noncyclic) systems. Asynchronous systems are divided into categories, and the categories to be treated are identified. Approximate models are presented. Chapter 11 is a prerequisite to this chapter.

2. ASYNCHRONOUS SYSTEMS IN PERSPECTIVE

2.1. Application Domain and General Characteristics

Asynchronous (noncylic) designs are used when one or more of the following conditions hold.

1. Short delays are required, even if at the expense of throughput.
2. Relatively little is known about the statistical characteristics of transactions.
3. The statistical characteristics of transactions are known to be very broad.
4. The system requirements imply a need for great flexibility.

On the basis of the last three characteristics, it is obvious why most commercial operating systems are asynchronous. Such systems must contend with a broad range of problems from a minor file update, to a compilation, to running a large batch program in background mode. The service time is measured by the running times of the programs being executed by the system; the transactions are program executions. Cyclic systems have a large inherent delay because transactions must pass through one or more cycles for completion. Asynchronous systems, by contrast, because a high priority can be assigned to critical transactions, can achieve relatively low delays at the cost of ultimate throughput. Above all, the asynchronous system is robust. There are few opportunities for critical timings that throw it out of kilter. A major increase in the processing time for one element does not affect the logic of the system. Asynchronous systems are effectively self-tuning and relatively impervious to the transaction statistics. Conversely, cyclic systems are well tuned at only one throughput. Actually, there are no cyclic systems or asynchronous systems as such. Cyclic systems will handle transactions for which small delays are desirable asynchronously at a high priority level, and asynchronous systems will perform system overhead, task/process assignments, input and/or output, or such, on a cyclic basis. A more detailed comparison of the two system types is given in Chapter 12.

2.2. Open versus Closed Networks

All effective models of asynchronous systems are based on a queueing network representation. A queueing network can be either **open** or **closed** (Figure 13-1). An open queueing network is one which has transactions arriving from the outside world at a rate λ, which ultimately leave the system at the same rate. An open queueing network may or may not have feedback.

A closed network (statistically) has no inputs or outputs. At any instant of time there are N transactions circulating on internal queues waiting for service. Service is granted to them for a short time, or **quantum**, whereupon they go back on queue to await a new service epoch. These transactions or jobs are presumed to have a infinite residence time. Small systems and special purpose systems (i.e., systems dedicated to a single application or a narrow set of applications) are most often best treated as open networks. Closed networks are convenient models for large scale time-sharing systems. The supposition in a closed network is that if a customer should leave, he is immediately replaced by another whose statistical characteristics are identical. The analysis and objectives for open and closed networks are distinctly different.

Open Network: find the relation between throughput and delay.

Closed Network: find the expected delay for service (i.e., mean time between quanta) given that there are N customers in circulation.

Open networks, therefore, are driven by an infinite population of customers, while closed networks work with a finite and fixed population of customers. Generally, queueing problems based on finite customer populations are more difficult than those based on infinite populations. Consequently, the analysis of closed networks is distinctly more difficult. If your system is best modeled as a closed queueing network, you have reached the limits of this book and should be prepared for a heavy labor in the fields of advanced queueing theory.

Before leaving closed networks forever, I would like to point out that there is an extensive literature pertaining to their analysis. In fact, most of the queueing

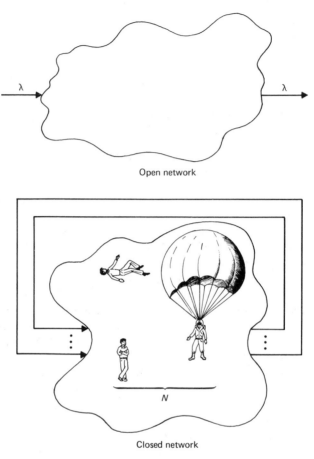

Figure 13-1. Open and closed queueing networks.

network models that have been applied to computer systems are of closed rather than open networks, so much so that casual survey of that literature might lead one to believe that the only models of computer systems are models of time-shared systems and their ilk. This is an unfortunate, but true situation— relatively little research effort has been spent on providing truly accurate models of asynchronous, open network systems; consequently we have to make do with simplifying assumptions, approximations, and heuristics. References to the more important sources on the theory of closed networks and time-shared systems are: BUZE71, COFF73, KLEI76, and WONG75.

3. THE BASIC MODEL

3.1. Overview of the Procedure

1. Develop appropriate models of all processes and resource usages identified on the transaction flows.
2. Using the transaction flows as a basis, set up and solve the flow balance equations to find the flows into each element of the network.
3. Using the results of steps 1 and 2 above, combine the subsidiary models into aggregate models where each aggregate corresponds to a physical server such as a CPU, I/O device, channel, etc.
4. Treat each aggregate model as appropriate as a $(M/M/1), (M/G/1),$ or $(GI/G/1)$ queueing system to obtain the relation between throughput and delay for the aggregate model.
5. If there is still a network at this point treat it as a queueing network problem, using the methodology of Section 7, Chapter 11, to obtain the over-all throughput–delay function. If there is no network left, skip to step 6.
6. Apply the throughput–delay functions derived in steps 4 or 5 above to the transaction flows. You now have an ordinary timing analysis to do, as described in Section 7 of Chapter 11.

While this sounds like a straightforward procedure, steps 3, 4, and 5 require simplifying assumptions and approximations, and there are possibilities for refinements that can substantially escalate the labor.

3.2. The Model, Its Limitations, and the Crux of the Problem

Figure 13-2 shows the transaction flow reinterpreted as a network of queueing subsystems. It is an ordinary timing analysis model (if flow is conserved). That is the first limitation. The model must consist of decisions, processes, and junctions. If it is a general activity network, in which time is determined by min or max terms, it cannot be handled by these techniques. The presence of AND junctions that lead to max functions, or OR junctions that lead to min functions and corresponding MUST branches (see Chapter 6 for a refresher), obviates these techniques.

A second problem is evident. I have labeled the queues in two sets, $A1, A2, A3, A4$ and $B1, B2, B3, B4$. Now let the A set correspond to different processes executed by the same CPU, and the B set correspond to different transfers to the same disc. The model does not fit any previously examined queueing network model. The individual queueing processes cannot be treated as separate, independent subsystems because that would be equivalent to assuming a multiserver model where one does not exist. Somehow, they must be treated as an

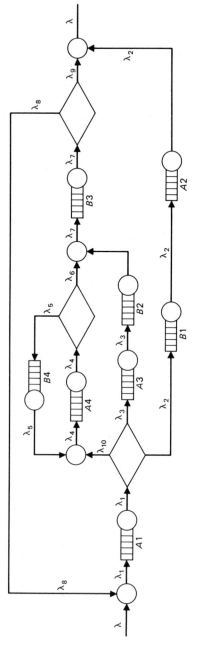

Figure 13-2. Transaction flow as a network of queueing subsystems.

aggregate without compromising the interrelation between the B components and the A components. Unfortunately, while they can be treated as an aggregate, the interrelation of the structure must be compromised.

There is a third limitation; there is no simple way of accurately including the effect of priority structures. You can think of the effect of priority structures as superimposing a set of quasi-dependent networks one at each priority level. The higher priority "networks" impact the lower, but not vice versa to any great degree. The A processes need not have priority structures that are compatable to those of the B processes, and passage of tasks between high priority level networks and low priority level networks can occur.

Summarizing these limitations and adding a few more:

1. The transaction flow must have been reduced to a simple timing analysis model with decisions, processes, and junctions.
2. The component queueing substystems must be aggregated and each set represented by an (almost) equivalent single server.
3. There is no way to rigorously handle multi-priority levels.
4. There is no way to reasonably handle multi-servers.
5. The arrivals at a junction from several different branches are not truly and completely independent.
6. If and when you do manage to reduce the problem to that of analyzing a queueing network, that entire treatment is approximate also.

But we're not downhearted, are we? As usual our approach will be based on four beliefs: (1) some answer is better than none; (2) uncertainty in the source data leads to bigger errors than most modeling assumptions; (3) if the structure is big enough, things will smooth out; and (4) most simplifications are pessimistic. We shall ignore analytical niceties and forge ahead with simplified models that yield workable answers.

3.3. Tasks, Transactions, and the Conservation of Flows

All the queueing network models have so far assumed that there is a single entrance and a single exit, and that for every input there is an output. In reality this is not the case, but it is relatively easy to get around that problem:

1. You can gather all the input rates into a single fictitious source node followed immediately by a decision that subdivides the input flow into the proper proportions.
2. You can gather all output rates to a fictitious junction node that leads them out of the system.
3. Non-outputs (i.e., transactions that are dropped) pass through fictitious processes that add nothing to the delay on their way to the unique, fictitious, outway junction.

With suitable transformations of this kind, you can always arrange to have the conservation of flow condition satisfied. Conservation of flow is probably the most basic assumption you have to make. However, it is *transaction* flows that are conserved; this does not necessarily correspond to the conservation of *task* flows. A transaction consists of a succession of tasks. That which constitutes a task is effectively arbitrary and chosen for convenience in modeling. Discrepancies between task flows and transaction flows can occur, as the following communications example shows. A transaction passes through the following processing phase: input, input processing, storage on disc, retrieval from disc, output processing, and output. From the point of view of transactions, there is one transaction in and one out. The task appearance is considerably different:

1. The disc model works in terms of storage blocks—each task to the disc queueing subsystem represents N blocks, where N is the average number of blocks per message.
2. Furthermore, a double copy of the message is written, but only one read. Consequently writing produces $2N$ blocks per task, while reading produces N blocks per task.
3. Even further yet, the average incoming message produces 1.7 outgoing messages. Consequently disc read operations are at a rate of 1.7 blocks per message. The same is true of output and output processing.

In principle, it may be desirable to express arrival rates differently for every queueing subsystem of the network, using that task definition which is most appropriate to the submodel under consideration. This represents a complication in the analysis, since potentially you may have to translate back and forth between definitions for every different queue type. Particular care must be taken with feedback loops and associated probabilities. You recall that you had to solve the flow balance equations to obtain the input rate for each queue in the network (see Chapter 11). Feedback loops must be expressed in terms of transactions and the flow equations solved accordingly. In the communications system described above, the analysis of flows was particularly simple—there was no feedback, there were no decisions, consequently the transaction arrival rates for all queueing subsystems were identical.

Consider a slight complication for Figure 13-2. Say that in the *A4–B4* loop the only probability we could get, the only sensible model, was to express the feedback in terms of tasks, say blocks, rather than transactions. Perhaps this shows that some block have to be reread because of malfunctions, or some other reason. To handle this case, solve a local flow balance based on identical tasks involving only those two subsystems. Since the flow balance has nothing to do with nature of the queueing process, but only the structure of the network and the probabilities, you will arrive at the proper task arrival rates for processes *A4* and *B4*.

4. THE PROCEDURE

4.1. Step 1—Develop the Subsidiary Models

That is what the first eleven chapters of this book are all about. Because these are queueing models, typically $(M/G/1)$ or $(GI/G/1)$, the variance of the service time is more important than it was for the analysis of cyclic systems. If you can't get those variances, because there are no equations for them, or because the work is gruesome and not worth it, then you might want to use an exponential assumption for the distribution. This is usually pessimistic. You can get a handle on the possible validity of such an assumption as follows.

1. If the flowchart is dominated by serial subprocesses, deterministic loops, and relatively few parallel paths, then the variance will be less than the mean and an exponential assumption will be pessimistic.
2. If the flowchart is dominated by parallel subprocesses with large variations in the processing time along different branches, the exponential assumption will be optimistic.
3. Look at the 10 most important paths, or that small set (if any) which account for 80-90% of the time spent in that process in order to judge if 1 or 2 above applies.
4. Use a simplified model of the process, find its mean and variance. Get the ratio of the square of the mean to the variance. This should be (in an asynchronous system) reasonably independent of the load. Express the variance as the product of the real mean and that ratio, rather than using an exact expression for the variance.

4.2. Step 2—Solve the Flow Balance Equations

Whatever task definitions might be convenient in the analysis of individual queueing subsystems, it must be related back to transaction definitions that are applicable system-wide. This is mostly a matter of bookkeeping rather than theory; it is a point where errors creep in. Check each one dimensionally before you solve the equations—you might be adding apples and oranges.

4.3. Step 3—Aggregate the Subsidiary Models

Let's take a closer look at server $A1$ and $A2$ of Figure 13-2 (see Figure 13-3). A is one server which, for convenience's sake, we had chosen to look at as four separate queueing subsystems. *All four subsystems are identical.* The difficulty with this model is twofold. There are four different arrival populations and the server treats each population differently. If we had nice general solutions for this situation, the only differences in delay would arise from the combination of arrival statistics and server behavior for each of the four different queues. Exact

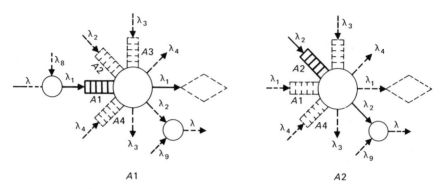

A1   A2

Figure 13-3. A closer look at servers *A1* and *A2* of Figure 13-2.

solutions are not available, and rigorous approximations are intractable. However, it is not all that difficult to approximate this model. Replace it with an $(M/G/1)$ model whose service behavior is defined by

$$\frac{1}{\mu} = \frac{\sum \lambda_i \frac{1}{\mu_i}}{\sum \lambda_i} \tag{13.1a}$$

$$\sigma_\mu{}^2 = \frac{\sum \lambda_i \sigma_{\mu i}{}^2}{\sum \lambda_i} + \frac{\sum \frac{\lambda_i}{\mu_i{}^2}}{\sum \lambda_i} - \left[\frac{\sum \frac{\lambda_i}{\mu_i}}{\sum \lambda_i}\right]^2 \tag{13.1b}$$

This is nothing more than the familiar parallel equations corresponding to a timing model of the form:

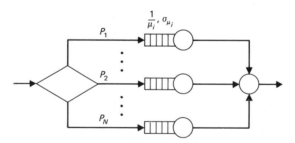

where $P_i = \lambda_i/\sum \lambda_i$.

You now have a mean service rate and variance suitable for use in an $(M/GI/1)$ or $(GI/G/1)$ queueing system model. The flow to that model is of course, $\sum \lambda_i$.

Do this for each model, the CPU, the channel(s), the disc, or whatever else may have been in the original queueing network based on the transaction flows.

4.4. Steps 4 and 6

Use the expression appropriate to each aggregate model to obtain the throughput-delay relation for that aggregate model. Replace every occurrence of a submodel of an aggregate in the transaction flow with its aggregate model and aggregate flows. For any throughput (system-wide arrival rate), these copies will give the correct mean delay, which you now interpret as a processing time. You now have an ordinary timing model with times, variances, and probabilities. Solve it in the ordinary way. The time obtained by this procedure is the mean transaction delay; the variance is the system-wide variance.

4.5. Step 5

Go back to Figure 13-2 and consider a slightly different situation depicted in Figure 13-4. It is clear that there are three essentially independent networks in operation here. $C1$, $B1/B2$, and $A1/A2/A3/A4/A5$. Any transaction that starts in one of these networks either remains in that queueing subsystem or leaves it before going to another queueing subsystem. The component networks are re-solvable into queueing subsystems. A more formal way of putting this is to say that a server with multiple appearances can be aggregated into an equivalent server with a single appearance if:

1. starting at the proposed aggregate inway it is possible to reach every component of the aggregate without passing through an intervening queue that belongs to some other aggregate;
2. the position within the resulting queueing network into which the aggregate is to be placed can be uniquely identified (all possible positions have identical effects on the resulting queueing network's behavior).

The A group of Figure 13-4 can be replaced by an equivalent queueing subsystem, as shown in Figure 13-5. However, if $C1/B1$ had been appearances of the same server they could not form an aggregate, because we would not know whether to place the aggregate in the $C1$ position or in the $B1$ position.

A closer approximation of the system's behavior can be obtained if all servers are resolvable in this way. The process then consists of aggregating the servers individually as in step 4, and then (here's the difference) using one of the network models described in Chapter 11, Section 7.2, or for more accuracy, Section 7.3.

Suppose the network is only resolvable in part? Split it into a resolvable portion and an unresolvable portion. Use step 4 analysis for the unresolvable portions and step 5 for the resolvable portions.

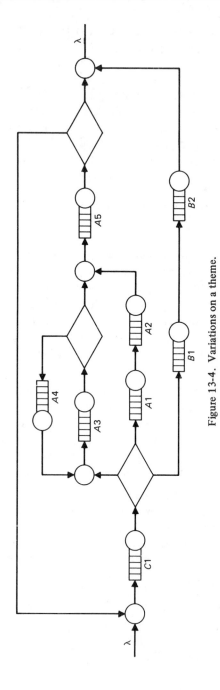

Figure 13-4. Variations on a theme.

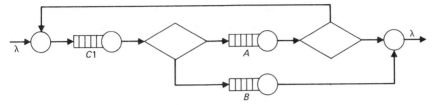

Figure 13-5. Variations on a theme simplified.

5. MULTI-PRIORITY MODELS

5.1. General

Servers, particularly CPUs, operate at several priority levels. A priority scheme is inherent in every asynchronous system. The CPU is a single server. It must process tasks on several different queues. There must be a rule by which the next task to be processed will be selected.

The priority scheme is often mechanized as software executed by a centralized executive program or "scheduler." The priority levels that the executive works with do not necessarily correspond to the physical priority levels that may be built into the hardware. Consequently, while there may be only two or three different hardware levels, operationally, through the action of the executive, there may be tens or hundreds. Thirty to forty levels would not be extreme in a moderately complicated system. Priorities need not be explicit; they can be implicit in the ordering of tasks on queues.

5.2. High Priority Functions, Stretch, and Global Stretch

The highest priority level is made up of hardware demands for memory, typically arising from DMA transfers. Following these are load independent interrupts and their associated processing. These can be treated as global stretch. Unlike cyclic systems in which it is possible to allocate stretch to various transfers and processing, the randomness of the asynchronous system implies that no such possibility will exist. In effect, all stretch is global. Every level of a priority queueing system, however, stretches every level beneath it—and some levels may be on the transaction flow path and others not. The distinction is important. Typically, interrupt processing, except for initial input, is not on the processing path in the transaction flow. For example, part of the transaction processing includes a write to memory. The completion of the write operation is signaled by an interrupt which is processed. If the transaction must wait for the completion of that interrupt processing to proceed to the next phase of its processing, the interrupt is on the path and should have been included. If, however, the purpose of the interrupt is not to block the transaction, but merely to cause the initiation of the next disc operation, it is not on the path and need not be considered except as a contribution to stretch. Recall the form for the priority queue equation (T11.42):

$$\frac{F(\lambda_i, \mu_i)}{2(1 - \sigma_i)(1 - \sigma_{i-1})}$$

where: $\sigma_i = \Sigma_{j=1}^{i} \rho_j$.

σ_{i-1} is recognizable as the sum of all demands higher than priority level i. It is precisely a stretch factor that can be applied to T_s. The first step, then, is to evaluate all high priority functions that cannot directly block the progress of a transaction through the queueing network. Calculate the associated stretch function; this will be used to multiply all timings obtained by the subsequent multi-priority analysis.

5.3. Separability by Levels

You have established the true, functionally distinct priority levels for the CPU. Each level consists of a number of different service routines, each with its own processing time and variance. Furthermore, because you have solved the flow equations, you know the arrival rates for each service module. You have eliminated all the levels that do not directly block the progress of a transaction flow diagram. Because of the priority scheme, you can apply separability considerations separately to each level. Thus, while levels 1, 2, and 4 may not be separable, and will therefore have to be treated as an aggregate server, level 3 might be separable and it is possible to obtain a more accurate model of that level's behavior. Since it is only the total resource utilization at the higher levels that matters as far as the lower levels are concerned, it does not matter what kind of model you use at each level—it cannot affect the results of the other levels. Figure 13-6 shows the situation. The subscript is the priority level. If this were not a priority system then it would not be possible to separate the A system because of the intervention of $B1$, $C1$, and $C2$. However, because the A's are operating at three different priority levels, $A1_2$ and $A2_2$ can be aggregated into a simpler subnetwork. Similarly, $A1_3$ can be treated separately. However, $A1_1$ and $A2_1$ must be averaged because of the intervention of the B's and C's. Note that in this type of treatment, a queue at a different priority level plays the same role as a queue belonging to an entirely different device. The resulting, simplified model is shown in Figure 13-7.

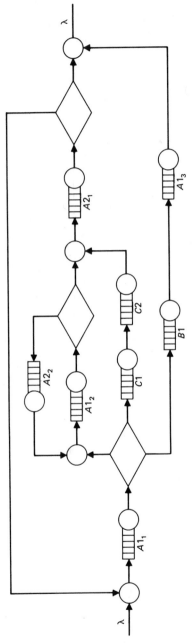

Figure 13-6. A multi-priority example.

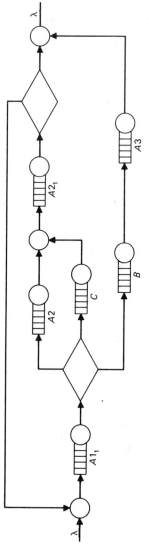

Figure 13-7. The multi-priority example simplified.

5.4. Analysis

1. Develop appropriate models of all processes and resource usages identified on the transaction flow.
2. Using the transaction flows as a basis, set up and solve the flow balance equations and find the flows into each element of the network where elements have been identified by functional priority levels for each serving device.
3. Examine the network for separability by device and by priority level within each device.
4. Simplify those subnetworks that are separable, using the timing analysis equations.
5. Replace each queue that was not separable by device/priority by an equivalent queueing subsystem whose parameters are those of the averages of its components.
6. For every device evaluate the utilization factors for every priority level and the stretch factors for every level. Apply these factors to the timing expressions for all affected queues.
7. If there is still a network at this point, treat it as a queueing network problem, using the methodology of Chapter 11, Section 7; then go to step 8. If there is no network, go directly to step 8.
8. Apply the throughput–delay functions obtained in steps 1–7 above to the transaction flows, and proceed as for an ordinary timing analysis model.

6. UTILIZATION VERSUS DEMAND AND MODEL VALIDITY

Cyclic systems are not necessarily bound by one resource, since the binding factor can change from point to point in the cycle. Usually such systems are out of tune (at least at that load level). Typically, one resource will be the ultimate limiting factor at high load. Differences between demand and utilizations come about because:

1. there is "make-work processing" that grows to fill the gaps;
2. there is batching overhead which becomes amortized over more and more tasks as load is increased;
3. there are "gaps" during which a resource is blocked and cannot be used by any other process—therefore, while not actually used, it is utilized.

None of the above situations exist in the ideal asynchronous system, and consequently the utilization of resources and the demands are identical. Unfortunately, all three of the above are operative in a real asynchronous system.

1. If there are no tasks to process, the executive will at least buzz around the system to check if there is something to do. Good design dictates that it continues to do so until interrupted. This policy will minimize reaction time, but provides a load dependent overhead, and therefore a difference between demand and utilization.
2. Batching is used for many things: interrupt processing, disc and drum optimization, some task processing, executive level functions, and the like.
3. There are gaps that can disable the use of a resource while waiting for completion of some task.

A reexamination of the numerous simplifying assumptions and the various models discussed for asynchronous systems should lead you to the conclusion that there is no mechanism in these techniques to incorporate such effects. How does that influence the resulting analysis? It tends to be optimistic at low load levels. The error is not significant, though—typically comparable to the mean processing time of uninterruptable overhead functions. As load is increased, the models become less optimistic. This optimism, however, must be balanced against the use of pessimistic, heavy load approximations for $(GI/G/1)$ queueing subsystems and disc/drum latency models.

7. EXERCISES

NOTE: All of these exercises are variations on the model described in exercise 1. Find the throughput/delay function, the SR function, and the total number of items queued. Transactions arrive at a rate of R per second.

1. An asynchronous system consists of five processes whose execution time is given by:

   T_a = 0.05 seconds, activated once per second;
   T_b = 0.026 seconds per transaction;
   T_c = 0.001 seconds per second, at random, at a high-priority level;
   T_d = 0.11 seconds per transaction;
   T_e = 0.022 seconds per transaction.

   A task first passes through process d and then through process b, after which it leaves the system. Process e, while depending on the transaction arrival rate, does not directly affect the processing delay.
2. Modify T_b so that it contains a loop with a looping probability of 0.01 and a new process T_f in the feedback loop that requires 0.2 seconds per transaction.
3. In exercises 1 and 2 above, assume that all processes except b and f can operate at different priority levels, with a the highest, b-f the next, followed by c, d, and e.

4. Continuation. If you have complete freedom to assign the priority levels, there are potentially 120 systems to work with. Assume rather, that you can assign the levels for processes b-f, c, d, and e. This is only 24 different systems to play with. A little bit of thinking should convince you that there are only two cases worth looking at. Determine which design has the better system behavior. Can the ultimate throughput be affected by your machinations? Investigate the system behavior with variations in the looping probability.

5. For the original system, with processes in the following order: a, b, d, c, e, replace process b with $T_b = 0.026 + 0.0005N_{qd}$, where N_{qd} is the number of items on the process d queue. (Estimate only.)

6. For the original system, with processes in the order a, b, d, c, e, replace process b with $T_b = 0.026 + 0.0005N_{qb}$.

7. Modify exercises 1–4 above by the addition of a drum write following process d. The drum rotates at 1800 rpm and has 16 sectors. Process b cannot be initiated until the write for that transaction is done. Investigate the system's behavior when each write is 1, 2, 4, 8, and 16 sectors long. Assume a scheduled drum.

8. Do exercise 7 assuming that the sector writes are sequential. That is, each transaction requires a write of 1, 2, 4, 8, or 16 contiguous sectors. (Careful!)

9. Do exercise 7 assuming a FIFO drum.

10. Repeat exercises 7–9 eliminating the restriction of waiting for the completion of drum write prior to the initiation of process b.

11. Repeat exercises 5 and 6 with the addition of the drum of exercise 7 and the restriction on the initiation of process b.

12. Repeat exercises 5 and 6 with the addition of the drum of exercise 7 and no restriction on the initiation of process b.

14
Static and Dynamic Memory Utilization

1. SYNOPSIS

Memory can be divided into two categories—static and dynamic. Static memory utilization is not load dependent. Dynamic memory utilization is. Static memory estimation is conceptually trivial, but practically difficult. Dynamic memory utilization is conceptually difficult, but practically simple. This chapter concerns some tips regarding the estimation of static memory and approaches to the formal analysis of dynamic memory requirements.

2. STATIC VERSUS DYNAMIC MEMORY

2.1. Which Memories?

Memory sizing is required for all storage devices, whether or not the designer has control over size. If the size is modifiable (as in main memory, or discs, or ROM), the object of memory analysis is to determine how much should be provided. If the size is not controllable, the objective is to determine the consequence of not having enough. The same approach is used for all memory devices—discs, tapes, main memory, bubble memories, whatnot.

2.2. Static Memory

Static memory refers to those portions of the memory (whatever device) whose size is independent of load. Examples of static memory are:

1. Program space in main, ROM, disc overlays, etc.
2. Fixed allocation tables and data base elements.
3. Working space for temporaries, buffers, etc., that are permanently assigned to processes or functions.

While the amount of memory allocated to a function may be variable, this does not in itself make it dynamic. For example, the size of the data base depends (among other things) on the number of terminals that are connected to the system. That number changes from day to day. This does not make that segment of the data base dynamic. From the point of view of performance issues, as measured over a period of seconds, the allocation of memory to this function is static. The test for static versus dynamic is load dependency; if the memory quantity does not change as a function of load it is static memory.

2.3. Dynamic Memory

Dynamic memory refers to those portions of the memory (in whatever device) for which demand is a function of load. Examples of dynamic memory are:

1. process queue space;
2. data buffers;
3. control stacks;
4. data stacks;
5. shared buffers, even if permanently allocated.

A memory location or segment may be taken out of a dynamically allocated pool but may functionally be static. For example, the first twenty queue blocks in a list of available queue blocks are permanently assigned to the executive or are assigned to the executive program at start-up time. They are continuously held by the executive for its own use. The usage is not dynamic, it is static. A disc storage area is used to store old transactions for thirty days. The usage is dynamic, because even though the data is held for a long period of time, the amount that is required depends on the average load over the thirty day period as a first approximation. A memory requirement is dynamic if the demand is zero at zero load, while any memory demand that remains at zero load is static, not dynamic.

2.4. Mixed Cases

Reconsider the example of the queue blocks assigned to the executive program. Two allocation policies are possible.

1. The identity of the assigned memory blocks is constant. That is, the executive hangs on to specific blocks, by name or number, and uses them. Those blocks are never available to another user.
2. The executive is assured (by means of some priority scheme) of having N blocks at all times, but the identity is allowed to change. The executive returns used blocks to the pool, but is always given new ones in return (at a later time, perhaps).

In both cases, using the criteria of Sections 2.2 and 2.3, we would say that the allocation was static, rather than dynamic. However, the treatment of the two cases is distinctly different. The first case is that of a private resource. The second case is that of a shared resource with priority. Shared resources are treated by dynamic memory analysis. The constant demand is simply added to the load dependent demand, for reasons that will become clear in the sequel. The real issue, then, is not simply whether or not the demand is load dependent, but whether or not the resource is shared. If a static shared demand is treated as static memory, then the analysis will be pessimistic. The degree of pessimism depends on just how big the total resource is (e.g., memory blocks) and the relative sizes of the static and dynamic components.

3. STATIC MEMORY ESTIMATION

3.1. General

There are no elegant analytical tools for the estimation of static memory requirements. Static memory is evaluated by the conceptually simple but practically difficult process of counting. There is no way to tell *a priori* how much static space will be required. It can, however, be accurately estimated given sufficient information.

3.2. Program Space

This is usually the largest segment of static storage. The analytical procedures used for timing analysis are not a proper guide here. Recall that we were able to ignore most of the code because it concerned statistically insignificant exception conditions. You cannot do this in estimating space, because all program space must be counted. The procedure is an exercise in bookkeeping.

1. Start at the lowest levels, with common subroutines and macros.
2. Macros can be insidious, since they result in code expansion.
3. Be sure to include space taken for calling sequences. They are easy to forget, but in a modular program can add up significantly.
4. Do not double count. Programs or routines that are overlaid should be ignored; the space is accounted for in the overlay buffer.
5. Be sure to properly account for jump tables, indirect memory locations, and other, similar operations that do not result in one-instruction-one-location.
6. Try to keep your estimates (i.e., guesses) to the lowest possible level in the call tree. A lot of errors will cancel themselves. The lower the level at which the guesses are made, the better the results. For example, an error of ± 10% at the subroutine level is not at all the same as a similar error at the top level. The 10% guess at the bottom level can result in a (statistical) error of only 1%.
7. Programmers are notorious for keeping contingency space; they pad their estimates to be on the safe side. If everybody is padding, you will overesti-

mate. Calibrate each estimate (and estimator); you want the most accurate estimate, not the worst-worst-worst estimate. One way around this problem is to ask each programmer to specify his expected value, worst value, and best value. You can then do the analysis three ways and do not have to bother with calibrations; you get a more honest answer this way.

8. If you have real code, use it as a basis; even if it is wrong and not yet debugged, it is better than a guess. Code can contract as often as expand during debugging. Keep records as to the state of the code or the source, as follows:

(a) sheer guess;
(b) extrapolation from similar routines on previous machines or similar applications;
(c) based on undebugged code;
(d) based on debugged code.

3.3. Date Base and Table Space

The data base can be subdivided into three categories of elements.

1. Absolutely fixed single entry: there is exactly one entry of the given type and it must exist.
2. Multiple entries set by environment: there are N entries of the given type. The number of entries depends on the installation and is related to some simple parameter (e.g., number of terminals, number of fixed records, number of formats, etc.).
3. Multiple entries—tuning dependent: there are N entries of a given type; the number of entries can be varied in the interest of changing the system's performance characteristics.

The elements of the data base should be contained in a master data base document, often called a data dictionary. The data dictionary will usually contain all type 2 and type 3 entries. Type 1 entries may have to be extracted from listings, typically in the declaration areas of the source code. Be sure you know how to read the declaration formats. As in estimating program space, this is an exercise in bookkeeping:

1. Identify all type 1 elements, either actual or arrived at by guesses. Get as microscopic as you can. Avoid statements like: "and 5000 words for miscellaneous. . . ." Break it down it down. The same principles that applied to code size estimation also work here. A lot of little guesses are better than a few big ones. Highest validity should be given to bona fide, debugged declarations— lowest to guesses. You will inevitably have to use a mix.
2. Type 2 entries are multiplied by a constant. Identify the constant. For type

2 entries, the constant (or constants) is (are) site dependent. Make sure that the model site is realistic and corresponds to that which is to be installed. You may have to keep the size parametric, since memory requirements could be what limits site capacity.

3. Type 3 entries are also multiplied by a constant; however, that constant is a tuning parameter. Estimate maximum, minimum, and expected values for all such parameters. You may (and probably will) have to go back after doing the performance analysis and modify the initial values (see Chapter 16 on tuning). The initial values are probably wrong.

3.4. Working Space

Working space is in principle and practice no different from estimating the table space. It is, however, more insidious. The primary sources of errors in this area are:

1. Failure to recognize numerous, small, private caches of temporary work space (this is especially common if the source language allows implicit declarations of temporaries, as FORTRAN does, for example).
2. Failure to recognize private work space invoked by macros.
3. Failure to account for temporaries generated by subroutine calls.
4. Failure to recognize that a whole bunch of private temporaries are equivalenced at a higher level.
5. Failure to recognize that a private area is defined in the data base.

3.5. Other Static Space

Static storage estimation is easiest done from assembly language source code. There is relatively little hidden space in such code. If a higher order source language is used, then there will be much hidden space, particularly in undeclared temporaries, calling sequences, private space for macros and built-in functions, and space reserved by the HOL and (as in FORTRAN for example) the run-time resident portion of the compiler. Documentation for this kind of static space is often sketchy. Two approaches are possible: you can badger the compiler designer, or you can look at the produced assembly level code. The latter is often the simpler approach. A representative sample of assembly language code can give you a handle on the expansion factor due to the HOL. Assembly languages, however, are not immune to the production of hidden space, and each must be examined in detail.

A second source of hidden static storage is that which is implicit in the hardware. The documentation of most computers identifies this storage. For example, "the first N words of memory are reserved for register storage," etc. Here again, there are no general principles, other than that a deep understanding of the system hardware and software is essential. The better the knowledge, the better the estimate.

4. DYNAMIC STORAGE ESTIMATION—GENERAL PRINCIPLES

4.1. Overview

Dynamic storage is subdivided into **pools** of identical elements or **blocks**. Pools have the following characteristics:

1. Their blocks are shared with no other pool.
2. All blocks in a pool are identical (i.e., the same size).
3. All blocks are statistically equivalent; any block is as good as any other, and assignment is random.
4. There is a functionally identifiable, centralized point (e.g., routine) that assigns blocks to users. There is another (possibly different) point to which blocks are returned. The assignment function and the return function need not use the same mechanism.

Each pool is treated separately. Examples of pools are: queue blocks, buffer blocks, and dynamically allocated work areas. A pool may reside on a disc, in main memory, or on another device. Each device is treated separately.

The models discussed here are variations on a theme first examined by A. K. Erlang around 1917 in conjunction with telephone exchange design problems. For this reason, most of the useful data, charts, tables, etc., are found in the telecommunications literature rather than in the computer literature. The problem considered by Erlang concerned determining the proper number of interexchange trunks. There are two telephone exchanges, say, each having a large number of directly connected subcribers. While most of the calls may be local to the exchange, a significant fraction of them will be routed to the other exchange over interexchange connections or **trunks**. If a trunk is not available, the call is said to be **blocked** and user gets a busy signal. The question is, how many trunks should be provided to handle a specified traffic load.

The above specification is incomplete; it lacks a probability. If the users are willing to accept a blocking probability of 1.0, then clearly, no interexchange trunks are required. Conversely, if the user demands zero blocking, then there must be a trunk for every user. Since the number of users for a typical telephone exchange is large (10,000-40,000) the number of trunks needed approaches (practically speaking) infinity. A complete specification of the problem, then, consists of the load, the blocking probability, and the number of trunks (servers).

The transformation of this problem to determining the pool size is direct:

trunks = blocks

traffic = demand

blocking probability = pool overflow probability.

Restating the problem, the objectives of memory analysis are as follows.

1. Given the demand (in blocks = erlangs) on the pool, and the size of the pool, find the overflow probability.
2. Given the demand and an acceptable overflow probability, find the size of the pool.
3. Given the size of the pool and an acceptable overflow probability, determine the maximum demand.

4.2. Oueue Block Analysis

It seems that there is a need for analyical techniques for buffer blocks, since this has not been covered elsewhere in this book. Why queue blocks? Is this not just the sum of the N_q (more precisely N_s) *for all the queues using the given pool? The answer is, yes and (mostly) no, because:

1. Not all usage of the queue blocks corresponds to the explicit number on queue as determined in Chapter 11 (optimistic).
2. Some of the "queues" determined by formulas from Chapter 11 could be in static space, rather than dynamic.
3. We must know the queue size distribution to get the probability of overflow, and this is available only for the simplest queueing system (generally, approximations must be used—optimistic or pessimistic).
4. The sum of the N_q treats each queue as an individual pool—the savings implicit in a shared resource are not analyzed (pessimistic).
5. While a task may spend N seconds on the queue, the queue block used to store the task was allocated before the task joined the queue and will be released only after the task leaves the queue (optimistic).
6. While a transaction may progress from queue to queue, the same queue block might be used throughout the task's lifetime (pessimistic).
7. A given transaction, while on a given queue, may consume one queue block, several queue blocks, or a fraction of a queue block (optimistic or pessimistic).

It should be clear from the above observations that the jumble of optimism and pessimism resulting from the assumption that the pool size is the sum of the individual queue sizes can lead to arbitrary answers.

---

*Because most routines hold on to the queue block while the task is being serviced.

4.3. Overflow, Real and Impending

A transaction is blocked because it cannot get a buffer block, a queue block, stack space, or some other dynamically allocated space resource. What does the system do with that transaction? Several options are possible.

1. The transaction or task is discarded.
2. The transaction is delayed until resources are available.
3. The transaction is temporarily handled by an overflow procedure.

All three are possible. A data-logging system or a process control system in which new transactions are generated automatically can afford to totally discard a blocked transaction. Blocking in such systems is equivalent to reducing the sample rate. A system that employs polling to obtain inputs from remotely located terminals can also discard a polling transaction. Blocking induces a lowered polling rate.

The second option is the most common one used in computer systems. The task or transaction is delayed until the resource again becomes available. Presumably the designers have reserved enough resources of the required type to prevent lock-up. The system can **lock-up** when a resource is needed (directly or indirectly) to free the same kind of resource. For example, a queue block is needed by the executive program to release low priority queue blocks. If one has not been reserved the system will lock, since it cannot release the block it needs.

The third option is common in communications systems. The transaction is shunted to an overflow medium (e.g., disc storage as overflow storage for main memory). When the resource next becomes available, the transaction or task will be returned to the mainstream.

Most systems will not allow actual overflow to occur. The system monitors the resource's availability. When that availability falls below specified threshold values, processing is altered to prevent the actual occurrence of overflow. Thus, the data logger or process control system will drop to a lower sampling rate when the available buffer blocks or queue blocks fall below the specified minimum. Communication systems will reduce polling rates, or start shutting traffic sources off, before running out of queue blocks or buffer blocks. Overflow or blocking probabilities, then, are really *impending* overflow probabilities, i.e., the probability that the overflow mechanism will be invoked in the absence of corrective measures.

4.4. Acceptable Probabilities

The common practice in telephony is to provide a blocking probability of 0.01 for trunks, and 0.001 for control equipment (that are analyzed the same way). These values are totally inadequate for most computer problems.

Queue blocks, stacks, and similar pools related to control issues are typically sized at very low probabilities, in the range of 10^{-6}-10^{-10}. In many systems, unavailability of queue blocks implies loss of control, since it may not be possible to even refuse the transaction because of lock-up problems. In systems where transaction loss cannot be tolerated (e.g., military communication systems) queue block overflow probabilities of 10^{-10} are not uncommon. The data logger example could tolerate higher queue block overflow probabilities. To get a handle on tolerable queue block overflow probabilities, consider the following.

1. Interpret the probabilities as a percentage of transaction (i.e., one transaction out of N). Knowing the transaction arrival rate, as averaged over long periods of time, translate the probability further into expected time between refusals—e.g., one transaction every thirty days, every century, etc. There are no general rules and the correct answer is application-specific.

2. What are the consequences of blocking? The system fails? The user is annoyed? There is a temporary loss of accuracy? The more dire the consequence the lower the required probability.

3. What is the cost in terms of processing time and space, and the development cost, to include a load-quenching mechanism that will prevent the overflow? Compare that to the cost of sufficient additional memory to provide blocking probability low enough to allow you to ignore the problem.

Much the same considerations apply to buffer blocks. In most systems, buffer block loss implies loss or delay of data. This is usually more tolerable than control loss. Consequently, overflow probabilities in the range of 10^{-3}-10^{-7} are typically acceptable. If the system has a back-up store (e.g., a disc) that can be used for overflow data, then high blocking probabilities (10^{-2}-10^{-4}) may be acceptable. A trade-off analysis is essential here to judge between low overflow probabilities (and large buffer areas) and high overflow probabilities with an overflow mechanism.

While in principle the probability of overflow should be specified by the buyer, it rarely is. That decision rests almost always with the designer; the most likely answer from the buyer is "never." As we know, "never" implies an infinite budget.

5. COMPONENTS OF THE MODELS

5.1. General

Each pool is treated as a multi-server queueing system. There are several different models, which reflect different user habits and different consequences of blocking. The models then, require:

1. the number of servers;
2. the request arrival rate;
3. the server time (distribution);
4. the overflow probability;
5. the characteristics of the servers and customers.

5.2. Number of Servers

The number of servers is the number of blocks in the pool. This does not neces-sarily correspond to the number of blocks programmed or declared. Effective use is what counts, not what may be declared. The following examples illustrate the source of potential differences:

1. A buffer block is subdivided into smaller blocks which are dynamically allocated. A pool is constructed out of a large, fixed array. The servers are the smaller blocks or the subdivisions of the array.
2. A transaction is forced, for whatever reason, to be allocated to a queue block and simultaneously to a buffer block. The server is the queue block–buffer block pair.
3. A transaction spans a fixed number of blocks, say N. The server is the N block set, not the individual blocks.

Identify the servers. They will usually correspond in a direct way to the declared queue or buffer block definition, but need not. The analysis must be done from the point of view of effective servers, rather than declared servers.

5.3. Request Arrival Rates

Redo the entire analysis of the system based on a simplified model in which you have identified all requests for a given pool. In principle, there will be a separate model for each pool. In the steady state, request rates must equal return rates, or else the system is destroying the pool or creating memory. Therefore, one is as good as the other. Since the requests are less likely to be forgotten, and since there are fewer bugs associated with requests than with returns, it is better to model the request instances than the return instances. Calculate in this manner the mean number of requests for the given pool as a function of the system-wide transaction arrival rate. Note that in cyclic sys-tems you will need the relation of cycle time to throughput to do this. There-fore, timing analysis must precede memory analysis.

This is less work than may appear at first because you have already done the tough analysis for time and delay, and only a small part of the model is involved in the request rate for a given pool. Furthermore, for many pools, the request rate is a simple multiple of the transaction arrival rate.

5.4. The Server Times—Holding Times

In most previous queueing systems we treated the server as an object that operated in accordance its own discipline. That is, its service time was dependent more on its design than on a characteristic of the customer. In general, the service time depends to a great extent on the customer rather than the server. Consider a supermarket checkout counter. The server (the checker/bagger) works at a more or less constant rate per item. However, the number of items that have to be served is a customer characteristic. In analyzing a supermarket checkout counter, then, the service time would be a simple multiple of the number of items bought by the customer. If the size of the grocery order is exponentially distributed, the checkout unit will exhibit an exponential service distribution. Similarly, if the size is narrowly distributed (as at a ticket counter) an Erlang service time distribution might be more appropriate. In all of these examples, the actual time taken by the server for a microscopic component of the task is constant. It is the variability of the number of such components that leads to a distributed service time.

The service time for dynamic memory is determined by the **holding time** for the block, i.e., the expected duration over which the block will be in use by the customer. Note that this has nothing to do with productive use. A block is considered to be in use as soon as its use by some other customer would be detrimental. It ceases to be in use when it is possible to fill it with random data without harm. This definition is important because it provides a more precise guideline for judging the period over which the block is held. While this usually corresponds to the time interval between formal allocation and release, as determined by the allocator and/or collector, it need not thus correspond. This kind of confusion can occur when a pool is shared by several users operating at different priority levels, when blocks can be reserved before actually being put to use, and when blocks are returned only long after they have ceased to be functionally useful.

Determining the mean holding time is not difficult if you keep the above principles in mind. The holding time is developed separately for every pool. The holding time is merely the elapsed time between the allocation point and the release point. This is clearly a variation on a theme of delay analysis, in which we assume the starting point (transaction arrival time) to be the allocation point, and the end time (the transaction departure point) to be the release point. You consider the transaction to be a buffer or queue block allocate/release cycle and analyze it as you would any other delay, basing it on an asynchronous or cyclic model as appropriate. This model is of course a submodel of the overall timing/delay model, and is consequently simpler. Usually, it follows directly from the over-all model.

5.5. Demand

The demand is defined as the ratio of the arrival rate to the service rate. The service rate in this case is the reciprocal of the holding time. Consequently, the demand in erlangs is simply the product of the block request rates and the holding times. For example, requests are made at a rate of 30 blocks per second. The mean holding time is 20 seconds (i.e., a service rate of one block per 20 seconds). Therefore, the demand in erlangs is 20 × 30 = 600 erlangs.

Most pools are shared by several users. This is particularly true of queue blocks and buffer blocks; the demand must be determined for each user group separately and then added, rather than the other way around. That is, the request rate for each user group must be multiplied by the holding time for that group. As an example:

Group	Request rate	Holding time	Group erlangs
1	0.001	500	0.5
2	0.1	50	5
3	10	0.5	5
4	100	0.0001	0.01
Correct total erlangs			10.51
Incorrect, average	27.53	137.63	3,788.16

Just so you don't jump to the conclusion that pre-averaging is pessimistic, consider the following example.

Group	Request rate	Holding times	Group erlangs
1	0.0001	0.0001	10^{-8}
2	0.001	0.001	10^{-6}
3	0.01	0.01	10^{-4}
4	0.1	0.1	10^{-2}
5	1	1	1
6	10	10	100
Correct total erlangs			101.010101
Incorrect, averaging	1.85	1.85	3.43

It may seem a trivial and obvious observation for the above cases. However, it is not always so clear when the data looks something like the following.

Group	Request rate	Holding times
1	37.3	10
2	39.4	1.5
3	60	2.2
4	45	3.7

6. THE MODELS

6.1. General Comments

Three different models are provided—Erlang-B, Poisson, and Erlang-C. They differ from the point of view of the customer's behavior. One model is not *a priori* better than the other. You must identify the model best suited to your situation. For large pools (thousands of blocks) and low probabilities (less than 10^{-6}) the three models give almost identical answers. In all cases the models produce a relation of the form

$$\text{overflow probability} = \text{a function (of demand and number of servers)}.$$

A FORTRAN program, fun36, that calculates any one of the three variables in terms of the other two is given in Appendix I. It is accurate to four significant digits for all values of probabilities (to 10^{-20}) and for servers up to 500,000, and probably beyond. The central Gaussian and chi-squared distributions are along for the ride, since they are used as (accurate) approximations for the extremes of the range.

6.2. Loss Systems versus Delay Systems

Consider the consequences of requesting a block and being refused.

1. The refused task disappears and never returns.
2. The refused task waits for service as long as, but no longer than, its expected portion of the service time.
3. The task will keep on trying until it is granted service. Once service is granted, it will take its full service time.

The first case is an example of a loss system, so called because the task is lost to the system. Case 2 and 3 are examples of delay systems, because the task is merely delayed, but not lost. It is intuitively obvious that case 1 is the least stringent, while case 3 is the most stringent. In loss systems, the probability of interest is the probability that a loss will occur. In delay systems, it is the probability of delay that is of interest. Furthermore, in delay systems it is desirable to know the expected duration of the delay as averaged over all transactions, and as averaged only over those transactions that were delayed.

6.3. Case 1—The Erlang-B Formula

This is a loss system. A refused task will disappear. Technically, it is a $(M/G/c)$: $(GI/c/\infty)$ system. Since the maximum queue size is c, and is equal to the number of servers, it is clear that no queue is allowed to form; therefore, it is a loss system. The probability of loss is

$$P_{\text{loss}} = \frac{\rho^c/c!}{\displaystyle\sum_{k=0}^{c} \rho^k/k!}.$$ (14.1)

where

ρ = the total load in erlangs,
c = the number of servers (blocks).

This formula is generally called the Erlang-B formula, or Erlang's second formula. A loss system analysis would be appropriate for a pool with overflow storage. The Erlang-B formula then gives you the probability that the overflow storage would be used. The exact treatment of the overflow storage is complicated and will not be given here. As a first order approximation, use the product of the loss probability and the load to obtain the expected load into the overflow storage medium. That overflow medium is then treated as a loss system or a delay system in its own right. This is a sufficient approximation for most memory problems, but should not be used in general.

6.4. Case 2—The Poisson Formula

This case is relatively rare in computer systems. It is interesting because it falls between the Erlang-B and the Erlang-C, and is easy to calculate. It is a delay system in which the user will spend only the amount of time they expected to spend, regardless of whether or not their service is complete. The delay probability is given by

$$P_{\text{delay}} = \sum_{k=c}^{\infty} \frac{\rho^k e^{-\rho}}{k!}.$$ (14.2)

Technically, this is an $(M/G/c):(GI/\infty/\infty)$ system. It can be shown to follow from the Erlang-B formula when the maximum queue size is allowed to go to infinity.

6.5. Case 3—The Erlang- C Formula

This formula applies in pure delay systems, where the fact that the customer was delayed does not influence the amount of time he will spend in service. The delay probability is given by

$$P_{\text{delay}} = \frac{\rho^c/c! \left(1 - \dfrac{\rho}{c}\right)^{-1}}{\rho^c/c! \left(1 - \dfrac{\rho}{c}\right)^{-1} + \displaystyle\sum_{k=0}^{c-1} \rho^k/k!}. \tag{14.3}$$

The expected delay averaged over all transactions is

$$T_{\text{all}} = \frac{h}{c - \rho} P_{\text{delay}}, \tag{14.4}$$

where h is the mean holding time. The expected delay for those transactions that are delayed is

$$T_{\text{delay}} = \frac{h}{c - \rho}. \tag{14.5}$$

This formula is known as the Erlang-C formula or Erlang's third formula.

6.6. Other Models

Equivalent models for blocking and delay systems exist when the user population must be treated as finite rather than infinite. Such models will not be presented here. The principal difference between finite source population models and infinite source population models is that in a finite source population a customer in service does not generate load. Therefore, the load effectively decreases as more customers are being served. The infinite population models, on the other hand, continue to generate load no matter what the state of the system. The infinite source population models are generally more stringent than the equivalent finite population models. There are significant difficulties in attempting to identify the number in the population—not the least of which is that the size of the calling population may be an output of the analysis and related back to itself in a nontrivial way. Using the infinite source model is slightly pessimistic. At large loads and low probabilities, these models do not differ significantly. For treatment of finite models, see [FRYT65].

6.7. Fixed-Length Buffers

It is not always obvious that something should be treated by this kind of analysis. Sometimes, it is desirable to size a fixed-length buffer. It can also be treated by this kind of analysis if conditions are correct. If the buffer is being used to hold a single transaction or data set, and the entire transaction or data set is read in at one time, then the sizing is also done as a function of overflow probability, but not by using one of the above three formulas. To do this, you must know the transaction length distribution. The overflow probability is then merely the probability that the transaction length will exceed a specified size; knowing the distribution allows you to calculate the required buffer length directly.

If the buffer is used to store information and:

1. it is of variable length,
2. the sources that use it are independent, and
3. the empty space is compacted (closed up) after a transaction leaves,

then, the entire buffer can be treated as a multi-server in which the server is an individual character. The Erlang-B, Erlang-C, or Poisson formulas are used in accordance with the peculiarities of the buffer's use and the user habits, as appropriate.

7. WHY NOT AVERAGES?

One of the more common, reprehensible practices in sizing dynamic memory is to calculate the expected load in erlangs, as discussed above, and use this as the "average" number of blocks required. Then, because experience has shown that this is not a safe number, that value is multiplied by a fat factor of, say, 50% or so. This is presumably safe. If the load is 150 erlangs, then 225 ought to do it. This is a truly miserable approach. It is hopelessly optimistic for small loads and grossly profligate for large loads. Figure 14-1 shows the Erlang-B formula over the range of interest expressed in terms of the fat factor. Assuming a constant overflow probability of 10^{-6}, the fat factors are as follows.

Load	Fat factor
1	9
5	3.7
10	2.8
50	1.7
100	1.5
500	1.2
1,000	1.15
5,000	1.06
10,000	1.04
50,000	1.017
100,000	1.013

A flat 50%, or any other flat percentage, grossly undersizes small pools (where

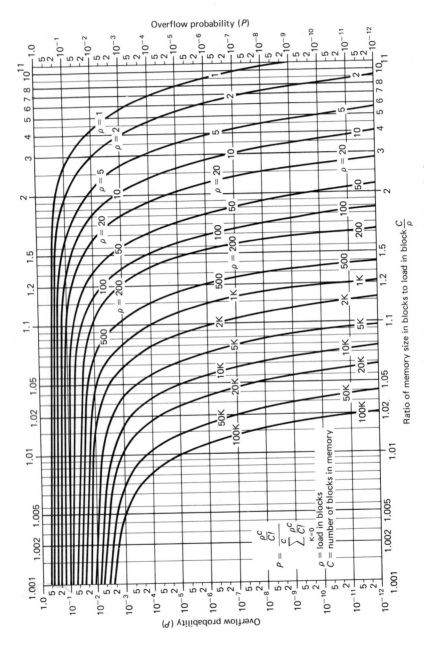

Figure 14-1. Plot of Erlang-B formula for different loads.

this is likely to cause performance problems) and grossly oversizes large pools (where this is likely to cost budget problems).

8. SUMMARY

1. Treat each pool on each device separately.
2. Use a modified system model to determine the request rate for each user population within the pool.
3. Use the delay model to determine the mean holding times for each user population within a pool.
4. The product of the request rate and the holding time is the number of erlangs of load for that user population.
5. Add the erlangs for the various populations to obtain the overall load in erlangs.
6. Determine or obtain a reasonable overflow probability.
7. For the given overflow probability and load, determine the required number of blocks for that pool.
8. For loss systems, obtain the approximate overflow traffic and analyze the requirements for the overflow medium, typically as one of several loads on the overflow medium pool which is used for other functions as well.
9. For a delay system, determine the mean delay and add that to the transaction delay (a very small number which can be safely ignored). Do this for all delay pools that the transaction might have to use.
10. Convert the individual pool requirements, given in blocks, to some common measure such as words or characters. The sum of all the pools is the dynamic memory required.

9. EXERCISES

1. Transactions whose length is L characters are stored in buffer blocks of length $l = c + a$ characters, where c is the number of working characters and a is the length of the administrative field used for link and status data. You want to pack transactions onto the blocks with a minimum of wasted space. Show that the optimum block length is $l = L + a$ characters.
2. Transactions whose mean length is L characters are stored in buffer blocks of length $l = c + a$ characters, where c is the number of working characters and a is the length of the administrative field used for link and status data. You want to pack transactions onto the blocks with a minimum of wasted space. Show that the optimum block length is $l = a + \sqrt{2La}$. You can

assume that blocks are short compared to L. Set up an expression for the wasted space and find the minimum. (Hint: If you follow this to the bitter end you may get only halfway.)

3. Transactions whose mean length . . . etc.   The transactions arrive on a communication line at a rate of s characters per second. Each block is held for a time interval of h seconds for processing over and above the time it takes to fill the block. The block is released immediately after processing. Show that the optimum block size is given by $l = a + \sqrt{sah}$. (Hint: How many erlangs of storage does it take to handle a transaction when they arrive at a rate r?)

4. Transactions whose mean length . . . etc. . . . characters per second. Each block is held for the time it takes to fill it, and is held until the last block has been filled.   The entire transaction is then held for an additional h seconds and is thereafter released. Show that the optimum block length is given by $l = a + \sqrt{2sah + La}$.   Reconcile the differences between your answers for exercises 1–4 and prove and/or disprove the rationality of the author. (Hint: On the last day of Christmas my true love gave me how many presents?)

5. Transactions whose mean length is L . . . etc. with a minimum of wasted space. The transaction length is distributed in accordance with an arbitrary but known distribution. Does the argument of exercise 2 necessarily lead to a correct optimum?   Suppose the pdf is bimodal with a peak at a small transaction length and another peak at very large transaction lengths? Flowchart a procedure to determine the optimum block length for arbitrary distributions.

6. A system provides a memory load of 50 erlangs for buffer blocks whose length is 32 characters, of which 2 characters are used for link data. Using the Erlang-B assumptions, how many characters are required for an overflow probability of 10^{-7}?

7. Assuming that the average transaction size is 128 characters, and that the load is 50 erlangs, examine the effect on memory size of using a block of 4, 8, 16, 24, 32, 48, 64, 96, 128, and 192 characters.   In all cases, two characters are required per block for administrative data. Which block size is optimum from the point of view of minimizing the total memory required for an overflow probability of 10^{-7}?   Repeat at loads of 100, 200, 500, 700, and 1000 erlangs. Use the Erlang-B formula.

8. If you can run the fun36 statistical routine of Appendix I or the equivalent, repeat exercise 7 using the Erlang-C and the Poisson formulas and compare the three sets of answers.

9. Under the assumption that you have done exercise 7 or 8, show why the answers to exercises 1–4 above are not quite correct—so I lied. Flowchart

a procedure that will find the optimum block size under the assumption that the total pool size (in characters) is to be minimized.

10. A cyclic system's cycle equation is given by:

$$L = \max (W, T_d + T_e + T_a + T_b) + T_c,$$

where:

$T_a = 0.05$ sec;
$T_b = 0.001 + 0.25RL + 0.0003R^2L^2$;
$T_c = 0.001L + 0.005RL$;
$T_d = 0.02 + 0.1RL$;
$T_e = 0.110$;
R = the load in transactions per second;
L = the cycle length in seconds;
W = is the expected duration of a write operation to a 16 sector drum rotating at 1800 rpm. Each transaction requires 16 sectors worth of data. The drum is optimally scheduled.

The cycle consists of the processes in the order a, b, c, d, e. A transaction first passes through process d, then b, and then the drum write operation. Once process d has started, it will accept no further transactions. Sixteen buffer blocks of sixteen characters each are assigned to each transaction at the instant it arrives. They are released after the transaction has passed through the system but not before the conclusion of process a. An additional 16 buffer blocks are assigned to each transaction while in process c. These are released at the conclusion of process e but not before the drum writes are completed. Furthermore, in addition to the buffer blocks, queue blocks 8 characters long are assigned at the same time as buffer blocks are assigned. Queue blocks are released at the conclusion of process e but two cycles after the system has finished processing the transaction. Determine the buffer block and queue block load in erlangs as a function of the transaction arrival rate. Determine, for all values of the load, the total memory required in characters to achieve an overflow probability of 10^{-5}, 10^{-7}, and 10^{-9}. Assume buffers and queues are taken from different pools. Use Erlang-B, unless you have access to a Poisson formula program, in which case use it.

11. *Continuation*. Assume that each block, buffer or queue, requires 4 characters of administrative data. Decide to use the buffer blocks for the queue block function despite the waste of space. Determine the total memory required for this shared pool and compare the results at various throughputs and the specified overflow probabilities of exercise 10.

12. It is decided to save program space in the system of exercise 10 by over-

laying processes a and c. The overlay is 64 sectors long and each sector is 64 characters long. Use of the overlay will save 4,096 characters of static space. The a overlay can be done during process d's execution but the c overlay can only occur at the conclusion of the drum write operation. For all throughput values from 0 to R_{max}, and an overflow probability of 10^{-7}, determine the total memory required for the overlay system and compare with the total memory required for the system without overlays. You can assume a sequential read operation for the overlays.

15
Testing and Validation—The Moment of Truth, or The Agony and The Ecstasy

1. SYNOPSIS

Models like programs are bug prone. The model must be tested, and eventually validated against a real system. A structured approach to model testing is as useful as a similar approach to system testing.

2. CATEGORIES OF BUGS

Program bugs are typically subdivided into: typographical errors, syntactic errors, specification errors, and bona fide design errors. Since much (if not most) of the model is based on the software, we can expect the same kinds of error to occur in models. The model situation is more complicated because the model is typically done before the system has been debugged. Consequently, the following error categories are to be faced:

1. typographical errors: "I meant '+' not '$\times$';"
2. computational errors: "'7,' not '70!'"
3. approximation errors: "You mean N^2 is not a good approximation for $N!$?"
4. dimensional errors: "meters/second = stone-furlongs/centimeter^2;"
5. simplification errors, "$(A + B)(A - B) = A^2 + B^2$;"
6. scaling errors: "3 centimeters + 14 meters = 17 kilometers;"
7. source errors: "The model is correct—the program has a bug!"

It is not possible in practice to apply different techniques to the discovery of the different error types. General techniques that will lead you to the discovery of errors of whatever type are presented below. A bug free model is no more likely than a bug free program; it occurs only for trivial models or for your first model—you will never be so lucky again. Testing is mandatory, since there is no other way (until validation) to tell if the model is correct. The same meticulous care that you take with program testing should be applied to model testing.

3. REVIEW OF UNIT LEVEL TESTING

Testing of models starts at the unit level. This corresponds almost directly to the unit level testing of software. The steps in unit level model testing are as follows.

1. Do a dimensional check on the final answer. If the result is a time, then all components should have the dimension of time. Any exception to dimensional consistency is a bug and should be rectified. Dimensional analysis is the quickest and most productive form of unit level testing and catches most of the bugs.

2. Do a scaling check. All components must be in the same units. You are working at the microsecond level and convert to milliseconds and then seconds. You will fail to convert properly at least once.

3. Do an extreme point probability check. Test all probabilities in all combinations of 0 and 1 (within reason). Are zero answers really zero or is there some overhead processing on all paths? Are infinite answers really infinite; is there really a loop in the routine?

4. Do sensibility checks. Try trial cases for reasonable answers. Are the results sensible? Examine all counterintuitive results.

5. Do a positive value check. Every submodel returns a positive value for all resource use for all values of parameters. A negative result is probably incorrect.

6. Test maxima and minima. Differentiate the submodel's equation with respect to a parameter of interest. Set the derivative to zero and solve for the conditions that give you a minimum or maximum. Most models have a minimum and maximum only at the endpoints (i.e., $p = 0, p = 1$) and are monotonic in between. A maximum or minimum not at the endpoints of the range of the parameter bears further investigation and validation that that is indeed the way the routine behaves.

The testing steps are repeated as units (i.e., submodel equations) are combined. Successful passage of unit level tests and of integrated unit tests does not guarantee the model's validity. System level testing is required for that.

4. SYSTEM LEVEL TESTING

4.1 Principles

System level testing presumes that unit level testing has been completed on all component submodels. Furthermore, the entire model runs to output. That is, you can and have substituted parameter values and solved the model equations for all numbers of interest, and have produced the entire throughput-delay curve. It is, however, more revealing to work with the subjective-objective rate (SR) curve, or for its cyclic system counterpart, the cycle frequency-throughput curve. System level testing is based on the following principles.

1. The final equations are relatively easy to solve numerically.
2. Is the overall curve reasonable and physically feasible?
3. Does the model behave properly at the endpoints?
4. Does the model behave as expected with respect to parameter changes?
5. Are all resources, demands and utilizations well behaved?

4.2 Solution Glitches

You are either using a model manipulation package, an equation solver, have programmed the model in some convenient language, or are sweating it out by hand with a calculator—the method of solution is not important. You start at zero load and solve for the delay or cycle length. Having found the solution at the first point you increment the load and proceed to another point. Occasionally, you find load values for which convergence is difficult or impossible. The equations simply will not solve at that point. Your first inclination is to skip that value and go on to the next. You should not. You should play around with the value and find the precise points at which solution is easy and tough (see Figure 15-1). The solution converged rapidly at all points up to X. At X, either you failed to get a solution or did so only after numerous attempts. Similarly for point Y. This kind of behavior occurs under two circumstances: a bug, or a change in the binding resource. When there is a change in the binding resource (e.g., going from CPU bound to channel bound) we can expect a change in the slope as well (see Chapter 4). If there is a slope change, then examine the solution in the neighborhood of the troubled point and confirm that indeed there was a binding resource change. If there is no binding resource change, then it is likely that there is a bug. Typically a typographical error, approximation error, dimensional error, but most likely, a simplification error.

The problem at point Y is a dead giveaway, since there was an unreasonable shift in the curve. Solution difficulties are not guarantees of bugs. It may just mean that the system is ill tuned in the region, with considerable jumping back and forth between binding resources, all of which lead to solution problems.

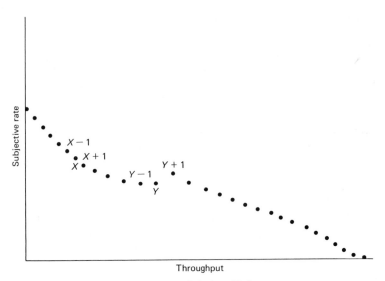

Figure 15-1. Solution glitches.

Just what "difficult" means depends on the complexity of the model. Moderate models will usually converge in a half a dozen Newton–Raphson iterations. Complicated models take more iterations. Our model manipulation/solution system allows us to keep track of the rate of convergence and to trace intermediate answers. If the solution is diverging rather than converging, or is getting into similar difficulties, we can find out in short order.

Given a troublesome point, it is effective to jump to a point beyond where a solution does come in short order. Then, approach the trouble spot from both directions, noting if things get suddenly worse or gradually worse. Gradual worsening is indicative of an approximation error. Sudden worsening, at a specific point, typically is some kind of an out-and-out goof. Modify the model one section at a time by making the values of major submodels constant (one at a time) and independent of load. Use the value near the trouble spot. If the problem goes away, then the submodel you just made constant is the culprit. Take it apart the same way. That is, make part of it constant and find the new trouble spot. Continued modification of the model in this manner will rapidly lead you to an identification of the bug.

4.3 Reasonable and Physical

Ultimately we are dealing with physical systems that cannot transcend physical laws, no matter how much we might wish to the contrary.* There are no time

---

*Alternate realities, notions of noncausality, Castaneda, Ram Dass, Zen, and the fourfold way notwithstanding.

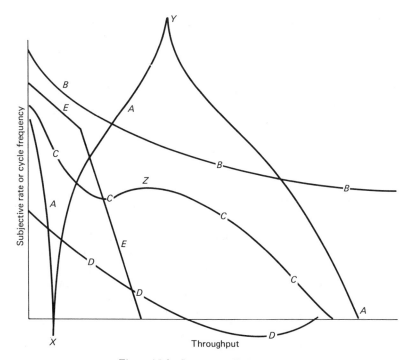

Figure 15-2. Some unrealistic models.

machines. You can't get something for nothing. And things can't better in order to get worse. Furthermore, to quote Scambia's theorem, "No matter how late you start in order to avoid the traffic, you won't get home earlier!" Occurrences of most impossibilities are obvious on the SR curve; the thoughput–delay curve may not show it all. Figure 15-2 shows some nonphysical behaviors.

Curve A has a pole at point X and another at point Y. Look for an erroneous analytical simplification. Again, examine the solution in those troubled regions, the same way you examined points that had solution problems. The behavior is not physical because it predicts physically impossible negative subjective rates at X and physically impossible overperformance at Y.

Curve B is another physical impossibility. It seems to imply that the system will never run out of resources; there is no blow-up point. The most likely cause of this anomaly is a scaling or dimensional error. There is a blow-up point, but it is so far out that you did not find it within the range of throughputs that you obtained by a simplified brick wall analysis. Set the subjective rate to zero and solve for the throughput that will give you that rate. This is probably a high level bug connected with scaling. You had the results in seconds already and multiplied by 0.001 to spuriously convert from milliseconds. Curve E is another nonphysical bug. It shows the system precipitously going to zero far earlier than expected. Probably another scaling error. At least one submodel is still expressed in microseconds or milliseconds. Find which one by setting the other submodels to zero, one at a time.

Curve C asks us to pump in extra transactions to achieve a desirable load which optimizes the systems' performance at point Z. This could be an analytical error, but it is equally likely to be a design bug. Blank out various submodels to home in on the culprit.

System D is not positive throughout the range of interest. It has multiple blow-up points. An analytical simplification error is indicated here.

4.4 Reasonable When Nonphysical

Just because the system's performance curve is physically sensible only in the first quadrant does not mean that it should not behave nicely in nonphysical areas. Figure 15-3 shows some variations. This section is not intended to expound some deep theorems—merely observations as to what to expect and what to test. Curve A shows the expected behavior of an ideal system in all regions. We have simply extended the curve to include negative throughputs and negative subjective rates. Most models will behave this way after they have been debugged. All four models seem to have reasonable behavior in the physical domain. We have already met curve B. In general, the existence of multiple

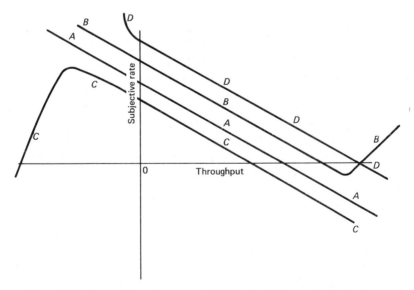

Figure 15-3. Reasonable and unreasonable behavior in the nonphysical regions.

blow-up points is indicative of erratic model behavior.   While the analytical simplifications that lead to this behavior may not invalidate the model, they must be examined in further detail to be sure that the behavior is reasonable. Intuition may be hard to come by in such nonphysical regions, but it does pay to try to see what would happen with negative throughputs and negative delays.   Reversals, such as those in curves B and C, are indicative of a modeling bug—although this is not guaranteed.   It makes sense to expect a system, when subjected to a negative load, to have improved performance.   A negative throughput should never cause a negative subjective rate, but merely an ever increasing positive rate.   Similarly, once beyond the blow-up point, further increases in throughput can only result in ever increasingly negative subjective rates.

Fanciful conjectures aside, the issue is that you cannot investigate the model for all combinations of parameter values.   If there is a point on the SR curve, even if not in the physically realizable region, that exhibits anomalous behavior, then might there not be a combination of parameter values that would bring that point into the physical region?   The function should be sensible, physical region or not.

4.5 Endpoint Behavior

The behavior of the system at the endpoints, meaning zero throughput and blow-up point, are the greatest bug catchers of them all.   The zero load model is easy to get.   You go through the equations manually, substitute zero for the load; all sorts of things cancel out, drop out, and what not.   Do this independently of the over-all model.   You must get the same value from the full model as you do from the zero load model, otherwise there is a modeling bug.   Check the utilizations.   The demands should be zero (or mostly zero).   The utilizations should still be greater than the demands.   Are they physical?   Are they all reasonable?   Can all nonzero utilizations be explained in terms of overhead or the system characteristics?

A comparison of the utilizations and demands at the blow-up point is also revealing.   Generally, there will be only one binding resource.   Its utilization and demand will be almost equal, or as equal as you want to make them by approaching the blow-up point more closely.   Is this really the binding resource? Have all overhead resources become insignificant?   This last observation can lead to a simplified model for the blow-up point.   Simply make all overhead functions zero.*   The proportion of demands to utilizations should then be similar to those of the blow-up point.

Compare the simplified blow-up model with the complete model.   Removal of the overhead functions does not generally move the blow-up point.   Compare with brick wall analyses.   Do the utilization ratios (demand/utilization) approach

---

*The overhead functions, of course, are those terms that remain at zero load.

constant values as you approach the blow-up point? They should! Or do they have discrete jumps in the neighborhood of the blow-up point? They should not.

4.6 Parameter Change Behavior

You have, or should have, a clear intuitive idea of the impact of various external parameters on performance. As a designer, you argued often enough that, "If such and such a parameter value was allowed, it would kill the system." Your intuition was probably correct. Does the model support your intuition? Does an increased error rate really make the system worse? Do longer holding times increase memory utilization? Play with the parameters of the problem and see how many different ways you can "kill" the system. Counterintuitive behavior bears further examination. The fault might lie with your intuition, or with the model. You have to win on this one, since either the model or your intuition will be improved as a result. Probe the entire solution curve over the range of physically realizable parameter values. Use an extreme point, midpoint, other extreme point approach. Is the behavior monotonic? (For example, increasing memory speed at some points of the curve decreases performance.) In most cases, such anomalous behavior indicates the existence of bugs.

4.7. Is Everything Else Well Behaved?

The same philosophy can be applied to all aspects of the model. We do not expect things to get nonphysical; we do not expect things to get better when they are getting worse. All such behavior must be explored. This goes for all resource utilizations, demands, and performance. A model that is well behaved over all parameter ranges in the physical and the nonphysical domain, while it may not be free of bugs, should inspire confidence on the part of others and should make it easier to sleep at night. Ultimate confirmation is obtainable only through validation against the real system. Since that may take place months or years after the model is built, you need something to tide you over until that time. Testing, as described here, might seem like a lot of work—it is. But then again, why should it not be? It is a model of what is predominantly a software system. Testing is the single largest part of software design, so let it be with models.

5. VALIDATION

5.1 General Principles

The object of validation is to confirm that the model tracks reality, and failing that, to find the reasons why it does not, or why it should not. This implies the following.

1. There is a model.
2. There is a system.
3. There is a way to generate a test load.
4. There is a way to measure the system's response to that load.
5. There is a way to compare the system and the model.

The above may seem obvious, and even trivial; however, that is not the case.

5.2. The Test Load

5.2.1. General

The ideal is to conduct a controlled experiment. There are two main sources of test loads—the real system environment, and a load generator. The environment, while seemingly ideal, is not the ideal source of load, for the following reasons.

1. Validation occurs early in the life of the system, typically before the load's characteristics have stabilized.
2. The real environment cannot be controlled.
3. It is not possible to play with different load characteristics.
4. The steady state assumptions are not necessarily valid.
5. It is difficult to measure the load without introducing code that affects performance.

Ultimately, validation should be conducted with a live load in the real environment. However, the first phase of system load testing, and also model validation, should be conducted with a load generator. The load generator, if properly constructed, is also the chief measuring tool for the system's performance. A load generator is not trivial. A block diagram is shown in Figure 15-4. It consists of three conceptual components: an off-line test data generator, an on-line load generator, and an off-line analyzer.

5.2.2. The Data Generator

The input to the data generator is a specification for a run, typically in terms of parameter values for transactions, including such things as mean arrival rate, distribution characteristics, special application-related probabilities, etc. In other words, all those data dependent probabilities that you used in the model must also appear in the test data generator. The test data generator, using a set of random number generation routines and built-in rules that define the structure of transactions, generates a historical scenario for a run that is in every way statistically equivalent to a real load. It is similar to the sequence of transactions generated by a simulation program. With proper design of the generator, there is no need to have this done on-line. In fact, if it were done on-line, in many cases the on-line load generator might not be able to keep

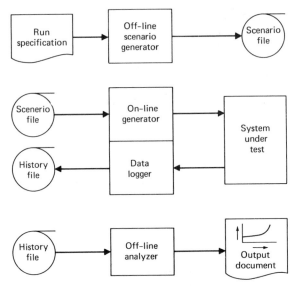

Figure 15-4. Load generator block diagram.

up with the system. It is desirable to have the scenario output to a permanent storage medium such as tape or removable disc. The statistical characteristics of a simulated load may take a long time to stabilize. If you make a correction to the model or to the system, you want to be sure that you are repeating the identical situation that led you to the change. Permanent storage of the scenario is the only sensible answer. Efficiency is not an issue in the off-line data generator. Consequently, it can be written in a higher order language with little or no sacrifice. Another approach is to design a specialized simulator that does nothing but create transactions. Simulation languages contain the facilities required to this.

5.2.3. The Load Generator

The load generator is a system in its own right. It can require the same resources as the system it is testing, or more. In some systems, particularly communications systems, it is possible to make the system be its own load generator. While the load generator is a system, it is typically simpler than that which is being tested, for the following reasons.

1. Recovery from malfunctions is not necessary. It is simpler to restart the test.
2. There are no error conditions or exception paths—the generator should not respond to the transactions, nor interpret them, but merely pass them to the tested system at the correct time.

3. Not all conditions and variations of the system being tested need be tested under load.

In some respects it is more complicated and must be more efficient than the system being tested, for the following reasons.

1. If the load generator reaches its blow-up point in the same neighborhood that the system does, it will not be possible to tell who is doing what and with which and to whom.
2. The load generator may require resources not available to the real system, such as input and output tapes and/or disc.
3. The load generator, in the interest of minimizing processing time, will tend to use as much memory as the real system, or more.
4. The load generator probably monitors the system's performance.

The load generator and the measurement facilities (the monitor, see below) are almost always the same unit, for the following reasons.

1. The scenario on the source file and the scenario as executed may differ because of loading effects in the system under test—e.g., it is throttling input. Consequently, the actual history must be measured. It cannot be presumed to be the same as on the scenario file.
2. Transactions involve interactions. Some performance factors, such as delays, can only be sensibly measured by the response that the system would make to the hypothetical set of users—the load generator.
3. Correlating driving transaction and response on a transaction-by-transaction basis between two separate computers (a load generator and a logger) is typically more processing than doing the logging in the generator in the first place.
4. Many of the facilities in a logger and a generator would be needlessly duplicated—e.g., interface software, device drivers, measuring software, etc.

The output of the generator/logger is a history file that combines (ideally) the original scenario and the history of the system's response to the scenario on a transaction-by-transaction basis. While some data reduction can be done in the on-line generator, this is best avoided, since such processing (like scenario generation) can materially increase the load.

5.2.4. The Analyzer

The analyzer is an off-line routine, again written in a higher order language, that accepts the history file, accumulates counts, performs elementary statistical analyses, and produces reports that allow a comparison of the system to the model (or the system against the specification).

5.2.5. Variations

A proper discussion of the load generator would take us far afield and would be tantamount to a moderate size book on simulation. The above load generator is not intended to be taken as a monolithic approach; however, all of these components must be present in any load generator. The most common approach to load generation, lacking a bona fide, separate load generator, is to fool the system by introducing prepackaged transactions directly on an internal queue. If this is all you can afford, it is better than nothing. However, you will have to find means to correct the results to the situation corresponding to a more realistic load. In many cases, it is possible to construct a load generator out of a copy of the real system, or to modify an existing system to which the subject system must communicate. The variations are endless. There is one approach, however, that is to be avoided—manual generation of load.

It is tempting, particularly for lightly loaded systems, to say that you will sit at the keyboard, or the console, or the whatnot, and manually simulate the load. This will not work for one or more of the following reasons.

1. You won't keep up.
2. You can't keep it up long enough.
3. You can't generate a random load, never mind one with prescribed statistical properties.
4. You'll never be able to repeat what you did.
5. Your logging will be sloppy.
6. Your records will be worse.
7. You will lie, cheat, ignore, be biased, shade and manipulate (unconsciously, of course) to prove (or disprove) the validity of the model and/or the system.

I've caught myself doing all of those things and I'm perfect.

5.3. Measurement

5.3.1. General

We want to measure everything that we predict with the model. This means: all throughput-delay functions, all demands, all utilizations, all processing times from the lowest level to the highest, the time spent in each state, the number of interrupts, the latencies, the probabilities, etc., etc., etc. Unfortunately, every act of measurement introduces **artifact**. This term originated in biology; it means the perturbation to a measurement brought about by the act of measurement. This is inherent in all measurements, but in many cases it can be ignored because it is small. Some examples may be instructive.

1. You measure voltage with a voltmeter. The voltmeter is a current drain and therefore introduces a voltage drop—artifact. You can ignore it when mea-

suring house voltage since a few million ohms are not going to materially affect the power station; you can't ignore it when measuring the voltage difference across the boundary of cell membrane.

2. You are measuring response time for a transaction. It takes 15 microseconds of processing to detect and log the occurrence—it is not a significant artifact.

3. You want to measure the processing time for an interrupt whose expected processing time is 25 microseconds. The logging and measurement takes 500 microseconds. That's a lot of artifact.

4. You are measuring how far a frog will jump when stimulated by an electric current. You strap a storage battery, a data logging unit, and a transmitter to the frog's back.

5. You are measuring the response of an aboriginal tribe to new foods (Western); you are there to record the results. They hate the stuff, but being extremely polite, eat it out of respect for you.

The single most common fault in any system measurement effort is to ignore artifact, to assume that it does not exist, or to falsely assume it to be negligible. The better the measurement, the more complete the data, the greater the artifact—period. There are two major methods used to measure things of interest—hardware monitors and software probes. Each has its value and limitations.

5.3.2. Hardware Monitors

A hardware monitor is typically a small computer outfitted with connectors that can be inserted into various parts of the system under test. The connectors function as probes and are integrated into a logic network, and/or software, that together can be used to detect the occurrence of previously defined events. Hardware monitors cause almost no artifact, but then again, they do not tell you a whole lot that is functionally related. Basically, they can count predefined events, and record the start and stop times of predefined events. A predefined event is one of the following kinds of things:

1. program state changes;
2. interrupts (physically oriented, not functionally);
3. access to prescribed memory locations or regions;
4. initiation and termination of I/O activities by channel;
5. bus activity.

The hardware monitor recognizes an event as a bit pattern on some specified group of wires. The more complicated that pattern (e.g., a sequence of characters) the more resources have to be provided in the monitor to detect that pattern. Practical limits are soon reached, and as a consequence artifact free measurements are of limited value. If you are willing to tolerate a minimal amount of artifact, you can insert instructions that will do unique things, typically to prescribed I/O channels, particularly direct channels. You issue the right instruction at the places in the program you want to record. The monitor can readily detect the event, and can do it with a minimum of artifact. Carry this approach too far, and as you increase the intelligibility of the event (vis-à-vis functions of the system under measurement) you increase the artifact.

5.3.3. Software Monitors

Software monitoring is primarily done by placing patches at strategic locations to measure things of interest. As such, there is no inherent limit to complexity (other than resource consumption) and the results can be made as intelligible as desired. The arrival rate of events can be obtained by counting the events over a prescribed time period. The elapsed time between events can be gotten by interrogating the clock at the beginning and end. Probes can be placed where desired, as desired. Software monitoring schemes have the following problems.

1. They must consume time and space resources; they inherently introduce artifact.
2. Very high time resolution is possible only at high priority levels. Probes placed at lower priority levels can and will have measured values stretched by higher priority functions.
3. They can introduce bugs because they are implemented as code.

It is important to get the data accumulated or measured in as direct a manner as possible. A minimum amount of processing should be done on-line. I/O operations to transfer measured data to another media for subsequent off-line processing should be minimized. Pre-averaging or accumulation over a specified time period is a useful technique to minimize the artifact. Event counts are accumulated in count buffers which are reset every N seconds. In cyclic systems, this can be done by resetting every N cycles. At the conclusion of the sampling period, the counts are transferred to the tape or disc used for monitor data storage. Off-line division by the sample time interval gives you the mean rate over the sample period. For steady state measurements, sample periods of 16–32 seconds are effective for most systems. Time intervals, such as length of a transfer, latencies, and measured delays, should also be accumulated. The length of the event is calculated on-line by subtracting the stop time from the start time. The event lengths for a particular kind of event are accumulated, as is the number of events. The division to obtain the mean is not done on-line. The accumulated event times and event counts are transmitted periodically to the storage medium. Conversion to rational units and scaling is done off-line.

If you want to get more than just the mean value (say, the distribution of a variable), then you could either place the measurements in different bins, or decrease the sample interval. The latter is usually preferable. Rather than accumulate events over a 30 second period, say, cut the sample time to one or two seconds. The minimum sample length should be several times larger than the typical transaction delay. Batch the results and transmit the group of measurements every 30 or 40 seconds. Build the distribution off-line. The following should be kept in mind.

1. Be sure you can relate the measurements to the transactions or to the transaction arrival rates. Measurements should be buffered and transmitted as a group for this reason alone.

2. Keep track, by means of counters, of exactly how many measurements of each type were made during the sample interval. This is essential if you are going to correct for artifact by analytical means. This information is usually available as a byproduct of the measurements.

3. It is better to repeat the experiment several times, with different sets of probes, thus minimizing artifact, than to try to measure everything at once.

4. Use indirect means where there are good analytical models available. For example, it is easier to sample the queue length, getting N_s*, than to measure the waiting time—Little's theorem allows you to deduce the one from the other.

5. Minimize the precision of the measurements. Eight bits is sufficient for most purposes; sixteen is lush. Use the number of bits that minimizes resource utilization. The final mean values can be significantly more accurate than the eight bit precision if enough samples are taken.

6. Use the method that is simple on-line, even if it does cause extensive off-line processing.

5.3.4. Data Reduction

The monitor, be it hardware, software, part of the load generator, or all three, creates a data base. Since measurements have been designed to minimize artifact, the raw data are crude and in several different, incompatible formats. Furthermore, they tend not to be directly correlated event-by-event. The ultimate objective of the off-line data reduction is to produce measurements in units that are useful and sensible, to the same scale factors, and directly related to interesting parameters of the system or its model. Data reduction consists of several phases.

---

*Recall that in most computer systems, $N_q = N_s$ because the transaction being processed is still stored on the physical queue.

Phase 1—*Completion of the calculations.* Divide the accumulated counts by the sample period to obtain rates. Subtract beginning and end points (if not done on-line) to obtain elapsed times; this may require searching for the corresponding beginning and end of an event. Add constants to convert relative values to absolute values (e.g., the measurement was taken N seconds after event Y).

Phase 2—*Scaling.* Perform all scale conversions by multiplying by the appropriate constant. Similar measurements taken from different sources should be presented the same way. For example, a rate is measured as time intervals; take the reciprocal to convert to a rate for all such measurements.

Phase 3—*Coordination.* The measurements concerning a given event may be splattered all over the data base; this is often the case for elapsed times and delays. Transaction arrival rates may be measured by the load generator and processing time by a software monitor. The transaction rate must be coordinated with the measured resource used over the same period. Sampling intervals might differ among the several data-gathering sources. The sample intervals must be coordinated so that final output data is based on the same sample interval. This kind of processing can be lengthy and can require a lot of searching. The output is a set of consistent self-contained records that are elapsed-time independent.

Do not destroy raw data records if you can possibly help it. You will invariably want to go back at a later time to massage the data in a different way.

6. COMPARISON AND EMPIRICAL MODELS

6.1. General

Look at the measured data points of the SR curve for Figure 3-7. There are a lot of points there, and it is not obvious just what the model is. Empirical data look like that—a scatter of points. The analytical model gives you a nice line. It is not obvious how to judge if the line fits the scatter of points. Prior to comparison of the model and the system, then, you have to convert the scatter of measured points to a continuous function which can be compared. What you are doing is creating an empirical model of the system, based on measurements. The primary tool for empirical model generation is **regression analysis**. You can, of course, overlay the model behavior on the empirical data and "eyeball" the results. This is not effective, except as a crude guide, because:

1. it does not allow you to correct for artifact;

2. it is useless when the "curve" is really a function of several variables (I don't know anybody who can "eyeball" a five dimensional surface);

3. such curves are not very good fits.

6.2. Linear Regression Analysis

Given a set of empirical data points, such as subjective and objective rate, find a straight line through those points that is "best fit" in accordance with some well defined criterion. The objective of a linear regression analysis is illustrated by Figure 15-5. The dependent variable Y is to be expressed as a linear function of the independent variable X, of the form $Y = a_0 + a_1 X$, such that some measure of fit is minimized. The most commonly used, and generally best measure is the "least squared deviation" measure. The **deviation** is the distance from an experimental point (x_i, y_i) to the line, and given by $(y_i - a_1 x_i)$. The function to be minimized is $\Sigma_i (y_i - a_1 x_i)^2$. The value of a_0 and a_1 that satisfy this criterion are given by

$$a_1 = \frac{n \sum_i x_i y_i - \sum_i x_i \sum_j y_j}{n \sum_i x_i^2 - \left(\sum_i x_i\right)^2} \qquad (15.1)$$

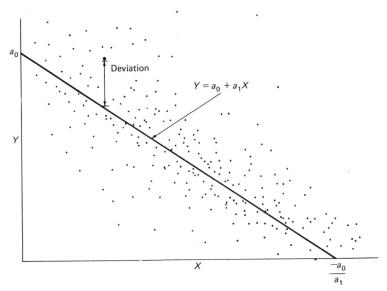

Figure 15-5. Linear regression analysis.

$$a_0 = \frac{\sum_i y_i - a_1 \sum x_i}{n}.$$

(15.2)

where

(x_i, y_i) are the values of a data point, and
n is the total number of data points.

These equations are available as built-in functions on many scientific and statistical calculators.

6.3. Piecewise Linearization

While the SR function is almost linear, it is not quite linear. A linear assumption, which is to say an assumption that the system is quasi-ideal, is not always tenable. We see by eyeballing that a linear fit is not really good enough.

Figure 15-6 shows a set of points for which a linear fit will not suffice. The dashed line shows a simple linear fit to the entire set of data. It is not a good fit. The solid lines are three different regions. Note that the regions chosen overlap. There is no simple way to tell you how to choose the regions and how much overlap to use. However, keep in mind that you have only a limited number of data points. As you increase the number of pieces, the number of data points available to each piece is reduced; consequently the fit over the more restrictive

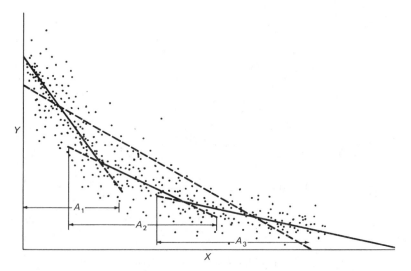

Figure 15-6. Piecewise linear fit.

set of points is not as good. Clearly if you reduced each range to just one datum point each, then you could not fit anything at all. It is better to use a few overlapping ranges, say less than five, than to use many ranges with fewer points in each.

6.4. Variable Transformation

Suppose you knew on the basis of the model that the correct form of the expression was:

$$Y = a_0 + a_1 X^2.$$

Let $W = X^2$. Then

$$Y = a_0 + a_1 W.$$

This is a linear fit in W. The essence of the technique is to transform one or the other, or both variables so that you have a linear form. As examples, consider the following.

Original	Transformation	Result
$X^2 + Y^2 = a^2$	$W = X^2, Z = Y^2$	$W + Z = a^2$
$Y = a_0 + a_1 \log X$	$W = \log X$	$Y = a_0 + a_1 W$
$Y = a_0 + \dfrac{a_1}{1 - a_2 X}$	$W = \dfrac{1}{1 - a_2 X}$	$Y = a_0 + a_1 W$
$Y = aX^n$	$W = \log Y, Z = \log X$	$W = \log a + nZ$

The SR function will be dominated by a strong linear component. A combination of linear and nonlinear fitting can be used. First find a linear regression fit to the entire data set. Then massage the source data to express the deviation from this linear function. Do this by subtracting the sample value of Y from the linear equation's value for Y. This gives you a new set of data points which you can linearize by variable transformation. The final result is expressed as the sum of the linear fit and the nonlinear fit for the deviation. If this does not suffice, then do it again. If you continue this often enough, you will be generating a series approximation to the points. While this method is not useful in general, it is reasonably easy when you know there is a strong linear component and you have the model to guide you in discovering the general form of the nonlinear components.

6.5. Multivariate Fits and the Elimination of Artifact

Generally, the delay or the subjective rate is not a function of a single variable. There is more than one kind of transaction; each transaction is another independent variable. A more complete picture of the subjective/objective rate function

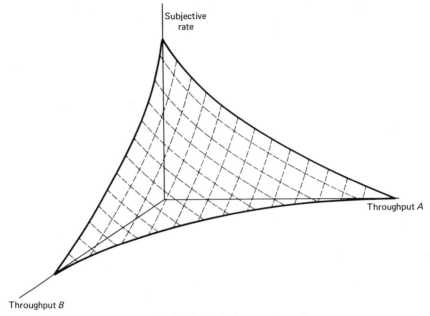

Figure 15-7. Subjective/objective rate surface.

for a system that has two kinds of transactions (with two potentially different rates) is given in Figure 15-7. The objective in this case is to fit a surface rather than a straight line. The approach is the same as for one independent variable but involves solving a set of simultaneous linear equations. The method is to be found in any good book on applied statistics, such as Sterling and Pollack [STERL68]. The same linearization methods can be used as were used for a single independent variable.

The importance of a multivariate fit is not that there are several components to the throughput, but that it allows us to correct for artifact. If you kept track of the number of measurements made, for each type of measurement, then the measurements can be treated as another type of transaction. If the measurement rate correlates directly with the throughput, artifact elimination will not be complete. If however, most of the measurement activities are independent of throughput, you will be able to almost completely eliminate their effect. One way to assure this is to make the large, time-consuming activities, such as outputting sample data records, resetting all counters, etc., occur periodically, and independently of the throughput. If, alternatively, you do your housekeeping only after a prescribed number of events or inputs have occurred, you will have inadvertently correlated this activity with throughput and will not be able to eliminate the artifact. It is not always possible to arrange things this way, but if the opportunity exists, it should be taken advantage of.

The output of the multivariate regression analysis (with possible linearization) is a model that expresses subjective rate (say) as a function of several throughput components and several artifact components. By eliminating the artifact terms you have created an artifact free (or at least an artifact reduced) model of the system which you can now compare with the model or with specified performance values.

6.6. How Good Is the Fit?

The goodness of the fit is measured by (among several alternatives) the **Pearson product moment correlation coefficient**. It is defined as:

$$r = \frac{\sum_i [(x_i - \overline{X})(y_i - \overline{Y})]}{\sqrt{[\sum(x_i - \overline{X})^2][\sum(y_i - \overline{Y})^2]}}$$

(15.3)

where

r is the correlation coefficient,
x_i, y_i is a sample point, and
$\overline{X}, \overline{Y}$ are the means of the sample
points, e.g., $\Sigma x_i/n$, $\Sigma y_i/n$.

The correlation coefficient is a number that lies between -1 and $+1$. Because the SR function has a negative slope, the correlation coefficient will lie between -1 and 0. A value of -1 indicates the best possible fit. A value of 0 indicates no fit at all. Go back now, to Figure 3-7. Note the scatter. Actually the throughput axis represented the sum of four different throughput components. A multivariate regression analysis showed a correlation coefficient of -0.994 for approximately 700 points. This means that there really was no scatter at all, but that we were looking at the projection of several independent variables onto a single axis. Put some dots on the surface in Figure 15-7 and project it against the back surface to see what this means (see Figure 15-8).

With a good model on which to base your empirical regression analysis, approximately 500 points, with suitable linearization, you can routinely expect correlation coefficients of the order of -0.9 or better. If you decrease the number of points below 200, the results become shaky. More than 1000 data points add nothing but cost. The more variables, the more points needed. As a rule of thumb, you can estimate that between 150 and 250 data points will be needed for each independent variable, if you are to get the correlation coefficient up into the 90s.

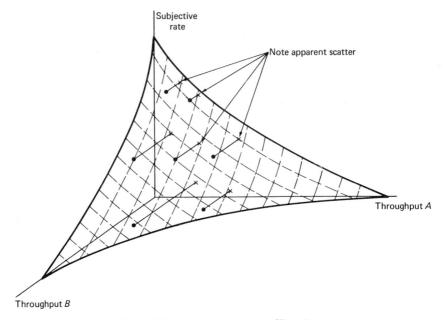

Figure 15-8. Apparent scatter on SR surface.

7. COMPARISONS

The empirical model and the analytical model do not match, of course. Since you have real data, might you not throw away that analytical model now? No, because it will be needed for tuning (see Chapter 16). Furthermore, the poor fit is probably due to some simple things you overlooked, a bug, or it isn't really a good fit.

1. The empirical model gives you a model for all combinations of throughput types. The analytical model is based on a predetermined or narrow set of combinations. Use the combinations assumed for the analysis in the empirical model before you compare.
2. Is the analytical model optimistic? If so, examine the artifact carefully. Revise the analytical model to include the processing and other resource consumption due to the artifact, and then compare.
3. Do the analytical model and empirical model check at the zero load point? They should, since this is the most reliable point of the model. Examine the model carefully in the zero load region to find the bug.

4. Do the models match at the blow-up point? They do not because you cannot get the real system to blow up, it has too many safeguards against that sort of thing. Try cutting some of these safeguards out with patches and see what happens.

5. Is the difference systematic? (i.e., the curves have the same shape, but they are displaced.) Fit a curve to the difference to create a model of the error. How does it behave with changing load? with changing parameters? If the displacement is vertical, look for a missing or spurious overhead function. If the displacement is horizontal (e.g., a constant multiplier) look for an improper probability.

6. Is the difference erratic? Look for different tuning assumptions and different tuning values. Rerun the model or the system, whichever is easier, so that they are operating with the same tuning parameters.

7. Compare the ratio of the resource utilization to the number of transactions in the system [utilization/throughput × delay)] for the empirical model and the analytical model. Examine the differences. It may guide you to spotting the error.

This last suggestion bears amplification. The throughput multiplied by the delay is a measure of the number of transactions in the system at the time. Dividing the utilization at a given throughput by the number of transactions in the system gives you a measure of the expected utilization per transaction. This is usually a more sensitive indicator of what is going on than raw utilizations. Nonmonotonic behavior here is suspicious, although not impossible (see Chapter 16). You can play the same games you played in debugging the model. Make a part of the resource demand constant and see how that affects the model with respect to its deviation from empirical data. By subdividing finely enough, you should be able to home in on the discrepancies. If the analytical model has a systematic difference, and has the same zero load point, and the deviation is of the order of 10% or less, I'm generally content to leave it alone and say that the model is adequate. If you spend too much time and effort reconciling the differences, the system will probabily be changing faster than you can change the model.

8. EXERCISES

1. A cyclic system has a clock that operates at a high priority level. A clock interrupt occurs every ten milliseconds. You use it to measure the duration of various processes. What is the smallest duration you can discern? For processes whose duration exceeds the smallest duration, how much accuracy can you

get in the measured time? Assuming that the durations are distributed and that you measure mean lengths, how much accuracy can you get? Several short processes occur sequentially such that any one of them is shorter than the smallest discernible interval, but such that the sum of any two of them is greater than the smallest discernible interval. For these processes, what is the smallest interval you measure and with what accuracy?

2. Repeat exercise 1 above given that you have both a 10 millisecond clock and an 11 millisecond clock.

3. You are measuring the performance of a real system. You can control only a small fraction of the load. Is there any benefit to introducing a small controlled load, even if it is insignificant compared to the total load? Specify conditions and justify your claim.

4. Use the models corresponding to the problems specified below as sources of data and fit an empirical function to that data using an appropriate form of regression analysis. Compare your empirically derived function with the actual function.

a. Chapter 6, exercise 5
b. (6-6)
c. (6-7)
d. (7-14a)
e. (7-14b)
f. (7-14c)

g. (11-12)
h. (12-1)
i. (12-4)
j. (12-5)
k. (12-7)
l. (12-8)

m. (12-9)
n. (12-10)
o. (13-1)
p. (13-7)
q. (14-10)

5. Consider any of the cyclic models of Chapter 12. Derive an expression for the zero-load cycle length. Derive other expressions for the ratios of all process durations to the cycle length at the blowup point. Sketch the expected unit utilizations and relate to the corresponding process equations.

6. You design a test data generator. It will place transactions on several lines at specified mean rates. Compare the following schemes for allocating transactions to lines: (a) a separate generator for each line; (b) a master generator for all lines and a process that distributes the transactions to the lines at random; (c) a master generator for all lines with transactions distributed to lines in cyclic order. All lines are to get transactions at the same mean rate.

7. Flowchart a transaction generator that produces transactions whose mean length is specified and that have a known but arbitrary length distribution.

8. A critical measurement introduces a lot of artifact. Furthermore, the artifact is proportional to the load. You cannot eliminate the artifact without eliminating the measurement. Describe an experimental procedure that will allow you to remove the artifact analytically. (Hint: It's not a question of too much of a good thing, but rather not enough of bad thing.)

9. The following table was obtained by measurement:

Throughput	Delay
0.00 transactions/sec	0.64 sec
0.24	0.82
0.70	1.14
1.14	1.40
1.73	1.50
1.98	1.82
2.42	1.98
2.87	1.30
3.21	2.68
3.24	2.78
3.28	2.80

Is the system well tuned throughout the range of measured values? Show that the ultimate throughput is approximately 4.2 transactions per second. Is the system probably ultimately CPU bound or I/O bound? Show that it is not likely that a very fast CPU would improve the ultimate throughput beyond 6 transactions per second. Show that with good tuning and a faster CPU it might be possible to push the system's ultimate throughput to 7 transactions per second. Compare the original capacity with that of the system with a fast CPU alone and with a well tuned I/O and a fast CPU. *Hint:* pseudo cyclic system.

10. I was particularly frustrated once with a set of very fine experimental data. Any one set of points, corresponding to a given set of parameter values, produced nice looking curves with little or no scatter. The experimental data should have allowed me to obtain values for various constants in a model. Every parameter was measured over a range of equally spaced values—for example: transaction length = 50, 100, 150, 200, . . . characters. Despite the vast amount of data it was not possible to solve for the constants. What was wrong with the experimental setup? *Hint:* it's a matter of what depends on what and how.

16

Tuning for Fun and Profit

1. SYNOPSIS

What tuning is and isn't. Why all systems are initially badly tuned; and how to use the model to support a tuning effort.

2. TUNING

2.1. Definition and Prerequisities

Tuning is the modification of the design and/or the parameters of an already working system in the interest of achieving a better fit of the system to its environment. While bugs may show up as a result of tuning, debugging is not the objective of tuning. Tuning is ideally done to take advantage of the system's robustness and may be a continual effort throughout the system's lifetime. There are three primary prerequisites to a tuning effort:

1. a stable system;
2. a stable operating environment;
3. a tuning goal.

2.2. A Stable System

A stable system is free of bugs and has stable functions. Tuning is ideally done on a bug free system. While this objective is never met in practice, it is a goal worth aspiring to. Rational tuning cannot be done in the presence of numerous bugs because their effect is haphazard. Bugs are to be distinguished from misconceptions regarding the application. That is, the programmer wrote a good program that does (in part) the wrong thing. This is middle ground between tuning and debugging. Tuning a system in the presence of bugs is like tuning an automobile in the presence of a malevolent demon that modifies settings at random. It cannot be done effectively.

Not only must the system be relatively bug free, but the application must be stable. Tuning cannot be effective if, during the course of it, the user is changing software to put in new functions, deleting old functions, etc. Tuning, like most experimental procedures, requires control over variables. Such control is impossible when applications are being changed. You can do one or the other, but not both simultaneously. A well run installation will alternate between tuning and changing.

2.3. A Stable Operating Environment

Systems, particularly those that interact with humans, are subjected to unnatural stresses early in life. Time-sharing systems are notorious for this. The day the system is put into operation is the day that the fun and games start. Users attempt to crash the system; to compromise its security; they investigate the limits of its capabilities in all directions; they exercise what should be low probability paths. In short, they do all sorts of things the system was not statistically designed to handle. Systems with human operators are also subject to this kind of abuse. The operators will likewise try strange functions and combinations, not necessarily maliciously, but as a means of learning the system's capabilities. Eventually, the users, operators, etc., find the most effective operating pattern and the environment stabilizes. This kind of stabilization may not come for three to six months after the system has been put into operation. The stability point is reached earlier with systems that have little or no human interaction. A replacement system fares better than a new system.

2.4. Tuning Goals

An engine can be tuned for maximum power, minimum fuel consumption, maximum lifetime, or some weighted combination of the three, but not for all of them simultaneously. A system can be tuned for minimum delay, maximum throughput, or capacity (however that is measured), but not for all of them simultaneously. Since the system's behavior is not characterized by a single point but by a function, typically of several input variables, it does not make sense to say, "Make it better." The system's performance is describable as a multidimensional surface (i.e., the throughput–delay function, or the subjective/objective rate function). Tuning is indicated when that surface is not satisfactory at one or more points. There is, therefore, a goal or set of goals, that indicate the specific, desirable performance characteristics to be obtained (or attempted) by the tuning exercise. A clear statement of purpose is essential if tuning is not to be aimless playing with the system in order to "make it better."

2.5. Why New Systems Are Always Badly Tuned

I am sure there are exceptions; they rank with bug free original code. A new system is always mistuned because:

1. Implicitly, or explicitly, consciously or subconsciously, the designer makes statistical assumptions about the characteristics of the load; these range from careful analyses to wild guesses. Some of the guesses and some of the analyses are wrong.

2. The source data on which the design was based were in turn based on the user's behavior under a previous system or in the absence of the system; the assumptions did not take into account the fact that the system itself would change the user's behavior. Furthermore, there was no rational way to predict such effects, even if their possibility had been considered.

3. The system's specifications changed throughout the development period; basic statistical assumptions were not (or rarely) changed to suit.

4. Design decisions were based on assumed performance, i.e., there was a feedback loop between performance and design. While there was a realization that the performance changed (not necessarily for the worse) basic assumptions regarding performance were not revised.

5. Hardware characteristics changed during development, some for the better, some for the worse. Again no revisions.

6. There were at least a half-dozen things left out of all models and analyses that turned out to be important; and a comparable number of things initially felt to be important that were reduced to trivia by somebody's astute design.

These observations are not truly universal; the system is not *always* badly tuned; but it will be badly tuned to the extent that the above are operative. No system is ever tuned to the optimum. The fact that the system is out of tune may or may not be obvious. External observations do not show it to be out of tune during simulated load tests because simulated loads *do* (by definition) behave as originally assumed. It is only after the system has been put into operation and the environment has stabilized that it becomes apparent that the system is out of tune. Realization emerges as gathered statistics show discrepancies between assumptions and reality. Realization emerges as the system's performance characteristics prove disappointing.

One can adopt a defensive or a positive attitude toward tuning. The defensive attitude is predicated on the false belief that the system will go into operation well tuned. Consequently, neither time, nor dollars, nor other resources are allocated by the builder to tuning. When the system does not function as expected, the defensive attitude results in a scrabble to "fix things up;" the tuning effort is haphazard, expensive, and not effective. Conversely, a positive attitude toward tuning is based on the presumption that it will be necessary. ("After you've driven it for 4000 miles, bring it back so we can tune it up for you.") This is not free, of course, and presumes a willingness on the part of the buyer to either directly or indirectly pay for the cost of tuning and the supporting instrumentation and analytical effort. Users, all too often, foster a defensive attitude toward tuning by expecting the system to be well tuned the day it is put into operation, by expecting the test setup and the real system to behave identically, and by not being willing to pay for a tuning effort even when stated explicitly.

Such attitudes are ineffective because it is the user that will have the greatest need for tuning. Just as the basic statistical assumptions on which the design, and therefore the initial tuning, was based changed over the course of the project's development, the same parameters can be expected to change over the system's lifetime. Therefore, it should be expected that the system will be in need of periodic tuning if it is to respond to a changing environment. Since the environment is continually changing, so is the tuning. Consequently, not only is the system initially out of tune, but is continuously getting out of tune throughout its life.

2.6. What Is Tuning?

Tuning, as an activity, consists of making changes almost exclusively to the software. The changes can be categorized as follows.

1. *Elimination of resource gaps:* This involves rearranging things to remove blockages or gaps in the resource.
2. *Elimination of stupidities:* These are not bugs—the system does do the right thing, only it does it ineffectively.
3. *Inappropriate tactics:* Code was optimized in the wrong direction.
4. *Inappropriate strategy:* Functions were assigned to the wrong place or in an ineffective manner.
5. *Trades:* Trade opportunities were resolved at a less than optimum point.
6. *Squeezing:* A scarce resource (high demand) is squeezed (at the expense of most other resources).

Terms like "inappropriate," "wrong," or "stupid" should be taken as retrospective observations. I am not saying that the designer was stupid or wrong; the type of things I have in mind are the things for which the responsible party (the designer) would say, "Hmm, that was a dumb thing to do. Now that I see what the load really looks like," etc.

3. CAPACITY AND TUNING OBJECTIVES

3.1. Definition of System Capacity

I have found it convenient and revealing to define the system's **capacity** as the area under the SR curve. For a quasi-ideal system, whose SR curve is given by

$$\frac{S}{S_{max}} + \frac{R}{R_{max}} = 1.$$

The area is

$$\int_0^{R\,max} S\,dR = S_{max} \int_0^{R\,max} \left(1 - \frac{R}{R_{max}}\right) dR = \frac{S_{max}\,R_{max}}{2}\frac{(\text{transactions})^2}{(\text{sec})^2}.$$

$$(16.1)$$

If the binding factor throughout the range from 0 to R_{max} throughput was the same resource, say memory speed, it is clear that doubling the memory speed would double both S_{max} and R_{max}, since a transaction would have half the delay at zero throughput and the ultimate throughput would be doubled. Consequently, the capacity as defined above would be quadrupled; the capacity is proportional to the square of the binding resource. This is a slightly less heuristic and intuitively satisfactory justification for "Grosch's square law" that relates "performance" (not formally defined) to the square of the cost. Beside being easy to evaluate once you have the SR curve, this definition of capacity has justice. Figure 16-1 shows several systems. System A is a base system to be used for comparison. System B has the same minimum delay, but double the throughput. From a user's point of view, with regard to throughput, it has double the effectiveness. One should not be surprised to pay double for a truck that can haul twice the load. System C has the same maximum throughput rate, but half the delay. It would be fair to pay twice as much for a car that can go twice as fast. In either case, systems B and C match our intuitive notion of what we expect in the way of a capacity measure. System D doubles both the subjective rate and the throughput, and by definition has four times the capacity; since two important parameters were doubled, we expect the capacity measure to quadruple.

3.2 Tuning Goals Revisited

You should distinguish between two types of tuning objectives: those that modify the curve without increasing capacity, and those that increase capacity. Clearly, we should expect the latter to be more difficult to achieve. Figure 16-2 shows a number of quasi-ideal systems, all of which have the same capacity. Conceptually, the high throughput system batches transactions over a period of months and

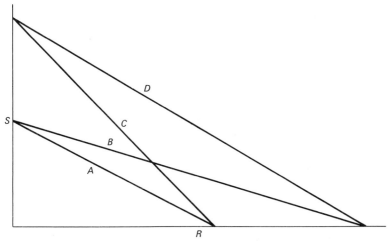

Figure 16-1. Several system capacities compared.

processes them with great efficiency. Conversely, the high subjective rate system goes to work on a task from beginning to end without interruption. Should any task arrive while it is busy, the system will reject it. In principle, the entire family of systems is achievable. That family creates a hyperbolic boundary curve, as shown in Figure 16-2. Any given system is defined by a tangent to that boundary curve. All systems have equal capacity. A second bounding curve, corresponding to a family of designs that have a higher capacity is also shown. In principle, achieving a design tangent to *that* boundary should require additional resources.

Undoubtedly there are deep theoretical issues at stake here, suitable to the production of innumerable esoteric theses in obscure technical journals, but that is not my point—the real point is that neither the designer nor the buyer should expect to get something for nothing, especially out of a tuning effort. In principle, tuning should be conducted along the following lines.

1. Develop the SR curve for the system before tuning.
2. Discuss the curve's deficiencies with the buyer and obtain agreement as to how it should be modified.
3. Measure the capacity of the old and the new SR curves.
4. If the new curve has significantly more capacity than you can expect to squeeze (assuming that the system met the original specifications) resolve appropriate financial issues before you begin the tuning effort.
5. Conversely, if you are the buyer, and the new curve has significantly more capacity, decide what functions you will sacrifice, or what additional resources you will obtain to achieve the higher capacity.

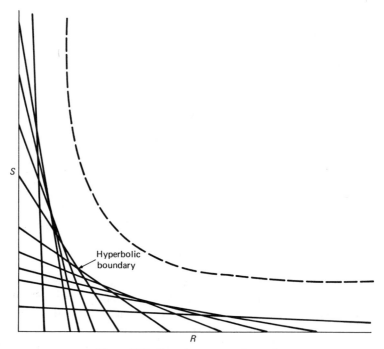

Figure 16-2. Capacity conservative tuning.

The state of the theory is simply too primitive to allow us to get quantitative about tuning expectations, except in highly restricted (and generally unrealistic) circumstances. We are barely beginning to understand quantitative system performance analysis; throwing a further optimization problem (for that is what tuning is all about) on top of this is too much at the moment.

3.3. The Binding Resource

At any given point on the SR curve, there is (typically) only one binding resource. As you move from the origin toward R_{max}, the binding resources may become, in turn, A, B, and C. If you look at the system's behavior as the superposition of several resources (see Figure 4-6) each one of which exhibits quasi-ideal behavior, it is clear that once a given resource has stopped binding, it will never bind again. Thus, if the binding resources in turn are A, B, C, A, D, it is clear that resource A is exhibiting anomolous behavior and bears further investigation. An alleged tuning change that does not affect the binding resource can have no effect on the system's performance at a given point of the SR curve. Suppose the system's characteristics are as shown in Figure 16-3. Suppose that we want to modify the

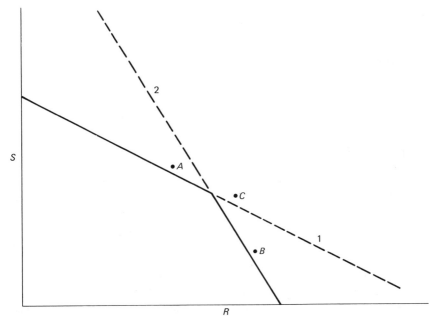

Figure 16-3. Binding resources.

design to surpass point A or point B. Point A can be achieved by tilting line 1 clockwise for a lower ultimate throughput and a higher subjective rate. Point B can be achieved by increasing ultimate throughput at the expense of delay (counterclockwise tilt). In both cases, only the binding resource is affected. If however, it is point C that is desired, then both lines 1 and 2 will have to be modified. In that case, not only must the binding resource be known, but the new binding resource must be predictable as well.

The binding resource at a point is clearly the resource that has the highest utilization. Utilization can be measured directly. A prerequisite, then, to rational tuning is the ability to determine the various utilizations in descending order at every point on the SR curve. Without this, you are tuning blind, and any changes you get are gratuitous, or due to complex interactions that are not readily understandable. The binding resource is, therefore, the single most important guide to tuning—it tells you what area to look for: memory, memory access rates, bus transfers, disc latency, processing, etc.

A second principle is to go after the big guy. Don't expect to win a $100 in a penny ante poker game. It might happen, but it probably won't. Break the binding resource down into its components by processing modules, transfer types, etc. Order the components and go for the statistically biggest one (at that throughput level). The relative mean size of the components may shift with throughput, so you must determine that relative size in the region of interest.

4. TUNING DIAGNOSTICS

4.1. Detection of Gaps

A gap in a resource is a period of inactivity for that resource. Since in general there is only one binding resource, all nonbinding resources can be expected to have gaps. Gaps as such do not present opportunities for tuning. A gap in the binding resource, however, is a prime prospect for tuning.* It says that something is wrong with our strategy. We are limited by resource X, but we occasionally waste it. A typical example of a binding resource gap occurs in a CPU bound system that suspends processing while waiting for an I/O transfer to complete. The presence of gaps can be detected by monitoring the resource's activity. If it is the binding resource at any given throughput, and it is inactive (at least statistically), then there is a gap someplace.

Location and isolation of gaps in cyclic systems is relatively trivial. They can be very elusive in an asynchronous system. In cyclic systems, the gap is discovered by using instrumentation (say a hardware monitor) to produce a detailed cycle chart. The gaps are self-evident. The presence of gaps can also be deduced from an examination of the SR curve. Consider Figure 16-4. The system is well tuned, except for a step in a mid-throughput region. While there is no absolute theoretical assurance that a resource gap will exist in that region, there are good reasons to suspect it. Changes of this kind come about through a local shift in binding resource. The binding resource is A on either side of the gap. A is the CPU, while B is, say, a disc transfer that exhibits latency. The gap begins at a throughput rate high enough to cause a discontinuous increase in the latency. Therefore, it temporarily becomes the binding resource. Once the penalty has been paid, there is no further latency increase, and, gradually, processing increases to fill the gap and reestablishes itself as the binding resource.

Even if there is no local shift in binding resource, gaps can be deduced from kinks in the curve. If the rate of change of the gap with respect to throughput and the rate of change of the binding resource with respect to throughput are not the same, then either the gap must overtake the resource or the resource must overtake the gap. Eventually, one or the other must become the binding factor. If the gap is growing faster than the resource, the over-all curve must be convex. Conversely, if the gap is being relatively diminished, the over-all curve must be concave (see Figure 16-5). If the relative size of the gap (compared to the resource utilization) is identical throughout the curve, then the SR curve will not tell you anything. Since gaps are caused by different devices, that have dif-

---

*By "gap," in what follows, I mean gaps in the binding resource.

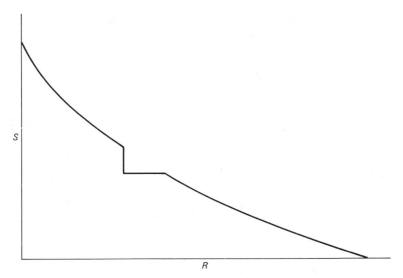

Figure 16-4. A gap?

ferent responses to demand, the likelihood of a constant size (proportional) gap is low. This diagnostic does not ensure the existence of a gap, because several resources could conspire to exhibit this behavior, or for that matter, as we shall see, one resource, with the right kind of characteristic, could do the same thing.

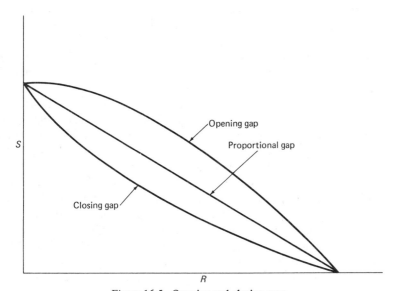

Figure 16-5. Opening and closing gaps.

Generally, notches in the SR curve are better indicators of gaps than global convexity or concavity. However, local convexity or concavity (a sort of smooth notch) are signposts of a gap. If a gap is detected, it should be confirmed by explicit measurements in the suspected region.

4.2. Unit Utilization

Measure, or calculate the resources consumed per unit transaction. To get this, divide the utilization by the number of transactions in the system. The number of transactions in the system is estimated by the transaction arrival rate multiplied by the delay:

$$\text{unit utilization} = \frac{\text{resource utilization}}{\text{arrival rate} \times \text{delay}}.$$

The unit utilization is a measure of how much effort is spent per transaction. This need be calculated only for the binding resource(s). Plot it as a function of throughput, and consider the possible alternative shapes to the curve (see Figure 16-6).

1. Curve A shows the unit utilization decreasing with increased throughput, and becoming asymptotically constant near the blow-up point. Not much opportunity for tuning here, since it is getting more efficient with increasing load. This is not likely for an asynchronous system, unless somebody has sneaked in some batch processing someplace. If the purpose of tuning was to increase the subjective rate at the expense of throughput, I would interpret this curve as representing such an opportunity (for an asynchronous system, but not for a cyclic system).
2. Curve B is independent of load and is the typical behavior one would expect for an asynchronous system. For a cyclic system, one would ask why the function was not batched; it would represent a tuning opportunity.
3. Curve C is peculiar. Processing is load dependent up to a point. This behavior is unusual because load dependent processing does not tend to stabilize as such. Curves D or E are more representative of a load dependent unit utilization. If I saw this kind of behavior (C) I would investigate it until I had a clear understanding of the mechanism that led to it.
4. Curves D and E are representative of load dependent unit utilizations. Load dependencies are always rich sources of tuning opportunities. They occur for sorts, queue scanning, and search operations among others. It pays to do a rough curve fit to these to find the growth law. It matters a whole lot if the growth is linear, quadratic, exponential, or what. Generally such load dependencies can be arranged to follow a $N \log N$ growth, so that anything that grows faster than that is suspected. Quadratics direct you to loops

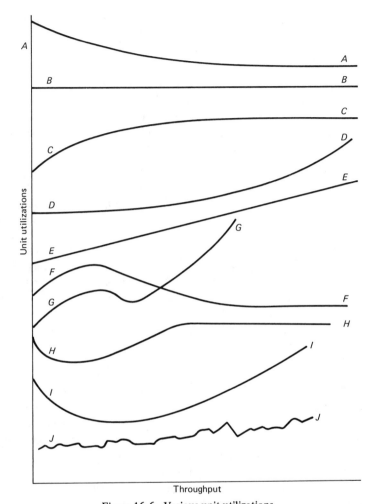

Figure 16-6. Various unit utilizations.

nested two deep, cubics to loops nested three deep, etc. The growth law gives you an insight to the mechanism; examine the mechanism to find out what is going on.

5. Curves F, G, H, and I could all come about from the superposition of several different processing components, each one of which was individually sensible. F and G, however, are suspect. You have to ask yourself about the clever thing that happened in the mid-region to reduce the processing per transaction, and why that clever thing could not have been done earlier

in the game, resulting in a curve like B or D, respectively. Such behavior bears more investigation.

6. Curve H is peculiar. It can be viewed as a combination of curve A, which has acceptable and understandable behavior, and curve C, which does not. Again, the presence of a reversal is a sign for investigation.

7. Curve I is not of the same ilk. It can be viewed as the superposition of curves A and D. There are two processes involved. One which gets more efficient with increasing load, and one which exhibits strong load dependencies. Find the components and treat them individually.

If the over-all resource does not exhibit strange behavior, it is no reason to set it aside and to look elsewhere. The over-all resource utilization is the superposition of many components; the components tend to compensate for each other.

The net result might be something like curve J. Furthermore, since you got this data from measured points and regression analyses, they don't look anywhere near as nice, or as solid as illustrated. Everything discussed above applies as well to a component of a resource utilization. If the over-all binding resource doesn't show it, go to the next level with the largest component first and see what you can find. Incidently, the same kind of analyses can be useful in debugging a system. Bugs, because of their haphazard nature, almost always show up as affecting performance. Usually, that effect is haphazard as well, leading to peculiar looking SR curves and more peculiar looking unit utilization curves.

4.3. An Empirical Observation

A bug free system (or model) that is well tuned has a smooth SR curve, generally slightly concave, without notches, and only one plateau, typically near the blowup point. The unit utilization curves tend to be monotonic and smooth. If not monotonic, they have a minimum (are concave upwards) and can be explained as the superposition of two processes, one of which is getting more efficient with load, and the other which is growing nonlinearly with load. Bugs and mistuning are most apparent in the rocky portions of the SR curve.

5. HOW TO TUNE

5.1. Delay–Throughput Trades

5.1.1. Asynchronous Systems
Delay can be reduced for some transactions, typically at the expense of increasing the delay for others. Shifting a high delay processing component to a higher functional priority level will decrease the delay for that transaction type at the

expense of lower priority transactions. If most of the processing occurs at one level, then the number of level shifts is minimized. As processing is distributed to more and more functional levels, the expected number of level shifts, or equivalently, the expected number of returns to a central dispatcher, increases. Consequently unit utilization increases, resulting in a reduced throughput. Transaction delays can be reduced by splitting functions into more microscopic pieces to take maximum advantage of wasted processing that might occur in gaps. This again increases unit utilizations. Generally, the trade between throughput and delay is difficult to observe in asynchronous systems, since the effect may be very diffuse.

5.1.2. Cyclic Systems

Throughput–delay trades are more obvious in cyclic systems. The trades are effected by one or more of the following tactics:

1. shifting a function from the cyclic base level to a higher priority, asynchronous level (global stretch is increased for all other functions);
2. invoking the routine several times in a cycle (overhead is increased, therefore the maximum throughput is decreased);
3. modifying the order of the cycle so that the number of cycles required to complete a given transaction is reduced (this generally increases delay for some other transactions, and may cause gaps);
4. allocating an incoming task to start processing if the input routine is active rather than waiting for the next cycle; similarly, issuing output commands as soon as the task has been processed rather than waiting until the end of the batch (unit processing is increased because batching advantages are discarded; furthermore, there are more priority level shifts, therefore more stretch);
5. forcibly curtailing the cycle or curtailing processing on some program after a fixed number of transactions have been processed (the system now goes through more cycles to handle the same load, and consequently has higher overhead).

Note that in all cases the delay was reduced in the cyclic system by increasing the per unit processing at the given throughput level—which is to say, by effectively *increasing* the cycle length.

5.1.3. The Other Way

If you want to increase throughput at the expense of delay, then the reverse of the above tactics can be employed: move things to lower priority levels, increase batch size, etc.

5.2. Gaps

5.2.1. General

Gaps in binding resources can either be eliminated or filled. They are usually easier to fill than to eliminate. They typically exist because you did not expect them to: "Who expected to have to seek across 40 tracks? When they said they would return the acknowledgment in more than 50 microseconds, I didn't expect it to be 500 milliseconds. I was sure that there was enough time to calculate the next position before the start of the next revolution"; etc.

You eliminate a binding resource gap by splitting a gap-causing function and invoking it twice. Since gaps are often I/O latency-related, such opportunities may not occur. If the system is I/O bound, and the gap is caused by processing, then the gap can be split. But if the system is CPU bound and the gap is a one-half revolution latency, there is not much you can do about it. You fill gaps by finding something for the bound resource to do within the gap.

5.2.2. Asynchronous Systems

Gap filling in asynchronous systems is accomplished by shifting task priority levels. Low priority tasks that had been blocked because the waiting task was of a higher priority are moved to a higher priority than the waiting task. If you move enough low priority tasks up, and enough stalled tasks down, you may eliminate the gap. If you overdo it, you will create new gaps. Monitoring activities at each priority level (functional, not physical) is an indispensable aid to gap filling.

5.2.3. Cyclic Systems

Gap filling in cyclic systems is done by moving processes around to different parts of the cycle.

1. Take a time-consuming process that is done at one point in the cycle and execute it whenever there is a gap, instead of going into a wait loop. Do one task, see if the I/O operation is done; if not, take another task; otherwise, go back to the mainstream process. Overhead will clearly increase but so will ultimate throughput. Not only have you eliminated the gap, but you have made the system self-tuning.
2. Rearrange the cycle so that the growth rate of the gap-causing function is comparable to the function being "gapped." This may mean combining functions, splitting functions, forcing extra cycles of delay, etc.
3. Accumulate tasks for the gapped process over a longer period of time, invoking it less frequently, or in alternation with some other function.

When you do invoke it, it will be larger than the "gapper." The cost is increased delay, and increased memory.

5.3. Code Bias

5.3.1. What Is It?

Branch instructions are typically asymmetrical. In many computers they are implemented as a skip to a jump instruction. Consequently, whatever you do for one path or the other, there is a time difference between the two paths by virtue of the branch. This may not seem like a lot of time, but it adds up because the typical program contains some 20% branch instructions. In designing the code then, you made numerous choices (almost subconsciously) at every decision, as to which should be the "normal path" and which should be the exception path. If those decisions are made haphazardly, or are based on what turn out to be inaccurate data, the code will be biased in favor of cases that are not statistically significant. Therein lies a tuning opportunity.

5.3.2. How to Find It and Fix It

You must know the instruction repertoire at the machine level, and you must examine the code. The modeling and validation effort gives you a guide as to which routines to examine. There is no point in spending time on small stuff. Having ordered the unit utilizations in decreasing order, and further broken this down to subsystems, subprograms, modules, subroutines, etc., using techniques that are now familiar, analyze the flows to find the statistically significant components. These are the ones to go after. At that point, assuming you have found something significant, you can redo those code segments. Ultimate throughput will be improved for the mix of transactions that you bias the code to, and decreased for all transactions on the exception paths. Similarly, delay will be decreased for the favored transactions at the expense of the unfavored ones.

5.3.3. A More Elegant Situation

In some cases, it is possible to rearrange a sequence of decisions to minimize the expected processing time for a set of operations. The model is shown in Figure 16-7. The flowchart consists of a sequence of decisions, 1, 2, 3, with associated processing $A1, B1, A2, B2$, and $A3, B3$, respectively. If the condition is met, for say, Decision 2, the process $B2$ will be executed and the program will be exited. Otherwise, process $A2$ will be executed and Decision 3 will be next executed. Assume that you have complete freedom in choosing the order of

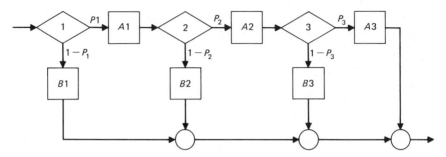

Figure 16-7. Code order optimization problem.

processing (e.g., 1, 2, 3 or 3, 1, 2, etc.). This situation and variations occur frequently.* You can examine N different permutations, but for even moderate N, say 7 or 8, this is unreasonable. The following algorithm will give you the optimum order directly:

1. Calculate $S_i = P_i(A_i - B_i) + B_i$ for all i.
2. For every pair of decisions, i and j, calculate $T_{ij} = S_i + P_i S_j$.
3. Compare T_{ij} with T_{ji} and discard the larger one.
4. Draw a graph with N nodes, one corresponding to each decision. If you kept T_{ij}, draw an arrow from i to j. If you kept T_{ji} draw an arrow from j to i. If you kept both (because they were equal) draw a double-headed arrow.
5. You must now examine only those permutations that can be obtained by following the arrows on the graph, starting with any node, and passing through each node once and only once.

Example:

Step 1: Calculate the S_i

P	A	B	$S = P(A - B) + B$
(1) 0.05	100	200	195
(2) 0.2	50	100	90
(3) 0.8	50	20	44

Steps 2, 3: Calculate the $T_{ij} = S_i + P_i S_j$ and discard the larger one.

$$T_{12} = 199.5 \qquad T_{21} = 129*$$
$$T_{13} = 197.2* \qquad T_{31} = 200$$
$$T_{23} = 98.8* \qquad T_{32} = 116$$

---

*For example, an IF-THEN-ELSEIF .... construct in structured code.

Step 4: Draw the graph in accordance to the values of T_{ij}.

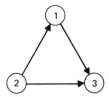

Step 5: Find the single covering paths corresponding to the permutations to be examined. There is only one path through this graph that covers each node once and only once. It is 2, 1, 3. Therefore, this is the optimum ordering.

A comparison of the optimum ordering (2, 1, 3) and the worst ordering shows mean times of 129.44 and 203.6, respectively. A sequence of 10 decisions requires only 90 comparisons and can be done in a fraction of an hour. Explicit examination of the permutations would require you to consider 3,628,800 different arrangements, heroic but unnecessary.

5.3.4. *Loop Trades and Further*

You have a loop as shown in Figure 16-8. Process C can be done either inside the loop (executed each time through) or outside the loop. Where should it be put? Compare the two cases:

$$\frac{A + PB}{1 - P} + C \sim \frac{A + PB + PC}{1 - P}$$

With a little algebra you can show that if $P > \frac{1}{2}$, the function should be placed outside the loop; otherwise it should be placed inside the loop.

The purpose of this exercise is to show that trades of this kind can be examined analytically. Application details will tell you how you can move functions about. You can model the alternatives and compare them algebraically or

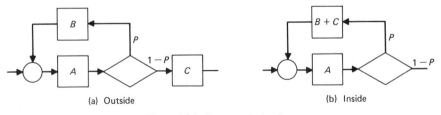

Figure 16-8. Loop optimization.

numerically in the regions of interest and obtain simple criteria for choosing the alternatives. Intuition tends to be a poor guide in choosing the optimum; formal methods are preferable.

5.3.5. Effect of Code Bias

As you tune tighter, providing more code bias to minimize desirable paths, you perforce increase the processing time on other paths. This has a twofold consequence. While the mean is reduced, the variance is increased. Depending on the specifics of the probabilities and the lengths of the off-paths, the simultaneous reduction in mean and increase in variance may result in either an increase or decrease in T_q, and therefore T_s. (Recall that the mean time in the queuing system depends on the variance of the service time.) Generally, you can expect that the service time variance will be increased. Therefore, while you are reducing the processing time, and therefore increasing the maximum throughput, you are doing it at the expense of increased delay. This delay increase acts to increase holding times, and therefore results in a simultaneous increase in dynamic memory. So code bias can result in the expected throughput–delay and throughput–memory trades also.

5.4. Memory and Overlay Trades

Static memory can be reduced by overlaying programs from an auxiliary store such as a disc or drum. This may or may not prove beneficial. The use of an overlay forces increased delays in both synchronous and asynchronous systems. This perforce increases holding times for dynamic memory; possibly by an amount equal to the expected latency and transfer time for the overlay. That increase in holding time may completely wipe out any static memory gains you may have obtained by virtue of increased dynamic memory. Furthermore, the overlay itself, through increased stretch and associated interrupts, reduces throughput and increases delay. It is not always obvious whether overlays will result in a net increase or decrease of memory. Here again, intuition is a poor guide because there are too many variables with too many subtle interactions. The alternatives should be examined analytically.

5.5. In-Line Code versus Subroutines

Processing time can be reduced by substituting in-line macros for common subroutines. It is not always obvious which subroutines should be treated this way. The steps, however are straightforward.

Annotate the model with subroutine call instances rather than processing time.

That is, substitute "1" for each subroutine call of interest, for a particular subroutine. Let all other calls and processing be set to zero. Alternatively, and sometimes more effectively, set the processing time for the subroutine of interest to zero, leaving the rest of the model the same. You cannot solve this model for the cycle length or delay as a function of throughput, since it will give you erroneous answers. However, you have solved the original model and therefore you have either the cycle length or delay as a function of throughput which you can substitute into the revised model. You can now use the revised model to determine the expected number of calls to the subroutine (the first approach) or the expected improvement due to the elimination of the subroutine (second approach). Comparing the revised model with the original gives you guidance as to whether or not straight-lining this subroutine is worthwhile. You can now go after the ones with the biggest payoff. The increase in static space is readily determined by counting the number of appearances of the subroutine in the listings or complete flowcharts. Here processing time is reduced and so is delay, at the expense of the static space. Therefore, dynamic space is decreased. Furthermore, since the in-line macro typically does not have as many explicit parameters to transfer, the space taken by the calling sequence may also be reduced. The space saved (dynamic and static) must be compared to the space increase caused by multiple appearances of the macro. It is often the case that the in-line macro reduces time, space, and delay; a fact that is rarely obvious.

Conversely, you can examine the replacement of a space-consuming macro with a common subroutine in order to save static space. Similarly, it is not usually intuitively obvious if such trades have a net payoff. It is clear that all such trades are correct only for certain probabilities, and that another set of probabilities could dictate that the trade go the other way.

6. HYPERTUNING

There is such a thing as going too far. As you tune tighter, code becomes "less natural" and subtler. Furthermore, it becomes increasingly vulnerable to environmental changes. If you overtune, that is, peak the system very sharply for optimum performance under a narrow set of assumed conditions, (i.e. probabilities), the system's performance degradation off that optimum point will be more disastrous. The system lacks robustness; the ability to take changes in stride. A system can be hypertuned with deleterious consequences throughout its lifetime. Sharp tuning increases maintenance costs, makes bugs subtler, and produces sharper breaks in the throughput–delay curve. These deleterious effects must be weighed against the marginal improvements of hypertuning.

7. PLAYING WITH THE MODEL

All proposed trades and tuning changes should be first examined by suitable modifications of the model. This is less costly, and often less embarrassing than doing it on the system directly. The model then, is not merely a tool used in the initial stages of design, or to determine the initial performance of the system. It is a living tool that can and should be used (and consequently should be maintained) throughout the system's lifetime.

8. EXERCISES

1. Tune the following systems in Chapter 12. You have complete freedom as to the order in which processes are invoked. Furthermore, you can split a process and invoke it more than once in a cycle. If you do so, however, the overhead will be incurred each time the operation is invoked. For example, if the process equation is $T_b = 0.001 + 0.025N$, splitting this function and invoking it twice does not change the equation, but rather the value of N that you will work with. Similarly, you can choose to invoke a function every other cycle, or every third cycle. In each case, develop the entire throughput delay curve and/or the SR curve. Measure the capacity of the system.

   a. (12-1)   c. (12-5)   e. (12-7)   g. (12-10)
   b. (12-4)   d. (12-6)   f. (12-9)

   Tune for minimum cycle length.
2. *Continuation.* Tune for minimum delay. Determine impact on cycle length and ultimate throughput.
3. *Continuation.* Tune for maximum ultimate throughput. Determine impact on cycle length and delay.
4. *Continuation.* Let the memory load in erlangs be proportional to the number of transactions in the system, which is in turn measured by the product of the delay and arrival rates. Tune for minimum memory load.
5. *Continuation.* Examine the impact on capacity, ultimate throughput, and cycle length as you tune for minimum, medial, and maximal delay. Similarly for throughput and memory.
6. *Continuation.* Tune to minimize the delay at that throughput corresponding to 65% of the untuned system's maximum throughput.
7. Tune the following systems in Chapter 13. You have freedom to order the priority levels of all processes.

   a. (13-5)   c. (13-7a)   e. (13-7c)
   b. (13-6)   d. (13-7b)   f. (13-7d)

Measure the capacity. With memory proportional to the product of the transaction arrival rates and the delay, tune for: minimum memory load, minimum delay, maximum throughput.

8. Tune the following systems in Chapter 14. You can rearrange or modify the cycle as in exercise 1 above. Determine the capacity of the tuned and untuned systems and tune for: minimum memory, maximum ultimate throughput, minimum delay, minimum initial delay.

a. (14-10)   b. (14-11)   c. (14-12)

9. A process consists of a simple loop, with function A in the forward part of the loop, B in the loopback position, and C following the exit of the loop. Process C can be combined with B. Prove that if the looping probability is greater than 0.5, C should be placed outside the loop to minimize the mean processing time.

10. The conditions of this problem are the same as that of exercise 9 above. Let the A and B processes be distributed with both mean and variance given. Let C be constant. It is desired to minimize the variance of the over-all process. Show that process C should always be placed outside of the loop.

11. Generalize exercises 9 and 10 above by considering the minimization of a function of the mean and standard deviation of the form: $\mu + k\sigma$, where μ is the process mean, k is an arbitrary integer constant, and σ is the process standard deviation. Show that the probability at which the inside and outside designs are the same is given by:

$$P = \frac{k^2 + 4 - k\sqrt{k^2 + 8}}{8}.$$

Particularize k to obtain the results of exercises 9 and 10.

12. A loop consists of three processes. Process C is an initialization process that could occur outside of the loop or inside the loop. The loop itself consists of process A followed by a test for terminating conditions. If the program loops, then process B is executed. C can be placed either with A or with B or remain outside. Establish the conditions under which you would pick each option.

13. Prove the validity of the ordering algorithm given in section 5.3.3. (Hint: It is isn't a question of which is the greater, but which doesn't dominate which.)

14. Show that the optimum order of the decisions are as given, where the A's and B's are defined in accordance with Figure 16-7.

Decision	Probability	A	B
1	0.001	1000.0	1.0010
2	0.002	500.0	1.0020
3	0.004	250.0	1.0040
4	0.005	125.0	1.0081

Compare the best order with the worst order.

15. Find the optimum order of these decisions:

Decision	Probability	A	B
1	0.4	200.0	500.0
2	0.6	300.0	500.0
3	0.8	400.0	500.0
4	0.2	100.0	500.0

16. Find the optimum order for these decisions:

Decision	Probability	A	B
1	0.05	500.0	450.0
2	0.1	250.0	475.0
3	0.15	166.7	425.0
4	0.2	125.0	450.0
5	0.4	62.5	425.0

Appendix I
Statistical Routines[†]
and Latency Models
Program Listings

NOTES:

$$\text{alog} = \log_{10}$$
$$\text{amax}1(a, b) = \max{(a, b)}$$

1. Drum latency model—fun23

    fsec   = number of sectors

    ftrs   = number of tasks in batch

    fun23 = the output, expected number of revolutions for the batch; multiply by the rotation time to get actual time rather than revolutions.

2. Statistical function model—fun36

    dlog = double precision $\log_{10}$

    dexp = double precision exponent (e)

    dsqrt = double precision square root

    prec = precision constant; i.e. 0.0001 is four significant digits. Processing time is proportional to the number of significant digits.

3. Disc latency model, fun32, fun33, fun34, binom. binom is a subroutine.

    fsec = number of sectors

    ftrs   = number of tasks in batch

    fcyl = number of cylinders on disc

    smin = minimum seek time on seek curve

    sdif = difference between minimum and maximum seek times

    trot = rotation time for disc.

expected time for batch = trot*fun32 + fun33 + fun34

Watch out for scaling errors.

[†]Thanks to Robert Rosenberg of Data Systems Analysts Inc. who wrote these routines.

drum latency model function

```
c drum latency model function
      function fun23(fsec,ftrs)
      data ftrm/.644/,strm/.0577/,frpr/.156/,five/-.0249/
      gtrs = amax1(ftrs,1.)
      nsec=fsec + .5
      conl=sqrt(3*fsec)
      con2 = 3422500/fsec/fsec
      slog=alog(fsec)
      tlog=alog(gtrs)
      if((gtrs.lt.conl.or.gtrs.gt.con2).and.gtrs.ge.64) go to 2000
      scpr=-.236
      rdpr=.0915
      four=-.01
      sixt=.0625
      sevn=-.0285
      pnin=.00338
      go to 3000
 2000 scpr=.0721
      rdpr=-.0517
      four=.00632
      sixt=-.0737
      sevn=.0316
      pnin=-.00326
 3000 eone = frpr+slog*(scpr+slog*(rdpr+slog*four))
      etwo = five+slog*(sixt+slog*(sevn+slog*pnin))
      exrt = (gtrs+.5+(fsec-1)/2*gtrs**(ftrm-strm*slog))/fsec
      fun23=exrt-(eone+tlog*etwo)*tlog*(tlog-4.159)
      return
      end
```

STATISTICAL SUBROUTINE PACKAGE

```
c does forward and 2 inverses for each of 5 distributions
      double precision prob,p,fprb,gprb,gtrm,gsum,hsum,fsum,prbl
      double precision prb2,prbh,drat
      fnxl(u)=u-(2.515517+u*(.802853+.010328*u))/
     *(1+u*(1.432788+u*(.189269+.001308*u)))
      fnul(p)=dsqrt(-2*dlog(1-p))
      fnx2(r,t)=((r/t)**e3-1+1/(9*t))*3*sqrt(t)
      fnu2(x)=1/(1+c*x)
      ftrm(r,x)=((sqrt(4*r)-x)**2+1)/4
      frat(t,x)=t*(1-1/(9*t)+x/sqrt(9*t))**3
      fprb(x,u)=ld0-a*exp(-aminl(x,13.)**2/2)*u*(bl+u*(b2+
     *u*(b3+u*(b4+b5*u))))
      gprb(x,u)=a*exp(-aminl(x,13.)**2/2)*(x*u*(bl+u*(b2+
     *u*(b3+u*(b4+b5*u))))
     *+c*(bl+u*(2*b2+u*(3*b3+u*(4*b4+5*b5*u))))/(1+c*x)**2)
      dprb(x,t,r,u)=t**el*r**e2*gprb(x,u)
      eprb(x,t,r,u)=t**-.5*(3*(r/t)**e3-9-1/t)*gprb(x,u)/6
      fsum(r,p)=exp(r)*(1-p)
      data a,bl,b2,b3,b4,b5,c,el,e2,e3/.39894228,.31938153,
     *-.356563782,1.781477937,-1.821255978,1.330274429,
     *.2316419,.1666666666,-.6666666666,.3333333333/
      data prec/.0001/

      kind=rind
c kind                      meaning
c ----                      -------
c   1      poisson: given items & prob find load
c   2      poisson: given load & prob find items
c   3      poisson: given load & items find prob
c   4      not used
c   5      erlang-b: given channels & prob find load
c   6      erlang-b: given load & prob find channels
c   7      erlang-b: given load & channels find prob
c   8      not used
c   9      erlang-c: given channels & prob find load
c  10      erlang-c: given load & prob find channels
c  11      erlang-c: given load & channels find prob
c  12      not used
c  13      chi-square: given d. 0f f. & prob find chi-sq.
c  14      chi-square: given chi-sq. & prob find d. of f.
c  15      chi-square: given chi-sq. & d. of f. find prob
c  16      not used
c  17      central gaussian: given sigma & prob find x
c  18      central gaussian: given x & prob find sigma
c  19      central gaussian: given x & sigma find prob
c  20      not used
      iprb=1
      if(kind.gt.4.and.kind.lt.13) iprb=2
      go to (1010,1020,1030,5000,1010,1020,2070,5000,1010,1020,
     *2070,5000,2130,2140,2150,5000,2180,2170,2190,5000),kind
c find rate
 1010 term=argl
      prbh=arg2
```

```
 2135 prbl=dlog(prbh)
      kont=0
      patl=term+180.5-9.5*sqrt(361+4*term)
      if(term.lt.10) patl=0
      pat2=term
      xxxx=fnxl(fnul(prbh))
      ratl=frat(term,xxxx)
      patl=aminl(patl,ratl)/2
      pat2=amaxl(pat2,ratl)*2
 1380 kont=kont+1
      if(kont.eq.15) go to 1060
      rate=ratl
      go to (1480,2480),iprb
 1300 continue
      if(prob.lt.le-15) go to 1305
      diff=dlog(prob)-prbl
      if(abs(diff).lt.prec) go to 1060
      if(derv.lt.le-15) go to 1305
      ratl=rate
      ratl=rate-prob*diff/derv
 1315 if(ratl.lt.patl) ratl=(rate+patl)/2
      if(ratl.gt.pat2) ratl=(rate+pat2)/2
      go to 1380
 1305 ratl=(rate+ratl)/2
      go to 1315
 1060 fun36=rate
      if(kind.eq.13) fun36=2*fun36
      return
c find first term
 1020 rate=arg1
      prbh=arg2
      go to (1105,1101),iprb
 1105 if(rate.gt.30)go to 1100
      hsum=fsum(rate,prbh)
      qsum=1
      qtrm=1
      do 1110 itrm=1,30
      if(qsum.gt.hsum)go to 1120
      qtrm=qtrm*rate/itrm
 1110 qsum=qsum+qtrm
 1100 prbl=dlog(prbh)
      kont=0
      prml=rate
      prm2=rate*(1+19/sqrt(rate))
      xxxx=fnxl(fnul(prbh))
      trml=ftrm(rate,xxxx)
      prml=aminl(prml,trml)/2
      prm2=amaxl(prm2,trml)*2
 1390 kont=kont+1
      if(kont.eq.15) go to 1160
      term=trml
      go to (1480,2480),iprb
 1500 continue
      if(prob.lt.le-15) go to 1505
```

```
           diff=dlog(prob)-prbl
           if(abs(diff).lt.prec) go to 1160
           if(derv.gt.-le-15) go to 1505
           trml=term
           trml=term-prob*diff/derv
     1515  if(trml.lt.prml) trml=(term+prml)/2
           if(trml.gt.prm2) trml=(term+prm2)/2
           go to 1390
     1505  trml=(term+trml)/2
           go to 1515
     1160  fun36=term
           go to 1165
     1120  fun36=itrm-(gsum-hsum)/gtrm
     1165  if(kind.eq.14) fun36=2*fun36
           return
     1101  if(rate.gt.100) go to 1100
           prbr=1/prbh
           gsum=1
           do 2510 itrm=1,100
           hsum=gsum
           gsum=gsum*itrm/rate+1
           if(kind.eq.10) go to 2500
           if(gsum.gt.prbr) go to 1125
     2510  continue
           go to 1100
     1126  gsum=gsum-hsum
           hsum=(1-rate/(itrm-1))*(hsum-1)+1
     1125  fun36=itrm-(1-prbh*gsum)/(1-gsum/hsum)
           return
     2500  if(gsum-hsum.gt.prbr) go to 1126
           go to 2510
c find probability
     1030  rate=argl
           term=arg2
     1480  ntrm=term-1
           if(ntrm.gt.30) go to 1220
           drat=rate
           gsum=1
           gtrm=1
           if(ntrm.lt.1)go to 1310
           do 1210 itrm=1,ntrm
           gtrm=gtrm*rate/itrm
           if(gtrm.lt.le-15) go to 1310
     1210  gsum=gsum+gtrm
     1310  prob=ld0-dexp(-drat)*gsum
           go to (1410,1415,1430,5000,1410,1415,1430,5000,1410,1415,
          *1430,5000,1410,1415,1435,5000),kind
     1415  derv=-dexp(-drat)*gtrm
           go to 2650
     1410  derv=dexp(-drat)*gtrm
     2650  go to (1300,1500,5000,5000,1300,1500,5000,5000,
          *1300,1500,5000,5000,1300,1500,5000,5000),kind
     1430  fun36=prob
           return
```

```
1220 xxxx=fnx2(rate,term)
     if(xxxx.lt.0) go to 1320
     uuuu=fnu2(xxxx)
     prob=fprb(xxxx,uuuu)
1605 go to (1600,1610,1430,5000,1600,1600,1600,5000,
    *1600,1600,1600,5000,1600,1610,1435,5000),kind
1320 xxxx=-xxxx
     uuuu=fnu2(xxxx)
     prob=1-fprb(xxxx,uuuu)
     go to 1605
1600 derv=dprb(xxxx,term,rate,uuuu)
     go to (1300,2600),iprb
1610 derv=eprb(xxxx,term,rate,uuuu)
     go to 1500
c find probability(erlang)
2070 rate=arg1
     term=arg2
2480 ntrm=term
     if(rate.eq.0) go to 2485
     tbyr=ntrm/rate
     if(kind.gt.8.and.tbyr.le.1) go to 2305
     if((kind.eq.6.or.kind.eq.10).and.rate.gt.100) go to 1220
     if(ntrm.gt.100) go to 1220
     if(kind.gt.8) go to 2300
     qsum=1
     qtrm=1
2310 if(ntrm.lt.1) go to 2315
     itrm=ntrm+1
     prop=1-prec
     hsum=0
     do 2210 ktrm=1,ntrm
     itrm=itrm-1
     qtrm=qtrm*itrm/rate
     qsum=qsum+qtrm
     if(hsum.gt.prop*qsum.or.qsum.gt.1e15) go to 2315
     hsum=qsum
2210 continue
2315 prob=1/qsum
2495 go to (2410,2410,1430,5000,2415,2415,1430,5000),kind-4
2485 prob=0
     go to 2495
2300 qsum=1
     qtrm=1-1/tbyr
     go to 2310
2305 prob=1
     go to 2495
2410 derv=(tbyr+prob-1)*prob
     if(kind.eq.6) derv=-derv
     go to 2650
2415 derv=(tbyr+(1-prob)/(ntrm-rate)-1)*prob
     if(kind.eq.10) derv=-derv
     go to 2650
2600 if(prob.lt.1) prob=derv/(1-prob)
     if(kind.gt.8) prob=tbyr/(1+(tbyr-1)/prob)
```

```
          go to 2495
c chi-square
 2130 term=arg1/2
      prbh=ld0-arg2
      go to 2135
 2140 rate=arg1/2
      prbh=ld0-arg2
      go to 1105
 2150 rate=arg1/2
      term=arg2/2
      go to 1480
 1435 fun36=1-prob
      return
c gaussian
 2170 prbh=ld0-arg2
      xxxx=fnxl(fnul(prbh))
      fun36=arg1/xxxx
 5000 return
 2180 prbh=ld0-arg2
      xxxx=fnxl(fnul(prbh))
      fun36=arg1*xxxx
      return
 2190 xxxx=arg2/arg1
      if(xxxx.lt.0) go to 2195
      fun36=1-fprb(xxxx,fnu2(xxxx))
      return
 2195 xxxx=-xxxx
      fun36=fprb(xxxx,fnu2(xxxx))
      return
      end
```

1st term of disk model function

```
c     portion of 1st term of disk model function
      function fun32(fsec,ftrs,fcvl)
      data scpl/-.236/,rdpl/.0915/,foul/-.01/,sixl/.0625/,
     *sevl/-.0285/,pnil/.00338/,scp2/.0721/,rdp2/-.0517/,
     *fou2/.00632/,six2/-.0737/,sev2/.0316/,pni2/-.00326/
      data ftrm/.644/,strm/.0577/,frpr/.156/,five/-.0249/
      data frev/.01/
      nsec = fsec + .5
      sloq = aloq(fsec)
      con1 = sqrt(3*fsec)
      con2 = 3422500/fsec/fsec
      eon1 = frpr+sloq*(scpl+sloq*(rdpl+sloq*foul))
      etwl = five+sloq*(sixl+sloq*(sevl+sloq*pnil))
      eon2 = frpr+sloq*(scp2+sloq*(rdp2+sloq*fou2))
      etw2 = five+sloq*(six2+sloq*(sev2+sloq*pni2))
      if(fcvl.le.1.) qo to 1000
      fcvl = fcvl - 1.
      ntrs = ftrs
      qtrs = ntrs
      qtrl = qtrs + 1.
      rcvl = 1./fcvl
      mean = qtrs/fcvl
      fmen = mean
      fact = binom(ntrs,mean,rcvl)
      tact = fact
      nret = 1
      ptrs = fmen
      qo to 5000
 5010 rvpc = exrt*fact
      rvpd = rvpc/(qtrl-fmen)
      pfac = 0
      if(ntrs.eq.0) qo to 1130
      nret = 2
      do 1010 itrs = mean+1,ntrs
      htrs = itrs
      fact = (qtrl-htrs)/htrs/fcvl*fact
      ptrs = htrs
      qo to 5000
 5020 term = exrt*fact
      rvpc = rvpc + term
      rvpd = rvpd + term/(qtrl-htrs)
      if(fact.qe.pfac) qo to 1010
      if(qtrs*(qtrs-htrs)*fact.lt.frev) qo to 1130
 1010 pfac = fact
 1130 if(mean.eq.0) qo to 1030
      fact = tact
      pfac = 0
      nret = 3
      do 1110 itrs = 1,mean
      itrs = mean - itrs
      htrs = itrs
      fact = (htrs+1.)*fcvl/(qtrs-htrs)*fact
      ptrs = htrs
      qo to 5000
```

```
5030 term = exrt*fact
     rvpc = rvpc + term
     rvpd = rvpd + term/(atrl-htrs)
    \if(fact.ge.pfac) go to 1110
     if(atrs*(atrs-htrs)*fact.lt.frev) go to 1030
1110 pfac = fact
1030 powr = 0
     expo = atrl*alog(rcvl)
     if(expo.gt.-88.) powr = exp(expo)
     nret = 4
     ptrs = atrl
     go to 5000
5040 fun32 = fcvl*(rvpc+(ftrs-atrs)*(powr*exrt
    *+atrl*(1-rcvl)*rvpd-rvpc))
     return
1000 ptrs = ftrs
     nret = 5
5000 atrs = amaxl(ptrs,1.)
     tlog=alog(atrs)
     if((atrs.lt.conl.or.atrs.gt.con2).and.atrs.ge.64) go to 2000
     eone = eonl
     etwo = etwl
     go to 3000
2000 eone = eon2
     etwo = etw2
3000 exrt = (atrs+.5+(fsec-1)/2*atrs**(ftrm-strm*slog))/fsec
    *-(eone+tlog*etwo)*tlog*(tlog-4.159)
     if(ptrs.lt.1.) exrt = ptrs*exrt + (1.-ptrs)*.5/fsec
     go to (5010,5020,5030,5040,5050),nret
5050 fun32 = exrt
     return
     end
```

second term of the disk model function.

```
c second term of the disk model function.
      function fun33(smin,ftrs,fcvl)
      data expl/88./
      if(fcvl.le.1.) ao to 1000
      expo = amaxl(ftrs-1.,0.)*aloa(1.-1./fcvl)
      if(expo.lt.-expl) ao to 1010
      fun33 = smin*(fcvl-(fcvl-1.)*exp(expo))
      return
 1000 fun33 = smin
      return
 1010 fun33 = smin*fcvl
      return
      end
```

3rd term of disk model function.

```
c 3rd term of disk model function.
      function fun34(ftrs,fcvl,sdif)
      data expl/88./
      if(fcvl.le.2.) go to 1000
      expo = amaxl(ftrs-1.,0.)*aloq(1.-1./fcvl)
      if(expo.lt.-expl) go to 1000
      acvl = fcvl - (fcvl-1.)*exp(expo)
      fun34 = sdif*acvl*(fcvl-acvl)/(acvl+1.)/(fcvl-1.)
      return
 1000 fun34 = 0
      return
      end
```

binomial function

```
      function binom(ntot,nchs,prob)
      data bian/1.e32/,smal/1.e-32/
      prcm=prob
      nsml=min0(nchs,ntot-nchs)
      if(nsml.eq.ntot-nchs)prcm=1.-prob
      prnc=1.-prcm
      nbia=ntot-nsml
      binom=1
      if(nsml.eq.0) ao to 1000
      kont=nsml-1
      fact=(nbia+1)*prcm
 1010 binom=binom*fact
      if(kont.eq.0)ao to 1000
      kont=kont-1
      fact=(ntot-kont)*prcm/(nsml-kont)
 1030 if(binom.le.smal/fact)ao to 1040
      if(binom.lt.bian/fact) ao to 1010
      binom=binom*prnc
      nbia=nbia-1
      ao to 1030
 1000 if(nbia.eq.0)return
      if(binom.lt.smal/prnc)ao to 1040
      binom=binom*prnc
      nbia=nbia-1
      ao to 1000
 1040 binom=0
      return
      end
```

Appendix II
Models[†]

The following models are used in various exercises in the book. The flowcharts are represented as a list of links. This is an alternative representation to flowcharts or matrices (see Chapter 8). The list representation is convenient for computer manipulation of models. A comparison of the first model flowchart with the corresponding list will help clarify the notation.

The flowchart consists of **links** and **nodes**. A link is represented as an ordered pair of nodes. For example $(D1, D2)$ is a link that joins node $D1$ to node $D2$. Each line of the list corresponds to a link. The meanings of the various columns are given below:

SEQ   sequence number of the link.
CODE   identifies the kind of node according to the following codes:
               INWA   an inway node, a flowchart entry point;
               LINK   an internal link of the flowchart;
               OUTW   an outway node, a flowchart exit point;
               ENDL   a control code signifying the end of the model or
                      answer.
ANODE   the first node in the ordered pair of nodes used to define a
               link. GILA is a special, fictitious node that connects to all
               inways. An asterisk (*) in this column signifies that the
               model entry program generated this name.
BNODE   the second node in the ordered pair of nodes used to define a
               link. ZEND is a fictitious node that connects all outways.
               An asterisk indicates the name was supplied by the program.
PROBABILITY   specifies the probability associated with the link. Ignore
               asterisks.
MEAN   specifies the mean value of the resource consumed by the
               given link. Ignore asterisks.
DEVIATION   specifies the standard deviation of the resource consumed by

---

[†]Thanks to Powell Arms of Data Systems Analysts Inc. who created and solved (by hand and by machine) most of these models.

the given link. The deviation field is not always present. If present on output and absent on the input, then it is assumed that all link deviations were zero.

CONTROL   used to indicate various things about the model output or input.

DIST   indicates that the normal calculation is to be used to determine the standard deviation for a loop. See Chapter 7, section 6.2.3.

FIXED   indicates that looping probabilities are to be interpreted as a shorthand for a count of the number of times the loop is traversed.

DEAD   the model analyzer discoverd that the link in question did not terminate in a declared outway by any available path.

NO PATH   the model program determined that there was no path between the specified node pair.

Inputs and outputs may appear either in fixed- or floating-point notation. The output format is almost the same as the input format. Note that in several models there are two sets of outputs, labeled INITIAL OUTPUT and FINAL OUTPUT. (See model T003 for an example). The first output is obtained by reducing the model (by whatever means) until only the declared inways and outways remain. If, at that point, there remain connections between the inways, or among the outways, or unreduced loops between inways and outways, the analysis is not complete. To complete the analysis, you consider every combination of inway and outway. Reduce the model one inway/outway pair at a time, treating the remaining inways and outways as internal nodes of the model. The INITIAL OUTPUT is the model reduced to the point where this procedure can be applied. The FINAL OUTPUT is the result of this procedure. In model T016, for example, the first phase reduces the model to nine links, of which only five belong in the final answer. Note the link between nodes C and $A1$. It must be removed for a final answer. In this case, the intermediate model is reduced four times, retaining node pairs $(A1, H)$, $(A1, I)$, (C, H), and (C, I) respectively. You will find it instructive to draw the flowcharts. Note that some of the lists in the T model series contain several models each. Comparison of these subsidiary models may be instructive.

Since you do not have a model manipulation and analysis program (about 6,000 statements in FORTRAN), you may find it instructive to "build" your own processor for this purpose. That's what we did before we built the beast. It was fairly good for small models (under 50 links). Furthermore, since we never did build an algebraic version of this package, the "processor" described below was used. It is, in fact, generally more convenient for algebraic models than the matrix method (see Chapter 8).

Lay in a good supply of index cards (3″ X 5″ for numerical models and 5″ X 7″ for algebraic models). Use one card for each link. Write the names of the nodes that define the link at the top of the card—e.g. ANODE, BNODE, and all appropriate numerical or algebraic data on the first line beneath. Sort the cards in alphabetic order by ANODE name and by BNODE name within ANODE name. Apply the reduction algorithm. The key is the selection of a node for the cross-term step. The cross-term step can be applied if you find a pair of cards whose names are (ANAME, BNAME), (BNAME, CNAME). This is why it pays to sort them in alphabetical order. If you find such a pair, then make sure to treat all cards involving BNAME in either the first or second position, since it is node BNAME that you are going to remove. Each combination of the above form creates a new card, to which you apply the cross-term equations to obtain the new probability, new mean, and new deviation values or expressions. Put the old cards of the removed node aside and resort the deck. The parallels will now be obvious, since they will have the same name pairs. Apply the parallel rules. Now look for loops. They will have both names the same, and apply the loop equation. Say the loop card is of the form (ANAME, ANAME); then there will be cards of the form (ANAME, BNAME) which must be corrected when the loop is removed.

All strategic considerations regarding the selection of a node for removal can be readily translated to an equivalent operation on the index cards. If you manipulate the cards correctly, you will not have to waste much time sorting them. A string sort algorithm, based on the assumption that cards are almost perfectly sorted, is ideal and most efficient. You can set things up so that you can eliminate several nodes per pass, but this requires complicated bookkeeping and is difficult to control by hand. Keep your decisions simple lest you get lost.

A36

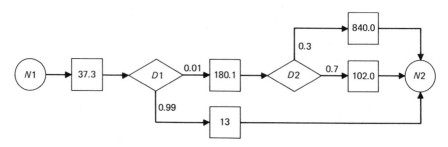

INPUT

SEQ.	CODE	ANODE	BNODE	PROBABILITY	MEAN	CONTROL
1	INWA	GILA*	N1	1.0000000*	0.0000000*	DIST.
2	LINK	N1	D1	1.0000000*	37.3	DIST.
3	"	D1	D2	.01	180.1	DIST.
4	"	"	N2	0.9900000*	13.0	DIST.
5	"	D2	"	.7	102.	DIST.
6	"	"	"	0.3000000*	840.	DIST.
7	OUTW	N2	ZEND*	1.0000000*	0.0000000*	DIST.
8	ENDL					

OUTPUT

SEQ.	CODE	ANODE	BNODE	PROBABILITY	MEAN	CONTROL
1	INWA	GILA	N1	1.000000	0.0000	DIST.
2	LINK	N1	N2	1.000000	0.5521E+02	DIST.
3	OUTW	N2	ZEND	1.000000	0.0000	DIST.

A44

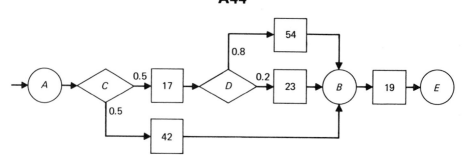

A44 (continued)

INPUT

SEQ.	CODE	ANODE	BNODE	PROBABILITY	MEAN	CONTROL
1	INWA	GILA*	A	1.0000000*	0.0000000*	DIST.
2	LINK	A	C	1.0000000*	0.0000000*	DIST.
3	"	C	D	.5	17.	DIST.
4	"	C	B	0.5000000*	42.	DIST.
5	"	D	"	.2	23.	DIST.
6	"	"	"	0.8000000*	54.	DIST.
7	"	B	E	1.0000000*	19.	DIST.
8	OUTW	E	ZEND*	1.0000000*	0.0000000*	DIST.
9	ENDL					

OUTPUT

SEQ.	CODE	ANODE	BNODE	PROBABILITY	MEAN	CONTROL
1	LINK	A	E	1.000000	0.7240E+02	DIST.
2	OUTW	E	ZEND	1.000000	0.0000	DIST.
3	INWA	GILA	A	1.000000	0.0000	DIST.

A41

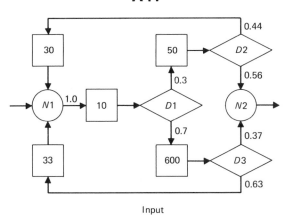

Input

A41 (continued)

INPUT

SEQ.	CODE	ANODE	BNODE	PROBABILITY	MEAN	CONTROL
1	INWA	GILA*	N1	1.0000000*	0.0000000*	DIST.
2	LINK	N1	D1	1.0000000*	10.	DIST.
3	"	D1	D2	.3	50.	DIST.
4	"	"	D3	0.7000000*	600.	DIST.
5	"	D2	N1	.44	30.	DIST.
6	"	"	N2	0.5600000*	0.0000000*	DIST.
7	"	D3	"	.37	0.0000000*	DIST.
8	"	"	N1	0.6300000*	33.	DIST.
9	OUTW	N2	ZEND*	1.0000000*	0.0000000*	DIST.
10	ENDL					

OUTPUT

SEQ.	CODE	ANODE	BNODE	PROBABILITY	MEAN	CONTROL
1	INWA	GILA	N1	1.000000	0.0000	DIST.
2	LINK	N1	N2	1.000000	0.1086E+04	DIST.
3	OUTW	N2	ZEND	1.000000	0.0000	DIST.

A5

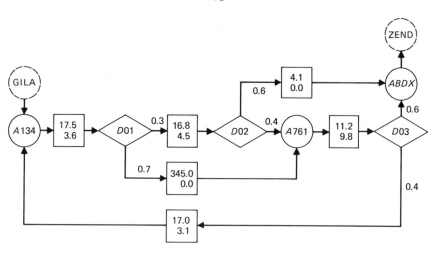

A5 (continued)

INPUT

SEQ.	CODE	ANODE	BNODE	PROBABILITY	MEAN	DEVIATION	CONTROL
1	INWA	GILA*	A134	1.0000000*	0.0000000*	0.0000000*	DIST.
2	LINK	A134	DO1	1.0000000*	17.5	3.6	DIST.
3	"	DO1	DO2	.3	16.8	4.5	DIST.
4	"	"	A761	0.7000000*	345.	0.0000000*	DIST.
5	"	DO2	"	.4	0.0000000*	0.0000000*	DIST.
6	"	"	ABDX	0.6000000*	4.1	0.0000000*	DIST.
7	"	A761	DO3	1.0000000*	11.2	9.8	DIST.
8	"	DO3	ABDX	.6	0.0000000*	0.0000000*	DIST.
9	"	"	A134	0.4000000*	17.	3.1	DIST.
10	OUTW	ABDX	ZEND*	1.0000000*	0.0000000*	0.0000000*	DIST.
11	ENDL						

OUTPUT

SEQ.	CODE	ANODE	BNODE	PROBABILITY	MEAN	DEVIATION	CONTROL
1	LINK	A134	ABDX	1.000000	0.4160E+03	0.2670E+03	DIST.
2	OUTW	ABDX	ZEND	1.000000	0.0000	0.0000	DIST.
3	INWA	GILA	A134	1.000000	0.0000	0.0000	DIST.

A39

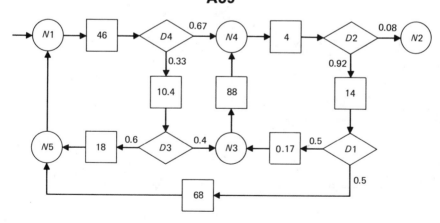

A39 (continued)

INPUT

SEQ.	CODE	ANODE	BNODE	PROBABILITY	MEAN	CONTROL
1	INWA	GILA*	N1	1.0000000*	0.0000000*	DIST.
2	LINK	N1	D4	1.0000000*	46.	DIST.
3	"	D4	D3	.33	10.4	DIST.
4	"	"	N4	0.6700000*	0.0000000*	DIST.
5	"	D3	N5	.60	18.	DIST.
6	"	"	N3	.40	0.0000000*	DIST.
7	"	N5	N1	1.0000000*	0.0000000*	DIST.
8	"	N3	N4	1.0000000*	88.	DIST.
9	"	N4	D2	1.0000000*	4.	DIST.
10	"	D2	N2	.08	0.0000000*	DIST.
11	"	"	D1	0.9200000*	14.	DIST.
12	"	D1	N3	.5	.17	DIST.
13	"	"	N5	0.5000000*	68.	DIST.
14	OUTW	N2	ZEND*	1.0000000*	0.0000000*	DIST.
15	ENDL					

OUTPUT

SEQ.	CODE	ANODE	BNODE	PROBABILITY	MEAN	CONTROL
1	INWA	GILA	N1	1.000000	0.0000	DIST.
2	LINK	N1	N2	1.000000	0.2263E+04	DIST.
3	OUTW	N2	ZEND	1.000000	0.0000	DIST.

A42

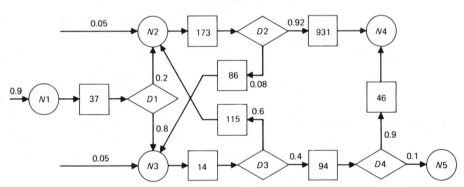

A42 (continued)

INPUT

SEQ.	CODE	ANODE	BNODE	PROBABILITY	MEAN	CONTROL
1	INWA	GILA*	N1	.90	0.0000000*	DIST.
2	"	GILA*	N2	.05	0.0000000*	DIST.
3	"	GILA*	N3	0.0500000*	0.0000000*	DIST.
4	LINK	N1	D1	1.0000000*	37.	DIST.
5	"	D1	N2	.2	0.0000000*	DIST.
6	"	"	N3	0.8000000*	0.0000000*	DIST.
7	"	N2	D2	1.0000000*	173.	DIST.
8	"	D2	N4	.92	931.	DIST.
9	"	"	N3	0.0800000*	86.	DIST.
10	"	N3	D3	1.0000000*	14.	DIST.
11	"	D3	N2	.6	115.	DIST.
12	"	"	D4	0.4000000*	94.	DIST.
13	"	D4	N5	.1	0.0000000*	DIST.
14	"	"	N4	0.9000000*	46.	DIST.
15	OUTW	N4	ZEND*	1.0000000*	0.0000000*	DIST.
16	"	N5	ZEND*	1.0000000*	0.0000000*	DIST.
17	ENDL					

OUTPUT

SEQ.	CODE	ANODE	BNODE	PROBABILITY	MEAN	CONTROL
1	INWA	GILA	N1	0.900000	0.0000	DIST.
2	INWA	GILA	N2	0.050000	0.0000	DIST.
3	INWA	GILA	N3	0.050000	0.0000	DIST.
4	LINK	N1	N2	0.200000	0.3700E+02	DIST.
5	LINK	N1	N3	0.800000	0.3700E+02	DIST.
6	LINK	N2	N3	0.080000	0.2590E+03	DIST.
7	LINK	N2	N4	0.920000	0.1104E+04	DIST.
8	LINK	N3	N2	0.600000	0.1290E+03	DIST.
9	LINK	N3	N4	0.360000	0.1540E+03	DIST.
10	LINK	N3	N5	0.040000	0.1080E+03	DIST.
11	OUTW	N4	ZEND	1.000000	0.0000	DIST.
12	OUTW	N5	ZEND	1.000000	0.0000	DIST.

A37

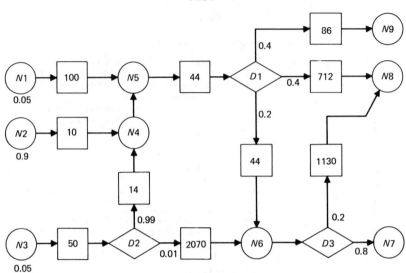

INPUT

SEQ.	CODE	ANODE	BNODE	PROBABILITY	MEAN	CONTROL
1	INWA	GILA*	N1	.05	0.0000000*	DIST.
2	"	GILA*	N2	.90	0.0000000*	DIST.
3	"	GILA*	N3	0.0500000*	0.0000000*	DIST.
4	LINK	N1	N5	1.0000000*	100.	DIST.
5	"	N2	N4	1.0000000*	10.	DIST.
6	"	N3	D2	1.0000000*	50.	DIST.
7	"	N5	D1	1.0000000*	44.	DIST.
8	"	N4	N5	1.0000000*	0.0000000*	DIST.
9	"	D2	N4	.99	14.	DIST.
10	"	"	N6	0.0100000*	2070.	DIST.
11	"	D1	N9	.40	86.	DIST.
12	"	"	N8	.40	712.	DIST.
13	"	"	N6	0.2000000*	44.	DIST.
14	"	N6	D3	1.0000000*	0.0000000*	DIST.
15	"	D3	N7	.80	0.0000000*	DIST.
16	"	"	N8	0.2000000*	1130.	DIST.
17	OUTW	N9	ZEND*	1.0000000*	0.0000000*	DIST.
18	"	N8	ZEND*	1.0000000*	0.0000000*	DIST.
19	"	N7	ZEND*	1.0000000*	0.0000000*	DIST.
20	ENDL					

A37 (continued)

OUTPUT

SEQ.	CODE	ANODE	BNODE	PROBABILITY	MEAN	CONTROL
1	INWA	GILA	N1	0.050000	0.0000	DIST.
2	INWA	GILA	N2	0.900000	0.0000	DIST.
3	INWA	GILA	N3	0.050000	0.0000	DIST.
4	LINK	N1	N7	0.160000	0.1880E+03	DIST.
5	LINK	N1	N8	0.440000	0.8980E+03	DIST.
6	LINK	N1	N9	0.400000	0.2300E+03	DIST.
7	LINK	N2	N7	0.160000	0.9800E+02	DIST.
8	LINK	N2	N8	0.440000	0.8080E+03	DIST.
9	LINK	N2	N9	0.400000	0.1400E+03	DIST.
10	LINK	N3	N7	0.166400	0.2466E+03	DIST.
11	LINK	N3	N8	0.437600	0.8729E+03	DIST.
12	LINK	N3	N9	0.396000	0.1940E+03	DIST.
13	OUTW	N7	ZEND	1.000000	0.0000	DIST.
14	OUTW	N8	ZEND	1.000000	0.0000	DIST.
15	OUTW	N9	ZEND	1.000000	0.0000	DIST.

A38

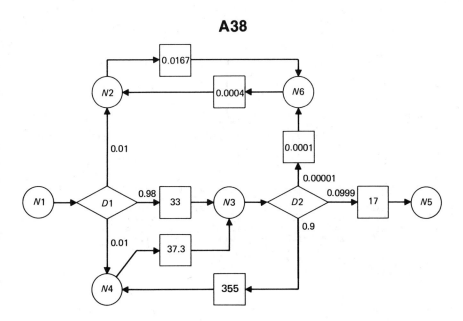

A38 (continued)

INPUT

SEQ.	CODE	ANODE	BNODE	PROBABILITY	MEAN	CONTROL
1	INWA	GILA*	N1	1.0000000*	0.0000000*	DIST.
2	LINK	N1	D1	1.0000000*	0.0000000*	DIST.
3	"	D1	N4	.01	0.0000000*	DIST.
4	"	"	N3	.98	33.	DIST.
5	"	"	N2	0.0100000*	0.0000000*	DIST.
6	"	N4	N3	1.0000000*	37.3	DIST.
7	"	N3	D2	1.0000000*	0.0000000*	DIST.
8	"	D2	N4	.9	355.	DIST.
9	"	"	N5	.09999	17.	DIST.
10	"	"	N6	0.0000100*	.0001	DIST.
11	"	N6	N2	1.0000000*	.0004	DIST.
12	"	N2	N6	1.0000000*	.0167	DIST.
13	OUTW	N5	ZEND*	1.0000000*	0.0000000*	DIST.
14	ENDL					

OUTPUT

DEAD END LOOP

SEQ	CODE	ANODE	BNODE	PROB.	MEAN	DEVIATION	CONTROL
8	LINK	N6	N6	1.000000	0.1710000E-01	0.0000000	DIST.

SEQ	CODE	ANODE	BNODE	PROB.	MEAN	DEVIATION	CONTROL
0	LINK	N1	N6	0.000000	0.0000000	0.0000000	DEAD
0	LINK	N3	N6	0.000000	0.0000000	0.0000000	DEAD
0	LINK	N1	N6	0.000000	0.0000000	0.0000000	DEAD

SEQ	CODE	ANODE	BNODE	PROB.	MEAN	DEVIATION	CONTROL
1	INWA	GILA	N1	1.000000	0.0000000	0.0000000	DIST.
2	LINK	N1	N5	0.989901	0.3581097E+04	0.3722057E+04	DIST.
3	LINK	N1	N6	0.010099	0.3461136E+06	0.5067730E+07	DIST.
4	OUTW	N5	ZEND	1.000000	0.0000000	0.0000000	DIST.

T003

INPUT

SEQ	CODE	ANODE	BNODE	PROB.	MEAN	DEVIATION	CONTROL
1	INWA	GILA	A1	0.500000	0.0000000	0.0000000	DIST.
2	INWA	GILA	AB	0.500000	0.0000000	0.0000000	DIST.
3	LINK	A1	A3	0.250000	0.1000000E+02	0.1000000E+01	DIST.
4	LINK	A1	A3	0.750000	0.1000000E+03	0.1000000E+02	DIST.
5	LINK	AB	123	0.250000	0.8000000E+01	0.1000000E+01	DIST.
6	LINK	AB	789	0.750000	0.5000000E+02	0.0000000	DIST.
7	LINK	123	AF	1.000000	0.2000000E+01	0.0000000	DIST.
8	LINK	789	AF	1.000000	0.5000000E+02	0.1000000E+02	DIST.
9	LINK	A3	ASD	1.000000	0.0000000	0.0000000	DIST.
10	LINK	AF	QWS	1.000000	0.0000000	0.0000000	DIST.
11	OUTW	ASD	ƵEND	1.000000	0.0000000	0.0000000	DIST.
12	OUTW	QWS	ƵEND	1.000000	0.0000000	0.0000000	DIST.

INITIAL OUTPUT

SEQ	CODE	ANODE	BNODE	PROB.	MEAN	DEVIATIMN	CONTROL
1	LINK	A1	ASD	1.000000	0.7750000E+02	0.3992493E+02	DIST.
2	LINK	AB	QWS	1.000000	0.7750000E+02	0.3992493E+02	DIST.
3	OUTW	ASD	ƵEND	1.000000	0.0000000	0.0000000	DIST.
4	INWA	GILA	A1	0.500000	0.0000000	0.0000000	DIST.
5	INWA	GILA	AB	0.500000	0.0000000	0.0000000	DIST.
6	OUTW	QWS	ƵEND	1.000000	0.0000000	0.0000000	DIST.

FINAL OUTPUT

ANODE	BNODE	PROBABILITY	MEAN	DEVIATION	
A1	ASD	0.500000	0.7750000E+02	0.3992493E+02	
A1	QWS	0.000000	0.0000000	0.0000000	NO PATH
AB	ASD	0.000000	0.0000000	0.0000000	NO PATH
AB	QWS	0.500000	0.7750000E+02	0.3992493E+02	

T004

INPUT

SEQ	CODE	ANODE	BNODE	PROB.	MEAN	DEVIATION	CONTROL
1	INWA	GILA	AB	0.500000	0.0000000	0.0000000	DIST.
2	LINK	AB	A2	1.000000	0.0000000	0.0000000	DIST.
3	LINK	A2	A2	0.800000	0.1000000E+02	0.1000000E+01	DIST.
4	LINK	A2	A3	0.200000	0.1000000E+03	0.1000000E+02	DIST.
5	OUTW	A3	ƵEND	1.000000	0.0000000	0.0000000	DIST.
6	INWA	GILA	A1	0.500000	0.0000000	0.0000000	DIST.
7	LINK	A1	C4	1.000000	0.0000000	0.0000000	DIST.
8	LINK	C4	72	0.800000	0.1000000E+02	0.1000000E+01	DIST.
9	LINK	C4	B3	0.200000	0.1000000E+03	0.1000000E+02	DIST.
10	LINK	72	C4	0.800000	0.1000000E+02	0.1000000E+01	DIST.
11	LINK	72	B3	0.200000	0.1000000E+03	0.1000000E+02	DIST.
12	OUTW	B3	ƵEND	1.000000	0.0000000	0.0000000	DIST.

T004 (continued)

INITIAL OUTPUT

SEQ	CODE	ANODE	BNODE	PROB.	MEAN	DEVIATION	CONTROL
1	LINK	A1	B3	1.000000	0.1400000E+03	0.4586938E+02	DIST.
2	OUTW	A3	ZEND	1.000000	0.0000000	0.0000000	DIST.
3	LINK	AB	A3	1.000000	0.1400000E+03	0.4586938E+02	DIST.
4	OUTW	B3	ZEND	1.000000	0.0000000	0.0000000	DIST.
5	INWA	GILA	A1	0.500000	0.0000000	0.0000000	DIST.
6	INWA	GILA	AB	0.500000	0.0000000	0.0000000	DIST.

FINAL OUTPUT

ANODE	BNODE	PROBABILITY	MEAN	DEVIATION	
A1	A3	0.000000	0.0000000	0.0000000	NO PATH
A1	B3	0.500000	0.1400000E+03	0.4586938E+02	
AB	A3	0.500000	0.1400000E+03	0.4586938E+02	
AB	B3	0.000000	0.0000000	0.0000000	NO PATH

T006

INPUT

SEQ	CODE	ANODE	BNODE	PROB.	MEAN	DEVIATION	CONTROL
1	INWA	GILA	Z1	0.333333	0.0000000	0.0000000	DIST.
2	INWA	GILA	LAM1	0.000000	0.0000000	0.0000000	FIXED
3	LINK	LAM1	BOY1	1.000000	0.0000000	0.0000000	DIST.
4	LINK	BOY1	GIRX	1.000000	0.0000000	0.0000000	DIST.
5	LINK	GIRX	FOX1	0.400000	0.0000000	0.0000000	FIXED
6	LINK	GIRX	BOY1	0.600000	0.1000000E+01	0.1000000E+01	FIXED
7	LINK	FOX1	BOY1	0.500000	0.1000000E+02	0.2000000E+01	FIXED
8	LINK	FOX1	LUX	0.500000	0.1000000E+02	0.1000000E+01	FIXED
9	OUTW	LUX	ZEND	1.000000	0.0000000	0.0000000	DIST.
10	LINK	Z1	C	1.000000	0.0000000	0.0000000	DIST.
11	LINK	C	B	0.800000	0.0000000	0.0000000	FIXED
12	LINK	C	A1	0.200000	0.1000000E+02	0.1000000E+01	FIXED
13	LINK	B	C	0.750000	0.1000000E+01	0.1000000E+01	FIXED
14	LINK	B	C	0.250000	0.1000000E+02	0.2000000E+01	FIXED
15	OUTW	A1	ZEND	1.000000	0.0000000	0.0000000	DIST.
16	INWA	GILA	71	0.333333	0.0000000	0.0000000	DIST.
17	LINK	71	C1	1.000000	0.0000000	0.0000000	DIST.
18	LINK	C1	C1	0.600000	0.1000000E+01	0.1000000E+01	FIXED
19	LINK	C1	C1	0.200000	0.1000000E+02	0.2000000E+01	FIXED
20	LINK	C1	D	0.200000	0.1000000E+02	0.1000000E+01	FIXED
21	OUTW	D	ZEND	1.000000	0.0000000	0.0000000	DIST.
22	INWA	GILA	LAM	0.333333	0.0000000	0.0000000	DIST.
23	LINK	LAM	BOY	1.000000	0.0000000	0.0000000	DIST.
24	LINK	BOY	GIRL	1.000000	0.0000000	0.0000000	DIST.
25	LINK	GIRL	BOY	0.200000	0.1000000E+02	0.2000000E+01	FIXED
26	LINK	GIRL	FOX	0.800000	0.0000000	0.0000000	FIXED
27	LINK	FOX	BOY	0.750000	0.1000000E+01	0.1000000E+01	FIXED
28	LINK	FOX	LU	0.250000	0.1000000E+02	0.1000000E+01	FIXED
29	OUTW	LU	ZEND	1.000000	0.0000000	0.0000000	DIST.

T006 (continued)

INITIAL OUTPUT

SEQ	CODE	ANODE	BNODE	PROB.	MEAN	DEVIATION	CONTROL
1	LINK	71	D	1.000000	0.230000E+02	0.2828427E+01	DIST.
2	OUTW	A1	ZEND	1.000000	0.0000000	0.0000000	DIST.
3	OUTW	D	ZEND	1.000000	0.0000000	0.0000000	DIST.
4	INWA	GILA	71	0.333333	0.0000000	0.0000000	DIST.
5	INWA	GILA	LAM	0.333333	0.0000000	0.0000000	DIST.
6	INWA	GILA	LAM1	0.000000	0.0000000	0.0000000	FIXED
7	INWA	GILA	Z1	0.333333	0.0000000	0.0000000	DIST.
8	LINK	LAM	LU	1.000000	0.230000E+02	0.2828427E+01	DIST.
9	LINK	LAM1	LUX	1.000000	0.230000E+02	0.2828427E+01	DIST.
10	OUTW	LU	ZEND	1.000000	0.0000000	0.0000000	DIST.
11	OUTW	LUX	ZEND	1.000000	0.0000000	0.0000000	DIST.
12	LINK	Z1	A1	1.000000	0.230000E+02	0.2828427E+01	DIST.

FINAL OUTPUT

ANODE	BNODE	PROBABILITY	MEAN	DEVIATION	
71	A1	0.000000	0.0000000	0.0000000	NO PATH
71	D	0.333333	0.230000E+02	0.2828427E+01	
71	LU	0.000000	0.0000000	0.0000000	NO PATH
71	LUX	0.000000	0.0000000	0.0000000	NO PATH
LAM	A1	0.000000	0.0000000	0.0000000	NO PATH
LAM	D	0.000000	0.0000000	0.0000000	NO PATH
LAM	LU	0.333333	0.230000E+02	0.2828427E+01	
LAM	LUX	0.000000	0.0000000	0.0000000	NO PATH
LAM1	A1	0.000000	0.0000000	0.0000000	NO PATH
LAM1	D	0.000000	0.0000000	0.0000000	NO PATH
LAM1	LU	0.000000	0.0000000	0.0000000	NO PATH
LAM1	LUX	0.000000	0.230000E+02	0.2828427E+01	
Z1	A1	0.333333	0.230000E+02	0.2828427E+01	
Z1	D	0.000000	0.0000000	0.0000000	NO PATH
Z1	LU	0.000000	0.0000000	0.0000000	NO PATH
Z1	LUX	0.000000	0.0000000	0.0000000	NO PATH

T008

INPUT

SEQ	CODE	ANODE	BNODE	PROB.	MEAN	DEVIATION	CONTROL
1	INWA	GILA	A1	0.600000	0.0000000	0.0000000	DIST.
2	INWA	GILA	G	0.400000	0.0000000	0.0000000	DIST.
3	LINK	A1	C	0.750000	0.1230000E+03	0.0000000	DIST.
4	LINK	A1	F	0.250000	0.4400000E+02	0.0000000	DIST.
5	LINK	G	F	1.000000	0.2200000E+02	0.0000000	DIST.
6	LINK	M	G	1.000000	0.9000000E+01	0.0000000	DIST.
7	LINK	D	M	1.000000	0.1120000E+03	0.0000000	DIST.
8	LINK	F	D	1.000000	0.3350000E+02	0.0000000	DIST.
9	OUTW	C	ZEND	1.000000	0.0000000	0.0000000	DIST.

T009

INPUT

SEQ	CODE	ANODE	BNODE	PROB.	MEAN	DEVIATION	CONTROL
1	INWA	GILA	A1	0.500000	0.0000000	0.0000000	DIST.
2	LINK	A1	B1	1.000000	0.1000000E+03	0.1000000E+01	DIST.
3	LINK	B1	B1	0.000000	0.1000000E+02	0.1000000E+01	FIXED
4	LINK	B1	9	1.000000	0.5000000E+02	0.3000000E+01	DIST.
5	OUTW	9	ZEND	1.000000	0.0000000	0.0000000	DIST.
6	INWA	GILA	8	0.500000	0.0000000	0.0000000	DIST.
7	LINK	8	4	1.000000	0.1000000E+02	0.2000000E+01	DIST.
8	LINK	4	4	1.000000	0.1000000E+02	0.1000000E+01	DIST.
9	LINK	4	7	0.000000	0.0000000	0.0000000	FIXED
10	OUTW	7	ZEND	1.000000	0.0000000	0.0000000	DIST.

T010

INPUT

SEQ	CODE	ANODE	BNODE	PROB.	MEAN	DEVIATION	CONTROL
1	INWA	GILA	P	0.200000	0.0000000	0.0000000	DIST.
2	LINK	P	R	1.000000	0.0000000	0.0000000	DIST.
3	LINK	R	F	0.250000	0.1000000E+01	0.1000000E+01	DIST.
4	LINK	R	F	0.400000	0.1000000E+02	0.1000000E+01	DIST.
5	LINK	R	F	0.350000	0.1000000E+03	0.1000000E+01	DIST.
6	OUTW	F	ZEND	1.000000	0.0000000	0.0000000	DIST.
7	INWA	GILA	P1	0.200000	0.0000000	0.0000000	DIST.
8	LINK	P1	R1	1.000000	0.0000000	0.0000000	DIST.
9	LINK	R1	X1	0.250000	0.1000000E+01	0.1000000E+01	DIST.
10	LINK	R1	F	0.400000	0.1000000E+02	0.1000000E+01	DIST.
11	LINK	R1	F	0.350000	0.1000000E+03	0.1000000E+01	DIST.
12	LINK	X1	F	1.000000	0.0000000	0.0000000	DIST.
13	INWA	GILA	P2	0.200000	0.0000000	0.0000000	DIST.
14	LINK	P2	R2	1.000000	0.0000000	0.0000000	DIST.
15	LINK	R2	X2	0.400000	0.1000000E+02	0.1000000E+01	DIST.
16	LINK	R2	F	0.250000	0.1000000E+01	0.1000000E+01	DIST.
17	LINK	R2	F	0.350000	0.1000000E+03	0.1000000E+01	DIST.
18	LINK	X2	F	1.000000	0.0000000	0.0000000	DIST.
19	INWA	GILA	P3	0.200000	0.0000000	0.0000000	DIST.
20	LINK	P3	R3	1.000000	0.0000000	0.0000000	DIST.
21	LINK	R3	X3	0.350000	0.1000000E+03	0.1000000E+01	DIST.
22	LINK	R3	F	0.250000	0.1000000E+01	0.1000000E+01	DIST.
23	LINK	R3	F	0.400000	0.1000000E+02	0.1000000E+01	DIST.
24	LINK	X3	F	1.000000	0.0000000	0.0000000	DIST.
25	INWA	GILA	P4	0.200000	0.0000000	0.0000000	DIST.
26	LINK	P4	R4	1.000000	0.0000000	0.0000000	DIST.
27	LINK	R4	X4	0.600000	0.0000000	0.0000000	DIST.
28	LINK	R4	F	0.400000	0.1000000E+02	0.1000000E+01	DIST.
29	LINK	X4	F	0.416667	0.1000000E+01	0.1000000E+01	DIST.
30	LINK	X4	F	0.583333	0.1000000E+03	0.1000000E+01	DIST.

T010 (continued)

INITIAL OUTPUT

SEQ	CODE	ANODE	BNODE	PROB.	MEAN	DEVIATION	CONTROL
1	OUTW	F	ZEND	1.000000	0.0000000	0.0000000	DIST.
2	INWA	GILA	P	0.200000	0.0000000	0.0000000	DIST.
3	INWA	GILA	P1	0.200000	0.0000000	0.0000000	DIST.
4	INWA	GILA	P2	0.200000	0.0000000	0.0000000	DIST.
5	INWA	GILA	P3	0.200000	0.0000000	0.0000000	DIST.
6	INWA	GILA	P4	0.200000	0.0000000	0.0000000	DIST.
7	LINK	P	F	1.000000	0.3925000E+02	0.4472905E+02	DIST.
8	LINK	P1	F	1.000000	0.3925000E+02	0.4472905E+02	DIST.
9	LINK	P2	F	1.000000	0.3925000E+02	0.4472905E+02	DIST.
10	LINK	P3	F	1.000000	0.3925000E+02	0.4472905E+02	DIST.
11	LINK	P4	F	1.000000	0.3925000E+02	0.4472905E+02	DIST.

FINAL OUTPUT

ANODE	BNODE	PROBABILITY	MEAN	DEVIATION
P	F	0.200000	0.3925000E+02	0.4472905E+02
P1	F	0.200000	0.3925000E+02	0.4472905E+02
P2	F	0.200000	0.3925000E+02	0.4472905E+02
P3	F	0.200000	0.3925000E+02	0.4472905E+02
P4	F	0.200000	0.3925000E+02	0.4472905E+02

T012

INPUT

SEQ	CODE	ANODE	BNODE	PROB.	MEAN	DEVIATION	CONTROL
1	INWA	GILA	P1	0.250000	0.0000000	0.0000000	DIST.
2	INWA	GILA	P2	0.250000	0.0000000	0.0000000	DIST.
3	INWA	GILA	P3	0.250000	0.0000000	0.0000000	DIST.
4	INWA	GILA	P4	0.250000	0.0000000	0.0000000	DIST.
5	OUTW	F	ZEND	1.000000	0.0000000	0.0000000	DIST.
6	LINK	P1	R1	1.000000	0.0000000	0.0000000	DIST.
7	LINK	R1	X1	0.250000	0.1000000E+01	0.1000000E+01	DIST.
8	LINK	R1	F	0.400000	0.1000000E+02	0.1000000E+01	DIST.
9	LINK	R1	F	0.350000	0.1000000E+03	0.1000000E+01	DIST.
10	LINK	X1	F	1.000000	0.0000000	0.0000000	DIST.
11	LINK	P2	X2	1.000000	0.0000000	0.0000000	DIST.
12	LINK	X2	R2	0.250000	0.1000000E+01	0.1000000E+01	DIST.
13	LINK	X2	F	0.400000	0.1000000E+02	0.1000000E+01	DIST.
14	LINK	X2	F	0.350000	0.1000000E+03	0.1000000E+01	DIST.
15	LINK	R2	F	1.000000	0.0000000	0.0000000	DIST.
16	LINK	P3	X3	1.000000	0.0000000	0.0000000	DIST.
17	LINK	X3	R3	0.600000	0.0000000	0.0000000	DIST.
18	LINK	X3	F	0.400000	0.1000000E+02	0.1000000E+01	DIST.
19	LINK	R3	F	0.416667	0.1000000E+01	0.1000000E+01	DIST.
20	LINK	R3	F	0.583333	0.1000000E+03	0.1000000E+01	DIST.
21	LINK	P4	R4	1.000000	0.0000000	0.0000000	DIST.
22	LINK	R4	X4	0.600000	0.0000000	0.0000000	DIST.
23	LINK	R4	F	0.400000	0.1000000E+02	0.1000000E+01	DIST.
24	LINK	X4	F	0.416667	0.1000000E+01	0.1000000E+01	DIST.
25	LINK	X4	F	0.583333	0.1000000E+03	0.1000000E+01	DIST.

T012 (continued)

INITIAL OUTPUT

SEQ	CODE	ANODE	BNODE	PROB.	MEAN	DEVIATION	CONTROL
1	OUTW	F	ZEND	1.000000	0.0000000	0.0000000	DIST.
2	INWA	GILA	P1	0.250000	0.0000000	0.0000000	DIST.
3	INWA	GILA	P2	0.250000	0.0000000	0.0000000	DIST.
4	INWA	GILA	P3	0.250000	0.0000000	0.0000000	DIST.
5	INWA	GILA	P4	0.250000	0.0000000	0.0000000	DIST.
6	LINK	P1	F	1.000000	0.3925000E+02	0.4472905E+02	DIST.
7	LINK	P2	F	1.000000	0.3925000E+02	0.4472905E+02	DIST.
8	LINK	P3	F	1.000000	0.3925000E+02	0.4472905E+02	DIST.
9	LINK	P4	F	1.000000	0.3925000E+02	0.4472905E+02	DIST.

FINAL OUTPUT

ANODE	BNODE	PROBABILITY	MEAN	DEVIATION
P1	F	0.250000	0.3925000E+02	0.4472905E+02
P2	F	0.250000	0.3925000E+02	0.4472905E+02
P3	F	0.250000	0.3925000E+02	0.4472905E+02
P4	F	0.250000	0.3925000E+02	0.4472905E+02

T016

INPUT

SEQ	CODE	ANODE	BNODE	PROB.	MEAN	DEVIATION	CONTROL
1	INWA	GILA	A1	0.500000	0.0000000	0.0000000	DIST.
2	INWA	GILA	C	0.500000	0.0000000	0.0000000	DIST.
3	LINK	A1	P1	1.000000	0.1000000E+02	0.1000000E+01	DIST.
4	LINK	P1	A1	0.500000	0.1000000E+03	0.2000000E+01	DIST.
5	LINK	P1	E	0.500000	0.1000000E+01	0.0000000	DIST.
6	LINK	C	F	1.000000	0.1000000E+02	0.3000000E+01	DIST.
7	LINK	F	P1	0.750000	0.1000000E+01	0.1000000E+01	DIST.
8	LINK	F	E	0.250000	0.1000000E+04	0.2000000E+01	DIST.
9	LINK	E	P1	0.500000	0.1000000E+02	0.1000000E+01	FIXED
10	LINK	E	R	0.250000	0.1000000E+03	0.0000000	FIXED
11	LINK	E	H	0.250000	0.0000000	0.0000000	FIXED
12	LINK	R	I	0.700000	0.1200000E+02	0.3000000E+01	DIST.
13	LINK	R	H	0.300000	0.1000000E+03	0.0000000	DIST.
14	OUTW	H	ZEND	1.000000	0.0000000	0.0000000	DIST.
15	OUTW	I	ZEND	1.000000	0.0000000	0.0000000	DIST.

T016 (continued)

INITIAL OUTPUT

SEQ	CODE	ANODE	BNODE	PROB.	MEAN	DEVIATION	CONTROL
1	LINK	A1	H	0.650000	0.2881538E+03	0.1607863E+03	FIXED
2	LINK	A1	I	0.350000	0.3540000E+03	0.1608142E+03	FIXED
3	LINK	C	A1	0.583333	0.2588095E+03	0.5451705E+01	DIST.
4	LINK	C	H	0.270833	0.4610205E+03	0.4680252E+01	FIXED
5	LINK	C	I	0.145833	0.5268667E+03	0.5559205E+01	FIXED
6	INWA	GILA	A1	0.500000	0.0000000	0.0000000	DIST.
7	INWA	GILA	C	0.500000	0.0000000	0.0000000	DIST.
8	OUTW	H	ZEND	1.000000	0.0000000	0.0000000	DIST.
9	OUTW	I	ZEND	1.000000	0.0000000	0.0000000	DIST.

FINAL OUTPUT

ANODE	BNODE	PROBABILITY	MEAN	DEVIATION
A1	H	0.325000	0.2881538E+03	0.1607863E+03
A1	I	0.175000	0.3540000E+03	0.1608142E+03
C	H	0.325000	0.5111539E+03	0.1229102E+03
C	I	0.175000	0.5770000E+03	0.1229468E+03

References

ABAT68   Abate, Joseph; Dubner, Harvey; Weinberg, Sheldon B. "Queueing Analysis of the IBM 2314 Disc Storage Facility," *Journal of the ACM*, Vol. 15, No. 4, October 1968, pp. 577–589.

Presents models for FIFO, file, continual arrival disc under various seek time functions and record length distributions. The approach leads to numerical procedures. Examples are worked out and presented.

AMER61   American Telephone and Telegraph Company. *Switching Systems*. American Telephone and Telegraph Company, New York, 1961.

Contains an excellent, clear introduction to the Poisson formula, the Erlang-*B* formula, and the Erlang-*C* formula. Charts covering up to 60 erlangs load with 80 servers and blocking (delay) probabilities down to 0.001. Comparison of the three formulas.

ARMS71   Arms, Powell, W. Jr. *Statistical Network Analysis*. MS thesis, University of Pennsylvania, Moore School of Electrical Engineering, Philadelphia, Pa. August 1971.

Derivation and proof of validity of the flow reduction algorithms.

BARN76   Barna, Arpad; Porat, Dan I. *Introduction to Microcomputers and Microprocessors*. Wiley–Interscience, New York, 1976. 108 + x pp.

General, elementary introduction to microcomputers.

BEIZ71   Beizer, Boris. *The Architecture and Engineering of Digital Computer Complexes*. Plenum Press, New York, 1971. Volume I, 394 + li pp; Volume II, 453 + xxxiii pp.

Overview of the architecture of large scale, real-time, multiple computer complexes. Survey of most important hardware features. Volume I contains derivations of flow reduction equations, program optimization techniques, application of linear programming to optimization. Volume II discusses communication functions, executive structures, operating systems.

BENW75   Benwell, Nicholas. *Benchmarking: Computer Evaluation and Measurement*. John Wiley & Sons, New York, 1975. 190 + xviii pp.

All about benchmarking, instruction mixes, etc. A conference proceeding including give-and-take among participants.

BUNY74   Bunyan, C. J. (Editor). *Computer Systems Measurement: Infotech State of the Art Report No. 18*. Infotech International Ltd, Maidenhead, Berks SL61LD, England. 1974, 701 + vii pp.

A panel of experts get together to discuss system performance, analysis, simulation, measurement, and tuning. An excellent overview. This is an expensive book and consequently will be found only in large university and corporate libraries. It's worth reading, though. Part of a continuing series of reports: further reports include performance modeling and prediction as such.

BURG71   Burge, William H.; Konheim, Alan G. "An Accessing Model," *Journal of the ACM*, Vol. 18, No. 3, July 1971, pp. 400–404.

Paged, scheduled, batch drum with constant batch size.

BUZE71   Buzen, Jeffrey P. *Queueing Network Models of Multi-Programming*. PhD dissertation, Harvard University, August 1971. Also USAF Electronics Systems Division, Hanscom Field, Bedford, Mass., report No. FF19628-70-C-0217, and Department of Commerce, National Technical Information Service report No. AD 731,575.

A seminal paper on the entire subject. Contains an excellent review of the state of the art as of 1971 and a complete bibliography.

CARN69   Carnahan, Brice; Luther, H. A.; Wilkes, James O. *Applied Numerical Methods*. John Wiley & Sons, 1969. 603 + xviii pp.

A big book with lots of information on numerical methods. Numerous programs, flowcharts, listings. A good source book.

CARS76   Carson, John H. (Editor). *Minicomputers and Microprocessors: A Tutorial*. Institute of Electrical and Electronics Engineers, New York, 1976. 282 + iv pp.

A collection of reprinted technical articles and conference papers dealing with most aspects of microcomputers, including: technology, programming, architecture, system development, and interfaces. Articles describing the architecture of most popular microcomputers are to be found here.

COFF69   Coffman, E. G., Jr. "Analysis of a Drum Input/Output Queue Under Scheduled Operation in a Paged Computer System," *Journal of the ACM*, Vol. 16, No. 1, January 1969, pp. 73–90.

Treats a paged, scheduled, continual arrival drum in which every sector can have its own arrival rate. The treatment is complete. Also considered is the precessing drum scheme which can be used when track switching time is high.

COFF73   Coffman, E. G., Jr; Denning, Peter J. *Operating Systems Theory*. Prentice-Hall, Englewood Cliffs, New Jersey, 1973. 331 + xvi pp.

This book is heavy in all aspects of queueing theory as applied to computer system performance analysis. Section 5.2 of Chapter 5 treats the FIFO unscheduled drum, the continual arrival, paged, scheduled drum, and the FIFO continual arrival drum. Also treated is the analysis of the bias of the SCAN procedure against the edge tasks. Discussion of closed queueing network models.

DAHL72   Dahl, O. J.; Dijkstra, E. W.; Hoare, C. A. R. *Structured Programming*. Academic Press, London, 1972. 220 + viii pp.

Modular programming (see MAYN72) only much more so. The how, what, when, and where of structured programming.

DENN65   Denning, Peter J. *Queueing Models for File Memory Operation*. M.S. thesis, MIT, Cambridge, Mass., May 1965.

A general discussion of the problem, its context, and a solution of the continual arrival sectored file drum. Results are given in terms of the numerical solution of an equation.

DENN67   Denning, Peter J. "Effects of Scheduling on File Memory Operation," *Transactions of the Spring Joint Computer Conference*, 1967, Vol. 30, AFIPS Press, Montvale N.J., pp. 9–21.

Examines the impact of read/write switching on drums; derives expected minimum access time (expected time to the beginning of the first task on a batch drum), an optimistic model for the batch drum, expected minimum seek time for a SSTF disc, waiting time for a single request under SCAN, and comparisons of various policies.

DRUM73   Drummond, Mansford, E. Jr. *Evaluation and Measurement Techniques for Digital Computer Systems*. Prentice-Hall, Englewood Cliffs, N.J., 1973. 338 + xiv pp.

Introduction to the entire field of performance analysis and measurement with the notable exception of analytical models and associated techniques. Use of benchmarks, simulation, and hardware and software instrumentation, are discussed in detail.

ELMA70   Elmaghraby, Salah, E. *Some Network Models in Management Science*. Springer-Verlag, New York, 1970. 176 pp.

Introduction to the theory of general activity networks; reduction procedures where applicable; applications.

EVER71   Everling, Wolfgang. *Exercises in Computer Systems Analysis*. Springer-Verlag, Berlin, 1975. 184 + vii pp.

Analysis of systems whose performance is dominated by queueing theoretic considerations and effects.

FRAN69   Frank, Howard. "Analysis and Optimization of Disc Storage Devices for Time-Sharing Systems," *Journal of the ACM*, Vol. 16, No. 4, October 1969, pp. 602–620.

Analysis of expected seek time and seek time distribution in general. Expected number of tracks traversed in a seek. Analysis of total seek time for file operations where a record can span several tracks. Analysis of problem when all locations are not equiprobable. Optimization strategies.

FIFE65   Fife, D. W.; Smith, J. L. "Transmission Capacity of Disc Storage Systems with Concurrent Arm Positioning," *IEEE Transactions on Electronic Computers*, Vol. 14, No. 4, August 1965, pp. 575–582.

Analysis of a multi-arm, FIFO, paging, continual arrival disc. Seeks can occur independently for several arms. A number of independent channels serve the disc.

FLOR69   Flores, Ivan. *Computer Organization*, Prentice-Hall, Englewood Cliffs, N.J., 1969. 371 + xii pp.

While old, this book remains one of the best introductions to the organization of computer hardware. Examples are drawn from many computers ranging from mini to macro.

FRYT65   Fry, Thornton, C. *Probability and Its Engineering Uses.* D. Van Nostrand, New York, 1965; first edition, 1928. 462 + xv pp.

Excellent introduction to probability. Many discussions of multi-server queueing systems that apply to dynamic storage problems. Comparisons of various formulas. A grand old book.

FULL75A   Fuller, Samuel H. *Analysis of Drum and Disc Storage Units.* Springer-Verlag, New York, 1975. 283 + ix pp.

Most complete treatment of continual arrival drums to date. Analysis of drum optimization in which both latency and processing time are minimized.

FULL75B   Fuller, Samuel, H. "An Analysis of Drum Storage Units," *Journal of the ACM,* Vol. 22, No. 1, January 1975, pp. 83–105.

FIFO sectored file drum, FIFO paging drum, scheduled paging drum, scheduled file drum. Simulation comparisons of various models. Empirical model for scheduled file drum, drum and CPU combined.

GILB77   Gilb, Tom. *Software Metrics.* Winthrop Publishers, Inc. Cambridge, Mass., 1977. 282 pp.

Measurement of software performance in the broad sense including reliability, maintainability in addition to throughput. Much philosophy and guidance relating to the value of additional performance vis-á-vis its actual or potential cost.

GORD69   Gordon, Geoffrey. *System Simulation.* Prentice-Hall, Englewood Cliffs, N.J., 1969. 303 + xvi pp.

Introductory book on system simulation which in many ways parallels this book. Applications are not, however, dominated by the simulation of computer systems. Simulation in DYNAMO, FORTRAN, GPSS, and SIMSCRIPT is discussed.

GOTL73   Gotlieb, Calvin C.; MacEwen, G. H. "Performance of Movable Head Disc Storage Devices," *Journal of the ACM,* Vol. 20, No. 4, October 1973, pp. 606–623.

Continual arrival FIFO disc with uniform distribution of tasks, SCAN disc, SCAN policy with nonuniform task distributions, FIFO with nonuniform task distributions, multi-mode disc systems, comparisons of FIFO, SCAN, and SSTF.

GROS74   Gross, Donald; Harris, Carl M. *Fundamentals of Queueing Theory.* John Wiley & Sons, New York, 1974. 556 + xvi pp.

An excellent introduction to the subject, although somewhat heavy for the uninitiated. Clearly and carefully written with consistent notation. An important feature is an excellent index that states just what solutions are available and in what form.

JOSL68   Joslin, Edward O. *Computer Selection.* Addison-Wesley, Reading, Mass., 1968. 172 + ix pp.

Discussion of benchmark techniques, primitive path tracing, and simulation, (especially with SCERT). Note that this book is aimed at the commercial data processing market and not the typical real-time, or mini/micro-based system designer.

KLEI76   Kleinrock, Leonard. *Queueing Systems*. John Wiley & Sons, New York, 1976. Volume I, 417 + xviii pp; Volume II, 549 + xx pp.

This is the definitive book on queueing theory and its application to computer systems analysis. Volume I concerns basic theory—it presumes a good deal of mathematics. The notation, while consistent, can take a lot of effort to get into, despite numerous excellent indexes. Approximately half of volume II concerns computer communication network problems. Volume II, however, does include a summary of most of the queueing theory models that have been developed for the analysis of computer systems. These volumes are a basic reference.

KUOS65   Kuo, Shan S. *Numerical Methods and Computers*. Addison-Wesley, Reading, Mass., 1965. 341 + x pp.

Source book on numerical analysis aimed at computer solutions with flow-charts and listings. Suitable to most of your needs.

MANG65   Mangulis, V. *Handbook of Series for Scientists and Engineers*. Academic Press, New York, 1965. 134 + viii pp.

MART72   Martin, James. *Systems Analysis for Data Transmission*. Prentice-Hall, Engle-wood Cliffs, N.J., 1972. 910 + xv pp.

There is a 68 page introduction to queueing theory in this book. I don't particularly recommend it for that because some of the formulas are not consistent with respect to the number on queue vs. the number in the system. Furthermore, the specification of the system being treated is not always clear. However, there are a lot of good tables and graphs (approximately 50 pages) that cover the more common and simpler queueing models. In all, this book does give you a good feel for queueing theory.

MAYE72   Mayeda, Wataru. *Graph Theory*. Wiley–Interscience, New York, 1972. 588 + x pp.

All around introduction to graph theory in all its glory. Readable.

MAYN72   Maynard, Jeff. *Modular Programming*. Auerbach, Princeton, 1972. 100 + iv pp.

A brief and readable introduction to modular programming techniques.

MCCR64   McCracken, David S.; Dorn, William S. *Numerical Methods and Fortran Programming*. John Wiley & Sons, New York, 1964. 457 + xii pp.

Good introduction to most numerical methods you are likely to need.

ONEY75   Oney, Walter C. "Queueing Analysis of the SCAN Policy for Moving Head Discs," *Journal of the ACM*, Vol. 22, No. 3, July 1975, pp. 397–412.

Continual arrival SCAN disc with general (approximate) solution for arbitrary seek functions. Analysis of edge bias for SCAN policies. Exact model for

SCAN disc with low and high load approximations. Batch disc without home position with FIFO within cylinders.

PARZ60   Parzen, Emanuel. *Modern Probability Theory and Its Applications.* John Wiley & Sons, New York, 1960. 464 + xiv pp.

Almost every queueing theory book has an introductory or supplementary section on probability, statistics, and prerequisite mathematics. In most cases, such introductions are useful only as a refresher if you already had the stuff. Parzen is a basic introduction and reference for probability theory.

PRIT69   Pritsker, A. Alan B. *GERT–Simulation program for GERT Network Analysis.* University of Georgia, COSMIC computer center, 1969. 39 pp.

This is the user's instruction manual for the GERT network analyzer. This program is written over the GASP IIA language.

PRIT74A   Pritsker, A. Alan B.; Sigal, C. Elliot. *The GERT IIIZ User's Manual.* Pritsker & Associates, Inc. West Lafayette, Indiana, 1974. 84 pp.

User's manual for GERTIIIZ proprietary software. Additional manuals for related proprietary software is also available from the publisher.

PRIT74B   Pritsker, A. Alan B. *The GASP IV Simulation Language.* John Wiley & Sons, New York, 1974. 451 + xvi pp.

Detailed description of the GASP IV simulation language and associated processing software. Examples and applications, but not to the analysis of computer systems.

RALL69   Rall, Louis B. *Computational Solution of NonLinear Operator Equations.* John Wiley & Sons, New York, 1969. 225 + viii pp.

Intermediate to advanced numerical analysis.

REIS74   Reiser, M.; Kobayashi, H. "Accuracy of the Diffusion Approximation for Some Queueing Systems." *IBM Journal of Research and Development*, Vol. 18, No. 2, March 1974, pp. 110–124.

REIT71   Reitman, Julian. *Computer Simulation Applications.* John Wiley & Sons, New York, 1971. 422 + xiv pp.

An introduction to simulation in FORTRAN, SIMSCRIPT, and GPSS. Only one application specifically to the performance of a computer system. Part III, "Commentary" deals with substantive issues in doing simulation and verifying the results. It is worth comparing the simulation methodology and problems as described in Reitman to the analytical methodology and problems as discussed in this book.

RIVE72   Rivett, Patrick. *Principles of Model Building.* John Wiley & Sons, London, 1972. 141 + iv pp.

A primarily philosophical book on the principles of mathematical modeling and simulation. Discussion of decision analysis models of the kind used to decide if an analysis is or is not worthwhile. Many other goodies.

ROSE74   Rosenberg, Robert. "Latency Models for Several Mass Memory Devices." Data Systems Analysts, Inc., Pennsauken, New Jersey, IM-5086, October 1974.

All batch models. Exact scheduled batch drum, approximate scheduled batch drum, scheduled batch disc with uniform tasks, linear seek function and optimized imbedded drum. Also two models for batch bubble or CCD memories.

SAAT61   Saaty, Thomas L. *Elements of Queueing Theory*. McGraw-Hill, New York, 1961. 423 + xv pp.

Contains a prodigious (910 entries) pre-1961 bibliography and solutions to many problems not readily available elsewhere. Generally reliable with occasional lapses in the distinction between "in the system" and "on the queue". Lots of goodies tucked away in the problem sections. For the hardy.

SAMM69   Sammet, Jean E. *Programming Languages: History and Fundamentals*. Prentice-Hall, Englewood Cliffs, N.J. 1969. 785 + xxx pp.

This is *the* reference work on programming languages. Short review of the DYNAMO, GPSS, SIMSCRIPT, MILITRAN, SIMULA, and OPS simulation languages.

SEAM66   Seaman, R. H.; Lind, R. A.; Wilson, T. L. "On Teleprocessing System Design— Part IV. An Analysis of Auxiliary Storage Activity," *IBM Systems Journal*, Vol. 5, No. 3, 1966. pp. 158–170.

Continual FIFO discs for multi-disc, multi-processor, with channel queueing. Analysis of mean seek time and seek time distribution.

SIEM70   Siemens AG. *Telephone Traffic Theory—Tables and Charts*. Siemens AG, Berlin–Munich, 1970. 420 pp.

Contains the most complete set of tables and graphs for the Poisson, Erlang-*B*, and Erlang-*C* formulas available. Tables for finite sources. Discussion of methods and tables for handling overflow calculations precisely.

SHAR69   Sharma, Roshan L. "Analysis of a Scheme for Information Organization and Retrieval from a Disc File." *IFIPS Conference Proceedings 1968*, North Holland Publishing, Amsterdam, 1969, pp. 853–859.

Analysis of batch scheduled disc by explicit enumeration of cases. Graphs for small number of tasks and sectors.

SOUC76   Soucek, Branko: *Microprocessors and Minicomputers*. John Wiley & Sons, New York, 1976. 607 + xv pp.

A comprehensive reference book on microcomputers including detailed discussions of the most popular types.

SPHI77   Sphicas, Georghios; "A conjecture on Dual ($M/G/1$) and ($G/M/1$) systems," Joint National ORSA/TIMS meeting, Atlanta, Georgia, November 7–9, 1977.

STER68   Sterling, Theodor D.; Pollack, Seymour V. *Introduction to Statistical Data Processing*. Prentice-Hall, Englewood Cliffs, N.J., 1968. 663 + xvii pp.

An excellent source book on most of the statistical analysis techniques you are ever likely to need in support of a performance analysis.

SVOB76   Svobodova, Liba. *Computer Performance Measurement and Evaluation Methods: Analysis and Applications*. American Elsevier, New York, 1976. 146 + xiii pp.

Overview of modeling and models, mixes, benchmarks, and simulation, but best on measurements and instrumentation. Good bibliography.

TEOR72   Teory, Toby J.; Pinkerton, Tad, B. "A Comparative Analysis of Disc Scheduling Policies," *Communications of the ACM*, Vol. 15, No. 3, March 1972, pp. 177–184.

Comparison of several continual arrival discs—FIFO, SSTF, and three different SCANs. Determination of expected seek time, correction to Denning's SSTF minimum seek time expression, simulation comparison of various policies.

WEIN66   Weingarten, Allen. "The Eschenbach Drum Scheme," *Communications of the ACM*, Vol. 9, No. 7, July 1966, pp. 509–512.

Mean time between accesses for FIFO drum including head switching time. Approximate analyses for continual drums. This is an historically important paper.

WEIN69   Weingarten, Allen. "The Analytical Design of Real-Time Disc Systems," *IFIPS Conference Proceedings, 1968*, North Holland Publishing, Amsterdam, 1969, pp. 860–866.

Mean number of cylinders scanned, mean seek time, and the Eschenbach strategy for discs.

WEIT74   Weitzman, Cay. *Minicomputer Systems*. Prentice-Hall, Englewood Cliffs, N.J., 1974. 367 + xii pp.

A readable introduction to minicomputer based systems. An understanding of Weitzman would provide a more than adequate background for the purposes of performance analysis.

WILH76   Wilhelm, Neil C. "An Anomaly in Disc Scheduling," *Communications of the ACM*, Vol. 19, No. 1, January 1976, pp. 13–17.

Shows that FIFO (continual disc) can have some advantages over SSTF. Analysis of FIFO disc. Comparison of FIFO and SSTF policies from several different points of view.

WILH77   Wilhelm, Neil C. "A General Model for the Performance of Disc Systems," *Journal of the ACM*, Vol. 24, No. 1, January 1977, pp. 14–31.

Multi-spindle discs with common channels. Comparison of various models, comparison with simulation. Much good stuff but most useful results are left as exercises for the reader.

WONG75   Wong, J. W. N. *Queueing Network Models for Computer Systems*. PhD dissertation, UCLA School of Engineering and Applied Sciences, University of California, Los Angeles, 1975. Also Department of Commerce, National Technical Information Service Document No. AD-A018657.

A more up to date review of queueing network models and their application to computer system performance than BUZE71. Emphasis is on commercial operating systems, time shared systems and similar applications.

WYMA70   Wyma, Forrest Paul. *Simulation Modeling: A Guide to Using SIMSCRIPT*. John Wiley & Sons, New York, 1970. 211 + xvi pp.

A textbook on the use and application of the SIMSCRIPT simulation language.

Index

Index